NIETZSCHE
AND THE
GERMAN TRADITION

NICHOLAS MARTIN (ED.)

NIETZSCHE
AND THE
GERMAN TRADITION

PETER LANG
Oxford • Bern • Berlin • Bruxelles • Frankfurt am Main • New York • Wien

Bibliographic information published by Die Deutsche Bibliothek
Die Deutsche Bibliothek lists this publication in the Deutsche National-
bibliografie; detailed bibliographic data is available on the Internet at
‹http://dnb.ddb.de›.

British Library and Library of Congress Cataloguing-in-Publication Data:
A catalogue record for this book is available from The British Library,
Great Britain, and from The Library of Congress, USA

Cover design: Thomas Jaberg, Peter Lang AG

ISBN 3-03910-060-2
US-ISBN 0-8204-6876-2

© Peter Lang AG, European Academic Publishers, Bern 2003
Hochfeldstrasse 32, Postfach 746, CH-3000 Bern 9, Switzerland
info@peterlang.com, www.peterlang.com, www.peterlang.net

Printed in Germany

Contents

vi

Acknowledgments

The editor would like to thank all the contributors to this volume for their goodwill and patience throughout the gestation of this project. In particular, I am grateful to them for their cooperation and willingness to answer queries and requests which arose at the editing stage.

I would also like to thank the Friedrich Nietzsche Society and the University of St Andrews, under whose joint auspices the conference was held, at which earlier versions of the papers in this volume were presented.

The editor owes a substantial debt of gratitude to The Carnegie Trust for the Universities of Scotland, and the School of Modern Languages of the University of St Andrews, for providing very generous financial assistance towards the cost of publishing this volume.

Finally, I would like to acknowledge the professionalism of the staff at Peter Lang, especially Graham Speake and Andrew Ivett, who patiently answered any number of queries and saw the volume through to its conclusion.

A Note on Sources and List of Abbreviations

Unless otherwise indicated, references to Nietzsche's writings are to the texts as they appear in the Colli-Montinari editions of his works and letters. For details of these, see below under KGB, KGW, KSA, and KSB. Citations are identified by abbreviations of the titles of the works in which they appear, followed by Arabic numerals referring to the relevant sections or paragraphs. Where necessary, Roman numerals are used to identify the parts of the works in which they are located. This form of citation should enable the reader to find the passages cited in German or English editions of Nietzsche's works.

AC   *Der Antichrist* (The Antichrist), 1888.

EH   *Ecce homo*, 1888.

FS   *Friedrich Nietzsche. Frühe Schriften*, ed. Hans Joachim Mette et al., 5 vols (Munich: Beck, 1994).

FW   *Die fröhliche Wissenschaft* (The Gay Science): Books I-IV, 1882; 2nd edn incorporating Book V and new Preface, 1887.

GD   *Götzen-Dämmerung* (Twilight of the Idols), 1888.

GM   *Zur Genealogie der Moral* (On the Genealogy of Morals / On the Genealogy of Morality), 1887.

GT   *Die Geburt der Tragödie* (The Birth of Tragedy), 1872.

GTVS 'Versuch einer Selbstkritik' ('Attempt at a Self-Criticism'), Preface to 1886 edition of GT.

HKP   'Homer und die klassische Philologie' (Homer and Classical Philology), 1869.

HW   *Homer's Wettkampf* (Homer's Contest), 1872.

JGB   *Jenseits von Gut und Böse* (Beyond Good and Evil), 1886.

KGB   *Friedrich Nietzsche. Briefwechsel. Kritische Gesamtausgabe* ed. Giorgio Colli, Mazzino Montinari et al. (Berlin and New York: de Gruyter, 1975–).

KGW   *Nietzsche. Werke. Kritische Gesamtausgabe*, ed. Giorgio Colli, Mazzino Montinari et al. (Berlin and New York: de Gruyter, 1967–).

KSA   *Friedrich Nietzsche. Sämtliche Werke. Kritische Studienausgabe*, ed. Giorgio Colli and Mazzino Montinari, 2nd edn, 15 vols (Munich: dtv; Berlin and New York: de Gruyter, 1988).

KSB   *Friedrich Nietzsche. Sämtliche Briefe. Kritische Studienausgabe*, ed. Giorgio Colli and Mazzino Montinari, 8 vols (Munich: dtv; Berlin and New York: de Gruyter, 1986).

M   *Morgenröthe* (Daybreak), 1881.

MA   *Menschliches, Allzumenschliches* (Human, All Too Human); I, 1878. II/1 – *Vermischte Meinungen und Sprüche* (Assorted Opinions and Maxims), 1879; II/2 – *Der Wanderer und sein Schatten* (The Wanderer and his Shadow), 1880. New edition of MA (I and II), 1886.

NF   *Nachgelassene Fragmente* (Notes and Fragments); the date, fragment number and KSA reference are given, e.g. NF 1871, 9[104]: KSA 7/312.

NW   *Nietzsche contra Wagner*, 1888.

UB   *Unzeitgemässe Betrachtungen* (Untimely Meditations); I – *David Strauss, der Bekenner und der Schriftsteller* (David Strauss, the Confessor and the Writer), 1873; II – *Vom Nutzen und Nachteil der Historie für das Leben* (On the Uses and Disadvantages of History for Life), 1874; III – *Schopenhauer als Erzieher* (Schopenhauer as Educator), 1874; IV – *Richard Wagner in Bayreuth*, 1876.

WA   *Der Fall Wagner* (The Wagner Case), 1888.

WL   'Über Wahrheit und Lüge im aussermoralischen Sinne' (On Truth and Lies in an Extra-Moral Sense), 1873.

WPh   *Wir Philologen* (We Philologists), 1875.

Za   *Also sprach Zarathustra* (Thus spake Zarathustra); Parts I–II, 1883; Part III, 1884; Part IV, 1885.

Notes on Contributors

CHRISTA DAVIS ACAMPORA is Assistant Professor of Philosophy at Hunter College of the City University of New York. She has published numerous articles on Nietzsche in a variety of publications, including *Journal of Nietzsche Studies*, *Nietzsche-forschung*, and *International Studies in Philosophy*. She is the co-editor, with Ralph Acampora, of *A Nietzschean Bestiary: Animality Beyond Docial and Brutal*, forthcoming from Rowman & Littlefield.

THOMAS H. BROBJER lectures in the history of ideas at the Universities of Uppsala and Stockholm. He is the author of *Nietzsche's Ethics of Character* (Uppsala 1995). He has published extensively on different aspects of Nietzsche's reading and extant library, in the following journals and others: *Journal of the History of Ideas*, *Journal of the History of Philosophy*, *Nietzsche-Studien*, *Journal of Nietzsche Studies*, *New Nietzsche Studies* and *International Studies in Philosophy*. He has also contributed to a number of books on Nietzsche.

DANIEL W. CONWAY is Professor of Philosophy and Director of Graduate Studies in Philosophy at The Pennsylvania State University. He has published widely on topics in political philosophy, contemporary European philosophy, and nineteenth-century philosophy. He is the author of *Nietzsche's Dangerous Game* (CUP 1997) and *Nietzsche and the Political* (Routledge 1997). He is also the editor of *Nietzsche: Critical Assessments* (Routledge 1998), and the co-editor of *Nietzsche, Philosophy, and the Arts* (CUP 1998).

MALCOLM HUMBLE studied Modern Languages at Emmanuel College, Cambridge, and was a Research Fellow there from 1966 to 1969. He was Lecturer in German at the University of St Andrews from 1969 to 2001. His publications include articles on Anglo-German literary relations, the reception of Nietzsche and Brecht, exile literature (1933–45), GDR literature, and (with Raymond Furness) *A Companion to Twentieth Century German Literature* (Routledge 1991, [2]1997) and *Introduction to German Literature 1871–1990* (Routledge 1994).

CHRISTOPHER JANAWAY is Professor of Philosophy at Birkbeck College, University of London. He specializes in philosophical aesthetics and the philosophies of Schopenhauer and Nietzsche. His publications include *Self and World in Schopenhauer's Philosophy* (OUP 1989), *Schopenhauer* (OUP 1994), and *Images of Excellence: Plato's Critique of the Arts* (OUP 1995). He is editor of the collections *Willing and Nothingness: Schopenhauer as Nietzsche's Educator* (OUP 1998) and *The Cambridge Companion to Schopenhauer* (CUP 1999).

DUNCAN LARGE is Senior Lecturer in German at University of Wales, Swansea, and Chairman of the Friedrich Nietzsche Society. He is the author of *Nietzsche and Proust: A Comparative Study* (OUP 2001), co-editor (with Keith Ansell-Pearson) of *The Nietzsche Reader* (Blackwell 2003), guest editor of 'Nietzsche and German Literature', *Journal of Nietzsche Studies*, 13 (Spring 1997), and has translated Sarah Kofman, *Nietzsche and Metaphor* (Athlone and Stanford UP 1993), as well as Nietzsche's *Twilight of the Idols* (OUP 1998) and *Ecce Homo* (OUP 2003). He is currently completing a monograph on *Nietzsche's Renaissance Figures*.

NICHOLAS MARTIN is Lecturer in German at the University of St Andrews. He is the author of *Nietzsche and Schiller: Untimely Aesthetics* (OUP 1996) and the translator of Gianni Vattimo, *Nietzsche: An Introduction* (Athlone and Stanford UP 2002). He has published articles on Nietzsche in *German Life and Letters*, *Nietzscheforschung*, *Journal of Nietzsche Studies*, *History of European Ideas*, and the *Times Literary Supplement*. His most recent publication on Nietzsche is '"Fighting a Philosophy": The Figure of Nietzsche in British Propaganda of the First World War', *Modern Language Review*, 98 (2003).

BEN MORGAN is a Fellow of Worcester College, Oxford, and Lecturer in German at the University of Oxford. His research interests include German intellectual history, German cinema and twentieth-century German philosophy. He has published widely on medieval mysticism, psychoanalysis, the Frankfurt School, and the films of Fritz Lang and Leni Riefenstahl.

GERD SCHANK studied linguistics, and German and Romance philology at Freiburg. Since 1977 he has been a lecturer at the University of Nijmegen (since 1988 in the Department of Philosophy, where he is a member of the Nietzsche Dictionary Project). His publications include: *'Rasse' und 'Züchtung' bei Nietzsche* (de Gruyter 2000); *Dionysos gegen den Gekreuzigten: Eine philologische und philosophische Studie zu Nietzsches 'Ecce homo'* (Lang 1993); and 'Dionysos und Ariadne im Gespräch: Subjektauflösung und Mehrstimmigkeit in Nietzsches Philosophie', *Tijdschrift voor Filosofie*, 53 (1991).

HANS-GERD von SEGGERN studied German literature, philosophy, and history in Berlin (Freie Universität) and Vienna from 1989–97. He held a Ph.D. scholarship from the Friedrich Ebert Foundation (1999–2001) and is completing a thesis on Nietzsche and Weimar classicism. Publications: *Nietzsches Philosophie des Scheins* (VDG 1999); 'Allen Tinten-Fischen feind: Metaphern der Melancholie in Nietzsches *Also sprach Zarathustra*', *Nietzscheforschung*, 9 (2002); 'Die Aura im Zeitalter ihrer theoretischen Beliebigkeit: Überlegungen zu einer untoten ästhetischen Kategorie', in Renate Reschke (ed.), *Ästhetik. Ephemeres und Historisches* (Kovač 2002).

PAUL J. M. van TONGEREN is Professor of Philosophical Ethics at the University of Nijmegen and Extraordinary Professor of Ethics at the Catholic University of Louvain. He is Director of the Nietzsche Research Group at Nijmegen, which is preparing a Nietzsche Dictionary (*Nietzsche-Wörterbuch*). He has recently published *Reinterpreting Modern Culture. An Introduction to Nietzsche's Philosophy* (Purdue UP 2000).

JIM URPETH is Senior Lecturer in Philosophy at the University of Greenwich, London. His research interests include Kant, Nietzsche, Heidegger, Bataille, Foucault, Deleuze, aesthetics, and the philosophy of religion. He is currently completing two books: *From Kant to Deleuze: The Renaturalisation of Aesthetics*; and *Nietzsche and French Religious Atheism*. He was co-editor (with John Lippitt) of *Nietzsche and the Divine* (Clinamen 2000) and guest editor of 'Nietzsche and Religion', *Journal of Nietzsche Studies*, 19 (Spring 2000). His other publications include '"Noble" *Ascesis*: Between Nietzsche and Foucault', *New Nietzsche Studies*, 2 (1998), and 'A "Sacred" Thrill: Presentation and Affectivity in the Analytic of the Sublime', in Rehberg and Jones (eds), *The Matter of Critique: Readings in Kant's Philosophy* (Clinamen 2000).

Preface

Nietzsche and the German Tradition. To those persuaded that Nietzsche is the anti-German, antitraditional thinker *par excellence,* this title may well appear contradictory. Just how potentially contradictory (but also fruitful) it is, can be gauged by recasting it as a series of questions, emphasising each word in turn: Nietzsche and the German *Tradition*? Nietzsche and the *German* Tradition? Nietzsche and *the* German Tradition? Nietzsche *and* the German Tradition? *Nietzsche* and the German Tradition?

Even without perplexed exclamation marks, each of these questions highlights different aspects of a central problem discussed in this collection of essays. This problem is the tension between Nietzsche's desire for a new beginning, a clean slate for (hu)mankind and his keen awareness that nineteenth-century humans are not a *tabula rasa*. Nietzsche himself is, of course, no different to his contemporaries. As he constantly reminds us, he carries an accumulated weight of psychological, cultural, political, religious and academic baggage. Much of Nietzsche's intellectual effort involves sorting through this 'traditional' baggage, attempting both to discard items likely to impede the journey and to repack those with the potential to enhance it. A difficulty for his interpreters is that Nietzsche's criteria for sorting, discarding and repacking tradition(s) undergo significant, though not constant, mutations.

This problem and its near-neighbour, the question of the extent to which Nietzsche and his legacies – and the study of them – have themselves become a 'tradition', are illuminated from a variety of perspectives in this volume. The contributors represent a wide range of disciplines (philosophy, cultural studies, the history of ideas, linguistics, history, and German studies), and they bring a refreshing diversity of methodological approaches to bear on the theme of Nietzsche and the German tradition.

The essays collected here, with the exception of the editor's, were first presented at the 7th Annual Conference of the Friedrich Nietzsche Society, which was held at the University of St Andrews in September 1997. All have since been revised and updated to take account of subsequent developments in Nietzsche studies and other relevant areas of scholarship. The conference itself attracted some sixty delegates, including nine from Scotland, eighteen from other parts of the UK, ten from other EU countries, and eleven from North America, as well as participants from South Africa, Australia and Switzerland.[1]

Three distinct, yet often overlapping, lines of inquiry emerged at the conference and are, quite naturally, reflected in this volume. The first is the investigation of Nietzsche's own engagement with various German traditions, including his battle with the tradition of German classical scholarship, re-assessed here by Christa Davis Acampora. Nietzsche's appropriation and reworking of German aesthetic traditions, particularly the 'classical' tradition of Schiller and Goethe, is the focus of Hans-Gerd von Seggern's essay. Duncan Large presents an illuminating and persuasive re-assessment of Nietzsche's ambivalent attitude to Martin Luther and to the tradition of German Protestantism he inaugurated. In his remarkably well-documented contribution, which is based, in part, on an exhaustive study of Nietzsche's library in Weimar, Thomas H. Brobjer traces Nietzsche's reading (and non-reading) of the German philosophical tradition from Leibniz to Marx. In his careful reconstruction of a question central to an understanding of Nietzsche's outlook, Christopher Janaway dispels many myths and misconceptions surrounding Nietzsche's complex attitude to Schopenhauer. Janaway rejects conventional arguments that Nietzsche is initially 'for' and then 'against' Schopen-

---

1   For an account of the conference proceedings, which includes brief summaries of many of the papers presented, see Uschi Nussbaumer-Benz, 'Bericht über die 7. und 8. Konferenz der englischen Friedrich Nietzsche Society', *Nietzsche-forschung*, 5 (2000), 393–97.

hauer, arguing instead, on the basis of firm textual evidence, that Nietzsche is able to reconcile these opposites.

The second line of inquiry pursued in this volume is an investigation of Nietzsche's attitudes to his German present. Daniel W. Conway's lucid essay, 'Nietzsche's Germano-mania', resists suggestions that Nietzsche can be easily pigeonholed as anti-German and philo-Semitic, by demonstrating the complex and often paradoxical nature of his pronouncements on Germans, 'Europeans' and Jews. Nietzsche's Prussian past and upbringing, and the impact of these on his personality (and his philosophy, its Siamese twin) are examined by Ben Morgan in his essay. The scars of this past are revealed in Nietzsche's most intemperate text, *The Antichrist*, in his 'frightened pursuit of mastery'.

The third important area investigated in this collection is what might be called the Nietzschean 'tradition', in other words Nietzsche's legacy, or legacies, as well as writing about him since *c.* 1890. Jim Urpeth's essay extends and amplifies Nietzsche's speculations on taste and aesthetic disinterestedness, by examining (and challenging) them through the prism of Heidegger's aesthetic theory. Malcolm Humble's thoughtful essay underscores the importance of Nietzsche to left-wing writers in Germany in the first half of the twentieth century. Humble shows how highly Nietzsche was regarded by Heinrich Mann and Arnold Zweig, for example, and demonstrates how, when in exile in the 1930s, these writers attempted to preserve and project an alternative image of Nietzsche to the one being paraded in Nazi Germany. Though none of the essays here engages exclusively with the thorny and emotionally charged issue of the National Socialists' use and abuse of Nietzsche, the issue is inevitably a subtext. Both Gerd Schank's and Paul J. M. van Tongeren's essays tackle and clarify issues in Nietzsche's thought which have led to (mis)appropriations, namely, his views on race and breeding, and his 'naturalism'. Another darker aspect of the Nietzschean 'tradition' is discussed in Nicholas Martin's essay on the interpretation of Nietzsche in the GDR.

The attentive reader will notice that the essays in this collection do not fall into these three lines of inquiry as neatly as has been suggested here. S/he will also see that there is healthy disagreement between contributors on a number of points. The essays presented here point to no collective conclusion. It would be strange, and strangely disappointing, if they did. They do, however, contribute to a better understanding both of the extent to which Nietzsche problematises 'tradition' and of the problems, and opportunities, arising from the Nietzschean 'tradition(s)' of the past hundred years.

Daniel W. Conway

Nietzsche's Germano-mania

> The German soul is above all manifold, of diverse origins, more put together and superimposed than actually built: that is due to where it comes from. A German who would make bold to say, 'Two souls, alas, are dwelling in my breast', would violate the truth grossly or, more precisely, would fall short of the truth by a good many souls. As a people of the most monstrous mixture and medley of races, perhaps even with a preponderance of the pre-Aryan element, as 'people of the middle' in every sense, the Germans are more incomprehensible, comprehensive, contradictory, unknown, incalculable, surprising, even frightening than other people are to themselves: they elude *definition* and would be on that account alone the despair of the French (JGB 244).

> It is part of my ambition to be considered a despiser of the Germans *par excellence*... The Germans have no idea how vulgar they are; but that is the superlative of vulgarity – they are not even ashamed of being merely Germans (EH 'WA' 4).

Nietzsche's relationship to his fellow Germans was famously vexed. On the one hand, he excoriated his contemporaries for their enthusiastic participation in the nationalism, anti-Semitism, xenophobia, and general pettiness that characterized European politics in the late nineteenth century. On the other hand, he unabashedly admired Goethe, Beethoven, and the 'blond beast' that still prowled the vanishing core of the German soul. He continued to write in his *Muttersprache*, delighting especially in those literary triumphs that were secured at the expense of his increasingly obtuse *Vaterland*.

However vexed it may have been, his relationship to his fellow Germans nevertheless reveals his allegiance to a particular ideal of Germanity. His hopes for the future of Germany are rooted in his idealized depiction of a soul multiply conflicted and productively at odds with itself. According to Nietzsche, in fact, the capacity of the

German soul to accommodate diverse, competing impulses is the generative source of the 'profundity' that it was once 'customary to attribute to the Germans, as a distinction' (JGB 244).[1] To cultivate within oneself a welter of competing passions is to nurture – and eventually to express – the dynamic strength of soul that he often associates with his favorite exemplars of the German people. At its world-historical best, the German soul translates its capacity for internal conflict into excess generative energy, of which its most enduring cultural triumphs have been born. What other nations and peoples have viewed as the signature mystery of (or defect in) the German soul, Nietzsche salutes as its greatest charm and attraction.

His idealized depiction of the German soul is best captured in his flattering sketch of Goethe, who is 'the last German for whom [he] feel[s] any reverence' (GD ix 51). According to Nietzsche, Goethe was a kind of self-overcoming on the part of the [eighteenth] century:

> [H]e was not fainthearted but took as much as possible upon himself, over himself, into himself. What he wanted was *totality* [...] he disciplined himself to wholeness, he *created* himself... Goethe conceived a human being who would be strong, highly educated, skillful in all bodily matters, self-controlled, reverent toward himself, and who might dare to afford the whole range and wealth of being natural... (GD ix 59)

I have cited this passage at length because it expresses Nietzsche's admiration for Goethe as an exemplary kind of German. Because Goethe was able to discipline and master his manifold impulses and talents, Germany was not able to contain him. An event so momentous and excessive required nothing less than the whole of Europe as its stage. In the person (or event) of Goethe, that is, the German soul exceeded its customary limits, reaching beyond Germany to Europe itself. Goethe may have written and lived in German, but he identified himself first and foremost as a citizen of *Europe*: 'Goethe was not a German event [*Ereigniss*], but a European

---

1   With the exception of occasional emendations, I rely throughout this essay on Walter Kaufmann's and R. J. Hollingdale's translations of Nietzsche's writings (see 'Works of Nietzsche Cited' for full citations).

one' (GD ix 49).[2] Nietzsche thus recalls with obvious delight those 'words of Goethe in which he deprecates with impatient hardness, *as if he belonged to a foreign country*, what the Germans take pride in' (JGB 244, emphasis added). As embodied by Goethe and idealized by Nietzsche, the multiplex German soul achieves its apotheosis in the cosmopolitanism of a 'good European'.

Nietzsche's contemporaries duly exhibit this capacity for internal conflict, but with an important difference: Their decadence renders them incapable of gathering and containing their manifold impulses within a functioning whole. What was once a productive, excessive regimen of internal conflict and self-aversion has degenerated into a destructive, implosive exercise in self-contempt. His goal, consequently, is to deliver Germany from self-contempt by placing it in a context – viz., that of a pan-European cosmopolitanism – in which it might learn once again to contain its inner contradictions and, so, to derive a surge of power from its internal conflicts. By restoring a splintered Europe to wholeness, that is, Nietzsche hopes to position Germany to restore itself as well. As it did so splendidly in the case of Goethe, the grander goal of a trans-national, pan-European culture will draw the German soul beyond itself and its familiar limits, which have been narrowed considerably by its recent dalliance with nationalism. As we shall see, moreover, Nietzsche can complete this ambitious task only if he avails himself of resources not presently in the possession of any European people or nation, the Germans included.

---

2   Nietzsche similarly describes Schopenhauer as 'the last German worthy of consideration (who represents a *European* event [*Ereigniss*] like Goethe, like Hegel, like Heinrich Heine, and not merely a local event, a "national" one)' (GD ix 21).

I.

Nietzsche's mixed review of his fellow Germans can be traced to his diagnosis of European decadence, which comes to dominate his post-Zarathustran writings. We know that he believes Europe to be sickly in general. Of all European nations, moreover, Germany figures most prominently in his diagnosis – either because the Germans are the sickest of European peoples, or the most likely to recover, or both. In one of his most damning indictments of his contemporaries, he identifies the Germans as the primary carriers of the nationalistic disease that threatens the disintegration of Europe:

> [W]e are not 'German' enough, in the sense in which the word 'German' is constantly being used nowadays, to advocate nationalism and race hatred and to be able to take pleasure in the national scabies of the heart and blood poisoning that now leads the nations of Europe to delimit and barricade themselves against each other as if it were a matter of quarantine (FW 377).

Although passages like this one suggest Nietzsche's outright dis-avowal of his Germanity, other passages are more balanced and thoughtful. In the following passage, for example, he diagnoses the Germans as spiritually exhausted following their successful bid to gain military power:

> Even a rapid estimate shows that it is not only obvious that German culture is declining but that there is sufficient reason for that. In the end, no one can spend more than he has: that is true of the individual, it is true of a people. If one spends oneself for power, for power politics, for economics, world trade, parliamentarianism, and military interests – if one spends in *this* direction the quantum of understanding, seriousness, will, and self-overcoming which one represents, then it will be lacking for the other direction. Culture and the state – one should not deceive oneself about this – are antagonists: '*Kultur-Staat*' is merely a modern idea. One lives off the other, one thrives at the expense of the other. All great ages of culture are ages of political decline: what is great culturally has always been unpolitical, even *anti-political* [...] In the history of European culture the rise of the 'Reich' means one thing above all: a displacement of the center of gravity. It is already known everywhere: in what

matters most – and that always remains culture – the Germans are no longer worthy of consideration (GD viii 4).

This lengthy passage illuminates four points that are crucial to an understanding of Nietzsche's Germanity. First of all, he attempts to present a balanced criticism of Germany rather than a wholesale dismissal of its aims and accomplishments. He judges Germany to be declining, but only relative to the goal of cultural advancement. In fact, the Germans are lacking in culture *because* they have spent themselves, successfully, in pursuit of extra-cultural ends. They consequently possess an abundance of resources that he believes can be productively diverted toward the restoration of German (and European) culture. Second, he identifies culture (*Kultur*) and state (*Staat*) as *antagonistic* goals for a single nation simultaneously to pursue. If Germany is to play the role that he has reserved for it in the restoration of a pan-European culture, then it must withdraw its current investment in the military and economic might of the Reich and reallocate its resources toward the restoration of culture. He consequently cites the current strength of the Reich as incontrovertible evidence of Germany's cultural decline. Third, he unambiguously aligns himself with the goal of cultural advancement, as opposed to the goal of military and economic expansion. Fourth, and perhaps most importantly, he explicitly links the cultural decline of Germany with the larger crisis of European decadence. The Reich has fortified itself at the expense not only of German culture, but of European culture as well. Nietzsche thus implies that a solution to the more local problem of German decline may also address the larger problem of European dis-integration. A rejuvenated Germany would stabilize Europe by restoring its displaced 'center of gravity'. As we shall see, in fact, his basic strategy for reintegrating Europe, and thereby renewing a distinctly European culture, is to arrange for Germany to receive an infusion of the spiritual and cultural resources that it presently lacks.

As this passage indicates, Nietzsche tends to situate his pro-German sentiments within the larger context of his pan-European cosmopolitanism. He wishes for Germany to thrive, but not on its own terms – this, after all, is the problem with the Reich. He consequently links the future of Germany to the future of Europe. Germany will become great once again only on the strength of its *refusal* of nationalism and the decadence it manifests. He consequently opposes the German nationalist movement of his day *not* for its Germano-centrism, but for its decadent embrace of disintegration and particularism (FW 377). Indeed, the nationalists and anti-Semites of his day ask too little of Germany rather than too much. In particular, they harbor no aspirations to restore Germany to the vital center of a distinctly European culture.[3]

Although Nietzsche is sharply critical of the Reich, he has not yet abandoned his hopes for the future of the German people. Germany may be sick, as evidenced by the attenuation of its identification with the whole of Europe, but it still possesses resources that can be applied productively toward cultural pursuits. In the case of Germany, that is, decadence manifests itself not as a loss or dissipation of strength, but as a misallocation of strength toward non-renewable expenditures. As he explains:

> The new Germany represents a large quantum of fitness, both inherited and acquired by training, so that for a time it may expend its accumulated store of strength, even squander it. It is *not* a high culture that has thus become the master, and even less a delicate taste, a noble 'beauty' of the instincts; but more *virile* virtues than any other country in Europe can show...One pays heavily for coming to power: power *makes stupid* (GD viii 1).

If Nietzsche is right, then the Germans are unlikely on their own to extricate themselves from this plight. Since they cannot spend themselves on culture – having squandered themselves elsewhere – they can contribute to the envisioned advancement of Europe only in the

---

3   For a persuasive account of Nietzsche's attempt to oppose nationalism with the ideal of 'Europeanism', see Yirmiyahu Yovel, *Dark Riddle: Hegel, Nietzsche, and the Jews* (University Park, PA: Penn State Press, 1998), pp. 132–36.

event that they acquire access to the spiritual resources of another people. They now require the services of someone who is decidedly *not* stupid – someone, that is, who is both 'clever' and 'wise', and a 'destiny' as well, even an author of many 'good books'. They now require, in short, the services of Nietzsche himself, who is uniquely positioned to correct for their stupidity and restore them to a place of cultural prominence in a rejuvenated European union.

With respect to the future of Germany, then, Nietzsche certainly protests too much. He would not be so critical of his German contemporaries if he did not think them capable once again, as he repeatedly hints, of assuming a position of cultural leadership over the unified Europe he envisions. In fact, his tirades against the Germans typically comprise equal parts ridicule and exhortation. Despite what he both says and implies about the Germans, he has by no means given up on them as *the* European people of world-historical destiny. At the end of the day, that is, he remains an inveterate – if complicated – Germanophile.

II.

Nietzsche addresses himself to the future of Germany in his discussion of 'Peoples and Fatherlands' in *Beyond Good and Evil*. Here he turns his hand to what he calls 'great politics', for his goal is nothing less than the restoration of a trans-national, pan-European culture. He presents his pan-European ideal, moreover, as consistent with the dominant trends of the late nineteenth century. Notwithstanding the widespread fascination with the exploits of independent nation-states, he maintains, '*Europe wants to become one*' (JGB 256). This fact, if that is what it is, not only validates his plan to revive a genuinely European culture, but also authorizes his attention to the question of how best to accommodate what Europe wants.

Since all appearances indicate that Europe does *not* 'want to become one', Nietzsche must account for his unique access to the genuine will of Europe. He is apparently able to penetrate beneath the surface squabbles and petty nationalisms of his day, arriving thereby at the underlying truth of European disintegration. As we have seen, he diagnoses Europe as locked in the throes of pandemic decay. Among other things, this diagnosis means that the constituent peoples and nations of Europe instinctively choose what is most harmful to them (GD ix 35). Rather than preserve their allegiance to the European culture that has nourished their aspirations to greatness, the newly emergent nations of Europe strike out on their own, convinced of the wisdom of their independence and autonomy. Nietzsche consequently interprets the impulse toward disintegration and 'particularism' as a symptom of decay. Each of the emerging nation-states has disastrously identified itself, rather than Europe, as the primary unit of political and cultural allegiance. He thus exposes nationalism as a pathological state of decline. As such, it expresses the contrary of the genuine will of Europe.

Nietzsche's diagnosis of European decay rests on what might be called his 'quantum theory' of race and racial development. As the name suggests, this theory allows Nietzsche to reduce all European races and peoples to their constituent 'quanta' of force. (He also speaks on occasion of quanta of 'strength', 'energy', 'will', 'self-overcoming', etc.) According to this theory, a people or race is nothing more than a transient configuration within a shifting field of contesting forces. As such, the endurance of a race is neither permanent nor eternal. As they become what they are, races are continually made, unmade, and remade over time. According to Nietzsche, then, race is not a natural kind, not a *res nata* (JGB 251).[4]

---

4   Nietzsche thus cleaves implicitly to something like Outlaw's distinction
     between 'race' and 'ethnie' (Lucius T. Outlaw, *On Race and Philosophy* (New
     York and London: Routledge, 1996), pp. 136–37), where the former includes
     'biologically transmitted physical factors' while in the latter 'the constitutive
     factors that are shared (more or less) by members of the group are for the most
     part cultural' (p. 136). Outlaw understands 'a "race" to be wider, more

Although the constancy of racial markers may lend an appearance of permanence to a particular configuration of forces, this appearance is easily explained as the prejudice or mistake of an insufficiently rigorous scientific approach. When viewed from the long-term perspective that Nietzsche favors for his anthropological and historical investigations, all races are seen to be works forever in progress.[5] This 'quantum theory' of racial development thus encourages him to treat all peoples and races as repositories of disposable, transferable force.

Nations, too, are reducible to their constituent configurations of force. According to Nietzsche, however, these configurations do not fit together into optimal interlocking relations. As we have seen, the emerging nation-states of Europe have collectively renounced their common European heritage in favor of an autonomous existence nourished by colonial expansion. What is wrong, misshapen, and objectionable about these nationalistic configurations is that they are no longer embedded to a larger constellation (viz., 'Europe') that enables in them the superadded amplification of force that, according to Nietzsche, makes possible a genuine culture. A 'nation' is therefore a people wrenched from the larger cultural context that formerly supported its highest aspirations.

The case of German nationalism is even more unfortunate in this respect, for the Germans have become a people estranged from their destiny. The title of 'Peoples and Fatherlands' thus refers to two kinds of configurations of force. 'Peoples' (*Völker*) are (ideally) enmeshed in a larger cultural context that allows them to interact productively with one another, while 'fatherlands' (*Vaterländer*) are separate and independent, deriving no renewal of forces from their autarkic

---

encompassing than an "ethnie" such that a particular "race" can have a number of "ethnies"' (p. 136). Nietzsche would presumably agree with Outlaw that race is a 'social-natural kind' (p. 7).

5　I discuss Nietzsche's theory of racial cultivation in my '"The Great Play and Fight of Forces": Nietzsche on Race', in Julie K. Ward and Tommy L. Lott (eds), *Philosophers on Race: Critical Essays* (Oxford: Blackwell, 2002), pp. 167–94 (pp. 168–75).

expenditures.[6] With particular reference to German music, Nietzsche thus explains that

> Schumann was already a merely *German* event [*Ereigniss*] in music, no longer a European one, as Beethoven was and, to a still greater extent, Mozart. With [Schumann] German music was threatened by its greatest danger: *losing the voice for the soul of Europe* and descending into mere fatherlandishness (JGB 245).

The background for this 'quantum theory' is a bit sketchy, and a full exposition of its details would exceed the scope of this essay. Nietzsche apparently conceives of the cosmos, or nature, as a plenum of amoral, non-purposive forces, for which he proposes the 'quantum' as a unit of measure and expression. Operating in the absence of final causality, divine providence, and pre-established order, these quanta of force continually arrange and re-arrange themselves into transient configurations. These configurations are in turn arrayed with one another (or not) in similarly transient constellations. Nietzsche thus refers to the collective activity of the cosmos as 'the great play and fight of forces' (JGB 251), wherein races are continually made and unmade. For the most part, these quanta of force organize themselves randomly, in accordance with the non-purposive mechanism of the cosmos.[7] There is no sense in which the cosmos, or nature, favors one configuration over another or displays anything but indifference toward the needs and desires of particular human beings.

In this era of 'great politics', however, it is possible that a canny legislator could enter 'the great play and fight of forces' and influence the remaking of particular races. This is precisely what Nietzsche proposes to do (whether directly or indirectly) in the case of contemporary Europe: he wishes to re-align the various peoples and races

6   On the difference between *Völker* and *Vaterländer*, see Conway, '"The Great Play and Fight of Forces": Nietzsche on Race', pp. 170–71.

7   For a provocative exploration of Nietzsche's attempt to conceive of human organisms and organizations on the model of machine systems, see Keith Ansell Pearson, *Viroid Life: Perspectives on Nietzsche and the Transhuman Condition* (London: Routledge, 1997), pp. 123–50.

of Europe so that they might partake of a post-nationalistic European culture. He thus conceives of the disintegration of European culture as a problem to be solved by a kind of racial engineering. Races and peoples must first be reduced to their constituent quanta, which will then be reassembled in more optimal configurations.

In 'Peoples and Fatherlands', Nietzsche offers his services as racial matchmaker, weighing the relative strengths and weaknesses of various European peoples and prescribing matches that are beneficial to all. If we adopt the hyperoptic perspective that he favors, surveying the totality of Europe's myriad resources and deficits, we too will see that all is not lost. If the relative strengths and weaknesses of the various European peoples and nations can be re-distributed, then a distinctly European culture can perhaps be restored. Here we see how readily Nietzsche transits from the role of cultural diagnostician to the role of political lawgiver – so readily, in fact, that we might suspect the influence of his vision of a new European order on the evaluations he advances of its constituent peoples.

Upon reducing all European nations to their constituent quanta of transferable force, Nietzsche assigns to each a strictly utilitarian value. He bases this value on the expected contribution of each nation to the renewal of a pan-European culture. He thereby subordinates the national interests of all Europeans to the prevailing, trans-national interests of the new pan-European order. Ostensibly, then, this means that he values no race or people in its own right, but only for its perceived contributions to the formation of a new European order. Racial diversity is undeniably important to Nietzsche, but only insofar as it facilitates the consolidation of a pan-European polity. (Nietzsche is occasionally praised for his apparently progressive celebration of the mingling of races that characterizes Europe in the late nineteenth century.[8] As far as I can tell, however, he does not so much celebrate the emerging racial diversity as acknowledge it as a fact of the

---

8   See Walter Kaufmann, *Nietzsche: Philosopher, Psychologist, Antichrist*, 4th edn (Princeton: Princeton University Press, 1974), pp. 284–306.

contemporary, i.e., decadent, political scene.) Indeed, he appreciates
the mingling of races only insofar as it provides the new ruling elite
with an adaptable, pliable mass, onto which it may stamp the imprint
of the new European order.[9] In 'the great play and fight of forces', it
would seem, everything is up for grabs.

In fact, however, not everything is up for grabs. That the
Germans will occupy the center of Nietzsche's Europe is treated as
settled and non-negotiable. In his mind, any progress toward the
restoration of Germany will necessarily involve progress toward the
restoration of Europe as a whole. In this light, it makes perfect sense
for him to attend so closely to the strengths and defects of the German
people. Other ethnic and racial markers may and will be preserved in
the 'great play and fight of forces', but only in the event that they
complement or enhance the Germanocentrism that Nietzsche envisions for the new European order. His 'Europe', in short, may be
little more than a metonym for a transfigured, fortified Germany.

Nietzsche's Germanocentrism thus imposes some formidable
constraints on the execution of his project of racial engineering.
Rather than conduct an objective survey of the quanta of force
configured throughout contemporary Europe, he stipulates that all
configurations must be rearranged to suit the anticipated restoration of
German culture. Rather than construct the new European order around
a center that is already rich in culture, subtlety, and spirituality, he
reserves the center for the Germans, whom he also diagnoses as

---

9   Nietzsche thus explains, for example, how the 'democratic' movement actually
    plays into his hands: 'the overall impression of such future Europeans will
    probably be that of manifold garrulous workers who will be poor in will,
    extremely employable, and as much in need of a master and commander as of
    their daily bread. But while the democratization of Europe leads to the
    production of a type that is prepared for *slavery* in the subtlest sense, in single,
    exceptional cases the *strong* human being will have to turn out stronger and
    richer than perhaps ever before – thanks to the absence of prejudice from his
    training, thanks to the tremendous manifoldness of practice, art, and mask. I
    meant to say: the democratization of Europe is at the same time an involuntary
    arrangement for the cultivation of *tyrants* – taking that word in every sense,
    including the most spiritual' (JGB 242).

culturally impoverished. While it is certainly possible that Germany could be restored to a position of cultural prominence, is it not the case that more promising candidates are available? Would it not be more efficient to remake Europe with an established cultural force (e.g. France) at its cultural center? In light of his unwavering Germanocentrism, Nietzsche must become unusually creative in his efforts at matchmaking.

With whom, then, does Nietzsche propose to match the culturally challenged Germans? As his diagnosis indicates, no other European nation or people possesses in abundance what Germany lacks. The French can contribute psychological subtlety, politesse, and an entrenched moralistic sense, but they cannot provide the infusion of spirit that the restoration of culture requires. The most obvious match, which he playfully considers before turning serious, is with the Jews, whom he describes as the 'strongest, toughest, and purest race now living in Europe' (JGB 251). Indeed, he observes that

> [a] thinker who has the development of Europe on his conscience will, in all his projects for this future, take into account the Jews as well as the Russians as the provisionally surest and most probable factors in the great play and fight of forces [...] That the Jews, if they wanted it – or if they were forced into it, which seems to be what the anti-Semites want – could even now have preponderance, indeed quite literally mastery over Europe, that is certain; that they are not working and planning for that is equally certain (ibid.).

Fortunately for the anti-Semites (and, for different reasons, for Nietzsche), the Jews have no interest in dominating Europe. Their main interest lies elsewhere – or so he claims. Although he does not say so, he apparently views their aversion to dominance as a weakness. Since the Jews are not leaders, they must be matched with a masterly people.

Articulating the terms of the match he proposes, Nietzsche explains how the Jews might figure in his plans for the future of Europe. Presenting himself as both a friend of European Jews and their spokesman, he avers that the Jews 'want and wish, even with some importunity, to be absorbed and assimilated (*ein- und auf-gesaugt*) by Europe' (JGB 251). He furthermore urges that this wish be granted, even recommending that Germany 'expel the anti-Semitic screamers' who oppose the assimilation of the Jews (ibid.). Because the Jews wish to be assimilated, in fact, the match that he proposes makes perfect sense: the Germans yearn to rule Europe but cannot, whereas the Jews could easily master Europe but have devoted their spiritual energies to the quest for a permanent European home. If these two peoples could somehow be persuaded to pool their respective resources, both would benefit from the collaboration, as would Europe as a whole. According to the terms of this proposed match, the 'nomadic' Jews would finally find a home at the spiritual center of a new European culture. All they need do in return is to share their potent spirituality with the dispirited nations of Europe, Germany in particular.

In a surprising development in an already surprising analysis, Nietzsche goes so far as to recommend that the Germans combat their cultural anemia by tapping into the overflowing spirit and vitality of the Jewish people. Toward that end, he proposes a program of intermarriage between Jewish women and officers from the Prussian military corps, which is the seat of the German nobility.[10] Since the Germans and Jews are unlikely to pursue this match on their own initiative, moreover, his recommendation also reserves for him a role as the arbiter of this pan-European order. He thus urges that the Jews' wish for assimilation be

> accommodated with all caution, with selection; approximately as the English nobility does. It is obvious that the stronger and already more clearly defined types of the new Germanism can enter into relations with them with the least hesitation; for example, officers of the nobility from the March Brandenburg: it would be interesting in many ways to see whether the hereditary art of commanding and obeying – in both of these the land just named is classical today – could not be enriched with the genius of money and patience (and above all a little spirituality, which is utterly lacking among these officers) (JGB 251).

10 My interpretation of this passage is indebted to Laurence Lampert, *Nietzsche's Task: An Interpretation of 'Beyond Good and Evil'* (New Haven and London: Yale University Press, 2001), pp. 256–57.

Especially when viewed against the backdrop of the Reich, aflame with nationalistic fervor, this is an extraordinarily bold recommendation. He clearly delights in the supposition that the Germans might revive themselves by mingling the supposedly pure blood of the Aryan race with the supposedly polluted blood of the Jews. The offspring of these proposed unions would not only spearhead the German renascence, but also expose the moral and scientific bankruptcy of German anti-Semitism. Of course, he also displays once again his weakness for stock racial stereotypes – a lingering symptom, perhaps, of his 'brief daring sojourn in [the] very infected territory' of anti-Semitism (ibid.). As this weakness confirms, his approach to racial engineering is by no means objective and disinterested. In fact, it seems that his prejudices motivate his 'quantum theory', and not the other way around.

To be sure, Nietzsche tenders this intermarriage proposal with his tongue planted firmly in his cheek.[11] He is only joking, as he immediately volunteers, merely indulging himself in a bit of 'cheerful Germano-mania and holiday oratory' (JGB 251). Calling himself to order, he immediately acknowledges that 'here it is proper to break off' his jest. As he explains, 'I am beginning to touch on what is serious for me, the "European problem" as I understand it, the cultivation of a new caste that will rule Europe' (ibid.).[12] This is

11 Nietzsche may not intend seriously his proposal that Jews and Germans intermarry, but in Nueva Germania, an Aryan colony founded in Paraguay by Nietzsche's sister Elisabeth and her husband, Bernhard Förster, the need for an expanded gene pool eventually became undeniable. After visiting the colony in 1991, Macintyre reports that several generations of inbreeding (and the genetic problems that invariably attend this dubious practice) have obliged the colonists of Nueva Germania to intermarry with the native Paraguayans (Ben Macintyre, *Forgotten Fatherland: The Search for Elisabeth Nietzsche* (London: Macmillan; New York: Farrar, Strauss, Giroux, 1992), pp. 202–18). If only the colonists had actually managed to read the 'cheerful' words of the philosopher whom they had uncritically adopted as their prophet!

12 As Nietzsche explains elsewhere, the task of this new ruling caste is to prepare Europe '*to acquire one will* [...] that would be able to cast its goals millennia hence – so the long-drawn-out comedy of its many splinter states as well as its

an important qualification, for it helpfully defines the focus of Nietzsche's own political interests. In the 'great play and fight of forces', the arranged pairing of Germans and Jews may indeed be a promising opening gambit, but it is not Nietzsche's move to make. A final determination of the optimal relations between Germans and Jews must be left to the ruling caste itself.

Laurence Lampert offers a persuasive and elegant account of Nietzsche's avowed turn to seriousness. According to Lampert:

> If Nietzsche's seriousness about the European future is not exactly to be sought in his matchmaking, his arrangement of marriages, how *is* the breeding of a ruling caste to be understood? [...] [The following sections of 'Peoples and Fatherlands'] show that the new ruling caste can be formed only through a marriage of minds; antimodern, anti-English ideas of German philosophy are to occasion marriages with the French in particular, a mothering people of genius involuntarily prey to the suitors of a fathering people.[13]

Lampert's interpretation has many merits. First of all, it faithfully accounts for the narrative continuity of the sections that follow JGB 251 in 'Peoples and Fatherlands'. As Lampert suggests, Nietzsche is involved there in a fairly detailed reckoning of the relative strengths and weaknesses of the English and French, respectively. He undertakes this reckoning, moreover, in order to determine an appropriate 'match' for the Germans. It is the French, he decides, who would best complement the Germans' unique strengths, compensate for their Reich-induced failings, and restore them to a place of European cultural prominence. He thus proposes a Franco-Prussian alliance to restore the cultural balance that the Franco-Prussian war destroyed.

Second, Lampert's interpretation is faithful to the restricted focus of Nietzsche's serious attention to the 'European problem'. Notwithstanding his manic proposal of intermarriage between Jews and Germans, he is expressly concerned only with the 'marriage of

---

dynastic and democratic splinter wills would come to an end. The time for petty politics is over: the very next century will bring the fight for the domination of the earth – the *compulsion* to large-scale politics' (JGB 208).

13   Lampert, p. 257.

minds' that will yield the new European elite. On this interpretation, Nietzsche's 'Germano-mania' appears as a temporary dereliction of his legislative duty, to which he was right to call a timely halt. He will contribute to the new European order not by prescribing actual matches between particular peoples, but by training the ruling elite to whom the task of racial matchmaking will eventually fall. Finally, Lampert's solution allows for Nietzsche to propose an essentially non-violent, non-manipulative solution to the 'European problem'. There is no suggestion here of using or abusing the Jews, no hint of the anti-Semitism in which Nietzsche earlier admitted his partial share. On this interpretation, any dark connotations that we may be tempted to associate with the task of 'cultivating a new ruling caste' are entirely unwarranted.

But Lampert's interpretation also raises a number of questions about Nietzsche's serious turn. A 'marriage of minds' would seem to be an unusually idealistic and ascetic solution for Nietzsche to propose. To put it bluntly: A 'marriage of minds' between Germans and French may yield wondrous offspring, but it will not solve the 'European problem' of decayed strength and atrophied spirituality. Indeed, what about the *bodies* of the Germans and the French and the physical maladies suffered by each nation? For that matter, what about the *bodies* of those Europeans over whom this new caste will exert its rule? How will a 'marriage of minds' reverse or arrest the decadence that Nietzsche locates in the jumbled instincts of con-temporary Europeans?

Lampert's explanation is faithful to the spirit of 'Peoples and Fatherlands', but it also illuminates an important limitation of Nietzsche's turn to seriousness:

> Nietzsche stands in a long tradition of political philosophy according to which fitness to rule is conferred by nature, by supremacy of spirit and intellect, and rule is won by words, persuasive words that create whole peoples.[14]

14   Lampert, p. 261.

To be sure, Nietzsche is nothing if not a man of words; he is therefore well suited to the task that Lampert describes. If Nietzsche is to 'create whole peoples', however, his words must eventually influence the actual mating arrangements that will produce the new breed of Europeans. After all, quanta of force can be redistributed, and races remade, only through the consummation of fully embodied unions. But Nietzsche seems more comfortable presiding over sanitized, disembodied unions.

While writing under the spell of his mania, Nietzsche proposed to accommodate the selective mating of Jews and Germans; he went so far as to target the officers of the March Brandenburg as likely candidates for his breeding program. In his more serious role, however, he now retreats to an abstract world of words and delegates to unnamed others the messy details of arranging fruitful unions. This gesture of deferral returns Nietzsche to a familiar, if disappointing, position. He apparently would prefer to devote his energies to a political prelude or preparation than to intervene directly as a political agent in his own right. Although he may have been manic to propose intermarriage between Germans and Jews, *someone,* at some point in the formation of the new European order, will need to prescribe similar 'matches' between complementary nations and peoples. Nietzsche's mania, that is, must eventually become the stuff of someone else's sober seriousness.

Is it possible that Nietzsche, the self-proclaimed champion of the body, is squeamish and shy precisely where the future of Europe is most clearly at stake? Has he grown serious precisely where a cheerful mania might be more productive?

III.

When Nietzsche breaks off his 'cheerful Germano-mania and holiday oratory', he claims to do so because seriousness is more 'proper' to his consideration of the 'European problem'. It is not entirely clear, however, why he believes that the seriousness of the ensuing discussion counts in its favor. It is by no means obvious, for example, that his serious solution to the 'European problem' yields a more practical or plausible alternative to his manic matchmaking. If anything, his 'serious' proposal of a Franco-German alliance may be more ridiculous than his 'cheerful' proposal of intermarriage between Jews and Germans. Moreover, he has avowed his seriousness before in *Beyond Good and Evil*, and with respect to a similarly dubious end: He claims to see 'new philosophers coming up' (JGB 2).

But apart from any doubts we might have about the aims that prompt his occasional turns to seriousness, we might also wonder more generally about his apparent respect for positions, ideas, goals and projects pursued under the banner of seriousness. Is seriousness not one of the more familiar targets of his ridicule and invective? Does he not associate seriousness with the 'spirit of gravity', the will to truth, the ascetic ideal, and other manifestations of nihilism and cultural decline? In particular, does he not ally himself more regularly with the forces of *Heiterkeit*, especially when they are arrayed against the forces of *Ernst*? If so, then why would he commend himself for squelching his cheerful mania and assuming the leaden countenance of the serious scholar?

Let us consider, for example, *On the Genealogy of Morals*, which Nietzsche describes as a supplementary, clarifying 'sequel' to *Beyond Good and Evil*. In this 'sequel', he clearly opposes *Heiterkeit* to *Ernst* and pledges allegiance to the former. In his Preface to the *Genealogy*, he allows that 'there seems to be nothing *more* worth taking seriously [than the problems of morality]' (GM Preface 7). 'Among the rewards' for doing so, he explains, is

> that some day one will perhaps be allowed to take them *cheerfully* [*heiter*]. For cheerfulness [*Heiterkeit*] – or in my own language *gay science* – is […] the reward

of a long, brave, industrious, and subterranean seriousness [*Ernst*], of which, to be
sure, not everyone is capable (ibid.).

As this passage suggests, Nietzsche's genealogy of morals is supposed
to be (or approximate) an exercise of the 'gay science', which he prescribes as an antidote to the grave seriousness of the dominant will to
truth. *Heiterkeit* is not merely his reward for seriousness, but also his
liberation from seriousness. He has crawled and slithered through the
muck of serious scholarship precisely so that he might someday rise
above it:

> But on the day we can say with all our hearts, 'Onwards! our old morality too is
> part *of the comedy!*', we shall have discovered a new complication and possibility
> for the Dionysian drama of 'The Destiny of the Soul' – and one can wager that the
> grand old comic poet of our existence will be quick to make use of it! (ibid.)

These passages by no means deny the importance to philosophy of
serious scholarship. In fact, they honor the seriousness of Nietzsche's
scholarly labors as unattainable by most. In doing so, however, they
also clarify the ideal relationship (for people like Nietzsche) of seriousness to cheerfulness: The former should precede, and prepare for, the
latter. Seriousness is a means to cheerfulness, and not the other way
around. Seriousness for its own sake, as an end unto itself, is both a
symptom of decline and a recipe for further ruin.

Later in the *Genealogy*, Nietzsche introduces the presumptive
villain of his narrative, the ascetic priest, as 'the actual *representative of
seriousness*' (GM III 11), to whom he opposes the artist (GM III 25)
and the comedians of the ascetic ideal (GM III 27). Although he does
not say so, we may plausibly infer that these designated opponents of
the ascetic priest are dangerous precisely insofar as they partake of
Heiterkeit. Their good cheer will presumably banish or temper the
gravity of the ascetic ideal and perhaps loosen its exclusive hold on us.
Their infectious levity may enable us to enclose even the ascetic priest
and his somber ministrations within the circle of our irreverent laughter.
For an example of the libratory power of *Heiterkeit*, we might consider
Nietzsche's irreverent wish on behalf of Wagner and his *Parsifal*:

Was this Parsifal meant *seriously* [*ernst*]? For one might be tempted to suppose the reverse, even to desire it – that the Wagnerian *Parsifal* was intended as a joke, as a kind of epilogue and satyr play with which the tragedian Wagner wanted to take leave of us, also of himself, above all *of tragedy* in a fitting manner worthy of himself, namely with an extravagance of wanton parody of the tragic itself, of the whole gruesome earthly seriousness [*Erden-Ernst*] and misery of his previous works, of the *crudest form*, overcome at last, of the anti-nature of the ascetic ideal (GM III 3).

Nietzsche furthermore implies that the ascetic priest may eventually contribute to the production of his dialectical other: the "'philosopher'", who is not to be confused with those 'philosophers' who swaddle themselves in 'ascetic wraps and cloaks' (GM III 10). Nietzsche likens this new breed of "'philosopher'" to a gloriously emergent butterfly, whose gravity-defying flight conveys the lightness associated with *Heiterkeit*. This hovering, fluttering butterfly thus provides a vivid contrast to the 'repulsive and gloomy caterpillar form' from which it evolves (GM III 10). In all of these passages from the *Genealogy*, seriousness is depicted as a means to and condition of cheerfulness. The collective implication of these passages is that seriousness, grave and constrictive in its own right, is redeemed only by the cheerfulness that it potentially enables.[15]

15   This identification of seriousness as a means to cheerfulness is corroborated in Book V of *The Gay Science*, which was added in 1886 along with a new Preface. Nietzsche recommends 'another ideal', whose exemplar, he conjectures 'confronts all earthly seriousness so far...as if it were [his] most incarnate and involuntary parody' (FW 382). While this formulation confirms the passages cited above from the *Genealogy*, Nietzsche immediately adds, with specific reference to the exemplar of his alternative ideal, that 'in spite of all of this, it is perhaps only with him that *great seriousness* really begins, that the real question mark is posed for the first time, that the destiny of the soul changes, the hand moves forward, the tragedy *begins*' (FW 382). This last qualifying clause recalls the '*Incipit tragoedia*' with which Nietzsche introduces FW 342, the section that marks the original conclusion to *The Gay Science*, and so identifies Zarathustra as the unnamed exemplar of the alternative ideal. It is interesting to note that in his Preface to the second edition of *The Gay Science*, Nietzsche offers his readers a beguiling admonition: '*Incipit tragoedia*' we read at the end of this awesomely aweless book. 'Beware! Something downright wicked and malicious

My interest in determining the ideal relationship of *Ernst* to *Heiterkeit* is not merely academic. Nor am I interested simply in exposing an inconsistency or vacillation on Nietzsche's part. Rather, it seems to me that he is simply mistaken in *Beyond Good and Evil* §251 if he means to suggest that his seriousness marks some kind of qualitative improvement upon his cheerful 'Germano-mania'. That his turn to seriousness is in fact a retrograde movement is evident in the discussion that follows his turn to seriousness in *Beyond Good and Evil* §251. As I hope to show, his plans for the future of Europe suffer precisely from a shortage of *Heiterkeit*, especially with respect to his own role as broker of the new European union. Like the Wagner who delivered *Parsifal*, he does not yet 'know how to laugh at himself' (GM III 3). In particular, he is not yet able to laugh at the Germanocentrism that motivates and distorts his vision of a Europe renewed.[16]

IV.

Charles Mills has recently claimed to expose the 'racial contract' that both antedates and enables the various social contracts to which enlightened citizens of liberal European polities (or their erstwhile imperial possessions) typically appeal when making claims about

---

is announced here: *incipit parodia*, no doubt' (FW Preface 1). Does this qualification mean that the 'great seriousness' that Zarathustra supposedly inaugurates is also, perhaps simultaneously, a parody? If so, then perhaps we are right after all to locate the value of seriousness in its capacity to yield or enable cheerfulness.

16   Acknowledging the ideal relationship between seriousness and cheerfulness, Lampert artfully portrays Nietzsche as concluding 'Peoples and Fatherlands' on a light note: 'So Nietzsche ends merrily, on a bit of clowning that twists a local prejudice in favor of the fatherland to his own vast barbarian trans-Christian, trans-German, deeply European end' (p. 261).

social justice.[17] According to Mills, the 'racial contract' functions to install a set of normative background conditions for the administration of a just society. He thus explains that

> the most important political system of recent global history – the system of domination by which white people have historically ruled over and, in important ways, continue to rule over nonwhite people – is not seen as a political system at all. It is just taken for granted; it is the background against which other systems, which we *are* to see as political, are highlighted.[18]

Foremost among these background conditions are the unstated (and unchallenged) grounds for the distinction between 'white' and 'non-white' citizens. Whereas the social contract promises justice to *all* citizens, the racial contract antecedently defines 'all' as *some* – namely, those deemed 'white'. Social justice is consequently guaranteed to all citizens but in fact delivered only to those (white) citizens who are also parties to the antecedent racial contract. Not all whites are signatories to the racial contract, but all are beneficiaries of its provisions.

The inevitable failure of the polity to deliver social justice to non-whites is customarily explained on the grounds that non-whites have failed – by dint of their indolence, ignorance, tribal nonage, or irrational preferences – to honor the social contract to which they are, supposedly, both signatories and beneficiaries. This reasoning, Mills believes, betrays a confusion of cause and effect. Non-whites are not excluded from the social contract because they fail to uphold their end of the bargain. They fail to uphold their end of the bargain because they have already been excluded from the social contract. Under the terms of the antecedent racial contract, non-whites were never allowed to become party to the agreement that they are subsequently

---

17 As Mills explains, '[T]he notion of a Racial Contract might be more revealing of the real character of the world we are living in, and the corresponding historical deficiencies of its normative theories and practices, than the raceless notions currently dominant in political theory' (Charles W. Mills, *The Racial Contract* (Ithaca, NY: Cornell University Press, 1997), p. 7).

18 Mills, pp. 1–2.

punished for violating.[19] Mills thus cautions that '[f]rom the inception, then, race is in no way an "afterthought", a "deviation" from ostensibly raceless Western ideals, but rather a central shaping constituent of those ideals'.[20]

As Mills persuasively shows, the alleged failure of non-whites to honor the social contract is in fact a result of their enforced exclusion from the benefits of social justice under the terms of the racial contract.[21] The dependence of the social contract on the racial contract thus leads Mills to conclude that

> [o]ne could say that the Racial Contract creates a transnational white polity, a virtual community of people linked by their citizenship in Europe at home and abroad (Europe proper, the colonial greater Europe, and the 'fragments' of Euro-America, Euro-Australia, etc.) and constituted an opposition to their indigenous subjects.[22]

When applied to the case of Nietzsche's plan for pan-European integration, Mills's analysis of the racial contract helps us to identify and illuminate the background conditions to which Nietzsche tacitly pledges allegiance. To be sure, Nietzsche does not propound a version of the social contract as a means of deriving a justification for the exercise of political power; in fact, he expressly ridicules the 'sentimentalism' that motivates all such theories (GM II 17). But he does articulate a vision of a unified Europe, which functions like a

19 Indeed, Mills believes that the perpetuation of this confusion of cause and effect continues to fault conventional moral and political theory: 'White moral theory's debates on justice in the state must therefore inevitably have a somewhat farcical air, since they ignore the central injustice on which the state rests.' (p. 39)

20 Mills, p. 14.

21 Mills goes on to claim that whites too are eventually victimized by the racial contract, in the sense that they too fail to understand the abstractly theorized world they have created: '[T]he Racial Contract prescribes for its signatories an inverted epistemology, an epistemology of ignorance, a particular pattern of localized and global cognitive dysfunctions (which are psychologically and socially functional), producing the ironic outcome that whites will in general be unable to understand the world they themselves have made.' (p. 18)

22 Mills, p. 29.

kind of contract between participating peoples and nations, especially those whose fortunes are most likely to improve in the new order he sketches. Moreover, his political thinking rests on various pre-suppositions about race, which contribute to the implementation of what Mills calls a 'racial contract'. As we have seen, the Germano-centrism of Nietzsche's Europe is not subject to challenge or revision. He also treats as non-negotiable his proposed shift in emphasis from *Staat* to *Kultur*, which will benefit only a few nations. These prejudices (and others) combine to form the 'racial contract' on which his social contract is silently predicated.

Having applied Mills's tools of analysis, we might now pose the following question to Nietzsche: What will be the defining racial identity of his pan-European polity? His repeated and hopeful references to a reunified Europe might lead us to conclude that the new order will include and honor *all* European nations and peoples. It would be natural, that is, to assume that what he means by 'Europe' bears a strong resemblance to what other Europeans understand it to mean. His cosmopolitan interest in surmounting the myriad problems associated with nationalism might also suggest that no single race will be allowed to dominate the new Europe. His attention to the principles of racial engineering furthermore indicates that he regards all European peoples objectively (if not equally), as possessing trans-ferable quanta of force.

As Mills demonstrates, however, it would be both naïve and dangerous to believe that a pan-European culture would be raceless, or that it would equally assimilate and distribute the disparate races and peoples blended into it. The myth of a deracinated, post-nationalistic Europe might serve Nietzsche as the 'noble lie' that cements the founding of his new order, but it would also belie the racial contract at work in this founding. If Mills's analysis of the racial contract is applicable in this case, then Nietzsche's rhetoric of European integration masks his expectation that the defining culture of this new European order will reflect a particular (and limited) racial composition. He may speak like a trans-national European cosmo-polite, but his vision of 'Europe' is surprisingly narrow and restricted.

His social contract welcomes all European nations as signatories and beneficiaries (even if their decadence requires him to serve as their proxy), while his racial contract identifies only the Germans and the French as deserving of the privileges pertaining to genuine European nations.

Mills's analysis thus helps us to distinguish between the social and racial contracts that underlie Nietzsche's plan for European re-integration. Whereas all European peoples and nations will contribute to the new order that he envisions, most of them will play no role whatsoever in the formation and composition of the new ruling elite. What is more, he does not attempt to hide his preference for a Europe dominated by the intertwined cultures of Germany and France. His discussion in 'Peoples and Fatherlands' conspicuously ignores most European peoples and nations and expressly yokes the destiny of Europe to the cultural promise of a Franco-German alliance. So although his social contract may promise an eclectic, cosmopolitan pan-European culture, his racial contract specifies the Germans and French as the true heirs and arbiters of European culture.

By means of this racial contract, Nietzsche effectively dis-tinguishes between 'Europeans' and 'non-Europeans'. All European peoples and nations will participate *politically* in Nietzsche's empire, but only the Germans and French will participate fully, i.e. *racially*, in the new European order.[23] Of course, even the French should be wary of the racial composition of the new Europe in which they are promised such a prominent appointment. The overwhelmingly dominant identity of Nietzsche's empire is Germanic, and the French have not fared well when paired with the Germans. Moreover, the French are needed only to supply the feminine touch that will temper the overwrought virility

---

23   As the restrictions of Nietzsche's 'racial contract' come more clearly into view, his relative lack of experience with European peoples and nations becomes an increasingly sensitive point of contention. Put quite simply, he possessed an extremely limited first-hand knowledge of Europe and Europeans. For a sobering account of these limitations, see David F. Krell and Donald L. Bates, *The Good European: Nietzsche's Work Sites in Word and Image* (Chicago: University of Chicago Press, 1997), p. 1.

of the Germans. Other than that assignment, he has no specific plans for them.

V.

While this racial contract certainly bodes ill for those peoples and nations who will not participate in the new ruling elite, an even darker cloud impends the future of those peoples and nations that Nietzsche expressly identifies as *non*-European. Here we might ask: What will become of the Jews in a Europe molded by a 'marriage of minds' consecrated by Nietzsche between the Germans and the French? He has already told us that:

> A thinker who has the development of Europe on his conscience will, in all his projects for this future, take into account the Jews [...] as the provisionally surest and most probable factors in the great play and fight of forces (JGB 251).

He furthermore has identified himself as this kind of thinker, especially in light of his 'serious' attention to 'the "European problem" as [he] understand[s] it' (JGB 251).

In the 'serious' discussion that follows, however, in which he arranges the 'marriage of minds' that will produce the new ruling elite, he makes no mention of the Jews.[24] This means that they will be

24 Lampert suggests that Nietzsche resumes his discussion of the Jews in the chapter following his turn to seriousness: 'But *noblesse* is now pronounced *Vornehmheit* so it's necessary [for Nietzsche] to add not only the final two sections on the Germans but a whole chapter – *Was ist vornehm?* – defining nobility in a new way, a chapter that peaks with the nobility of the philosopher, the solitary German wanderer who aims to give the European people a new direction loyal to what mothered and fathered it, Greeks, Romans, and Jews' (p. 258). As far as I can discern, however, and Lampert's commentary provides no contradiction, this 'new direction' is 'loyal' to the Jews only in the negative sense that it continues to overcome – and thereby distance European civilization from – the Jews' apostasy from nature in the Second Temple period.

party neither to the 'marriage of minds' nor to the new ruling caste that this spiritual union will produce. How, then, does the serious Nietzsche propose to take them into account as he plans the future of Europe?

The Jews are of interest to Nietzsche primarily because they are *not* a European race. (Despite their long history in Europe, he continues to treat them as a foreign people.)[25] Owing to their extra-European origins, the Jews are untouched, or so he believes, by the decadence that now grips Europe as a whole. Like the Russians, whom Nietzsche also views as a non-European people,[26] the Jews have amassed a comparative advantage in spiritual resources. He thus regards the Russians and the Jews as 'the provisionally surest and most probable factors in the great play and fight of forces' (JGB 251). He consequently hopes to harness their strength and spirit in his efforts to resuscitate the declining nations and peoples of Europe – hence his supposedly joking proposal of intermarriage between Jews and Germans.

Against the backdrop of his plans for the new Europe, however, Nietzsche's praise for the Jews appears distinctly double-edged. When he describes the Jews as the 'strongest, toughest, and purest race now living in Europe' (ibid.), he clearly means to salute them for resisting the decay that afflicts Europe as a whole. But he just as

25   Simon thus notes Nietzsche's resentment (or 'counter-resentment') of the Jews: 'Anyone who attempts to experience this particularity as an outsider inevitably finds that he has no access to this intellectual spirit. Rather, the experience that one has here is of the *other*, of an alienating way of behaving that calls forth a counterresentment.' (Josef Simon, 'Nietzsche on Judaism and Europe', in Jacob Golomb (ed.), *Nietzsche and Jewish Culture* (London: Routledge, 1997), pp. 101–116 (p. 107)).

26   As dangerous as it may be to the new European order that Nietzsche envisions, relying on the Jews is apparently preferable to relying on the Russians. In an alternative account of how an extra-European people might help Europe to acquire a single will and purpose, he speculates on the possible influence of Russia: 'I do not say this because I want it to happen: the opposite would be rather more after my heart – I mean such an increase in the menace of Russia that Europe would have to resolve to become menacing, too' (JGB 208).

clearly intends to deliver a backhanded compliment, for he is comparing the Jews to once great nations now grown decadent and dissolute. That the Jews are 'now living in Europe', he further speculates, may have something to do with the decadence that has secured their comparative advantage vis-à-vis all European nations and peoples.

In general, his approbatory references to the Jews – for their strength, spirit, resiliency, adaptability, etc. – are premised on an important caveat – namely, that they have prospered only at the expense of the advancement of European culture. In fact, he never completely renounces his suspicion that the Jews have deprived Europe of its birthright and defrauded the 'good Europeans' of their rightful legacy.

As the non-European parties to Nietzsche's social contract, the Jews would do well to examine the fine print on the racial contract that silently informs his plan for European re-integration. As a 'strong' race, they are expected both to assimilate into the new European union and to share their spirituality with lesser races and peoples. In exchange for these sacrifices they will supposedly be granted a home in the new European order, which, Nietzsche assures us, they desire most of all.

Let us set aside the questions of whether the Jews want a home in Europe and how Nietzsche would have knowledge of such a wish. What kind of home could they expect to enjoy in the pan-European union he envisions? According to Nietzsche, of course, the Jews *want* to be 'absorbed and assimilated', and he proposes to accommodate their wish. However, he does not specify what he takes this supposed wish to entail. *Assimilation* is a notoriously charged term of political discourse, for it seems to cover everything from the peaceful co-existence of diverse races and nations to the systematic deracination of alien peoples and cultures. Especially in light of Nietzsche's imperialistic designs, what he means by 'assimilation' may have little in common with the Jews' wish to make a home in Europe.

Everything, it would seem, turns on what he does and does not mean by the 'absorption and assimilation' of the Jews into Europe.[27]

We know that Nietzsche plans to select for and against various racial traits when matching complementary peoples and nations. While he certainly aims to preserve some elements of these various cultures and heritages, it is not obviously clear (or even plausible) that these elements can be selectively excised without destroying the racial identity of the people in question. Can he reasonably expect the desirable racial characteristics that he selects to thrive outside the cultural contexts from which he intends to pluck them? Whence the enduring value, for example, of Jewish 'spirituality' in the multiplex soul of a German, or of the German 'hereditary art of commanding and obeying' when transplanted into a culture of Jewish provenance? If a race properly constitutes a genuine whole or unity, then the selective assimilation he recommends may not only destroy the identity and integrity of the races involved, but also dilute the value of the racial traits he wishes to incorporate into his new European order. If racial identities are cut from something like whole cloth, as Nietzsche's analysis of racial cultivation indicates, then his proposed alterations threaten to destroy the fabric altogether.[28]

Perhaps, however, we are simply mistaken to assume that Nietzsche is concerned to preserve the racial identity of the Jews whom he hopes to absorb into his new European order. Perhaps, that is, he would not mind if the Jews were to disappear *qua* race once

---

27 Yovel advances a relatively charitable account of what Nietzsche has in mind, calling his solution to the problem of the Jews in Europe a '*creative assimilation*, in which the Jews are secularized, excel in all European matters and serve as catalysts in a new revaluation of values – this time a curative, Dionysian revolution – that will overcome the Christian culture and the "modern ideas" born of it' (p. 129).

28 Yovel records a similar concern, with respect specifically to the Jews in the 'creative assimilation' Nietzsche intends for them: 'The Jews' role is certainly not to 'Judaize' Europe in a religious sense. But *Nietzsche seems to believe that their existential qualities can be extracted regardless of the content of their belief*. Nietzsche would rather expect them to *secularize* and practice creative assimilation in the framework of an atheistic Europe' (p. 130).

they have distributed their spirit, strength, and resiliency to the decadent nations of Europe. This outcome, after all, would solve the 'European problem' *and* the 'Jewish question' in a single stroke. Europe would obtain the transfusion of spirit that it needs, and it would no longer face the obstacle posed by the non-negotiable tribalism of the Jews. The Jews in turn would be 'absorbed and assimilated' into Europe, in accordance with their supposed wish. To what extent they would continue to be identifiable as Jews, however, remains to be seen.

Nietzsche's ambivalence toward the Jews is well documented.[29] He admires their strength, resiliency, adaptability, and perseverance, but he also blames them for stalling the advance of European culture. In the *Genealogy*, for example, he identifies the Jews as the instigators of the 'slave revolt in morality' (GM I 7); the opponents of noble ideals (GM I 8); the enemies of Rome and all things imperial (GM I 16); and the architects of the Reformation and the French Revolution (GM I 16). As these passages indicate, he blames the Jews for every major historical setback to the cultural/social/political values that he expressly champions. He goes so far as to propose 'Rome against Judea, Judea against Rome' as a 'symbol' for the ongoing struggle that has defined the course of Western history (GM I 16).

Although he often uses 'Judea' and 'the Jews' as metonyms for the Jews of the Second Temple period,[30] whom he explicitly blames for the 'falsification of nature' that engendered Christianity,[31] he also regards contemporary Jews as sharing to some unspecified degree in (and, so, as propagating) the anti-naturalism of the Second Temple

---

29   See, for example, Yovel, ch. 9.
30   I am indebted for this line of argument to Yovel, pp. 152–63.
31   Nietzsche identifies the Jews as 'the strangest people in world history because, confronted with the question whether to be or not to be, they chose, with a perfectly uncanny deliberateness, to be *at any price*: this price was the *falsification* of all nature, all naturalness, all reality, of the whole inner world as well as the outer' (AC 24).

period.[32] As a consequence, his praise for the Jews of late nineteenth century Europe is always measured and conditional. Modern Jews have developed and matured in a number of impressive ways, but he nevertheless suspects that they have not fully extricated themselves from the anti-naturalism of the Second Temple period.

It seems likely, in fact, that Nietzsche's plan for the assimilation of the Jews *must* also involve their political neutralization, lest they frustrate him as they have frustrated predecessor champions of 'noble' values. His plan for Jewish assimilation is therefore quite complicated, for he regards the Jews as the most formidable opponents *both* to the spread of European decadence *and* to the consolidation of trans-national power.[33] He must somehow unleash – and subsequently harness – their spirituality in its former mode of expression without also authorizing its latter mode of expression. That is, he must somehow tame the oppositional power of the Jews, but only after first channeling this power toward the formation of a new European order.

His best option for ensuring the political neutralization of the Jews may be to encourage or allow their racial neutralization. Whatever it is that makes the Jews a difficult people to 'digest' must be mitigated, even if they are obliged in the process to forfeit their racial identity. In that event, the 'absorption and assimilation' of the Jews would likely involve their eventual deracination. To be sure, Nietzsche did not actively seek this outcome, for he did not hate the

---

32 See my '*Ecce Caesar*: Nietzsche's Imperial Aspirations', in Jacob Golomb and Robert S. Wistrich (eds), *Nietzsche, Godfather of Fascism? On the Uses and Abuses of a Philosophy* (Princeton: Princeton University Press, 2002), pp. 173–95 (pp. 185–90).

33 In one of his most straightforward accounts of the oppositional power that he attributes to the Jews, Nietzsche explains that 'The Jews are the antithesis of all decadents: they have had to *represent* decadents to the point of illusion; with a *non plus ultra* of histrionic genius they have known how to place themselves at the head of all movements of decadence (as the Christianity of *Paul* –), in order to create something out of them which is stronger than any *Yes-saying* party of life' (AC 24).

Jews. He feared them, and his fear was predicated on his ignorance of them. At the same time, however, he also said nothing that would forbid or prevent the deracination of those Jews whose assimilation he promised to facilitate. As we have seen, his 'racial contract' includes no provisions for preserving the racial identity of the Jews. If he expected or hoped for the Jews *qua* race to play a prominent role in his Europe, he kept these expectations and hopes to himself. A new Europe without the Germans at its center would be unthinkable, but a Europe devoid of a distinctly Jewish presence was apparently tolerable, if not preferable, to him.

As Yovel instructively suggests, Nietzsche was at best an 'anti-anti-Semite', for he proposed no positive or constructive alternative that might have completed or complemented his opposition to German anti-Semitism.[34] This double negation not only fails to yield a positive formulation of the optimal relationship of Germans (or Europeans) to Jews, but also reveals the persistence of his dependence on the cultural basis of the anti-Semitism to which he opposes himself. He may have objected to the common practices of demonizing and scapegoating the Jews, but he did not necessarily object to the cultural distance at which European cosmopolitanism typically holds the Jews. He too held the Jews at arm's length,[35] even as he complimented them for positioning and maintaining themselves at that distance. His fear of the Jews thus placed him in the passive service of hateful prejudices circulated by others. A thinker who was not himself an enemy of the Jews consequently became engulfed in the larger anti-Semitic animus of his day.

This, I suspect, is the hard truth lurking behind Nietzsche's seemingly generous offer to provide the Jews with a home at the spiritual center of a new European union. The costs to the Jews of this

---

34 Yovel, ch. 8.
35 In one of his least enlightened comparisons, Nietzsche proudly maintains that: 'We would no more choose the "first Christians" to associate with than Polish Jews – not that one even required any objection to them: they both do not smell good' (AC 46).

new home would have been prohibitive, for Nietzsche had no intention of allowing them to remain 'undigested' and politically troublesome. In the envisioned re-spiritualization of Europe, they were apparently to be used and used up.

Conclusion

By way of conclusion, let us briefly revisit Lampert's image of a 'marriage of minds' between the Germans and the French. The Germans presumably occupy the position of 'husband' in this union, for they display 'more *virile* virtues than any other country in Europe can show' (GD viii 1). The French, in turn, occupy the position of 'wife' in this union, for they are, as Lampert suggests, a motherly, nurturing people.[36]

If Nietzsche's diagnosis of the Germans is accurate, however, then an arranged 'marriage' to a receptive, wifely people will not be sufficient to restore them to a position of cultural prominence. The Germans, he insists, are not merely in need of the refined taste, psychological finesse, and complementary receptivity that the French can provide. The Germans are also lacking in spirit, which the French cannot provide. As Mills's analysis confirms, Nietzsche's social contract is therefore inadequate to found the trans-national polity he seeks to establish. He must consequently rely as well on a racial contract, which essentially licenses the Germans to help themselves to extra-European sources of spirit.

The proposed 'marriage of minds' will consequently require the support and sustenance of an 'extra-marital' arrangement. And this is precisely where the Jews figure in Nietzsche's plan: not as a nurturing 'wife' to the manly Germans, but as a seductive 'mistress' or 'temptress'. We know that he regards the Jews, like the French, as

36   Lampert, pp. 257–58.

an overly feminized people.[37] The Jews are neither masterly nor preponderant, and they are primarily concerned with the prospect of homemaking (JGB 251). They furthermore excel at the 'feminine' arts of masquerade, duplicity, dissembling, and mendacity. They possess 'a *non plus ultra* of histrionic genius' (AC 24), which befits what is essentially a race of 'actors' (FW 361).[38]

Unlike the French, however, the Jews derive excess spirit and strength from their cultivation of these 'feminine' arts. They are able thereby to transform their apparent powerlessness into power over their more virile, noble, imperial opponents. Unlike the harmless French, then, the Jews are resilient, unpredictable, and, so, eminently *dangerous*. (This is simultaneously the highest compliment and the meanest slight that Nietzsche can bestow upon a people or race.) While the French are like those foolish, gossipy women whom Nietzsche ridicules for the superficial ends to which they devote their plastic powers, the Jews remind him of those complex, seductive, predatory women who always attract – and routinely entrap – the best of men.[39] (This distinction between the harmlessly feminized French

37 An expression of his ambivalence toward the Jews is found in his occasional attempts to categorize the Jews as a more manly type of people. He suggests, for example, that the Jews belong, along with the Romans (and perhaps the Germans), to the type of 'peoples of genius' 'who must fertilize and become the causes of new orders of life' (JGB 248). As I maintain below, however, Nietzsche more characteristically figures the Jews on the model of an aggressive, seductive, dangerous type of woman – a type that treats men as men treat women.

38 In this section from *The Gay Science*, which addresses 'The problem of the actor [*Schauspieler*]', Nietzsche moves immediately from a discussion of the Jews, 'the people who possess the art of adaptability *par excellence*', to a discussion of women, who '*must* be first of all and above all else actresses' (FW 361).

39 Commenting on the same collection of passages from *The Gay Science*, Derrida conjectures, 'That Jews and women should be thus associated does not seem at all insignificant and the fact that Nietzsche often considers them in parallel roles might in fact be related to the motif of castration and simulacrum for which circumcision is the mark, indeed the name of the mark' (Jacques Derrida, *Spurs:*

and the perilously feminized Jews thus illuminates the twin poles between which Nietzsche's thoughts on women – and, so, his misogyny – typically oscillate.)

Although the virile Germans may need to mate chastely with the refined, sophisticated French, they will also need to mate sensuously with the seductive, enlivening Jews.[40] It is this latter union, in fact, that will enable the former union to succeed as planned. Whereas the former arrangement will be official, permanent, public, and entirely above board, the latter arrangement must remain illicit, temporary, furtive, and disavowed. Nietzsche's social contract may promise the Jews a home at the center of a restored Europe, but his racial contract prohibits them from participating openly in the new order.

If this sort of analysis is remotely accurate, then our attention to Nietzsche's racial contract helps to illuminate the likely status of the Jews in his envisioned European order. Although he sides against the hyper-virile Germans, this does not mean that he sides with the feminized Jews. He still fears the Jews for their womanly wiles, even as he acknowledges the surpassing value of their unique accomplishments. The Jews will be the saviors of Nietzsche's Europe, but because they are extra-European in origin, their contributions must be minimized. Like all 'mistresses', in fact, the Jews are ultimately dispensable to Nietzsche's Europe. They are needed simply to enliven the Germans and tempt them to their destined greatness. Apart from catalyzing the desired transition from *Staat* to *Kultur*, the Jews are of no further use to him. On the contrary, as we have seen, he suspects

---

Nietzsche's Styles, trans. Barbara Harlow (Chicago: University of Chicago Press, 1979), p. 69).

40   Nietzsche's 'manic' enthusiasm for a union between the virile Germans and the feminized Jews is captured in the following citation: 'Woman wants to be taken and accepted as a possession, wants to be absorbed into the concept of possession, possessed. Consequently, she wants someone who takes, who does not give himself or give himself away; on the contrary, he is supposed to become richer in "himself" – through the accretion of strength, happiness, and faith given him by the woman who gives herself' (FW 363).

that their unrivaled spirit and vitality pose a threat to the consolidation of his trans-national, pan-European polity.

Nietzsche may present himself only jokingly as a racial match-maker, but his more 'serious' plan for the spiritual renewal of Europe would seem to cast him in precisely this role. As it turns out, his joke is not so far removed from his more 'serious' consideration of 'the "European problem"' (JGB 251). His turn to seriousness does not so much veto the union he cheerfully proposes between Jews and Germans as it removes this union from public view and discussion. If anything, in fact, his 'cheerful Germano-mania' yields a more honest account of his dependency on the contributions of extra-European races like the Jews. Although he does not seriously expect the German nobility to take Jewish wives (not, at least, for the reasons he specifies), he *does* expect the Germans to revitalize themselves by borrowing as they please from the spiritual resources of 'strong' races like the Jews. He furthermore expects the Jews to disseminate their spirit and culture in the racial intermingling that he proposes as his solution to the 'European problem'. Nietzsche's intermarriage pro-posal is therefore only slightly less offensive when interpreted figurally, as a call for spiritual and cultural assimilation, for it still obliges the Jews to sacrifice their identity and heritage for the sake of a larger goal of dubious value.

Thomas H. Brobjer

Nietzsche as German Philosopher: His Reading of the Classical German Philosophers

Nietzsche's final view of the more important of the classical German philosophers is expressed in *Ecce homo*:

> In the history of knowledge the Germans are represented by nothing but ambiguous names, they have ever produced only 'unconscious' false-coiners (– Fichte, Schelling, Schopenhauer, Hegel, Schleiermacher deserve this description as well as Kant and Leibniz; they are all mere *Schleiermacher*, mere veilmakers –) (EH 'WA' 3).

In this essay I will briefly examine what lies behind this outright rejection of them and more extensively discuss and emphasize the evidence we have of what Nietzsche had read by, and to a lesser extent about, them. This has received little attention but is important both for understanding the reasons for Nietzsche's rejection and critique of them, as well as for judging the seriousness and depth of Nietzsche's views. I will also discuss his first impressions of these classical German philosophers, which in most cases were much more positive than his later, more well-known views. The results presented here are to a large extent based on work on Nietzsche's library and reading, with which I have been concerned for the past few years. Surprisingly, no such overall investigation seems to have been carried out previously.

Nietzsche implicitly divides German philosophers into three groups: firstly, the classical German philosophers whom he refers to as 'German philosophers' and whom the middle and late Nietzsche criticizes severely for being metaphysicians and, essentially, Christians; secondly, a disparate group of thinkers and philosophers whom he read but rarely referred to and, finally, the 'implicit' group of

German philosophers whom he neither read nor referred to, such as Wolff, Mendelssohn, Jacobi and, of course, many others.

The second group includes German thinkers whom he praises but does not refer to as philosophers, such as Lichtenberg and Lessing, a group of philosophers whom he criticizes but rarely read or mentions individually, the materialists, and a disparate group of philosophers whom he read intensively, but rarely, if ever, mentions in the published works, such as Lange, Liebmann, Dühring, Mainländer, Hartmann, Bahnsen and Teichmüller.[1]

I will discuss Nietzsche's view of, relation to and reading of the classical German philosophers Leibniz, Herder, Kant, Fichte, Schelling, Hegel, Herbart, Schopenhauer, Schleiermacher, Marx and Feuerbach. Nietzsche's relation to these thinkers are often discussed, and some of them, like Schopenhauer and Kant, were essential to Nietzsche's intellectual development. Others, like Feuerbach and Hegel, may have been, but the majority were of little importance to him. Nonetheless, they constitute an important background to Nietzsche's philosophy and thinking, and he refers to them relatively frequently.

Nietzsche as German philosopher

It could be argued that Nietzsche should not be regarded as a German philosopher at all. Firstly, at the age of twenty-four he 'resigned' his Prussian citizenship and thereafter remained stateless for the rest of his life. Secondly, the strongest early philosophical influences on him were not German but Greek and American, in the form of Plato (and other ancient Greeks) and Emerson. He will soon thereafter become

---

1   I will discuss Nietzsche's knowledge and reading of these philosophers in a forthcoming book, *Nietzsche's Knowledge of Philosophy: A Study and Survey of the Philosophical Influences on Nietzsche.*

strongly influenced by Schopenhauer, Lange and Kant, but this influence he will later reject, which was not true for the influence of Emerson and the Greeks. Thirdly, he never even mentions a number of important German philosophers such as Wolff, Mendelssohn, Thomasius, Jacobi and others, and he apparently has not read anything at all, or only very limited amounts of Leibniz, Fichte, Schelling, Herbart and others. Fourthly, Nietzsche himself did not want to be a German philosopher. He was the most anti-German of all German philosophers and suggested 'German' as a new four-letter word suitable for something very superficial (EH 'WA' 3),[2] and he claimed that it would be easier to translate his books into French than into German. Instead he referred to himself as a good European. Fifthly, the Germans themselves do not wish to regard him as German, at least in the general sense which is reflected in the fact that many Germans are ashamed of him and that Berlin not only has one, or several, Kant, Schopenhauer and Fichte streets etc., and also one or two Hartmann, Stirner and Treitschke streets, but no Nietzsche street.[3]

The claim that Nietzsche was not a German philosopher is perhaps a possible and reasonable claim with regard to the classical German philosophers discussed in this paper, but with regard to the second group of lesser known German philosophers this claim has essentially no validity. In fact, a critique or a disinterestedness towards the great German philosophers was more the norm than the exception among professional philosophers in the second half of the nineteenth century. Yet Nietzsche, in spite of his critique, was a German philosopher, spoke and wrote in German, and lived in a German cultural climate which becomes evident when one looks more closely at his thinking. Nietzsche was at the same time immensely concerned about German culture which is reflected in the fact that

2   Cf. also KSA 11, 37[4].

3   There is also no Nietzsche street in Weimar, for example, but Nietzsche streets do exist. With the help of a postcode catalogue I have found about fifteen, and there are almost certainly more.

German and Germany are two of the most frequently occurring words in his writings, that he wrote a chapter entitled 'What the Germans Lack' (GD viii) and planned to write whole books on this theme. It is true that Nietzsche's first closer encounter with philosophy seems to have been through Emerson and Plato rather than through specifically German philosophers, but soon thereafter he became influenced in a stronger sense by Schopenhauer, Kant and Lange.

The young Nietzsche had a relatively limited knowledge of philosophy as is shown when we examine his reading. His reading was very much more extensive in the fields of classical philology and literature, including literary criticism, than in philosophy. Furthermore, the word 'philosophy', or 'philosopher', does not occur in Nietzsche's letters at all until he has turned twenty, and in no important sense until after his discovery of Schopenhauer. Likewise, when one examines what journals Nietzsche read, one finds that journals in each of the fields of philology, literature, music and general culture outnumber the journals of philosophy that he read. Moreover, the only classical German philosopher to be found in Nietzsche's private library is Schopenhauer.

Thus, one should be wary of assuming that Nietzsche had a very close knowledge and first-hand experience of the great German philosophers. On the other hand, the *Zeitgeist* of the second half of the nineteenth century was so steeped in metaphysical philosophy and the great German philosophers that, even without first-hand reading, a German student or intellectual would have been relatively well acquainted with them.

Nietzsche's View of German Philosophy and German Philosophers as a Group

Nietzsche's repeated and strongly hostile critique of German philosophy and the great German philosophers – with such statements as 'German philosophy is at bottom – a *cunning* theology' (AC 10), and 'the erring instinct in all and everything, *anti-naturalness* as instinct, German décadence as philosophy' (AC 11) – can easily lead one to the impression that Nietzsche was well-informed, involved and consistently hostile to German philosophy and philosophers. This, however, is far from correct.

The early Nietzsche had a positive view of German philosophy, based mainly on his high regard for Kant and Schopenhauer, but also influenced by Wagner and the nationalism which he adopted under his influence, which even included a positive view of the Reformation. At this time Nietzsche associates German philosophy with German music and with Greek antiquity, including tragedy. German philosophy (Kant) had shown the limits of science and thus given us a possibility to curb Socratic optimism and scientism.[4] In his most optimistic moods Nietzsche then saw a possibility of the birth of a new tragic age in Germany.[5] However, in general Nietzsche says relatively little about German philosophy and philosophers, and his statements are, on the whole, mild, suggesting that he was not particularly involved with German philosophy at this time.

Around 1876 Nietzsche 'breaks' with Schopenhauer, Kant and Wagner and becomes more positivistically and scientifically oriented. This will inevitably lead to a more critical view of German meta-

---

4   For a time Nietzsche makes such strong connections between German philosophy (Kant) and the pre-Socratics – often to the advantage of the Germans – that he felt that the pre-Socratics ought to have realized some of the problems and solutions presented by Kant.

5   This is especially visible in GT 19, but also in other sections of this work, in UB III (*Schopenhauer als Erzieher*), *Ueber die Zukunft unserer Bildungsanstalten* and in some notes from this time.

physical philosophy. However, due to his non-involvement with German philosophy this is not visible for some time. Not until *Daybreak* (1881) does he explicitly express definite and relatively strong critique of it, and even then these statements are very few implying a disinterest and non-involvement with German philosophy. It seems likely that Nietzsche read little by, and about, the German metaphysical philosophers between *c.* 1874 and 1884:

> *German hostility to the Enlightenment.* – Let us consider the intellectual contribution to general culture made by the Germans of the first half of this century, and let us take first the German philosophers: they retreated to the first and oldest stage of speculation, for, like the thinkers of dreamy ages, they were content with concepts instead of explanations – they brought to life again a pre-scientific species of philosophy (M 197).[6]

The period of strong and consistent hostility towards German metaphysical philosophy began early in 1884 and continued to the end of his active life. However, it seems as if it is only during the early part of this period, during 1884 and 1885, that Nietzsche actively concerns himself with German philosophy, for it is only then that his notebooks contain a larger number of notes discussing and criticizing them.[7] It seems likely that this is the result of reading during this period, and since he almost always speaks of them as a group, it seems highly unlikely that he read works by them individually (without this leaving any other traces) and far more likely that he read one or several books about them as a group. He read a number of books about philosophy at this time, but none of the ones which have been identified seems likely to have elicited these views and comments. Thus, the source or origin to which these comments probably was a response was a work which remains for the time being unidentified. In these notes the 'great' German philosophers are seen as religious, theological, romantic and metaphysical. After September

---

6   Nietzsche's critique of German philosophers is also visible in sections 167 and 190 of this work, and in three notes from 1880 and 1881 (KSA 9, 3[31], 7[125], 12[151]).

7   For example, KSA 11, 25[303], 26[8, 412, 445], 34[157], 38[7], 41[4], 42[3, 6].

1885 there are again very few explicit references to German philosophy or to German philosophers as a group in his notebooks until the second half of 1888. However, the views Nietzsche wrote down in the notes from 1884–85 do occasionally become visible in the later published books, especially *Beyond Good and Evil* (1886) and the fifth book of *The Gay Science* (1887). But it is not until the books of the last year, 1888, (*The Wagner Case, Twilight of the Idols, The Antichrist* and *Ecce homo*) that the critique becomes explicit and highly hostile.

Nietzsche's Knowledge and Reading of Individual Great German Philosophers

Nietzsche's Philosophical Inspiration and Teacher: Schopenhauer

Nietzsche's more intensive interest in philosophy began with the discovery and reading of Schopenhauer's *Die Welt als Wille und Vorstellung* (*The World as Will and Representation*) in late 1865 and of F. A. Lange's *Geschichte des Materialismus* (*History of Materialism*) the following year. Before then his interest in philosophy had been limited, but that which he had expressed had probably been furnished by broad general interests, by an interest in Plato during 1863 and 1864 and the ancient *Weltanschauung* in general, possibly by his reading of Emerson from 1862 and onwards, and most importantly, by the inner conflict caused by the strain between intellectual integrity and truth on the one hand and the demands of Christian faith on the other.[8] His discovery of Schopenhauer would change all that.

---

8   Nietzsche was later to explain that the main reason Schopenhauer was so important for him, was that he was an atheist (EH 'UB' 2). Nietzsche seems to have broken with the Christian faith between 1862 and 1865, shortly before he

At the age of twenty-one Nietzsche discovered Schopenhauer's *magnum opus*, *Die Welt als Wille und Vorstellung*, in a bookshop in Leipzig in October or November 1865, and immediately became a Schopenhauerian and would remain one for the next ten years.[9] Two years later Nietzsche described the discovery with the words:

> I do not know what daemon whispered to me: 'Take this book home with you' [...] At home I threw myself into the sofa corner with the treasure I had acquired, and started to allow that energetic, sombre genius to work upon me. Here every line screamed renunciation, denial, resignation, here I saw a mirror in which I caught sight of world, of life, and of my own mind in terrifying

found Schopenhauer, but it would take more than a decade before he became hostile towards it.

9   Nietzsche describes his 'discovery' of Schopenhauer as sudden and unexpected: 'One day I found in the old Rohn's second-hand bookshop this book by Schopenhauer, took it in my hand, although it was completely unknown to me, and briefly examined it.' (FS 3/297–99, and KGW I.4 506–30, 60[1]) However, it seems as if he, in fact, had encountered Schopenhauer's philosophy before then. He may have heard a lecture about Schopenhauer's aesthetics, when one of Nietzsche's teachers at Pforta, Franz Kern, gave a lecture at the Literaria which was open to the citizens of Naumburg, with the title 'Die Grundzüge der Schopenhauerschen Aesthetik' sometime between 1860 and 1866 (the exact date and year of the lecture is not known). Furthermore, the journal *Anregungen für Kunst, Leben und Wissenschaft*, which Nietzsche read and subscribed to (at least for a year in 1861–62 together with his friends Pinder and Krug) published a number of articles about Schopenhauer (especially relating to his view of music). More certain is that Nietzsche listened and noted down references to Schopenhauer in the university course 'Outline of the History of Philosophy' by Schaarschmidt which he attended during the 1865 summer semester in Bonn. Nietzsche's as yet unpublished notes on this course contain no German philosophy with the exception of Kant and a one-page summary of Schopenhauer's critique of Kant's philosophy. Nietzsche also read Karl Fortlage's *Genetische Geschichte der Philosophie seit Kant* (Leipzig, 1852) in 1864–65. In this work he is likely to have read the chapter on Schopenhauer, which consists of a relatively neutral account of Schopenhauer's philosophy.

grandeur. Here the full, disinterested, sun-like eye of art looked upon me, here I saw sickness and healing, exile and sanctuary, hell and heaven (FS 3/298).[10]

This immediate affinity with Schopenhauer is not all that surprising, for Schopenhauer's philosophy goes well with Nietzsche's cultural, musical and aesthetic interests and values, and with his liking of Plato and Emerson, with their metaphysical philosophy, their emphasis on a sort of philosophy of life and with their literary and 'existential' manner of writing. Furthermore, it seems correct, as Nietzsche later claimed, that Schopenhauer's atheism (but still with a kinship to Christianity) further attracted Nietzsche who had lost his Christian faith shortly before.[11]

The discovery of Schopenhauer profoundly strengthened the philosophical tendency in Nietzsche's thinking. Nietzsche's relation to Schopenhauer in 1865–69 is one of extreme enthusiasm. He frequently read Schopenhauer, he persuaded his friends to read him (and to become Schopenhauerians), he continually praised Schopenhauer in his letters, referring to him as a demi-god, the greatest philosopher of the last thousand years etc., and he treated critics of Schopenhauer as personal enemies. Schopenhauer came to affect all of his thinking and he wished, against the advice and inclination of his teacher Ritschl, to let this philosophy affect his philological writings. He began to write philological work on more philosophical themes, such as Democritus and Diogenes Laertius, and he planned to write a history of literature from a Schopenhauerian perspective. The discovery of Schopenhauer not only changed Nietzsche's way of thinking and pushed it in a philosophical direction generally, but also very directly influenced his thinking, attitude and reading. In his letters from late 1865 and 1866 he suddenly becomes pessimistic and life-denying and appears to regard life as necessary suffering. The majority of the non-philological books Nietzsche read the following years were recommended to him in the works by Schopenhauer, or

10   I am using Janaway's translation in Christopher Janaway (ed.), *Willing and Nothingness: Schopenhauer as Nietzsche's Educator* (Oxford: Oxford University Press, 1998), p. 16. Cf. also EH ii 1.

11   See note 8 above.

were about Schopenhauer or were written by Schopenhauerians who elaborated on his philosophy.

Nietzsche's reading of Schopenhauer also strongly improved and influenced his interest in and knowledge of philosophy in general and the history of philosophy. Schopenhauer continually discusses philosophical questions and other philosophers' views in his works. His *Parerga und Paralipomena* also contains, apart from such general comments and many more special philosophical essays, a chapter of over one hundred pages, entitled 'Fragment zur Geschichte der Philosophie'.

What Nietzsche most clearly affirms is Schopenhauer as a person, his general *Weltanschauung* and his pessimism, but also a number of more specific aspects of his philosophy, including his view of art, of music, of language and style, and of pity.[12]

However, among Nietzsche's many enthusiastic notes and comments in letters we also find a number of connected notes, covering about ten published pages, written sometime between the autumn of 1867 and early 1868 in which Schopenhauer's philosophy is severely criticized.[13] In these notes Nietzsche seems to be rejecting the whole basis of Schopenhauer's philosophy:

---

12 In a letter to Rohde of 8 Oct. 1868 Nietzsche gives some of the reasons why he values Schopenhauer: 'Mir behagt an Wagner, was mir an Schopenhauer behagt, die ethische Luft, der faustische Duft, Kreuz, Tod und Gruft etc.' (KSB 2/322). The late Nietzsche is extremely critical of pity ('Mitleid'), but the early Nietzsche affirms, with Schopenhauer, the feeling and affect of pity.

13 KGW I.4 57[51–55, 61]. The same notes, though less complete and reliable, were also published in FS (3/352–62). Two translations of these notes into English have be published, by Crawford and Janaway, both from the earlier FS version. Karl Schlechta discusses these notes in his article 'Der junge Nietzsche und Schopenhauer', *Jahrbuch der Schopenhauer-Gesellschaft*, 26 (1939), 289–300.

On Schopenhauer.
An attempt to explain the world using a single assumed factor.
The thing in itself takes on one of its possible forms.
The attempt is unsuccessful.
Schopenhauer did not regard it as an attempt. [...]

If the discussion and analysis in these notes are Nietzsche's own (rather than being based on literature critical of Schopenhauer) it is probably Nietzsche's first extended, detailed and independent philosophical analysis. However, it is surprising that Nietzsche's attitude towards Schopenhauer does not seem to change in the slightest after making this analysis. One answer to this is that what Nietzsche affirms is Schopenhauer's style and general *Weltanschauung*, and therefore other aspects are of little consequence. Nietzsche suggests such a solution in letters to Deussen (see below) and this is how Schlechta seems to regard it.[14] However, such an answer seems to me unsatisfactory both in regard to Nietzsche's intellectual integrity and since his later break with Schopenhauer's thinking in 1875–76 has such profound consequences for his thinking then.

Another surprising aspect of these notes is that, in Nietzsche's response to two letters from Paul Deussen (both have unfortunately been lost) in which he attempts to persuade Nietzsche to write an apology or critique of Schopenhauer, Nietzsche claims to have no interest in doing so and that it would furthermore be futile, for either one accepts the overall view of a philosopher or not (the way one

---

14   'Daß diese soeben kurz skizzierte Kritik in die Zeit von Nietzsches leidenschaftlichster Schopenhauerverehrung fällt, ist öfter bemerkt und immer nach Äußerungen des älteren Nietzsche über die letzten Gründe seiner jugendlichen Begeisterung erklärt worden. Eine solche Interpretation aber der an sich gewiß merkwürdigen Tatsache ist, wie insbesondere die oben anmerkungsweise erwähnten Briefe an Paul Deussen beweisen, gar nicht nötig: der junge Nietzsche schon verlangt von dem Philosophen keine Lösung, sondern eine verdichtete Darstellung des Rätsels der Welt, und tritt damit bereits aus einem geistigen Raume heraus, in dem der von ihm geliebte Meister selbst noch atmete' (Schlechta, 'Der junge Nietzsche und Schopenhauer', p. 298).

either smells a rose or not), but nonetheless Nietzsche wrote these rather extensive notes on the theme.[15]

The reason to believe that the critique is essentially Nietzsche's own – and it has been regarded as such by all commentators so far, as far as I am aware – is that no major source (or inspiration) for the notes has been found, and because Nietzsche makes continual references to specific pages in Schopenhauer's works.

On the other hand, I find it surprising that, if Nietzsche had worked out the critique himself, it did not affect his view and evaluation of Schopenhauer at all. However, if he is basically summarizing critiques put forward by others, this lack of effect and emotional consequences is less surprising. Further research is needed to settle this point, but until more evidence is forthcoming, we probably need to assume that the critique was conducted by Nietzsche himself. I find it surprising that no serious attempt seems to have been made to carry out a thorough examination of this important question. Our view of these notes, and our understanding of Nietzsche's whole relation to Schopenhauer, depends on whether this is Nietzsche's own critique or a summary of other persons' critiques. It is, in fact, not even altogether impossible that Nietzsche wrote down these notes for the purpose of writing a defence of Schopenhauer, as Deussen had challenged him to do, though it is then surprising that he does not give the sources he used, i.e. the attack he was defending Schopenhauer against. However, in the notes Nietzsche does refer to Überweg's critique of Schopenhauer, presumably in his *Grundriss* in which his critique is fairly harsh, but not sufficiently similar to Nietzsche's to explain the fundamental drive behind Nietzsche's critique. In the letter Nietzsche wrote to Deussen in October 1868, i.e. after he had written the notes, he critically refers to two critics of Schopenhauer, Überweg and Haym:

> Indem ich so an den Schluß Deines Briefes anknüpfe, erledige ich zugleich den dort mir zugemutheten Vorschlag. Lieber Freund, 'gut schreiben' (wenn anders

---

15 Nietzsche replies to Deussen were written in Oct. 1867 and Oct. 1868, i.e. either side of the notes criticizing Schopenhauer.

ich dies Lob verdiene: nego ac pernego) berechtigt doch wahrhaftig nicht, eine Kritik des Schopenhauerschen Systems zu schreiben: im Übrigen kannst Du Dir von dem Respekt, den ich vor diesem 'Genius ersten Ranges' habe, gar keine Vorstellung machen, wenn Du *mir* (i.e. homini pusillullullo!) die Fähigkeiten zutraust, jenen besagten Riesen über den Haufen zu werfen: denn hoffentlich verstehst Du unter einer Kritik seines Systems nicht nur die Hervorhebung irgend welcher schadhaften Stellen, mißlungner Beweisführungen, taktischer Ungeschicktheiten: womit allerdings gewisse überverwegne Überwege und in der Philosophie nicht heimische Hayme alles gethan zu haben glauben. Man schreibt überhaupt nicht die Kritik einer Weltanschauung: sondern man begreift sie oder begreift sie eben nicht, ein dritter Standpunkt ist mir unergründlich. Jemand, der den Duft einer Rose nicht riecht, wird doch wahrhaftig nicht darüber kritisieren dürfen: und riecht er ihn: à la bonheur! Dann wird ihm die Lust vergehn, zu kritisieren (KSB 2/328).

There are significant similarities between Haym's severe critique of Schopenhauer's philosophy in his *Arthur Schopenhauer* (1864), which Nietzsche read in 1866, and possibly again in 1868, when he refers to one of Haym's expressions, and Nietzsche's critique in these notes, but I have in spite of this been unable, after a superficial examination, to conclude that Nietzsche's critique is directly based on Haym's or inspired by it.

Many other possible sources also need to be examined – many are mentioned in Überweg's account of Schopenhauer in his *Grundriss* – especially Victor Kiy's *Der Pessimismus und die Ethik Schopenhauer's* (1866), which Nietzsche seems to have read in 1866 (though Kiy's approach and critique is rather different to Nietzsche's), and Rudolf Seydel, *Schopenhauer's System dargestellt und beurtheilt* (1857), which Überweg refers to as one of the most critical of Schopenhauer; we have no certain knowledge that Nietzsche read this work. Furthermore, Otto Liebmann's severe critique of Schopenhauer in the chapter 'Die transcendente Richtung: Schopenhauer' of his work *Kant und die Epigonen* (1865) may also be of importance, as suggested by the commentary in Nietzsche's *Frühe Schriften* (FS 3/452), though Liebmann's critique is rather different from Nietzsche's.

Another source may be Lange, and at least one of Nietzsche's comments seems to have its origin in his reading of his *Geschichte des Materialismus*, for his reference to Überweg and to 'versteckte Kategorie' comes from Lange's work,[16] but Schopenhauer is not explicitly discussed in these pages. However, although Lange seems critical of Schopenhauer, he hardly ever mentions him at all in his *Geschichte des Materialismus* (1866), so this cannot be a major source. In the preface Lange writes:

> Mit Befremden wird vielleicht mancher Leser in meiner Darstellung den Namen Schopenhauer vermissen, um so mehr, da manche Anhänger dieses Mannes in meiner Anschauungsweise viel Verwandtes finden dürften. Ich muss offen gestehen, dass mir viele Schüler dieses Philosophen lieber sind, als der Meister. Schopenhauer selbst konnte ich in meiner Arbeit deshalb keinen Platz einräumen, weil ich in seiner Philosophie einen entschiednen Rückschritt hinter Kant finde.[17]

Furthermore, Nietzsche does not seem to change his view of Schopenhauer after reading Lange:

> Finally, Schopenhauer must be mentioned, for whom I still have every sympathy. What we possess in him was recently made quite clear to me by another work, which is excellent of its kind and very instructive: F. A. Lange's *History of Materialism and Critique of Its Meaning in the Present* (1866). Here we have an extremely enlightened Kantian and natural scientist. [...] Consequently, Lange thinks, one should give philosophers a free hand as long as they edify us in this sense. Art is free, also in the domain of concepts. Who would refute a phrase by Beethoven, and who would find error in Raphael's Madonna? You see, even with this severely critical standpoint our Schopenhauer stands firm; he becomes even almost more important to us. If philosophy is art, then even Haym should submit himself to Schopenhauer; if philosophy should edify, I know no more edifying philosopher than our Schopenhauer (letter to Gersdorff, end Aug. 1866: KSB 2/159–60).

---

16   F. A. Lange, *Geschichte des Materialismus und Kritik seiner Bedeutung in der Gegenwart* (Iserlohn: Baedeker, 1866), pp. 267–68.

17   Ibid., p. v.

And shortly thereafter he writes in another letter: 'Kant, Schopenhauer und dies Buch von Lange – mehr brauche ich nicht' (to Mushacke, Nov. 1866: KSB 2/184).

As stated above, Nietzsche acquired Schopenhauer's *Die Welt als Wille und Vorstellung* (2nd edn, 1844) in the late autumn of 1865 and read it intensively. He seems thereafter to have acquired a number of other works by Schopenhauer – most likely all the major works – but almost all of his references and discussions refer to *Die Welt als Wille und Vorstellung* and *Parerga und Paralipomena* (1851). None of these editions are in his library today. It seems likely that Nietzsche either lost them, or gave them away, in or around 1875. At this time, when Nietzsche was soon to begin breaking away from Schopenhauer, he copied down a fairly large number of notes from Schopenhauer's writings specifically relating to the Greeks (for his planned critique of classical philologists, *Wir Philologen*).[18] It seems likely that this reading and use of Schopenhauer reminded Nietzsche of his doubts about Schopenhauer's metaphysics (and his philosophy generally) which he had already expressed in 1868 and felt while writing *Schopenhauer als Erzieher* the previous year,[19] for shortly thereafter, during the summer of 1875, Nietzsche wrote a note entitled 'All sorts of plans' which lists as the third point 'to thoroughly read Dühring', a Schopenhauerian philosopher, 'to see what I have of Schopenhauer, and what not. Thereafter, read Schopenhauer yet again' (KSA 8, 8[4]).[20] Nietzsche also spent some considerable

18 See, for example, KSA 8, 5[72–83], notes which are all based on the second volume of Schopenhauer's *Die Welt als Wille und Vorstellung*.
19 See FS 3/352–61, and his letter to Cosima Wagner of 19 Dec. 1876: '[Sie werden] sich wundern, wenn ich Ihnen eine allmählich entstandene, mir fast plötzlich in's Bewußtsein getretene Differenz mit Schopenhauer's Lehre eingestehe? Ich stehe fast in allen allgemeinen Sätzen nicht auf seiner Seite; schon als ich über Sch. schrieb, merkte ich, daß ich über alles Dogmatische daran hinweg sei; mir lag alles am Menschen. In der Zwischenzeit ist meine "Vernunft" sehr thätig gewesen – damit ist denn das Leben wieder um einen Grad schwieriger, die Last größer geworden! Wie wird man's nur am Ende aushalten?' (KSB 5/210).
20 Cf. also ibid., 8[3] and 9[1].

energy to fulfil these plans during the summer of 1875, including reading both Dühring's *Der Werth des Lebens* (1865) and Schopenhauer carefully. His breach with Schopenhauer becomes clearly visible shortly thereafter in 1876.

It seems in fact to be possible to follow Nietzsche's breach with Schopenhauer in much more detail than has been done thus far and hence to understand better both the reasons for it and some of its consequences. By following Nietzsche's excerpts and extensive commentary to Dühring's *Der Werth des Lebens* and by examining Nietzsche's annotations in his complete works of Schopenhauer,[21] which he bought in the summer of 1875, and which are still in his library today, we are able to follow his increasing distance and critique.[22]

---

21   *Arthur Schopenhauer's Sämmtliche Werke*, ed. Julius Frauenstädt, 6 vols (Leipzig, 1873–74).

22   Three of these volumes contain annotations. The first volume of *Die Welt als Wille und Vorstellung* (WWV) contains a few annotations in the fourth book, para. 54 (and one annotation in para. 55), while the second volume is fairly heavily annotated throughout. The second volume of *Parerga...* contains a few annotations in the chapter 'Ueber Schriftstellerei und Stil'. Nietzsche's annotations in the second volume of WWV can with profit be used to better understand the reasons why Nietzsche broke away from Schopenhauer's philosophy. Nietzsche's copy is full of underlinings, marginal lines, exclamation marks and NB's [nota benes], but also with more direct comments which enable us to more concretely follow his response to the reading. I will here list some of Nietzsche's more informative comments (without being exhaustive) and the page on which they are made, to allow the reader to see what sort of response Nietzsche made while re-reading this work in 1875: 'aber das ist kein Einwand' (page 46), 'ecce' (222), 'folglich?' (260), 'im gegentheil!' (278), 'folglich!' (421), 'falsch' (438), 'falsch' (439), 'falsch' (440), 'also umgekehrt'/ 'ist Unsinn' / 'also' (441), 'ist Unsinn' (444), 'Unsinn' (450), 'sehr gut' (452), 'ja' / 'falsch' (497), 'ego' (513), 'warum' (531), 'Ist Unsinn' (543), 'Unsinn' (547), 'als ob' (548), 'also' (566), 'falsch' (583), 'Hierbei ist immer die Hauptsache übersehn: dass das neue Indiv. nicht das alte, sondern das (alte+x) ist – dass in der Gewachen [uncertain reading] sich ein Gesamtwachsthumsprocess vollzieht' (586), 'aber [–] nach Erhaltung der Gattung existiert gar nicht' [uncertain reading] (588), 'falsch' (592), 'ja!' (671), 'Unsinn' (678), 'ist Sinnloß' [uncertain reading] (688), 'ist Unsinn' (689) and 'falsch' (698).

Nietzsche's library contains one further book by Schopenhauer, also edited by Frauenstädt, namely *Aus Arthur Schopenhauer's handschriftlichem Nachlaß: Abhandlungen, Anmerkungen, Aphorismen und Fragmente* (1864). It is not known when he acquired this work, but it contains annotations (including exclamation marks) throughout.

Nietzsche continued to read, annotate and copy down passages from Schopenhauer's writings almost every year, even after his break with Schopenhauer, until the very end of his life. He continued to have respect for the person Schopenhauer, but regarded his philosophy as antipodal. For example, Nietzsche came after his break with Schopenhauer in 1875–76 to be much more sceptical towards metaphysics, towards art as the justification of life and he completely changed his view of ethics and pity.

Most of Nietzsche's continued reading of Schopenhauer was of his two main works, *Die Welt als Wille und Vorstellung* and *Parerga und Paralipomena*, but he also continued to read (and even study) other texts by Schopenhauer. As one example of Nietzsche's frequent reading of Schopenhauer after 1876, we can look at his detailed reading of Schopenhauer's *Preisschrift über die Grundlage der Moral* which gave rise to many excerpts in his notebooks in or around 1884,[23] and an increased discussion of Kant after this time. There are no annotations in Nietzsche's copy of this work, which is less than two hundred pages long and contains four parts. Part Two of this work, covering about seventy-five pages, is called 'Kritik des von Kant der Ethik gegebenen Fundaments' ('Critique of Kant's Foundation of Ethics') and is a detailed discussion and critique, including many quotations, of Kant's ethics, especially his *Grundlegung der Metaphysik der Sitten*.[24] This also reveals that much of

---

23 See, for example, KSA 11, 25[351, 437, 441–42] from early 1884, and KSA 11, 26[78, 84, 85, 96] from summer-autumn 1884.

24 In the preface Schopenhauer writes of Kant: 'Glücklicherweise hat er der Darstellung des Fundaments seines Ethik abgesondert von dieses selbst ein eigenes Werk gewidmet, die Grundlegung zur Metaphysik der Sitten, deren Thema also genau dasselbe ist mit dem Gegenstand unserer Preisfrage. [...] Aus

Nietzsche's understanding and discussion of Kant is conducted from a Schopenhauerian perspective (see discussion below).

Rationalist Philosophy: Leibniz

The father of German philosophy is without doubt Leibniz, but Nietzsche shows very limited interest in and knowledge of him, at least until 1884. In 1866 and 1867 Nietzsche would have read a few words about Leibniz in Lange's *Geschichte des Materialismus* and a more detailed description in Überweg's *Grundriss der Geschichte der Philosophie von Thales bis auf die Gegenwart* (1863–66), but this seems to have left no traces in Nietzsche's thinking, for Leibniz is never mentioned by the young Nietzsche. We have no evidence that Nietzsche read or had any more detailed knowledge of Leibniz until 1884 when he either read Leibniz, or more probably, an exposition of his thinking.[25] In fact, he refers to Leibniz only twice before then; there is a general statement in section 7 of *Die Philosophie im tragischen Zeitalter der Griechen* (1872–73) and a more specific one, with a quotation, at the end of the section on the Pythagoreans in his lectures 'Die vorplatonischen Philosophen', which were probably held during the 1869–70 winter semester and certainly held in the summer semester of 1872, the 1875–76 winter semester and the summer semester of 1876.[26] As we will see below, the increased reference to Leibniz in 1884–85 follows a general pattern, for there is a marked

allen diesen Gründen nehme ich in gegenwärtiger Kritik die zuerst gennante Grundlegung zur Metaphysik der Sitten zu meinem Leitfaden, und auf diese beziehn sich alle ohne weitern Beisatz von mir angeführten Seitenzahlen, welches ich zu merken bitte.' (Arthur Schopenhauer, *Sämtliche Werke*, ed. W. Frhr. von Löhneysen, 5 vols (Frankfurt a.M.: Suhrkamp, 1986), iii, 643–45).

25   I have attempted to identify this source, but so far without success.
26   'Das Werden erschien als ein Rechnen. Dies erinnert an den Spruch des Leibniz (epistol. collectio Kortholti ep. 154.) die Musik sei exercitium arithmeticae occultum nescientis se numerare animi. Dies hätten die Pythagor. wohl auch von der Welt sagen können: freilich nicht, was eigentlich rechne' (KGW II.4 350).

increase in Nietzsche's references to almost all 'great' German philosophers at this time. This is most probably due to his reading of an as yet unidentified source or sources. Nietzsche makes a reference to this reading in a letter to Overbeck of 22 December 1884. Speaking about his eye problems, he writes: 'Perhaps I have also this summer read too many badly printed books (*German* books about metaphysics!)' (KSB 6/572). This may perhaps refer to primary sources, but since Nietzsche's references to almost all German philosophers increase at this time, and the fact that he so often in the notes refers to them as a group, makes it much more likely that it refers to secondary sources.

In 1887 Nietzsche quotes a sentence from Leibniz's argument that this is the best of all possible worlds from *Essais de Théodicée* and gives a page reference to this work (KSA 12/264, 7[4]). This has sometimes been taken as evidence that Nietzsche then read Leibniz, but this is unlikely to be correct. Almost certainly, Nietzsche excerpted this note, like the nearby notes, from Kuno Fischer's *Geschichte der neuern Philosophie*.[27] We thus have no evidence that Nietzsche ever read Leibniz or showed any interest in him.

The Philosophers of the Counter-Enlightenment: Hamann, Jacobi and Herder

Hamann and Jacobi

It would not have been inconceivable that Nietzsche could have shown an interest in the philosophers of the counter-Enlightenment, with their critique of reason and utility. However, although he read Hamann and probably Herder, he seems to have shown no special interest in this tradition.

---

27 See 'Beiträge zur Quellenforschung mitgeteilt von Thomas H. Brobjer', *Nietzsche-Studien*, 30 (2001), 418–21.

Nietzsche wrote down a six-line quotation from Hamann in 1867–68 about his critique of Kant's optimism, and this critique Nietzsche takes to hold for optimism in general, which indicates a certain interest in and approval of Hamann's thinking (FS 3/392). However, the quotation is not taken from Hamann directly but from Überweg's *Grundriss der Geschichte der Philosophie*. In 1873 Nietzsche borrowed Hamann's *Schriften und Briefe* and read Hamann's *Sokratische Denkwurdigkeiten* with appreciation and quoted him in section 2 of *Die Philosophie im tragischen Zeitalter der Griechen*, at the same time objecting to his style.[28] He also makes one reference to Hamann and quotes a short sentence from him in his lectures 'Darstellung der antiken Rhetorik' which he held during the 1874 summer semester (KGW II.2 437). We have no evidence of any further reading, nor does Nietzsche refer to him again.[29]

This limited interest in the thinkers of the counter-Enlightenment is further confirmed by the fact that Nietzsche neither read nor ever mentioned (with one exception) the related thinker, Friedrich Heinrich Jacobi (1743–1819). Nietzsche's only reference to him was in the form of part of a paraphrase and summary of Viktor Hehn's *Gedanken über Goethe* (1888) which he read and paraphrased in the summer of 1888 (KSA 13, 16[36]).

---

28   Cf. KSA 7/509, and letter to Rohde, 31 Jan. 1873.
29   There are probably many additional sources to Nietzsche's knowledge of Hamann but which were not 'strong' enough to stimulate him to make explicit statements referring to it. For example, next to a review of Nietzsche's first *Unzeitgemäße Betrachtungen* in the journal *Zeitschrift für Philosophie und philosophische Kritik*, 64 (1874), 153–58, there is a review of Hamann's *Schriften und Briefe* by the same reviewer. It seems very likely that Nietzsche had read it, though we have no evidence of this and it has not left any traces.

Herder

The young Nietzsche frequently refers to *Der Cid* and seems to have both read and possessed it. It is not clear which *Der Cid* this refers to. The only *Der Cid* in Nietzsche's library today is Corneille's play with this name in a German translation. However, although this work is without year of publication, it belongs to a series which was published in 1871–76, i.e. too late to be the one Nietzsche referred to. Furthermore, in his catalogue of Nietzsche's library, which was compiled as early as 1892, Steiner lists this work as not cut open. It seems most likely that the *Cid* which Nietzsche refers to and possessed was Herder's *Der Cid*. This work consists of a free poetic rendering of a French prose version of the Spanish *El Cid* and is the most widely read of all Herder's works.

As early as 1858 Nietzsche had wished to receive *Der Cid*, and perhaps this wish was granted, for certainly by 1861–62 he possessed the work. In a note from October 1862 Nietzsche speaks of a reading of *Der Cid*, which was probably a reference to a second or third reading of the work, and in a long poem of April 1864 Nietzsche refers to Herder's spiritual greatness. Sometime between 1860 and 1864 Nietzsche also copied out extracts from Herder on parts of a single page but it is not clear from which work.[30] Nietzsche's notes from this rather ill-defined period, 1858–1864, also contains a list of ten books and compositions – possibly a list of what he wished for his birthday or for Christmas. The fourth item on this list is 'Herders Biographie'. We do not know if Nietzsche was given or read this work but its presence on the list certainly seems to reflect an interest in Herder at this time.

This interest continues, for in 1867 or 1868 Nietzsche writes an ambitious list of philosophical books which he wanted to read.

---

30 These as yet unpublished extracts are held in the Goethe-Schiller Archive (GSA) in Weimar under signum Mp V 27 (GSA 71/220). The FS edition simply states that they are there (FS 2/458). Nietzsche here quotes what appear to be four lines of poetry from Herder.

Herder's *Ideen zur Philosophie der Geschichte der Menschheit* is listed among these some thirty titles. We have no evidence that he read this work, and he seems to have read few, if any, of the titles listed.

In Nietzsche's 'Vorlesungen über lateinische Grammatik', which he held during the 1869–70 winter semester in Basle, he refers to and quotes one sentence from Herder's *Abhandlung über den Ursprung der Sprache* (1772), possibly but not necessarily implying a reading of it (KGW II.2 187).[31] There are also a few general notes to Herder in Nietzsche's early notes (1869–73), but which are probably only a reflection of his earlier interest and reading of Herder. That is probably also the background to the long section entitled 'Herder' in *The Wanderer and his Shadow* in 1880 (MA II/2 118). Thereafter, but probably already from the early 1870s, we no longer see any active interest in or reading of Herder.

The Great German Philosopher: Kant

Nietzsche's reading of Kant

Nietzsche's reading of Kant is an important and much discussed issue, for, with the exception of Schopenhauer and Plato, Kant is the philosopher to whom Nietzsche refers most often, and he constitutes the background and starting-point for almost all later German philosophy, including Schopenhauer's and Lange's. However, unlike Schopenhauer and Plato, whom Nietzsche knew well, his first-hand knowledge of Kant appears to have been slight. An awareness of Nietzsche's knowledge of Kant is important, for much of his later critique of modern philosophy, and especially German philosophy, was directed at Kant, or at least presented through his critique of Kant. Furthermore, Nietzsche's attitude towards Kant changed more

31   In his lectures 'Einleitung in das Studium der platonischen Dialogue' he also makes a brief reference to Herder (KGW II.4 41), but this probably does not reflect any reading of him.

than his attitude towards probably any other person; the early Nietzsche, i.e. until about 1876, held him in high esteem while after that period he became Nietzsche's main philosophical enemy. One cannot understand the reasons either for Nietzsche's esteem or critique or for his change of attitude, without a reasonable knowledge of Nietzsche's reading and knowledge of Kant.

The best starting-point is probably Janz's statement in his standard biography of Nietzsche, in which he claims that Nietzsche acquired his first impression of Kant's works through Lange's *Geschichte des Materialismus* which was then followed by the reading of the two-volume study of Kant by Kuno Fischer in his series *Geschichte der neuern Philosophie*. Thereafter he read Kant's *Kritik der Urteilskraft* (the Third Critique, dealing with aesthetic and teleological judgement) in late 1867 and early 1868.[32] Janz further claims that it is taken for granted in Nietzsche research that he had never read Kant in the original, with the exception of the *Kritik der Urteilskraft*. However, he adds that Nietzsche's dialogue with Kant is so strong, so detailed that surely a more cautious formulation is to be recommended: it has not yet been possible to prove a direct reading of Kant but equally it cannot be excluded.[33] Two sources need to be added to Janz's account. Schopenhauer was not only profoundly influenced by Kant, but also often discusses his philosophy explicitly and in some detail in his writings. This is likely to have been a major source of knowledge and interest for the young Nietzsche even before he read Lange. Among the secondary literature on Kant which Nietzsche read early, apart from Schopenhauer, Lange and Fischer, Überweg ought also to be mentioned. In 1868 Nietzsche read and studied his *Grundriss der Geschichte der*

---

32 Curt Paul Janz, *Friedrich Nietzsche. Biographie*, 3 vols (Munich and Vienna: Hanser, 1978–79), i, 199.

33 'Es gilt in der Nietzscheforschung als ausgemacht, daß Nietzsche nie Kant im Original gelesen habe – außer der "Kritik der Urteilskraft". [...] Der Dialog mit Kant ist aber so stark, so ins Detail greifend, daß wohl die vorsichtigere Formulierung sich empfiehlt: eine direkte Kantlektüre ließ sich bis jetzt nicht nachweisen, ist aber nicht auszuschließen' (Janz, i, 504).

Philosophie von Thales bis auf die Gegenwart (1863–66) which also contains an extensive running bibliography, in which Kant has a prominent place.

There is no work by Kant in Nietzsche's library and he almost certainly never possessed any work by him. The reason for believing that Nietzsche had read Kant is his enthusiasm for Kant at this time, including his plan to write his doctoral dissertation on Kantian themes and such statements as 'Kant, Schopenhauer and this book by Lange – I do not need anything else'.[34] Moreover, when Nietzsche asked to be transferred from the chair of philology to the chair of philosophy at Basle in 1871 he wrote to the authorities there and claimed that among the modern philosophers he had studied with special interest were Kant and Schopenhauer.[35] This view is further strengthened by the fact that we know that several of his friends read Kant at this time. The counter-argument is that we have no evidence of any such reading, with the exception of the Third Critique in 1867–68 and some very limited reading much later.

Nietzsche's interest in Kant was at its strongest in the late 1860s. A list of intended reading under the title 'Zur Teleologie' from that time contains seven titles, four of which relate to Kant: Rosenkranz, *Geschichte der Kant. Philosophie*; Fischer, *Kant*; and two works by Kant himself (*Kritik der reinen Vernunft* and *Kritik der Urtheilskraft*). We know that he then read Fischer's book and probably Kant's *Urtheilskraft* but probably not the other two works. Another longer list of intended reading from the same period, includes two works by Kant: *Allgemeine Naturgeschichte und Theorie des Himmels* and *Kritik der Urtheilskraft* again (FS 3/393–94).[36]

In the notes for Nietzsche's lectures at Basle in the 1870s we see his great respect for and affirmation of Kant, and we get further possible indications of his reading of Kant from several long

---

34   Letter to Mushacke, Nov. 1866 (KSB 2/184).
35   Letter to W. Vischer(-Bilfinger), (probably) Jan. 1871 (KSB 3/177).
36   It seems as if all but a very few of these titles are taken from Überweg.

quotations. These occur, for example, at the very beginning of his lectures 'Vorlesungen über lateinische Grammatik' and 'Darstellung der antiken Rhetorik'. However, the likelihood is that these quotations are taken from the secondary literature Nietzsche used when preparing his lectures, rather than from his reading of Kant himself.

In his lectures 'Encyclopädie der klassischen Philologie', first held in the summer of 1871 (and possibly repeated in 1873–74), Nietzsche recommended that philologists study philosophy and see the grand perspectives. For this he especially recommended the unity of Plato's and Kant's thinking and he affirms their idealism. The same spirit is apparent in the lectures 'Einführung in das Studium der platonischen Dialogue':

> The theory of ideas is something enormous, an invaluable preparation for Kantian idealism. Here is taught, with every means, including that of myths, the correct opposition between the Ding-an-sich and appearance: with which every more profound philosophy begins (KGW II.4 7).[37]

In his lectures 'Die vorplatonischen Philosophen', first given in 1869–70 or 1872 (repeated in 1875–76, and again in 1876) Nietzsche states that it is only with Kantian philosophy that we have realized the importance of Eleatic thinking. (KGW II.4 213–14) Later in the lectures Nietzsche emphasizes that in several important ways Kantian idealism occupies the opposite position to that of Parmenides (ibid., 294–95), and he goes so far as to claim that: 'if there had been a seed of profundity in Eleatic thinking, then he [Zeno] would from it inevitably have glimpsed the Kantian problem' (ibid., 301).

We have no definite evidence that Nietzsche read Kant first-hand after 1869, although his references to him in the early 1870s may suggest such reading.[38] Most importantly, we have no evidence or

---

37   This is the very first page of the lecture notes. A similar statement is made later, in a footnote, about the relation between Plato and Kant, but in connection with morality and a moral 'beyond' (KGW II.4 88).

38   A long quotation in 1872 from *Allgemeine Naturgeschichte und Theorie des Himmels* and several short quotations in 1886, with page references, from *Kritik der reinen Vernunft* possibly imply at least a partial reading of these works. A

indication of such a reading at the time when he 'breaks' with much of his earlier thinking, including Kant's, around 1876.

The references to Kant in Nietzsche's published works and notebooks reflect his importance for the late Nietzsche, with approximately forty, twenty-five, and one hundred and fifty respectively for the early, middle and late periods.[39] The late Nietzsche's interest is likely to be due to reading of secondary sources discussing Kant and to Nietzsche's own increasing critique of Kantian inspired thinking, rather than any reading of Kant himself.

References to Kant begin to increase in 1883, become most frequent during 1884–85 and decrease somewhat thereafter (there are some fifty references to Kant in the notebooks covering the period 1884–85). Whether this is mere coincidence or reflects either an independent increase of interest in Kantian (or rather anti-Kantian) problems or a response to reading Kant or some book about Kant remains to be determined. I would like to suggest that the main reason for Nietzsche's increased references to Kant at this time is due to his reading. In 1883 he read and annotated heavily Hartmann's *Phänomenologie des sittlichen Bewußtseins* (1879) which contains much about Kant. In the same year he also read and extensively annotated L. Dumont's *Vergnügen und Schmerz* (1876) which contains less about Kant, but which mentions Kant and several of Nietzsche's notes in his notebooks, including some concerning Kant, comes from this work.[40] He also probably read two Kantian works by

more detailed study is required to confirm this. The quotation from *Allgemeine Naturgeschichte...* could perhaps come from Zöllner whom Nietzsche read at this time and who deals with Kant's relevance and importance for the natural sciences. The quotations from *Kritik der reinen Vernunft* could possibly come from Romundt's *Grundlegung zur Reform der Philosophie: Vereinfachte und erweiterte Darstellung von Immanuel Kants Kritik der reinen Vernunft* (1885).

39   Kant is mentioned in thirteen letters during the period 1864 to Jan. 1871; there are only six mentions in the period 1872–1887 (in fact only four, since two are the same reference sent to different recipients). During the last year and a half there are five references to Kant.

40   See KSA 10, 7[233,234], and other notes nearby.

his friend Romundt this year. The most important reading at this time, around 1884, is, I believe, his detailed reading of Schopenhauer's *Preisschrift über die Grundlage der Moral*, with its detailed discussion of Kant, which gave rise to many excerpts in his notebooks.[41] The following year Nietzsche also read several books containing much on Kant, by Spir, Widemann and probably one by Romundt. For example, during a visit to the library at Chur, Switzerland, in May and June 1887, Nietzsche re-read Kuno Fischer's *Geschichte der neuern Philosophie: Bd. 5: Immanuel Kant und seine Lehre*, and excerpted seven pages of discussions, summaries and quotations from this work, based on five of Kant's works.[42]

There is no evidence that Nietzsche read Kant's best-known ethical work, *Grundlegung zur Metaphysik der Sitten*, but in 1884 he read closely Schopenhauer's detailed discussion and critique of this work, as mentioned above.[43]

Nietzsche's reading on Kant

Considering Kant's enormous stature it follows that Nietzsche's reading about him was extensive. Probably the earliest and most important influences were, as mentioned above, Schopenhauer, Lange, Überweg and Fischer. Furthermore, Nietzsche returned to Schopenhauer and Lange and re-read their works many times

---

41   See note 23 above.
42   See KSA 12, 7[4]. The five works are *Kritik der praktischen Vernunft, Kritik der Urteilskraft, Der Streit der Fakultäten, Grundlegung zur Metaphysik der Sitten*, and *Die Religion innerhalb der Grenzen der bloßen Vernunft*. Four of these sources have been determined and published by the editors of KSA (see Vol. 14). I have been able to confirm that the one section, of about 13 lines (p. 268f.), which has not been identified in KSA, comes originally from Kant's *Grundlegung...*, but Nietzsche has taken them all from Fischer's account; see my 'Beiträge zur Quellenforschung', *Nietzsche-Studien*, 30 (2001), 418–21.
43   It should be noted that Nietzsche's reading of Kant may have been much more extensive. Most reading does not result in specific comments or quotations. On the other hand, we have no indications that Nietzsche ever owned any work by Kant.

throughout his life. Two of Nietzsche's early friends, Deussen and Romundt, were deeply influenced by Kant and wrote books about Kant's philosophy. Nietzsche possessed four books on Kant by Romundt and one by Deussen. There are no annotations in these, but Nietzsche probably read them carefully. The first book by Romundt, his 'Habilitationsschrift' at the University of Basle, where Nietzsche worked, entitled *Die menschliche Erkenntniß und das Wesen der Dinge* (1872) deals mainly with Kant and the published version is dedicated to 'My friend Friedrich Nietzsche'.[44] Another work which the early Nietzsche read is Otto Kohl's dissertation: *I. Kant's Ansicht von der Willensfreiheit* (Leipzig, 1868), in which Kohl defends Kant's view of free will against Schopenhauer's determinism. Many other works by Julius Bahnsen, Johan Carl Friedrich Zöllner, Afrikan Spir, Rudolf Lehmann, Otto Liebmann, Philipp Mainländer and Eduard von Hartmann and others are likely to have been important for Nietzsche's knowledge of Kant. This list is, however, far from exhaustive. Some other books in Nietzsche's library may have been important, and books not in his library have not been discussed (with a few exceptions). Kant is also mentioned or discussed briefly in many other books in Nietzsche's library, some important for covering more specialized aspects of his thinking.[45]

---

44 Nietzsche also possessed three other books by Romundt, and it seems likely that he read them in the same years that they appeared: *Antäus. Neuer Aufbau der Lehre Kants über Seele, Freiheit und Gott* (1882); *Die Herstellung der Lehre Jesu durch Kants Reform der Philosophie* (1883); and *Grundlegung zur Reform der Philosophie. Vereinfachte und erweiterte Darstellung von Immanuel Kants Kritik der reinen Vernunft* (1885). Nietzsche possessed three books by Paul Deussen, his friend and a specialist on Schopenhauer and oriental philosophy. Deussen's first book, *Die Elemente der Metaphysik* (1877) deals extensively with Kant, and its Kantian and Schopenhauerian stance is reflected in the preface: 'Diesen Standpunkt der Versöhnung aller Gegensätze hat, wie wir glauben, die Menschheit der Hauptsache nach erreicht in dem von Kant begründeten, von Schopenhauer zu Ende gedachten Idealismus'.

45 The following eight books, for example all contain some information about Kant: J. J. Baumann, *Handbuch der Moral* (1879); Lecky, *Geschichte des Ursprungs und Einflusses der Aufklärung in Europa* (1873 or 1879); A.

German Idealist Philosophy:
Fichte, Schelling, Hegel and Herbart

Fichte

Nietzsche refers critically to German Idealist philosophy fairly frequently, but his reading of its most important representatives was limited. Nietzsche's only known relation to Fichte is that he, like all the pupils at Pforta, took part in the centenary celebrations of Fichte's birth in 1862, which were especially intense at Pforta as Fichte had been a pupil there. Later Nietzsche makes eight hostile and general statements about Fichte in his books and *Nachlass*, but none of these necessarily implies a reading of him.[46] He refers to Fichte, together with several other German philosophers, as essentially a theologian and he refers with hostility to Fichte's *Reden an die deutsche Nation*, one of Fichte's most well-known works, which is often seen as the beginning of German nationalism. Possibly Nietzsche heard or read these at the centenary celebrations, but more important is the fact that, in 1885 or 1886, he refers to Jean Paul's critique of the speeches which Nietzsche may have read, or learned about through Goethe. Nietzsche's library also contains a work about Fichte by Ernst Ebeling but which does not show any signs of having been read.[47]

Espinas, *Die tierischen Gesellschaften* (1879); J. Sully, *Le Pessimisme* (1882); Caspari, *Der Zusammenhang der Dinge* (1881); J. G. Vogt, *Die Kraft* (1878); E. du Bois-Reymond, *Über die Grenzen des Naturerkennens* (1884); F. Ratzel, *Anthropogeographie* (1882).

46　The majority of these occur after 1884. The earlier ones are two general statements in MA, II/1 216, and M 353, respectively.

47　E. Ebeling, *Darstellung und Beurteilung der religionsphilosophischen Lehren J. G. Fichtes*, dissertation, University of Halle, 1886. On the cover is a dedication by the author (23.6.1886), which has, however, been partially cut by the bookbinder.

Schelling

We have no definite evidence that the young Nietzsche read the works of Fichte's successor at Jena, Schelling (1775–1854), but we do have an indication that he may have read him in 1869. He would have read scathing remarks about him in Schopenhauer's works and a more 'objective' outline of his thinking in Überweg. After or during his reading of Überweg in 1867–68 he wrote down a list of intended reading with about twenty-five titles of a philosophical and scientific nature, in which two works by and one about Schelling are mentioned: *Ideen zu einer Philosophie der Natur, System des transcendenten Idealismus* and Rosenkranz's *Schelling Vorlesungen* (FS 3/394). We have no evidence that Nietzsche read any of these works, as is also the case with most of the entries in this list, and it seems highly unlikely that he did so.

Thus, in Nietzsche's notebooks, books and letters there is no evidence that Nietzsche had read Schelling. In a recent, massive study J. E. Wilson has been unable to show any such evidence, but he none the less argues that it seems very likely.[48] However, one such piece of evidence does exist, which Wilson has missed, and this is in Nietzsche's lecture notes. He begins his 'Vorlesungen über lateinische Grammatik', held in the 1869–70 winter semester with a short section on the origin of language, which he ends with a long quotation from Schelling:

> Zum Schluß Worte von Schelling (Abth. II. Bd. I S. 52) 'Da sich ohne Sprache nicht nur kein philosophisches, sondern überhaupt kein menschliches Bewußtsein denken läßt, so konnte der Grund der Sprache nicht mit Bewußtsein gelegt werden; und dennoch, je tiefer wir in sie eindringen, desto bestimmter entdeckt sich, daß ihre Tiefe die des bewußtvollsten Erzeugnisses noch bei weitem übertrifft. Er ist mir der Sprache, wie mit den organischen Wesen; wir glauben diese blindlings entstehen zu sehen und können die unergründliche

---

48   John Elbert Wilson, *Schelling und Nietzsche. Zur Auslegung der frühen Werke Friedrich Nietzsches*, Monographien und Texte zur Nietzsche-Forschung, 33 (Berlin and New York: de Gruyter, 1996).

Absichtlichkeit ihrer Bildung bis ins Einzelnste nicht in Abrede ziehen' (KGW II.2 188).[49]

Schelling is referred to at least another three times in Nietzsche's lectures, but none of these references suggests a reading of him.

Later, especially in 1884–86, Schelling becomes the butt of Nietzsche's criticism and ridicule relatively often – but none of these statements requires first-hand reading of him. Nietzsche's very first reference to Schelling in his *Nachlass* and books comes as a response to reading Max Müller's *Essays: 1. Beiträge zur vergleichenden Religionswissenschaft* (Leipzig, 1869) in 1870 or 1871, where Nietzsche defends Schopenhauer in relation to Schelling (and Hegel), but it says little about his view of Schelling *per se*. (KSA 7, 5[71]) His second reference comes in *Daybreak* (1881). By this time Nietzsche's anti-metaphysical and anti-romantic tendency is well established and, as expected, he criticizes Schelling and a number of other German thinkers harshly and without hesitation:

> Let us today take a look at Schiller, Wilhelm von Humboldt, Schleiermacher, Hegel, Schelling, read their correspondence and familiarise ourselves with their large circle of adherents: what do they have in common, what is it in them that seems to us, as we are today, now so insupportable, now so pitiable and moving? Firstly, their thirst for appearing morally *excited* at all costs; then, their desire for brilliant, boneless generalities, together with the intention of seeing everything (character, passions, ages, customs) in as beautiful a light as possible [...] It is a soft, good-natured, silver-glistering idealism which wants above all to affect noble gestures and a noble voice, a thing as presumptuous as it is harmless, infused with a heartfelt repugnance for 'cold' or 'dry' reality, for the anatomy, for wholehearted passion, for every kind of philosophical temperance and scepticism, but especially for the natural science except when it is amenable to being employed as religious symbolism (M 190).

He continues in this vein, contrasting Goethe and Schopenhauer favourably with this group of thinkers.

---

49   This may indicate a reading of Schelling in 1869, but it is perhaps more likely that he merely borrowed the quotation from a book he used in preparing his lectures.

In 1884 Nietzsche writes down a number of notes in which Schelling is mentioned in general terms. The first one is characteristic of Nietzsche's view of 'German philosophers' at this time and later: '– Fichte, Schelling, Hegel, Schleiermacher, Feuerbach, Strauß – all of them theologians' (KSA 11, 26[8]).[50] These comments and the simultaneous relatively intensive discussion of German philosophy almost certainly comes as a response to an as yet unidentified work which Nietzsche probably read at this time.

Nietzsche's two comments about Schelling in *Beyond Good and Evil* (1886) merely echo these notes:

> The honeymoon time of German philosophy arrived [after Kant]; and the young theologians of the College of Tübingen went straightway off into the bushes – all in search of 'faculties'. [...] Schelling baptized it intellectual intuition, and therewith satisfied the most heartfelt longings of his Germans, which longings were fundamentally pious (JGB 11).[51]

We can here clearly see how Nietzsche has gone from seeing them as harmless idealists in 1882 to, from 1884 onwards, regarding them as more dangerous, Christian, falsifiers of reality.

We can thus conclude that Nietzsche possibly read some Schelling in 1869, but his statement thereafter does not require or imply any reading or closer knowledge of him. Apart from the possible reading in 1869, it seems most probable that Nietzsche's knowledge of Schelling comes primarily from Schopenhauer, Überweg and an unidentified book which he read in 1884.

Hegel

With the exception of Schopenhauer and Kant, Hegel is the great German philosopher to whom Nietzsche refers most frequently. He also belongs, with Schopenhauer and Kant, to the few German

---

50 Other related notes from this time are: KSA 11, 25[303], 26[445, 412], 34[82], 38[7]; and KSA 12, 2[131].

51 See also JGB 252.

philosophers Nietzsche discusses, at least in part, in their own right. He is one of the first philosophers Nietzsche read – in 1865 – and in 1875 he ordered Hegel's *Encyklopädie*, though it is not clear if he read it or not. The later Nietzsche will refer to his own early writings, at least *The Birth of Tragedy*, as smelling 'offensively Hegelian', implying a rather strong Hegelian influence, although Nietzsche may well be referring more to a general *Zeitgeist* than to specific reading or acquaintance with Hegel's works. Although critical of Hegel, he is perhaps less critical than one might expect, especially considering Schopenhauer's hostility.

Nietzsche read Hegel before he read Schopenhauer, but we have no evidence of what he read, nor are any more obvious effects of this reading visible. Nietzsche had studied the history of philosophy under Schaarschmidt in Bonn, but in the rather sparse notes he took during the lectures there is no section dealing with Hegel. However, he seems to have continued reading philosophy privately after the end of term, for in September 1865, shortly before he was to move to Leipzig, he wrote to his friend Mushacke: 'To coffee I take a bit of Hegelian philosophy, and if I have a poor appetite then I take Straussian pills, perhaps "die Ganzen und die Halben"'.[52] The following month he discovered Schopenhauer in a bookshop and became influenced by his hostility towards Hegel. In the preface to *Die Welt als Wille und Vorstellung* Schopenhauer refers to Hegelian philosophy as absurd and senseless, as charlatanry and to Hegel as a sophist and 'that intellectual Caliban'. That Nietzsche was influenced by Schopenhauer's negative view is evident in a short outline entitled 'Über die Universitätsphilosophie', which Nietzsche wrote in 1867–68 under the direct influence of Schopenhauer's essay about academic philosophy and philosophers in *Parerga and Paralipomena* (FS

---

52   Nietzsche is here referring to David Friedrich Strauss's book *Die Halben und die Ganzen* (1865). It seems likely that Nietzsche read a work by Hegel at this time, but it is not known which. It is, however, also possible that he did not read Hegel first-hand, but rather read about him in a history of philosophy – possibly the account in Fortlage's *Genetische Geschichte der Philosophie seit Kant* which he read at this time.

3/395). Schopenhauer and Nietzsche here use 'die Hegelei' as an example of how academic philosophy is always in accordance with state religion, which is, of course, a denigration of philosophy.

Other early references to Hegel are more general and less evaluative, except the last one, written at the end of 1868, in which he refers to two intellectual traditions, the romantic movement and Hegelian philosophy which, although different, are at one in denying the value of personality – the one through the idea of 'Volksseele' and the other through 'Zeitgeist'. Contrary to this both Schopenhauer and Nietzsche would always strongly emphasize the importance of personality (FS 5/193).

Another source of information about Hegelian philosophy is Nietzsche's friendship with the pastor Friedrich August Wenkel from 1866 to 1868. Wenkel had been a follower of Hegel, Schleiermacher and Strauss, but inclined at this time more and more towards Kant's and Schopenhauer's philosophies. In a letter to Gersdorff of 22 June 1868 Nietzsche writes: 'We [i.e. Nietzsche and Wenkel] often together discussed philosophy etc., and I could never deny him my highest veneration, although he was an Hegelian'.

There is only one general statement in Nietzsche's lectures regarding Hegel, and although after 1869 there are many references to and discussions of Hegel in Nietzsche's books and *Nachlass* (and a few in letters), none of them implies a reading of him, with the exception of a few notes of 1873, when Nietzsche was preparing his second *Unzeitgemässe Betrachtung*, which suggest a reading of the *Vorlesungen über die Philosophie der Geschichte*. A receipt from 1875 also exists, which seems to show that Nietzsche ordered or bought Hegel's *Encyklopädie der philosophischen Wissenschaften* that year.[53] Most of Nietzsche's later discussions of Hegel seems to

---

53   The receipt is among Nietzsche's unpublished papers in the Goethe-Schiller Archive in Weimar and seems not previously to have been discovered. I am not aware of any evidence that Nietzsche actually read Hegel's *Encyklopädie*, and the book is not in his library, but future searches for hidden allusions, quotations or references to this work may well be able to establish such a reading.

be based on generalities and on general discussions in secondary literature.

We can thus conclude that Nietzsche had a reasonable knowledge of Hegel's philosophy through secondary sources. However, his direct reading of him seems to be limited – an unidentified work in 1865, his *Vorlesungen über die Philosophie der Geschichte* in 1873, and possibly the *Encyklopädie* in 1875 or later – but sufficient for him to claim with justification some first-hand knowledge of him.

Herbart

The German philosopher and educationalist Johann Friedrich Herbart (1776–1841) was a student of Fichte's but later broke with him and developed his own philosophy and educational system. He steered Kant's philosophy in another direction by stressing the existence of a world of real things behind the world of appearances. Herbart is a philosopher of lesser stature than the Idealists mentioned above but he is discussed here, for he, like the Idealists, was a post-Kantian and because he was much discussed by both Lange, Überweg (who had been a student of his) and other philosophers. Nietzsche refers to him but only rarely; the first time is in a list he wrote down from Überweg's study in 1867–68 of books he intended to read. The work he there listed was: 'Herbart analyt. Beleuchtung des Naturrechts und der Moral'.[54] He later refers to Herbartians once in a letter, once in his books and once in the *Nachlass*, but none of these statements is important and none implies any reading of Herbart's philosophy.[55] However, in the notes to the lectures 'Einleitung in das Studium der platonischen Dialogue' Nietzsche quotes four lines of text from Herbart where Herbart discusses the nature of Platonic ideas (KGW

---

54 He may well have read many of the titles on this list had he not been called to Basle, but as it was, he seems to have read very few of them.

55 See letter to Rohde, 4 Feb. 1872; *Schopenhauer als Erzieher* (UB III 8); and KSA 13, 16[29].

II.4 149). This could be an indication that Nietzsche had read Herbart, but I think it more likely that it is taken from books Nietzsche read while preparing the lectures.

Schleiermacher

Schleiermacher philosophized in the tradition of Kant, Fichte, Schelling and Hegel, but the essence of his thought was more theological than philosophical. Apart from being the most important Protestant systematic theologian of the nineteenth century he was also a philosopher, educator, Church minister and classical philologist. The young Nietzsche's few references to Schleiermacher are essentially to him as a classical philologist, though not primarily as the famous translator of Plato, but to his writings on early Greek philosophy, especially Democritus.[56] These statements are sometimes coloured by clearly negative value-judgements:

> I am personally extremely fond of the figure of Democritus, admittedly, I have reconstructed it completely new, since our historians of philosophy can neither do him nor Epicurus justice, because they are 'frumb' and like Jews before the master; least of all the womanly, snobbish, untrue and obscure Schleiermacher, whom one everywhere praises or criticizes in a disgusting manner, both with the greatest possible stupidity [a reference to the celebrations of the centenary of Schleiermacher's birth, 21 Nov. 1868]; the truth does not lie in the middle, but somewhere completely different (letter to Rohde, 9 Dec. 1868: KSB 2/350).[57]

The only other context in which Schleiermacher is mentioned by the young Nietzsche and his friends is when Gersdorff, who wrote in a letter to Nietzsche of 18 December 1864, that he had wished for Christmas, among other books, the *Monologe* by Schleiermacher, and

---

56   Nietzsche clearly read this material and, at least once or twice, quotes and gives page references to Schleiermacher's philological works, e.g. in FS 3/256, where he quotes from the third part of vol. III, p. 301, of Schleiermacher's collected works.

57   I have left the word 'frumb' untranslated, as I have been unable to find a satisfactory rendering for it.

Nietzsche who in letters to Deussen and Rohde, of 2 and 6 June 1868 respectively, wrote with obvious pleasure that the pastor Friedrich August Wenkel, with whom Nietzsche often discussed philosophy, had lately turned away from Hegel, Schleiermacher and Strauss to instead claim allegiance to Kant and Schopenhauer.

Nietzsche would continue to read Schleiermacher's philological works in Basle and often refer to him in his lectures and sometimes in his early notes from the Basle period. These frequent references to Schleiermacher in the lecture notes, especially the lectures about Plato and the pre-Platonic philosophers, is not surprising. Nor is it surprising that most of the references and discussions are critical.

However, if we limit our examination to Nietzsche's references and possible reading of non-philological works by Schleiermacher, the lecture notes still give us more information than Nietzsche's books, *Nachlass* and letters. Twice in his discussions of Schleiermacher's style he refers to his *Über die Religion*. He writes that Schleiermacher's translation of Plato is the best so far, but it is a turgid German '(one recognizes the author of "Reden über Religion" etc.)'[58] and a bit later on he writes that Schleiermacher saw in Plato a literary teacher, with an ideal audience of readers whom he attempted methodically to educate: i.e. about the same way in which Schleiermacher himself 'wrote for the educated in the "Reden über die Religion"' (KGW II.4 13).[59]

Nietzsche's first more general references to Schleiermacher were made in 1873 and 1874, in the first two *Untimely Meditations* (*Unzeitgemässe Betrachtungen*). In the first he critically discusses Strauss's dependence on Schleiermacher, and in *On the Uses and Disadvantages of History for Life* he criticizes Schleiermacher's ethnocentric

---

58   KGW II.4 10. This is at the beginning of his lectures 'Einleitung in das Studium der platonischen Dialogue', which he gave for the first time in the 1871–72 winter semester.

59   In his lectures about the pre-Platonic philosophers Nietzsche refers and gives a page reference to Schleiermacher's collected works, which shows that he had made use of them, even if here only of the philological parts.

view of Christianity more generally.[60] A few of these more general statements regarding Schleiermacher's view of Christianity continue in *Human, All Too Human*.[61] Thereafter Nietzsche begins to treat him with open hostility, but these references are few and not directed individually at Schleiermacher, but only as one of several German philosophers.[62]

It is clear that the late Nietzsche had no special interest in Schleiermacher and did not read him. Although the late Nietzsche was intensively concerned with Christianity and wrote *The Antichrist*, he makes no public comment on the theological aspect of Schleiermacher's thinking.

Nietzsche did not possess any work by Schleiermacher, but he did possess his translation of Plato. Schleiermacher was also discussed in some detail in issues of the *Philosophische Monatshefte* which we know that Nietzsche read in the early 1870s, though we do not know if he read specifically the articles about Schleiermacher.

Feuerbach

The young Nietzsche's relation to Ludwig Feuerbach (1804–72) may be an interesting one, but owing to a lack of hard evidence it remains an object of speculation. Feuerbach had first studied theology and then gone to Berlin to study philosophy under Hegel. There he reacted against philosophical idealism and began to argue that all religious feelings were only projections of human needs or wish-fulfilments and that God was a deification of the self. Later he worked out a philosophy of naturalistic materialism. Aspects of Nietzsche's view and critique of religion echo Feuerbach's and it is also possible that Nietzsche was in fact influenced by him at the time of his rejection of

60   See UB I 6 and 11; UB II 7 and 9.
61   See MA I 132, and MA II/2 216.
62   See M 190, and EH 'WA' 3.

the Christian faith in 1862.[63] We do know that Nietzsche listed two works by Feuerbach in a rather long birthday wish-list in October 1861: *Das Wesen des Christenthums* and *Gedanken über Tod und Unsterblichkeit*.[64] We have no direct evidence that Nietzsche received any of these works, but we have one indication that he read the former. In a fragment of a letter to his friends Gustav Krug and Wilhelm Pinder, dated 27 April 1862, he quotes a central statement from *Das Wesen des Christenthums*, namely, that man is the 'beginning, the middle and the end of religion', and the whole letter is Feuerbachian in spirit. He claims further that 'the illusion of a supernatural world had brought the human spirit to a false conception of the earthly world: it was the result of a childishness of peoples' (KSB 1/201–02).[65]

The only other reference to Feuerbach in the young Nietzsche's writings is a brief, rather Nietzschean, quotation from Feuerbach, 'be satisfied with the given world', six or seven years later, though this has its source not in Feuerbach directly but in Lange's *Geschichte des Materialismus* where Lange refers to it several times (FS 3/335, 449).

---

63   Jörg Salaquarda writes: 'Disagreement persists among Nietzsche scholars as to when, and for what reasons exactly, Nietzsche broke with Christianity. In the corpus of his early notes, we find testimonies of a living faith as late as 1861. But these notes conflict with other texts in which Nietzsche submitted Christian teachings to a sober analysis or penned rather blasphemous remarks. At any rate, from 1862 or so, Nietzsche was clearly estranged from Christianity, and in 1865, when he confined his studies exclusively to classics, he overtly broke with it irrevocably.' ('Nietzsche and the Judaeo-Christian Tradition', in Bernd Magnus and Kathleen M. Higgins (eds), *The Cambridge Companion to Nietzsche* (Cambridge: Cambridge University Press, 1996), p. 92). For a more detailed discussion of Nietzsche's loss of faith in 1861–65, see my 'Nietzsche's Changing Relation to Christianity: Nietzsche as Christian, Atheist and Anti-christ', in Weaver Santaniello (ed.), *Nietzsche and the Gods* (Albany: SUNY Press, 2001), pp. 137–57.

64   The list consists of eleven titles of books, one magazine subscription and two musical compositions; see FS 1/251.

65   This fragment is also published in FS 2/63 as a note, without indication that it was part of a letter.

Schopenhauer and Überweg hardly mention Feuerbach at all, but Lange discusses his thinking in some detail, and Wagner, who had held Feuerbach in high regard before encountering Schopenhauer, was later to be a source of interest in and knowledge about Feuerbach for Nietzsche. A later account by Ida Overbeck seems to confirm that Nietzsche was interested in and influenced by Feuerbach. She writes:

> Nietzsche at that time [1880–83] also quoted ideas of Ludwig Feuerbach's. He criticized Wagner for having turned from Feuerbach to Schopenhauer. Not as if he himself had undergone the opposite process; for Feuerbach had influenced him long ago, perhaps even before Schopenhauer.[66]

In 1875, while reading Dühring, Nietzsche notes that Dühring sympathizes with Feuerbach. There is then a silence until 1884 when he is treated *en masse* together with other German thinkers (compare Fichte, Leibniz and Schelling above), which is probably due to the reading of an as yet unidentified work about philosophy or German philosophy at this time. In May and June 1887 Nietzsche read in the library at Chur and wrote down a large number of notes and excerpts. Many of these notes were taken down by Nietzsche while reading Kuno Fischer's *Geschichte der neuern Philosophie*.[67] Among these are the title of a third work by Feuerbach, *Grundsätze der Philosophie der Zukunft*, where Nietzsche has underlined the first 'der'.[68] He adds immediately below this line, 'against "the abstract philosophy"', and above it, 'Feuerbach's "gesunde und frische Sinnlichkeit"' (KSA 12, 7[4]). The last line here is later used by Nietzsche in the only two published statements regarding Feuerbach, which both refer to Wagner's sympathy with Feuerbach.[69]

---

66   Quoted in Sander L. Gilman (ed.), *Conversations with Nietzsche: A Life in the Words of His Contemporaries*, trans. David J. Parent (New York and Oxford: Oxford University Press, 1987), p. 114.

67   See 'Beiträge zur Quellenforschung mitgeteilt von Thomas H. Brobjer', *Nietzsche-Studien*, 30 (2001), 421.

68   Nietzsche would, of course, think of his own, different 'Vorspiel einer Philosophie der Zukunft', i.e. his *Beyond Good and Evil* (1886).

69   See GM III 2, and NW viii.

In conclusion, it is possible that Nietzsche read Feuerbach's *Das Wesen des Christenthums* in 1861–62, at the time he lost his Christian faith and it is thus possible that Feuerbach was of enormous importance for Nietzsche's intellectual development. However, if this was the case, it is surprising how rarely Nietzsche refers to Feuerbach in general[70] and especially that there are no references to him when Nietzsche speaks of his own development. Furthermore, it has been impossible to substantiate this reading (and its importance), which however, remains possible and perhaps even probable. It is possible that Nietzsche did not have first-hand knowledge of Feuerbach but did have sufficient knowledge of him both to list two of his works as birthday wishes, and for his comments in that letter and the essays. This would allow for a possible important influence of Feuerbach on Nietzsche, and at the same time make his absence in Nietzsche's writings more comprehensible. Certainly, Nietzsche's later references to Feuerbach would seem to indicate that he had been important for Nietzsche's early development. Nietzsche did not read Feuerbach at any later date and did not show any special interest in his thinking.

Marx

Nietzsche never mentions Karl Marx or Friedrich Engels and it is generally assumed that he had no knowledge of them and their kind of thinking and socialism. However, this is not correct. Marx is referred to in at least thirteen books, by ten different authors, which Nietzsche read or possessed, and in six of them he is discussed and quoted extensively, and in one of them Nietzsche has underlined Karl Marx's name.[71]

---

70 There is, for example, no reference to Feuerbach in Nietzsche's lecture notes.
71 For a more extensive discussion of Nietzsche's knowledge of Marx, see my article 'Nietzsche's Knowledge of Marx and Marxism', forthcoming in *Nietzsche-Studien*.

The ten authors who mention or discuss Marx, and whose works we know that Nietzsche either possessed or had read, are Jörg, Lange, Dühring, Meysenbug, Frantz, Schäffle, Frary, Bahnsen, Bebel and Jacoby. Of these, the books by Lange, Dühring, Frantz, Schäffle, Bebel and Jacoby contain extensive discussions and long quotations.

A receipt shows that Nietzsche bought the third edition of Lange's *Die Arbeiterfrage* of 1875 in that year, and this work contains extensive positive discussions of Marx, whom Lange refers to as being 'well known for having probably a more thorough knowledge of the history of political economy than anyone else currently alive'.[72]

In the same year, 1875, Nietzsche also bought, read and annotated the German socialist and anti-Semite Eugen Dühring's *Kritische Geschichte der Nationalökonomie und des Sozialismus* (Berlin, [2]1875). This work contains a detailed hostile account of Marx' views in the chapter 'Der neuere Socialismus: Zweites Capitel: Gestaltungen in Deutschland', and Marx (and Engels) are also mentioned and discussed in other parts of the work.[73] A copy of this work is still in Nietzsche's library in Weimar and contains sparse annotations, but none relating directly to Dühring's discussions of Marx.

In 1879 or later Nietzsche acquired and probably read the philosopher and political writer Constantin Frantz's *Der Föderalismus als das leitende Prinzip für die soziale, staatliche und internationale Organisation, unter besonderer Bezugnahme auf Deutschland* (Mainz, 1879). The first chapter, 'Kritik des Socialismus', is essentially a detailed critique of Marx's view of political economy. This

---

72 The table of contents of Lange's *Die Arbeiterfrage* lists the following chapters: I. Der Kampf um das Dasein; II. Der Kampf um die bevorzugte Stellung; III. Glück und Glückseligkeit; IV. Die Lebenshaltung (standard of life); V. Kapital und Arbeit; VI. Eigenthum, Erbrecht und Bodenrente; VII. Von der Lösung der Arbeiterfrage. Chapter V especially contains extensive sympathetic discussions of Marx: 'In diesem Kapitel haben wir es hauptsächlich mit der Marx'schen Anschauung von der kapitalistischen Produktionsweise zu thun'.

73 Nietzsche possessed and read this book. Of particular interest is its conclusion (pp. 569–76).

book is still in Nietzsche's library, but contains no annotations. At this time Nietzsche probably also acquired the German-Austrian political economist Albert Schäffle's *Quintessenz des Sozialismus* (first published in 1875, with many later editions) which 'did more than any other publication to enlighten the educated and privileged classes in Germany and Austria about the true nature of socialism' (Redlich), for his library once contained the edition from 1879 but this has since been lost. Schäffle gives a detailed sympathetic account of Marx's views. Together with Gast in Venice in 1885 Nietzsche read one of the more well-known works in the Marxist and socialist tradition, August Bebel's *Die Frau in der Vergangenheit, Gegenwart und Zukunft* (^{2}1883), a work more commonly known as *Die Frau und der Sozialismus*, which is a socialist polemic and contains much discussion of political economy and many references to Marx's works, including the *Communist Manifesto* and *Das Kapital*. Finally, in 1887 or 1888, Nietzsche read and underlined the name Karl Marx in the enthusiastic Marxist Leopold Jacoby's *Die Idee der Ent-wicklung: Eine sozial-philosophische Darstellung* (Zurich, ^{2}1886–87). In this work Jacoby enthusiastically praises Darwin and Marx as the two great thinkers of development, Darwin in the field of biology and Marx in the human field, and several times he quotes passages of several pages from Marx's *Das Kapital* and Engels' *Die Lage der arbeitenden Klasse in England* (Leipzig, ^{2}1848).

Nietzsche is thus likely to have had a reasonable knowledge of Marx (and Engels) and of their kind of socialism. He never explicitly refers to them, but their kind of socialism is likely to be included in Nietzsche's harsh critique of socialism.

Nietzsche, like any German intellectual active during the second half of the nineteenth century, would continually encounter references to and discussions of the great German philosophers, and thus in some way be acquainted with their thinking generally. However, Nietzsche, who to a large extent was an autodidact in regard to philosophy, seems to have read very few philosophical works by most of them. His reading of contemporary – and today much less well known – philosophers was much more extensive and active. We have no evidence that he had read any relevant work by Leibniz, Herder, Jacobi, Fichte, Herbart and Marx, and probably also not by Schelling and Scheiermacher. However, he knew Schopenhauer well and continued to read him even after his 'break' with him in 1875–76. Kant was important for Nietzsche's thinking, and he encountered a large number of discussions of Kant's philosophy, but he seems to have had remarkably little first-hand knowledge of Kant's texts. He read Hegel, Feuerbach and Hamann before the mid-1870s (although there is some uncertainty regarding Feuerbach), and they may have been important for Nietzsche's thinking and development.

Christa Davis Acampora

'The Contest Between Nietzsche and Homer': Revaluing the Homeric Question[1]

> However, the greater and more sublime a Greek is, the brighter the ambitious flame breaks out of him, consuming everyone who runs with him on the same path. Aristotle once made a list of such hostile contestants in the great styles: among them is the most striking example – that even a dead man can still excite a living one to burning jealousy. Thus Aristotle designated the relation of Xenophanes of Colophon to Homer. We do not understand the strength of Xenophanes', and later Plato's, attack on the national hero of poetry, if we do not also think of the monstrous desire at the root of these attacks to assume the place of the overthrown poet and inherit his fame. Every great Hellene passes on the torch of the contest; every great virtue sets afire new greatness (HW: KSA 1/787–88).[2]

Nietzsche introduced himself to his Basle colleagues and the larger community of philologists by tackling what was arguably *the* most central and vexing question for those studying the texts of ancient Greece: the so-called 'Homeric Question'. In his inaugural lecture, *Homer and Classical Philology*, Nietzsche summoned the diverse approaches that defined nearly a century of German philological and philosophical scholarship addressing the authenticity, authorship, and significance of Homeric literature.[3] The task he set for himself was to

---

1   While the bulk of this paper is the text presented at the 1997 meeting of the Friedrich Nietzsche Society at St Andrews, this version has been modified in light of subsequently published research and the development of my own ideas.

2   The translation is my own, which also appears in my 'Re/Introducing "Homer's Contest": A new translation with notes and commentary', *Nietzscheana*, 5 (Fall 1996), i–iv and 1–8.

3   The lecture was entitled *Über die Persönlichkeit Homers* (On the Personality of Homer) when it was first presented. The title *Homer and Classical Philology*

bring about a tense reconciliation of opposing approaches, which was to be accomplished by asking the question anew, by setting the inquiry on a different course. Nietzsche sought not merely to introduce new evidence regarding the authorship and dating of the texts that were attributed to Homer, but rather to redefine the significance of asking the question 'Who is the real Homer, and what did he write?', in order to indicate its contemporary relevance, in short, to *revalue the Homeric Question*. Nietzsche saw the revaluation of the Homeric Question as relevant not only to providing a basis for understanding ancient Greek culture but also for defining the role such texts might play in the development of contemporary culture, especially the role they might play in the activity of *Bildung*, broadly conceived.

The tasks of this paper are, first, to situate Nietzsche's early accounts of Homeric significance (in his *Homer and Classical Philology* and his study of the anonymous ancient text 'The Contest Between Homer and Hesiod') in the philological tradition from which Nietzsche's ideas emerged and, second, to indicate the relevance of that work for ideas that Nietzsche later developed about aesthetics and his own practice of philosophy. Nietzsche's refashioning of the contest with Homer, in which he places himself in the role of an agonist, forms the basis of his lifelong engagements not only with Homer but also with other agonists he draws into skirmishes throughout his writings. Finally, I consider the culmination of Nietzsche's own contest with Homer in his effort to recreate for modern German culture what he thought Homeric literature provided for ancient Greek culture, namely, the opportunity to cultivate a kind of taste, the possibility of

appeared on the subsequent, privately published version. Nietzsche had already begun to develop his lecture while he was a student at Leipzig, and he had made a similar presentation to the Philology Club at Leipzig in 1866 (reported by Heinrich Stürenberg in *Conversations with Nietzsche: A Life in the Words of His Contemporaries*, ed. Sander L. Gilman, trans. David J. Parent (New York and Oxford: Oxford University Press, 1987), p. 29).

an exercise of judgement, which could provide the basis of a superior cultural formation.[4]

The first section of the paper briefly sketches Nietzsche's revision of the 'Homeric Question' and the relevance of Homer for Nietzsche's views on competition. In the second, I explore Nietzsche's rather traditional views on education and cultivation – *Bildung*, broadly conceived – and the ways in which those views were shaped by his conception of *agon* (contest). Finally, I conclude with some suggestions regarding how Nietzsche *qua* agonist strove to enact those ideas, when, in his *Thus spake Zarathustra*, he endeavored to challenge the monumental educator of the Greeks he so greatly admired in pursuit of a culture that would better even that of his rival.

I.

Nietzsche's approach to the 'Homeric Question' is driven by his concern with questions of taste and the goal of cultivation or *Bildung*. The intersection of these two concerns illuminates numerous aspects of Nietzsche's allegiance and antagonism with the German tradition. Wholly steeped in those conventions, Nietzsche's work still challenges that of his predecessors on several key points. The most significant is his characterization of the goal of aesthetic cultivation. While Schiller and Humboldt strive for harmonization, Nietzsche seeks perpetual and renewable tension and conflict. This difference shapes both the divergence of their ends and Nietzsche's vision of his own philosophical practice. Nietzsche not only praises agonistic interaction, his treatment of his predecessors, including the exemplars

---

4   I further develop these ideas in my 'Nietzsche's Problem of Homer', in *Nietzscheforschung*, 5–6 (2000), 553–74, and my 'Nietzsche Contra Homer, Socrates, and Paul', forthcoming in *The Journal of Nietzsche Studies*.

he finds in antiquity, reflects his efforts to practice a serious but playful, agonistic – contestatory – mode of philosophical engagement.

Throughout his career, Nietzsche wrestles with temptations to portray the Greeks either as idealized genteel noblemen or as exotic primitive human beings. He particularly opposes the view that the legacy of the Greeks is the 'noble simplicity and serene greatness' they exhibited, a thesis developed by Winckelmann and those who followed him. Nietzsche writes, 'One sort of consideration is left: to *understand* how the greatest creations of the spirit have evil and terror as their background' (NF 1875: KSA 8/19, 3[17]).[5] He strives to see the ancient Greeks as real human beings, whose greatness was not so miraculous but rather reflected their struggles and political turmoil, their sensuality, and their decadence in addition to their excellence: 'The *human element* that the classics show us is not to be confused with the *humane*. The antithesis to be strongly emphasized; what ails philology is its effort to smuggle in the humane'(ibid., 3[12]). In an effort to try to make sense of what appeared to many to be the 'miracle' of the development of classical Greek culture, Nietzsche aims to cast it in the light of what preceded it. His explanation is similar to the one Jacob Burckhardt suggests in lectures that form the basis of his *History of Ancient Greek Culture*: the principle around which the entire culture evolved was a competitive drive to excel.

Nietzsche did not simply inherit the idea from Burckhardt. Nietzsche's most extended work on the significance of *agon*, *Homer's Contest*, dates back at least as far as two years prior to his appointment at Basle where he was Burckhardt's colleague. Nietzsche also had occasion to think about the role of *agon* in Greek culture as he edited the ancient text *The Contest Between Homer and Hesiod* (anonymous author) and as he prepared his commentary on the same while a student at Leipzig. Burckhardt's lectures did not begin until 1870 (although he had been working on them since the early 1860s)

---

5   See the previous note (3[16]): *'Escape from reality* to the classics: hasn't the understanding of antiquity already been falsified in this manner?'

and there is no evidence that Nietzsche had any knowledge of Burckhardt's thesis before he came to Basle. Although Burckhardt is credited by classicists with 'discovering' the agonistic element of the so-called 'Greek spirit', Nietzsche had earlier recognized and began to trace its serious dangers.[6] Homer figures prominently in Nietzsche's account of how that culture came to be organized.

In his inaugural lecture of 28 May 1869, Nietzsche challenges two prevailing approaches to the question of the authorial unity and transmission of the writings attributed to Homer: first, the 'scientific' approach, which aims to dissect and catalogue every detail and to expose every possible corruption of the text not attributable to 'the real Homer' and, second, the approach characterized by its efforts to generate a 'beautiful' and 'complete' Homer regardless of the degree to which such a project requires pure fabrications.[7] Nietzsche's understanding of what is at stake in investigating Homeric literature and Greek history is informed by a variety of traditions in classical scholarship, including humanism, idealism, and realism. Neo-hellenism in Germany came to fruition in the eighteenth century in the work of Johann Joachim Winckelmann (1717–68), whose work represented a break from the then current Latin humanism and served to revive the study of Greek literature. His principal concern is to elucidate the harmonic coordination of individual artistic achievements with cultural and social advancement. Winckelmann's chief work, *Geschichte der Kunst des Altertums* (1764), was well-received. Lessing, Herder, Goethe, Humboldt, and many others took interest in and were significantly influenced by his writing. Winckelmann's texts are versatile: he employs a literary approach to his study of art, and

6   See Nietzsche's article, 'Der Florentinische Tractat über Homer und Hesiod, ihr Geschlecht und ihren Wettkampf', I–II. *Rheinisches Museum*, 25 [1870], 528–40; repr. in KGW II.1 271–337.

7   A good summary of the tensions, especially between classicism and historicism, and Nietzsche's attempts to address them is found in James I. Porter, *Nietzsche and the Philology of the Future* (Stanford: Stanford University Press, 2000), pp. 68–70.

this framework has proven fruitful for the study of literature, history, and philosophy.[8]

Winckelmann's biographer and devotee, Friedrich August Wolf (1759–1824) made significant contributions to the study of Homer and of Plato. The best known is his *Prolegomena ad Homerum* (1795). In that work Wolf employs various literary and linguistic tests to determine the authenticity of the Homeric epics, concluding that they were not the products of a single individual but of a group of rhapsodes. Although a great number of those principles were actually formulated by J. G. Eichhorn,[9] classical philology credits Wolf with formalizing the methods and approaches to the study of classical texts. And while many of his specific arguments were subsequently refuted or undermined, Wolf's work was extremely influential in his day, and continues to be so. It intensified a long-standing debate that continued for more than a century following concerning the authorship, authenticity, and dating of the so-called Homeric corpus.[10]

8   See Rudolf Pfeiffer, *History of Classical Scholarship from 1300–1850* (Oxford: Clarendon Press, 1976) p. 171.

9   For an elaboration of the similarities between Wolf's *Prolegomena* and Eichhorn's earlier *Einleitung ins Alte Testament* (1780–83), see Wolf's introduction to his *Prolegomena to Homer*, trans. and ed. Anthony Grafton et al. (Princeton: Princeton University Press, 1985), esp. pp. 18–26.

10   Pfeiffer, p. 175. Wolf's line of argument was supported and expanded in the twentieth century by Milman Parry, *The Making of Homeric Verse*, ed. A. Parry (Oxford: Oxford University Press, 1987). Additional studies of the controversy can be found in: J. Russo, 'Homer Against His Tradition', *Arion*, (Summer 1968), 275–95; Norman Austin, *Archery at the Dark of the Moon: Poetic Problems in Homer's Odyssey* (Stanford: Stanford University Press, 1975); Piero Pucci, *Odysseus Polytropos. Intertextual Readings in the Odyssey and the Iliad* (Ithaca, NY: Cornell University Press, 1987); David Shive, *Naming Achilles* (Oxford: Oxford University Press, 1987); and Richard P. Martin, *The Language of Heroes: Speech and Performance in the Iliad* (Ithaca, NY: Cornell University Press, 1989). See also David R. Lachterman, '*Die ewige Wiederkehr der Griechen*: Nietzsche and the Homeric Question', *International Studies in Philosophy*, 23 (1991), no. 2, 90–91. For a recent discussion of the debate, see Gregory Nagy, *Homeric Questions* (Austin: University of Texas Press, 1996).

Against those contemporaries whom Nietzsche describes as realists, whose primary interest was applying a strictly scientific approach to the study of antiquity, and those he describes as artists, whose aim was to capture the 'wonderful creative force; the real fragrance, of the atmosphere of antiquity' (HKP: KGW II.1, 252), Nietzsche argues that the most important concern with regard to the study of the texts to which we append the name 'Homer' is not whether there were one or several authors but what kind of personality the epics suggest, what judgment the appearance of Homeric literature reflects. As the inaugural lecture makes clear, Homer represents for Nietzsche what he describes as 'a productive point of view'. His interest in Homeric literature focuses upon the cultivation of a particular taste or judgement. The value of Homeric literature for contemporary audiences, Nietzsche suggests, lies not in determining the history of the transmission of the text, but in the ways in which it serves as an instrument for creating and shaping values. Nietzsche's abiding aim is to reveal that mechanism in hopes of utilizing it for the enhancement of his own culture.[11]

The upshot of Nietzsche's lecture seems to be that the so-called 'problem of Homer', that had significantly defined and directed the efforts of many of his fellow philologists is 'like a coin long passed from hand to hand, [and consequently] has lost its original and highly conspicuous stamp'. The 'real' Homer, the 'truth' of the Homeric works is like those metaphors described in Nietzsche's drafts for the essay 'On Truth and Lies in an Extra-Moral Sense': 'metaphors that have become worn out and have been drained of sensuous force, coins which have lost their embossing and are now considered as metal and no longer as coins' (WL: KSA 1/881). Both the realists and the idealists obscure the aesthetic qualities of the work, either by draining

---

11   In his *Nietzsche and the Philology of the Future*, Porter explains Nietzsche's solution as an outrageous attempt to reconcile or at least unite Wolf and Goethe (see pp. 68–78). My focus centers less on the Homeric Question as it was traditionally conceived and more on Nietzsche's concern with generating new problems that the phenomenon of Homeric literature potentially presents.

it of its life through dissection, or by obscuring it completely through fabrication in the interest of rendering it as a unified whole, obscuring its joints perceived as blemishes. Nietzsche writes:

> Poetical works, which cause the hearts of even the greatest geniuses to fail when they endeavor to vie with them, and in which unsurpassable images are held up for the admiration of posterity – and yet the poet who wrote them with only a hollow, shaky name, whenever we do lay hold on him; nowhere the solid kernel of a powerful personality. 'For who would wage war with the gods: who, even with the one god?' asks Goethe even, who, though a genius, strove in vain to solve that mysterious problem of the Homeric inaccessibility. (HKP: KGW II.1, 258)[12]

The task, then, is to make the personality of Homer accessible, not by picking apart the epics to show that, in fact, no 'Homer' exists, and not by so embellishing the work, covering over its blemishes, that we replace it with something it is not. Rather, the challenge for philologists who wish to tackle the Homeric question is to *play* the works, that is, to serve as the virtuoso who 'let[s] the world for the first time hear that music which lay so long in obscurity, despised and undecipherable' (HKP: KGW II.1, 268). And this requires a 'philosophical view of things' that organizes those principles of performance. In other words, what is needed are philosophical concepts that guide the hermeneutic activities that invariably come with bringing forth the meaning of 'Homer', thereby reanimating, reinvigorating the 'sensuous force' of Homeric literature. In his lecture, Nietzsche claims that such an approach would unite or mollify the differences between the diverse aims and methods of the idealist and realist approaches in his discipline. But as he himself then strives to 'restamp' the name Homer, it is unclear that he heeds his own call. Nietzsche's Homer seems to belong nearly entirely to the idealist camp even though he takes on some different qualities under Nietzsche's gaze.

---

12 Porter interestingly connects Nietzsche's emphasis on personality in this lecture with Nietzsche's later pervasive interest in the personality of Socrates and with Nietzsche's reception of F. A. Lange. See his discussion of Lange's conception of *Persönlichkeit*, pp. 58–60.

In *The Birth of Tragedy*, Nietzsche portrays Homer as the embodiment of the first artist of values. His artistic feat is accomplished through his reversal of the so-called wisdom of Silenus. Both Sophocles and Theognis testify to Silenus's grim view of the character of human existence. When Midas encounters Silenus in the forest, he tells him that what is best for humankind is not to be born and second-best is to die soon.[13] Through his depiction of human life as extending the possibility of exceptional glory, Homer, as Nietzsche reads him, effects a reversal of Silenus's judgement such that '"to die soon is worst of all for [human beings], the next worst – to die at all"' (GT 3). At their most basic core, namely the value of human existence as such, the values available to the Greeks were set upon a new axis following this transformation. It is *that* accomplishment to which Nietzsche seeks to draw attention and to have it serve as a model for the formation or cultivation of judgement generally. Nietzsche's revaluation of the 'Homeric Question' is an effort to redirect our concern about Homer from the authenticity of what are designated as Homeric texts to an investigation of both the specific values that Homer transformed and the structure of revaluation that we might be able to recognize in the process of our pursuits. Nietzsche's essay 'Homer's Contest' sketches those features, which he further develops and explores in greater detail in the contexts of the studies of other monumental shifts in values that form the basis of his subsequent writings.

Homer's revaluation took the form of a contest in several ways. In addition to portraying life as a series of contests through which circulated the honor and prestige that gave meaning to one's life, Homer's crafting of a contesting spirit resulted in the proliferation of agonistic institutions. Those institutions effectively tapped the

---

13   See 'Oedipus at Colonus', ll. 1224ff. Theognis expresses a similar view in his *Elegies*: 'For man the best thing is never to be born, / Never to look upon the hot sun's rays, / Next best, to speed at once through Hades' gates / And lie beneath a piled-up heap of earth' (ll. 425–28), in *Hesiod and Theognis*, trans. Dorothea Wender (New York: Penguin Books, 1973) p. 111.

productive possibilities of that spirit through appropriate *Bildung*, by cultivating a mode of action that supported the maintenance of those structures. In other words, the effect of introducing contest as a means to honor was twofold: first, it articulated a structure through which meaning (e.g. excellence) could be created and meted out; and, second, it simultaneously cultivated a commitment to a certain way of competing within those structures. That combination, Nietzsche claims, accounts for the exceptional accomplishments of later Greek culture. A brief review of the main arguments of 'Homer's Contest' illuminates these points.

At the beginning of 'Homer's Contest' Nietzsche reflects on what is ordinarily understood as 'humanity':

> underlying this idea is the belief that it is humanity that *separates* and distinguishes human beings from nature. But, there is, in reality, no such distinction: the 'natural' qualities and those properly called 'human' grow inseparably (HW: KSA 1/783).

He highlights the 'uncanny dual character' of human beings: while capable of nobility, we also bear the capacity for the terrifying and the inhuman. This curious entanglement of the great and the vile leads Nietzsche to reconsider traits ordinarily conceived of as bad, or perhaps even evil, in order to explore whether they might spring from the same soil as some other good. As evidence that others have held such views, Nietzsche cites Hesiod's passages about the good and bad Eris-goddesses – who shared the same origin but who were regarded quite differently.

What distinguishes the two, Nietzsche claims, are their associations with the different kinds of actions they inspire: one promotes destruction, the obliteration of its opposition, what Nietzsche characterizes as 'Vernichtungslust'. The other Eris draws inspiration, propelling human beings to strive to better their opposition in fights of contest (*Wettkämpfe*). In the second volume of *Human All Too Human*, Nietzsche further distinguishes those two actions when he writes, 'Someone who is envious senses every way in which another protrudes beyond the common measure and wants to force him back to it [*bis dahin herabdrücken*] – or to elevate himself to it [*sich bis dorthin erheben*]: out of which there arise two different modes of action [*Handlungsweisen*], which Hesiod designated as the evil and the good Eris' (MA II/2 29).[14] These modes of action – *forcing back* and *elevating above* – distinguish not only individuals, but also varieties of culture. Nietzsche argues that the achievements of Greek culture were made possible by the proliferation of outlets organized on an *agonistic* model in which praiseworthy accomplishments (in art, politics, education, etc.) were determined through public contestation that encouraged competitors to express their desire for recognition by rising above one another rather than seeking the destruction of their opposition. By simultaneously cultivating not only a desire to win, but a desire to compete well (which included respect for one's competitor and the institutions that sets forth the terms of the engagement),[15] the Greeks established a culture capable of deriving their standards of excellence internally and of renewing and revaluing those standards according to changes in needs and interests of the community. Throughout much of his career, Nietzsche appears optimistic that this legacy of the Greeks might be claimed.

So what does it mean for Nietzsche to 'revalue Homer'? Nietzsche's revaluation aims both to reorient the 'Homeric Question' and to restore the value of that which Homer represents: a particular taste that informed a capacity for making judgements. In *The Birth of Tragedy*, Nietzsche writes:

> In the Greeks the 'will' wished to contemplate itself in the transfiguration of genius and the world of art; in order to glorify themselves, its creatures had to feel themselves worthy of glory; they had to behold themselves again in a higher sphere, without this perfect world of contemplation acting as a command or a reproach. This is the sphere of beauty, in which they saw their mirror images, the Olympians. With this mirroring of beauty the Hellenic will combated its artistically correlative talent for suffering and for the wisdom of

14   The translation is my own.
15   For a brief but insightful discussion of the virtues of agonistic engagement that can be derived from Nietzsche's conception, see David Owen, *Nietzsche, Politics and Modernity* (London: Sage Publications, 1995), pp. 139–46.

suffering – and, as a monument of its victory, we have Homer, the naïve artist (GT 3).[16]

The taste for the preferences embodied in Homeric literature is not the only fruit of this victory. What fascinates Nietzsche is also the way in which the victory was achieved. *Agon*, Nietzsche argues, was not only a way of achieving honor but also provided an arena in which the standards of excellence could be negotiated and transmitted. In other words, agonistic interactions provided opportunities both for applying standards of measure and judgement and for determining, revising, and recreating what those standards would be. Hence, perpetuating the *agon* was important for having access to the means for distinguishing oneself and for claiming one's place in the community that authorizes those standards and judges the outcomes of other contests.

But, even if we find Nietzsche's account of the utility of competition compelling, we nevertheless might be unwilling to go so far as to say that the kinds of contests Homer displayed are appropriate models for emulation. The struggles that earned Homer's heroes their honor and glory were anything but productive. They were bloody, ruthless, and fraught with cruelty, more closely resembling what Nietzsche associates with the blood-lust of the original Eris than

---

16   This passage begins with an indication that it is qualifying the sense in which Homer is a naïve artist: 'The Homeric "naïveté" can be understood only as the complete victory of Apollinian illusion [...]'. Schiller draws the distinction between naïve and sentimental poetry in his *On Naïve and Sentimental Poetry* (1795). When Nietzsche characterizes Homer as a so-called 'naïve' artist, he is challenging Schiller's assessment. Schiller appears to have believed that the vision of the beautiful found in Homeric literature somehow stems from a greater proximity to nature that lends greater access to it; hence its naïveté refers to the fact that it is less mature, that its worldview is less complex. Naïve artists stand in contrast to those Schiller designates as 'sentimental'; they must successfully overcome certain cultural impediments that mediate their access to nature. Schiller appears to have thought that sentimental poetry was more admirable because it represented a more significant accomplishment (overcoming the obstacles to nature). Nietzsche's emphasis on Homer's exemplary status as a revaluator depicts Homer's *apparent* naïveté as *accomplished*.

the healthy inspiration her sister allegedly provided. Homer supplies not only the images of victory associated with the sacred games but also the agony of fights to the death on the battlefield. Accounts of how productive competition can be cultivated and the ways in which it can contribute to the development of a healthy culture still remain to be given. Nietzsche's attempts to do so are found in his efforts to adopt and adapt the agonistic model in his views on education and cultural development, particularly in his concerns for *Bildung*.

II.

The concept of *Bildung* as a personal and cultural ideal has a long tradition in German culture. The design of the German university system in the late eighteenth and early nineteenth centuries was strongly linked to the cultural programs of intellectuals such as Humboldt. Revival of interest in myths about the origins of Germanic peoples, the evolution of the German language, and the characteristics of 'what is German?' – a question Nietzsche often posed – preoccupied much reflection on the status of German culture and its future as the modern state of Germany was organized. How to shape 'the German soul', how to put it in a productive relation to society at large were concerns that echoed in much of the work written during the period of German Romanticism. *Bildung* was understood as a process, a way of effecting the sought for harmony and unity of cultural ideals that were perceived to be lacking in the wake of the significant influence of French culture.

It is unsurprising, then, that the German romantics would draw on conceptual traditions that had their roots in fourteenth-century German mysticism. '*Bildung*' was a figurative term used to describe the advance toward and the goal of becoming united with God, becoming complete – whole. It was a process of striving for perfection, an activity of transcending the discordant chaos and frailties of life. The German Romantics adopted and adapted that language for secular purposes as *Bildung* came to mean 'formation, education, constitution, cultivation, culture, personality development, learning, knowledge, good breeding, refinement,' and more.[17]

Bildung was a theme, which reverberated not only in what we might call educational theory, but also in political theory, religion, philosophy, drama, and literature. Fichte (1762–1814) provided an account of how the ego realizes itself through resistance and struggle with the non-ego. Hegel (1770–1831) articulated the universal and historical unfolding of the *Bildung*-process in *The Phenomenology of Spirit*, in which he described the manner in which the individual evolves from his *ungebildete* condition to a state of absolute consciousness. Hegel described his work as providing an account of the spirit's *Bildung*. Schlegel (1772–1829) likened the process of self-development, *sich bilden*, to becoming divine. Goethe's *Wilhelm Meister* (1795–96) exhibited striving that aimed not at becoming a deity of the heavens but at becoming 'a god of the earth'. Related to striving to attain divinity is the goal of securing absolute mastery. In the work of Novalis (1772–1801), one finds *Bildung* linked with both mastery and freedom. In *Heinrich von Ofterdingen*, *Bildung* is understood as leading to a heightened power of creativity, which in turn is identified as the fundamental principle of all being.[18]

17 Klaus Vondung, 'Unity through *Bildung*: A German Dream of Perfection', *Journal of Independent Philosophy*, 5–6 (1988), 47–55 (47). I am indebted to this article for providing most of the references cited in the next paragraph.

18 See J. G. Fichte, *Das System der Sittenlehre nach den Prinzipien der Wissenschaftslehre*, in *Werke. Auswahl*, ed. Fritz Medicus, 6 vols (Hamburg: Meiner, 1962), ii, 485–87; G. W. F. Hegel, *Phänomenologie des Geistes*, ed. Johannes Hoffmeister, 6th edn (Hamburg: Meiner, 1952), p. 26 (for Hegel's own description of his project); Friedrich Schlegel, 'Athenäums-Fragmente', in *Schriften zur Literatur*, ed. Wolfdietrich Rasch (Munich: Hanser, 1972), p. 54.; J. W. Goethe, *Wilhelm Meisters Lehrjahre*, in *Goethes Werke*, ed. Erich Trunz, 12th edn, 14 vols (Munich: Beck, 1981), vii, 71 and 82; and Novalis, *Heinrich von Ofterdingen*, ed. Wolfgang Frühwald (Stuttgart: Reclam, 1978), pp. 173–74. It is important to note that, in *Wilhelm Meister*, the goal of reaching the status of

Schiller argues that cultural and individual development are best achieved through conflict. In the context of discussing why the Greeks excelled in so many cultural and intellectual endeavors, Schiller writes: 'There was no other way of developing the manifold capacities of Man than by placing them in opposition to each other.'[19] But for Schiller, that dynamic cannot last if we are to achieve the ideal state toward which we strive: the individual as 'constant unity' (Schiller §11). Schiller frequently refers to the ideal model for life as one who is far along the endless path in pursuit of the 'divinity within himself' (Schiller §11), one who holds 'a pure ideal man within himself, with whose unalterable unity it is the great task of his existence, throughout all his vicissitudes, to harmonize' (Schiller §4). Disharmony, discord, and opposition are useful but not ideal; the 'antagonism of powers is the great instrument of culture, but it is only the instrument; for as long as it persists, we are only on the way towards culture' (Schiller §6). The best life, as well as the most advanced culture, according to Schiller, is one in which the developmental force of opposition is exhausted and overcome and a harmonic ideal is realized.

For Schiller, the Greeks are exemplary models of a harmonic ideal; relating them in a critical way to his own time facilitates the progress of his own culture toward the same goal. Schiller, like Humboldt, understands harmonization as a complicated dynamic. He identifies two fundamental principles at work in human life and the world as a whole. One aims at mutation and the other is inclined

a divinity is not attained and that the definition of the goal of *Bildung* shifts such that, by the end of the novel, the aim bildung is defined as 'being active in a dignified way', 'without wanting to dominate' (see Vondung, p. 49, and *Goethes Werke*, vii, 608). For a concise and useful account of *Bildung* in the plays of Schiller, Goethe, and Kleist, see Margaret Scholl, *The Bildungsdrama of the Age of Goethe* (Frankfurt a.M.: Lang, 1976).

19   Friedrich Schiller, *On the Aesthetic Education of Man in a Series of Letters*, trans. Reginald Snell (New York: Ungar, 1965), Letter 6, p. 43. Subsequent references, cited in the text, are drawn from this translation and indicate the letter in which the citation appears (e.g. Schiller §12).

toward immutability (Schiller §13). The first Schiller designates the
'sense impulse', the second, the 'form impulse'. The sense impulse
facilitates the development of ourselves as matter, which Schiller
describes as 'alteration, or reality which occupies time' (Schiller §12).
When occupied only by the sense impulse, 'Man [...] is nothing but a
unit of magnitude, an occupied moment of time – or rather, *he* is not,
for his personality is extinguished so long as sense perception governs
him and time whirls him along with itself' (Schiller §12).[20] The
formal impulse aims at harmonizing the diversity that the sensuous
impulse encourages. The formal springs from our rational nature, and
its goal is to inhibit change so that what is proper to our individuality
will be stabilized.

Although these impulses are generally opposed, they need not
come into direct conflict, Schiller claims, because they do not abide
within the same entity. Schiller seems to think that to the degree to
which these two impulses are manifest in different aspects of human
existence, they are able to simultaneously achieve their aims. The two
forces are mutually subordinate, and here Schiller distinguishes
between 'uniformity' and 'harmony'. Citing Fichte, Schiller calls for
'reciprocal action' between the two impulses, claiming that this notion
marks an improvement over what is implied by some forms of
transcendental philosophy in which the material, sensuous impulse is
an impediment to the rational, the formal, and therefore was to be
minimized and held as an object of disdain. Genuine *Bildung*, Schiller
claims, strives for a coordination in which the sensuous impulse is
amply stimulated by a variety of experiences, and the formal impulse
is permitted independence from the sensuous. 'Where both qualities
are united, Man will combine the greatest fullness of existence with
the utmost self-dependence and freedom, and instead of abandoning

20   Schiller describes the sense impulse as that 'in which the whole phenomenon of
     mankind is ultimately rooted'. He further claims that the sensuous 'absence-of-
     self' is what is ordinarily described as being '*beside oneself* – that is, to be
     outside one's ego', as one is when one is overwhelmed by some kind of
     sensation. Schiller argued that we are always only 'beside' ourselves so long as
     we only perceive; see Schiller's note at §12.

himself to the world he will rather draw it into himself with the whole infinity of its phenomena, and subject it to the unity of his reason' (Schiller §13). That process allows us to incorporate and to fully become united with the multiplicity that is characteristic of the totality of existence. Only through this transformation, Schiller claims, can we become the kind of people who rightly deserve recognition as 'humane'. Schiller writes:

> In order to make us cooperative, helpful, active people, feeling and character must be united, just as susceptibility of sense must combine with rigour of intellect in order to furnish us with experience. How can we be fair, kindly and humane towards others, let our maxims be as praiseworthy as they may, if we lack the capacity to make strange natures genuinely and truly a part of ourselves, appropriate strange situations, make strange feelings our own? [...] In this operation, then, consists for the most part what we call the forming of a human being; and that in the best sense of the term, as signifying the cultivation of the inner, not merely the outward, man (Schiller §13, n. 1).

Bildung is a transformative process that shapes the kind of people we are. It organizes *who* we are by coordinating without stultifying *what* we are.

Tragic art in Nietzsche's *The Birth of Tragedy* educates its participants by engaging them in a highly charged and tautly strained reconciliation of the Dionysian and the Apollinian, which are dangerously disposed toward eradicating each other. Tragic art is transformative for Nietzsche because the process of its enactment renders a similar union in the psyches of its audience. Organized in this way, Nietzsche thinks such people are in the best possible condition to find their own life and the world justified: it reconciles them to life. Agonistic *Bildung*, at least in Nietzsche's early writings, both facilitates our internal development and synchronizes us to the whole of nature.

Nietzsche and Schiller part company regarding the conception of how the impulses interact in play and how play is achieved.[21] We

---

21 I do not suggest that there are not significant similarities between Nietzsche's and Schiller's views. For a more thorough account of the similarities and

recall that the kind of play manifest in tragic art, as described in *The Birth of Tragedy*, is one in which the two opposed impulses harness their opposition in such ways that they ultimately advance each other's ends while remaining essentially distinct. What makes the experience of tragedy fruitful is that through it the opposing needs of unification and distinction that the impulses express are simultaneously met. The union of the Dionysian and the Apollinian does not destroy either one. In Schiller's work, by contrast, the Beauty that results from play yields the elimination of opposition – a third condition, which marks the annihilation, or in Schiller's terms, the cancellation (*Aufhebung*) of the sensual and formal impulses:

> Beauty *combines* those two opposite conditions, and thus removes the opposition. But since both conditions remain eternally opposed to one another, they can only be combined by cancellation. Our second business, then, is to make this combination perfect, to accomplish it so purely and completely that both conditions entirely disappear in a third [...] (Schiller §18).

Freedom achieved in play, Schiller claims, is freedom from the constraint of incessant striving for satisfaction, which the two drives necessarily manifest.[22] Clearly the kind of harmony that Schiller seeks is more complex than a simple cessation of struggle or a kind of relaxation and abdication of the difficulties of life. Still, the ideal toward which he strives is *annihilation* of the need to resist and oppose purchased at the expense of *overcoming* struggle. In his early writings, at least, Nietzsche denies both the possibility and the desirability of the kind of perfection that is the object of Schiller's work. The drives that call us to play, the exercise of impulses that find their fulfillment in that experience, are what make us human; to eliminate those drives is to cease to be humane. Freedom for

differences, see Nicholas Martin's valuable work, *Nietzsche and Schiller: Untimely Aesthetics* (Oxford: Clarendon Press, 1996).

22   See Schiller §19: 'Each of these two fundamental impulses, as soon as it has developed, strives by its nature and by necessity towards satisfaction; but just because both are necessary and both are yet striving towards opposite objectives, this twofold constraint naturally cancels itself, and the will preserves complete freedom between them both.'

Nietzsche is the free expression of these drives,[23] which is not our right but our earned accomplishment.

We can look to Nietzsche's 'Homer's Contest' for his view that agonistic institutions contribute to the health of individuals and the culture in which these institutions are organized. By extending the means for attaining personal distinction by defining oneself creatively through resistance to what one is not the *agon* provides outlets for the acquisition of meaningful freedom. Nietzsche takes upon himself, in his own writing, the task of making these kinds of challenges for his readers: 'To make the individual *uncomfortable*: my mission! Appeal of liberating the individual by struggling!' (NF 1875, 5[178]: KSA 8/91).[24] Providing the conditions for the acquisition of strength through endurance and the overcoming of significant challenge is what Nietzsche conceives as the mission of culture, broadly construed. That is the mission of *Bildung*, a transformative activity of cultivating individuals as well as cultures, that Nietzsche sought to effect.

III.

Rather than abandoning or rejecting the traditions of his discipline and vocation, Nietzsche engages that intellectual heritage – making it 'groan', as Foucault describes his appropriation of Nietzsche's work – and adapts it to fit his own concerns. The strategy Nietzsche uses in revaluing the Homeric Question is one that he employs throughout his works: he seeks to make Homer problematic in order to contest

---

23   Nietzsche qualifies this sense of freedom. It is not simply freedom from restraint: each depends upon the opposition of the other, in the context of the art of tragedy, in order to achieve its free expression.

24   'Das Individuum *unbehaglich* zu machen: meine Aufgabe! Reiz der Befreiung des Einzelnen im Kampfe!'

prevailing interpretations of the significance of Homer and to introduce new perspectives as potential opponents of other contemporary ideas. Another way in which we might make Nietzsche's work 'groan' is to read him in the context of the agonistic models discussed above. It is clear that Nietzsche views his own writing as playing a role in creating a contentious arena for the pursuit of new standards of literary and philosophical excellence. Among the numerous opponents Nietzsche seeks (e.g. Socrates, Plato, Paul, Wagner), we find Homer. Although the confines of this article do not permit an extensive account, I wish to explore several possible ways in which such a reading might be pursued and the fruit it might bear.

Nietzsche seeks to rival Homer in his creation of a work of art that would both cultivate a taste for new values and would enhance the critical faculties of those affected to make future judgements. These twin objectives are the same as those in his *agones* with his other rivals, but Nietzsche's approach to Homer is uniquely different: in the case of Homer, Nietzsche's actions do not take the form of an attack. To read Nietzsche as a contestant with Homer is, in part, to see him joined with the group named in the epigraph at the beginning of the paper – Xenophanes and Plato, who were consumed by 'the monstrous desire [...] to assume the place of the overthrown poet [Homer] and inherit his fame'. Nietzsche longs to pick up the 'torch of contest' he claims to receive from Homer in order to 'set afire new greatness'. But we would be hard-pressed to argue that Nietzsche's contest of Homer is organized on terms similar to those found in his contest with Socrates. The contest with Homer lacks the kind of attacks characteristic of his *agones* with others. Why? Part of the reason, it seems, is that unlike the others *it is not necessary to defeat Homer*. As we learn in *The Birth of Tragedy*, optimism of the sort that Homer is supposed to have embodied was replaced by a Socratic form of optimism. Nietzsche himself writes in *Ecce homo* that he only attacks causes that are victorious (EH i 7). Instead of assaulting Homer, Nietzsche strives to surpass him. We witness this both in his creation of the literary work *Thus spake Zarathustra*, which depicts a modern Odyssey, and in his numerous efforts to engage his readers in revaluations.

I have already claimed that Nietzsche's contest with Homer is one in which Nietzsche attempts not so much to overthrow Homer as he seeks to excel the standards that he set. Another reason for that difference is the fact that Homeric values are not radically opposed to those Zarathustra espouses.[25] Of the contest between Plato and Homer, Nietzsche writes, 'Plato versus Homer: that is the complete, the genuine antagonism – there the sincerest advocate of the "beyond", the great slanderer of life; here the instinctive deifier, the golden nature' (GM III 25). Nietzsche's contest with Homer does not take a form similar to that between Plato and Homer (or even that of Nietzsche and Plato), because unlike Plato, Nietzsche has no 'genuine antagonism' with Homer. Nietzsche and Homer are not opposed in that way. In *Thus spake Zarathustra*, Nietzsche is more interested in the *form* of valuation and the ways in which judgements regarding values are legislated and transformed. So, what is the form of the contest with Homer? What are its outcomes? And what bearing does this have for the questions of taste and judgement mentioned above? A brief glance at *Zarathustra* should enable us to make some general claims and indicate several preliminary conclusions.

---

25   This is not to say that Nietzsche advocates a 'return' to ancient Greek culture. There is ample evidence that Nietzsche thinks it is neither possible nor desirable to do so. However, consider a few examples from *Thus spake Zarathustra*: Zarathustra's citation of the Greek 'law of overcoming' in Za I xv: 'be bravest and pre-eminent above all' (Homer, *Iliad*, 6.208 and 11.784); Zarathustra's allegiance with Achilles when he claims that he would rather be a day laborer in Hades than join the chairs of higher education (cf. GT 3); Zarathustra's estimation of life and the importance of death at the right time (see Za I xxi; Za III x, xii, xiii; and GT 3). Even his reversals of Homeric material appear as coy word-play: In 'The Tomb Song' (Za II xi), Zarathustra tells us that, unlike the hero Achilles, he is invulnerable 'only in the heel'.

IV.

Zarathustra is less concerned about the specific values his disciples will eventually have than he is about whether they will become legislators of values, that is, that they will: 1) have opportunities to engage in revaluation (i.e. that they will have institutions that facilitate the creation of values); and 2) be enabled to participate in what he describes as redemption (i.e. that they will be able to engage in a productive mode of acting within the new contest). Zarathustra's new form of contest (self-overcoming) transforms the destructive internalized contests that Nietzsche associates with Platonic and Christian moralities by harnessing the productive features of what he earlier describes as Homeric forms of contest.

We recall from the discussion of 'Homer's Contest' above, that Nietzsche identifies two important features of the kind of competition that propelled ancient Greek culture: 1) the proliferation of formal structures that provided opportunities for competitors to meet and be judged by their communities; and 2) the cultivation of a productive way of acting within those institutions. Zarathustra shares these concerns. Self-overcoming aims to provide the *structure* of the new form of contest, and what Zarathustra describes as a new kind of redemption (in the form of a backwards willing) provides the proposed *mode of action* within that new structure.[26]

The objective of self-overcoming is to strive for what Zarathustra describes as a 'comprehensive soul': the 'soul that has the longest ladder and reaches down deepest'; it 'can run and stray and roam farthest within itself'. It tests values and its strength as a value creator. It is selfish in the sense of self-loving and 'self-enjoying' (Za III xii).

---

26 I elaborate these ideas in the context of articulating Nietzsche's alternative conception of individual development in my 'Nietzsche's *Thus Spoke Zarathustra* as Postmodern *Bildungsroman*', in Endre Kiss and Uschi Nussbaumer-Benz (eds), *Nietzsche, Postmodernismus und was nach ihnen kommt* (Cuxhaven and Dartford: Junghans, 2000).

The comprehensive soul 'out of sheer joy plunges itself into chance' (ibid.). It challenges itself; it risks itself. It is the soul that

> having being, dives into becoming; the soul which *has*, but *wants* to want and will; the soul which flees itself and catches up with itself in the widest circle; the wisest soul, which folly exhorts most sweetly; the soul which loves itself most, in which all things have their sweep and counter sweep and ebb and flood (ibid.).

That is certainly one form of the loving (as esteeming) message Zarathustra brings to his pupils. One cannot give another a comprehensive soul, nor can one instruct another to develop it. The comprehensive soul has and exercises certain capacities to enhance its own growth. Throughout *Thus spake Zarathustra*, Zarathustra wrestles with activating such capacities in himself and others.

Redemption for Zarathustra is a creative backward willing, such that one wills the past as if it were one's own responsibility, as if it were the result of one's own willing it to be so. It is not simply a reconciliation with suffering, not a passive acceptance of the past, but a passionate affirmation of the present and past: 'All "it was" is a fragment, a riddle, a dreadful accident – until the creative will says to it, "But thus I willed it". Until the creative will says to it, "But thus I will it; thus shall I will it"' (Za II xx). Zarathustra's redemption consists in a mode of esteeming, from which value can be self-generated.

It is only through this kind of willing that we are able to overcome revenge, Zarathustra believes. Revenge is the by-product of our impotency with regard to the past. The unliberated will is powerless in the face of history. The inability to undo what has already been done provokes anger and incites revenge against any and all that do not experience the same sense of hopelessness. Zarathustra speaks, 'This, indeed this alone, is what *revenge* is: the will's ill will against time and its "it was"' (ibid.). Zarathustra describes the propensity to punish as a futile and destructive attempt to undo the past: 'No deed can be annihilated: how could it be undone by punishment?' (ibid.). Interpretations of life that hold that existence is a form of punishment show themselves to be motivated by revenge:

'this is what is eternal in the punishment called existence, that existence must eternally become deed and guilt again. Unless the will should at last redeem himself, and willing should become not willing' (ibid.). At this point Zarathustra recognizes that his portrayal of the overman as a future goal needs to be abandoned. What he must do is communicate the urgency of redeeming the human past and present, thereby creating the conditions in which all life can be affirmed: its past, present, and future. The philosophers of the future that Nietzsche anticipates are of this sort: they are oriented toward becoming; they *are* the future. As creators of values, they provide an opening to the future for themselves and for others. Zarathustra later contrasts them with others who are unable to create: 'they are always the beginning of the end: they crucify him who writes new values on new tablets; they sacrifice the future to themselves – they crucify all man's future' (Za III xii). The creators of new values are capable of esteeming and thereby also giving meaning to the past. As they value the past, they redeem it: 'To redeem those who lived in the past and to recreate all "it was" into "thus I willed it" – that alone should I call redemption' (Za II xx).

Zarathustra conceives of authentic human existence as an ongoing activity that amounts to an exercise of taste – pursuing what is esteemed and valued in the activity of willing. Willing as esteeming is an exercise of taste, according to Zarathustra: 'all of life is a dispute over taste and tasting. Taste – that is at the same time weight and scales and weigher; and woe unto all the living that would live without disputes over weight and scales and weighers!' (Za II xiii). In Nietzsche's *Zarathustra* we find examples of the development and cultivation of taste. As Zarathustra acquires that sensibility, he also comes to learn that it is through that kind of transformation that he advances the goal of attaining a higher form of life. Nietzsche tells us that 'Zarathustra was the first to consider the fight of good and evil the very wheel in the machinery of things' (EH iv 3). It is Socrates' absolute and dogmatic insistence on the use of those standards that explains why it is that Nietzsche finds his practice so corrupt, and hence, in need of an attack. It excludes the critique of those standards and pretends that they do not need justification whereas Zarathustra's new contest requires that such standards be subject to constant revaluation or perish when that is no longer possible.

Recall the passage from *Beyond Good and Evil* in which Nietzsche, reflecting on the philosophers of the future, asks:

> Are these coming philosophers new friends of 'truth'? That is probable enough, for all philosophers so far have loved their truths. But they will certainly not be dogmatists. It must offend their pride, also their taste, if their truth is supposed to be a truth for everyman – which has so far been the secret wish and hidden meaning of all dogmatic aspirations. 'My judgment is *my* judgment': no one else is easily entitled to it – that is what such a philosopher of the future may perhaps say of himself (JGB 43).

The elitism of the passage should not cloud our understanding of what having judgements and acquiring them meant to Nietzsche. One's judgements, one's values, as I have argued, are the products and projects of one's will. To be entitled to those values is to have willed them, to have participated in the struggle for their creation. It is not merely ignoble to adopt the values of others *carte blanche*, it is an offense to taste itself, to the very activity of esteeming. That is what Nietzsche strives to resist.

Nietzsche attempts to enact similar struggles in his own writings.[27] In *Ecce homo* Nietzsche describes himself as 'warlike by nature', but he qualifies this claim with a description of how strength is developed in opposition and how he chooses his battles:

> The strength of those who attack can be measured in a way by the opposition they require: every growth is indicated by the search for a mighty opponent – or problem; for a warlike philosopher challenges problems, too, to single combat. The task is *not* simply to master whatever happens to resist, but what requires us to stake all our strength, suppleness, and fighting skill – opponents that are our equals (EH i 7).

He claims to temper his combative practice with four propositions: 1) he attacks only 'causes that are victorious'; 2) he compromises only

---

27 I develop these ideas in my 'Nietzsche's Agonal Wisdom', forthcoming in *International Studies in Philosophy*.

himself in his attacks and does not attack causes that others are eager
to challenge; 3) he aims to attack cultural deficiencies, not the
shortcomings of individuals – when he calls people by name in these
attacks, it is not the person he aims to fight but the ideal his opponent
embodies; and 4) he never attacks in the interest of settling some
personal dispute (ibid.). Nietzsche has an interest in what he calls 'an
honest duel': 'Where one feels contempt, one *cannot* wage war;
where one commands, where one sees something beneath oneself, one
has no business waging war' (ibid.). We might challenge Nietzsche by
claiming that his work offers evidence that he did not always act on
these principles, but we can still read these remarks, especially in the
light of his earlier work, as clarifying Nietzsche's conception of the
practice of agonistic philosophy as an endeavor that was meant to be
life-enhancing and enabling.[28]

Nietzsche's contest with Homer perhaps realizes the enabling
features of contest more than his other battles. It is in the contest
that follows from Nietzsche's revaluation of the Homeric Question
that Nietzsche truly appears to strive to surpass without destroying
that with which he wrestles. As evidence of my claim, I have sought
to identify several necessary, if not also sufficient, features of a
creative and productive contest, and I have provided examples from
Nietzsche's texts in which, I argue, he aims to meet precisely those
criteria: the creation of an appropriate arena of contention, and the
achievement of a productive mode of action. The contest with Homer

---

28 Compare these passages with Foucault's description of the task of his writing:
    'It is thus necessary to bring into struggle as much gaiety, lucidity and
    determination as possible. The only sad thing is not to fight. [...] Writing
    interests me only in the measure that it incorporates the reality of combat, as an
    instrument, a tactic, scouting. I would like my books to be like lancets, Molotov
    cocktails, or minefields, and have them burn up after use in the manner of
    fireworks.' ('An Interview with Michel Foucault', *History of the Present*, 1
    (1985), 14) For an insightful account of how Nietzsche's agonistic philosophical
    praxis aims to empower, see Herman Siemens, 'Nietzsche's Hammer:
    Philosophy, Destruction, or the Art of Limited Warfare', *Tijdschrift voor
    Filosofie*, 2 (June 1998), 321–47.

is but one of numerous matches Nietzsche arranges in his works. The result, if not a victory, is the illumination of some of Nietzsche's most affirmative formulations of the alternatives he envisions for contemporary culture. Finally, the contest between Nietzsche and Homer serves as a useful model with which we might contrast his other duels as we continue to evaluate Nietzsche's own philosophical practice and its legacy for a future philosophy.

Duncan Large

'Der Bauernaufstand des Geistes': Nietzsche, Luther and the Reformation

Introduction: Luther's Legacy

In the history of German culture, Martin Luther (1483–1546) serves as the 'representative man' *par excellence*, 'father' not only of an indigenous German religion but of several other German traditions to which Nietzsche very much saw himself as heir. In a wide-ranging overview of 'Luther and the Culture of the Germans', Thomas Nipperdey traces back to Luther and his 'church of the word' the roots of the German school and university systems, of German 'intellectuals' and intellectualism, of German traditions of pluralism, 'personalism' and inwardness; indeed he finds in Lutheran teaching nothing less than 'the beginnings of modern behaviour, regulated from within'.[1] In *Der Antichrist*, Nietzsche himself rails against Leibniz, Kant and the philosophers of the 'Tübinger Stift' for their continued adherence to Lutheran values in their practice of philosophy, remarking – archly, but with a fair degree of historical

---

1   Thomas Nipperdey, 'The Protestant Unrest: Luther and the Culture of the Germans', in Thomas Nipperdey et al., *Martin Luther and the Formation of the Germans*, trans. Patricia Crampton (Bonn: Inter Nationes, 1983), pp. 7–24 (p. 8). On Luther's cultural impact in general, see also: Heinrich Bornkamm, *Luther im Spiegel der deutschen Geistesgeschichte: mit ausgewählten Texten von Lessing bis zur Gegenwart* (Heidelberg: Quelle & Meyer, 1955); Gerhard Ebeling, 'Luther und der Anbruch der Neuzeit', *Zeitschrift für Theologie und Kirche*, 69 (1972), 185–213; and Johann Baptist Müller (ed.), *Die Deutschen und Luther. Texte zur Geschichte und Wirkung* (Stuttgart: Reclam, 1983).

accuracy: 'Der protestantische Pfarrer ist Grossvater der deutschen Philosophie, der Protestantismus selbst ihr peccatum originale' (AC 10).

Linguistically, Luther's voluminous writings had a key signi-ficance in hastening the transition from Latin to the vernacular as the language of intellectual life in Germany,[2] and the influence of his Bible translations in particular can scarcely be overestimated. Modern linguistic commentators have sought to qualify earlier arguments for Luther's status as 'father of the German language', but there remains little doubt that in an age, the sixteenth century, when Germany's political fragmentation was matched by an equal diversity of geo-graphically determined linguistic norms, Luther, his translator and printer colleagues, and the German Bible translation they collectively produced, played a major role in the establishment of the East Central dialect of New High German as the basis of the standard written language.[3] Similarly, although the title is more often conferred on Lessing in the eighteenth century, Luther can with some justification lay claim to the designation 'father (or perhaps grandfather) of German literature', for the literary impact of his writings has been acknowledged by successive generations of German writers ever since his time. Particularly at moments when a re-establishment or regener-ation of German literature has been perceived as necessary, time and again it is Luther's Bible and other writings to which writers have turned. From Lessing himself, who worked at one stage on a 'Luther-

2   See Herbert Wolf, 'Pioneer of Modern German: The Significance of Martin Luther in the History of Language', in Nipperdey et al., pp. 25–34: 'even by 1520 the Reformer had become the best-read German author, who until 1546 produced on an annual average one-third of all German-language publications' (p. 30). The Weimar edition of Luther's writings (in German and Latin) runs to 127 volumes.

3   On Luther's role in the development of the German language, see also Herbert Wolf, *Martin Luther. Eine Einführung in germanistische Luther-Studien* (Stuttgart: Metzler, 1980), pp. 89–92; C. J. Wells, *German: A Linguistic History to 1945* (Oxford: Clarendon Press, 1985), pp. 179–209; and, especially, the collection *Luthers Deutsch. Sprachliche Leistung und Wirkung*, ed. Herbert Wolf (Frankfurt a.M.: Lang, 1996).

Wörterbuch',[4] through Goethe and Nietzsche in the nineteenth century, to writers as diverse as Brecht and Thomas Mann in the twentieth – to name but a few – the characteristic stylistic stamp of Luther's prose cadences and verse rhythms is discernible, the inimitable combination of down-to-earth directness with flights of the highest spirituality and lyricism.[5]

Luther was adopted as a political icon in Nietzsche's own time, even before the 1871 unification,[6] and by 1883, the 400th anniversary of Luther's birth, he was duly celebrated at the highest official levels as one of the 'fathers of the German nation' – again with some justification, for in sixteenth-century Germany, when culture to a large extent *was* politics, when 'Germany' only really existed as a 'Cultur-nation', a figure of Luther's immense cultural importance inevitably bulked large in the political arena, too.[7] Nationalistic appropriations of Luther continued into the twentieth century, and the rise of the National Socialist regime led many commentators – both inside and outside Germany, from correspondingly different viewpoints – to

---

4   See Wolf, *Martin Luther*, p. 168.
5   On Nietzsche's use (and abuse) of language derived from Luther's Bible translations, see my 'Nietzsche's Use of Biblical Language', *Journal of Nietzsche Studies*, 22 (Autumn 2001), 88–115. On Luther's literary impact more generally, see Wolf, *Martin Luther*, pp. 77–78 and 167–70, and Martin Brecht, *Luther als Schriftsteller. Zeugnisse seines dichterischen Gestaltens* (Stuttgart: Calwer, 1990).
6   See Max L. Baeumer, 'Nietzsche and Luther: A Testimony to Germanophilia', in James C. O'Flaherty et al. (eds), *Studies in Nietzsche and the Judaeo-Christian Tradition* (Chapel Hill and London: University of North Carolina Press, 1985), pp. 143–60: 'in 1867/68 when Nietzsche joined the Prussian army, the combined 350th anniversary of the Reformation and dedication of the Luther Monument in Worms marked the climax of the many national festivals of that time' (p. 146). See also Baeumer, 'Lutherfeiern und ihre politische Manipulation', in Reinhold Grimm and Jost Hermand (eds), *Deutsche Feiern* (Wiesbaden: Athenaion, 1977), pp. 46–61.
7   On Luther's politics, see W. D. J. Cargill Thompson, *The Political Thought of Martin Luther*, ed. Philip Broadhead (Brighton: Harvester Press, 1984).

trace a direct line of ideological descent from Luther to Hitler.[8] Yet Luther's direct interventions in the political sphere, his condemnation of the Peasants' War and of course his 'Reformation' itself – however conservative in intent, however much they may honestly been directed at consolidation – were nevertheless anything but unifying in their effects, and instead left the German states with a schismatic religious legacy which by no means played itself out in the seventeenth century's Thirty Years War, or even the so-called 'Kulturkampf' of the Bismarck era.[9] Religious differences have plausibly been suggested as one of the contributory factors in the twentieth century, for example, to the decision by Konrad Adenauer, a Rhineland Catholic, to turn his back in the late 1940s on the 'Soviet Zone of Occupation', with its predominantly Protestant population, and thus cement the political division of Germany for the next forty years.[10]

Even in the wake of the re-unification of Germany in our time, then, the problematic ambivalences of Luther's cultural and ideological legacy are still needing to be negotiated, and the most recent

8   See W. M. McGovern, *From Luther to Hitler: The History of Fascist-Nazi Political Philosophy* (London: Harrap, 1941); Peter F. Wiener, *Martin Luther: Hitler's Spiritual Ancestor* (London and New York: Hutchinson, 1945); Gordon Rupp, *Martin Luther: Hitler's Cause – Or Cure? In Reply to Peter F. Wiener* (London: Lutterworth, 1945); Müller (ed.), *Die Deutschen und Luther*, pp. 195–204 ('Luther und das Luthertum als Wegbereiter Hitlers?'); Barbro Eberan, *Luther? Friedrich 'der Grosse'? Wagner? Nietzsche? ...? ...? Wer war an Hitler schuld? Die Debatte um die Schuldfrage 1945–1949*, 2nd edn (Munich: Minerva, 1985), pp. 110–15; Uwe Siemon-Netto, *Luther als Wegbereiter Hitlers? Zur Geschichte eines Vorurteils* (Gütersloh: Gütersloher Verlagshaus, 1993).

9   On Nietzsche's changing relation to Bismarck, see my 'The Aristocratic Radical and the White Revolutionary: Nietzsche's Bismarck', in Jürgen Barkhoff et al. (eds), *Das schwierige neunzehnte Jahrhundert. Germanistische Tagung zum 65. Geburtstag von Eda Sagarra im August 1998* (Tübingen: Niemeyer, 2000), pp. 101–13.

10   See Mary Fulbrook, *The Two Germanies, 1945–1990: Problems of Interpretation* (Basingstoke: Macmillan, 1992), p. 17.

major Luther anniversary – the 450th of his death in 1996 – only fuelled the disputes over Luther's role in a resurgent Germany on the verge of the twenty-first century, particularly now that, in the wake of the Nazi experience, Luther's overt anti-Semitism has become an aspect of his complex character which it is no longer possible to overlook.[11]

Nietzsche's Lutheranism

Given the problems which Germany as a whole, and its theologians and historians in particular, have had with evaluating Luther's uncomfortable legacy over the years, it should come as no surprise that Nietzsche's image of Luther is conflicted and unstable, an uneasy mixture of identification and rejection which serves as a microcosm of the larger picture. With Luther being cited in such a plethora of cultural paternity suits, it is hardly surprising that Nietzsche's image of him should be marked by a combination of filial devotion and Oedipal revolt. Nietzsche's engagement with Luther is of course determined by a number of factors rather closer to home, though, too – we should recall that when Nietzsche writes 'Der protestantische Pfarrer ist Grossvater der deutschen Philosophie', this particular German philosopher had not just one but two Protestant pastors as grandfathers, and a Protestant pastor father, to boot. What is more, he grew up – in Röcken, Naumburg and Pforta – in the very heartland of the Lutheran faith, close by all the most important landmarks on what one would now call (and what eastern German travel agents doubtless do call) 'The Luther Heritage Trail': Luther's birthplace in Eisleben, where Nietzsche makes a dutiful pilgrimage on his summer holidays in 1860 (FS 1/205–06, 218); Erfurt, where Luther went to university

11 See Andreas Späth, *Luther und die Juden* (Bonn: Verlag für Kultur und Wissenschaft, 2001).

and spent three years as a monk in the Augustinian monastery; Wittenberg, where he taught, preached and infamously nailed his Ninety-Five Theses to the church door; the Wartburg near Eisenach where Luther was 'taken into protective custody' on his way home from the Diet of Worms in 1521, to emerge the following year with the first version of his New Testament translation, and so on.[12]

Nietzsche is perhaps best known for the militant atheism of his mature years, summed up in the celebrated formulation 'Gott ist todt' (FW 125). The late polemic *Der Antichrist: Fluch auf das Christentum* pulls no punches in lambasting the Christian faith, and in *Ecce homo* Nietzsche even confesses to a rare feeling of envy, towards Stendhal, for stealing a march on him in cracking the best atheistic joke: '"die einzige Entschuldigung Gottes ist, dass er nicht existirt"' (EH ii 3). Nietzsche's upbringing was, however, strictly Lutheran: his parents' only surviving son, he was expected by his family to follow in his father's and grandfathers' footsteps and go into the church, a first career plan which he adopted enthusiastically in the piety of his youth. He was confirmed at the age of sixteen in March 1861,[13] and studied a year of theology at Bonn University in 1864–65, even if by this stage he was already beset by serious religious doubts and becoming more and more interested in pursuing the career in which he would eventually excel: classical philology. In his biography of Nietzsche, Ronald Hayman gives a telling impression of Nietzsche's spiritual confusion during this period:

12   The 'rebranding' of many of these places as 'Lutherstädte' is a 1990s phenom-
      enon, mostly associated with the 1996 anniversary, but even in 1983 the GDR
      was seeking to attract tourist dollars by promoting Luther-related destinations.
      See, for example, Paul Ambros and Udo Rössling, *Reisen zu Luther. Wirkungs-
      und Gedenkstätten* (Berlin and Leipzig: VEB Tourist Verlag, 1983).
13   Nietzsche's letter to his uncle Edmund Oehler from the beginning of the next
      month includes the pious hope: 'Dieser ernste und heilige Tag möge mir in
      meinen ganzen künftigen Leben immer vor der Seele schweben und mich an die
      feierlichen Gelöbnisse und Bekenntnisse erinnern, die ich damals abgelegt
      habe!' (KSB 1/151).

In spite of his commitment to philology, he had found himself incapable of breaking completely with the family's past, and he had registered as a theology student, intending to compromise by concentrating on 'the philological side of Gospel criticism and the investigation of the New Testament's sources'. He may have had some idea of resolving his religious doubts by confronting the theological problems, but his motives were also confused not only by his continuing veneration of his father, whose photograph was placed over the piano, underneath a painting of the deposition from the cross, but also by procrastination over telling his mother that he was not going to become a clergyman.[14]

Although Nietzsche would later devote the first of his *Unzeitgemässe Betrachtungen* to the merciless criticism of *David Strauss, der Bekenner und der Schriftsteller*, his reading of the second (1864) edition of Strauss's *Leben Jesu* had a profound impact on him and effectively crystallised his religious doubts into a decision to renounce the faith. By Easter 1865 he was ready to abandon the study of theology, and when he returned home that vacation he refused even to attend church services, much to the distress of his adoring and intensely pious sister and mother; the following year he sealed his decision by registering to study classical philology in Leipzig.

The impact of his decision to abandon the faith can be felt when one considers his writings of the period, and here I would cite in particular a few pages from his notebook of August–December 1865 (FS 3/125–28). Here Nietzsche charts a four-stage development in cultural history from 'Die Weltanschauung des katholischen Mittelalters' through 'Die Weltanschauung der protestantischen Orthodoxie' and 'Einiges aus der biblischen Weltanschauung' to 'Die moderne Weltanschauung', rejoicing in the last as a triumph of secularism and Copernican scientific empiricism. In this short narrative, not only is the impact of the Reformation itself very much played down, but Luther himself is effectively sidelined:

Die Reformation war zunächst nur eine Veränderung in dem prakt[ischen] Verhältniß des Mensche[n] zu Gott. Allerdings wurde[n] einige Stücke wie

14 Ronald Hayman, *Nietzsche: A Critical Life* (London: Weidenfeld and Nicolson, 1980), p. 60.

Feg[e]feuer, Messe die Macht der Heiligen fortgeräumt. Aber die Lehre blieb
übereinstimmend im Wesentl[ichen] mit dem Glaube[n] der alte[n] Kirche
vom 4t. bis 6t. J[ahr]h[undert]. Trotz Kopernikus behielt man seine[n] alte[n]
Himmel, sein[e] alte Erde seine alte Hölle. Weit ausgesponne[n] ist die
Mythologie des Teufels. Luther darin nur ein Kind seiner Zeit (FS 3/125–26).

At this stage, one can sense that Nietzsche is engaged in a period of
reassessment marked by a backlash against *any* type of religious
world-view, so that even in Luther's case he does not spare the
whip.

By the late 1860s/early 1870s this phase of what one might call
Luther-scepticism comes to an end, however, under the twin pressures
of Nietzsche's more overt nationalism and especially his contact
with Wagner, for as Nietzsche reports much later on, in *Zur
Genealogie der Moral* (GM III, 2), Wagner was himself interested in
Luther as a worthy spiritual forebear, and for a time planned a music-
drama on the theme of *Luthers Hochzeit*.[15] Although this, like so
many others of Wagner's projects, was ultimately abandoned, in the
early 1870s Nietzsche takes up where Wagner himself left off,
forging a link between Wagner and his illustrious predecessor in the
name of Dionysian music. Here, then, in his first serious engagement
with Luther, Nietzsche focuses on yet another aspect of the great
Reformer's polymathic productivity, Luther as composer of some of
the most famous and enduring of German music, chorales such as
'Vom Himmel hoch' and 'Ein' feste Burg ist unser Gott' which not
only survive to this day as some of the best-loved hymn tunes – in
Germany and, through translations of the texts, beyond – but, through
their re-use and reworking by Bach in particular, entered the very
lifeblood of the German musical tradition.[16]

Luther makes his grand entrance in *Die Geburt der Tragödie* in
section 23, an intensely nationalistic passage in which he figures as

15   On Wagner, Luther and the critique of chastity, see Sarah Kofman, 'Nietzsche et
     Wagner: Comment la musique devient bonne pour les cochons', in *L'imposture
     de la beauté et autres textes* (Paris: Galilée, 1995), pp. 75–103 (pp. 84–85).
16   See Oskar Söhngen, 'The Word of God in Song: The Significance of Luther in
     the History of Music', in Nipperdey et al., pp. 35–45.

one of the 'erhabene Vorkämpfer' who have paved the way for the triumphant appearance on the scene of Richard Wagner, the spiritual regenerator *par excellence* who will lift Germany out of its slough of cultural despond:

> Alle unsere Hoffnungen strecken sich vielmehr sehnsuchtsvoll nach jener Wahrnehmung aus, dass unter diesem unruhig auf und nieder zuckenden Culturleben und Bildungskrampfe eine herrliche, innerlich gesunde, uralte Kraft verborgen liegt, die freilich nur in ungeheuren Momenten sich gewaltig einmal bewegt und dann wieder einem zukünftigen Erwachen entgegenträumt. Aus diesem Abgrunde ist die deutsche Reformation hervorgewachsen: in deren Choral die Zukunftsweise der deutschen Musik zuerst erklang. So tief, muthig und seelenvoll, so überschwänglich gut und zart tönte dieser Choral Luther's, als der erste dionysische Lockruf, der aus dichtverwachsenem Gebüsch, im Nahen des Frühlings, hervordringt. Ihm antwortete in wetteiferndem Widerhall jener weihevoll übermüthige Festzug dionysischer Schwärmer, denen wir die deutsche Musik danken – und denen wir *die Wiedergeburt des deutschen Mythus* danken werden! (GT 23; cf. KSA 7/275)

In this period of overt cultural nationalism, Nietzsche co-opts Luther for his cause. In Bonn he had joined the 'Burschenschaft Franconia' and even acquired the prerequisite duelling scar; immediately after *Die Geburt der Tragödie*, in the fifth of his 1872 lectures 'Über die Zukunft unserer Bildungsanstalten', he writes with pride of the 'Burschenschaften' as manifesting 'jenen männlich ernsten, schwer- gemuthen, harten und kühnen deutschen Geist, jenen aus der Reformation her gesund bewahrten Geist des Bergmannssohnes Luther' (KSA 1/749).

In these early days of his philosophical career, Luther is an integral part of Nietzsche's highly restricted pantheon of Germanic culture, and he appears in all the lists of 'German greats' which Nietzsche was fond of drawing up at the time (so as to give Wagner and Schopenhauer some company). Again in 1872, for example, just after *Die Geburt der Tragödie*, we find a notebook entry stating simply: 'Schopenhauer. Wagner. Goethe. Schiller. Luther. Beethoven' (KSA 7/260; cf. 7/645); by 1875, when he is working on *Richard Wagner in Bayreuth*, only the order has changed – 'Luther Goethe Schiller Schopenhauer Beethoven Wagner' – as he contemplates a

historical movement of 'Progeneration' which involves the 'Fort-
pflanzung des deutschen Wesens *hoch über* allem (Nach-Luther)'
(KSA 8/248). In *Richard Wagner in Bayreuth* itself, Luther is cited
together with Beethoven and Wagner as one of the 'wahrhaft großen
Deutschen' who exhibited 'jene eigentlich und einzig *deutsche
Heiterkeit*' (UB IV 8).

The mid-1870s are in fact the high-water mark in Nietzsche's
appreciation of Luther: he writes to his friend Erwin Rohde in the
February of that year, concerned that their mutual friend Romundt has
converted to Roman Catholicism:

> Unsre gute reine protestantische Luft! Ich habe nie bis jetzt stärker meine
> innigste Abhängigkeit von dem Geiste Luthers gefühlt als jetzt, und allen diesen
> befreienden Genien will der unglückliche den Rücken wenden? (KSB 5/27–28)

Soon after this, though, the 'gute reine protestantische Luft' is
poisoned and the whole complexion of Nietzsche's attitude to Luther
changes. The reasons for Nietzsche's volte-face are not hard to find,
and his alienation from Wagner certainly played an important role, for
admiration of Luther had been part of the cultural inheritance which
Nietzsche shared with the Wagner circle – when he writes to Wagner
in 1870 on Luther's birthday, 10 November, he is careful to date his
letter 'am Luthertage' (KSB 3/156), for example – so that on his
break from Wagner, Nietzsche's conception of Luther is forced to
undergo the same revision as his conception of all the other figures
whom he had previously linked with the progressivism of Wagnerian
music-drama in the heady days, now far off, when he had been a
frequent house-guest of the Wagners at their villa Tribschen on Lake
Lucerne.[17] I have explored elsewhere the similar fates which befall his
conceptions of Shakespeare and Laurence Sterne, for example, and

---

17 I disagree here with Baeumer, who claims that 'Nietzsche was, in his
   nationalistic attitude [...] little influenced by Richard Wagner' ('Nietzsche and
   Luther', p. 148) and argues on the basis of some of Nietzsche's notes towards
   Richard Wagner in Bayreuth from early 1874 (KSA 7:762-63, 774) that his
   break with Wagner was not a factor in his turn against Luther (pp. 150–51).

there are many other casualties who succumb to Nietzsche's revisionist impulse in this momentous revaluation.[18]

Revaluing Luther

His split with Wagner and with the patriotic peccadilloes of the
Wagner period is of course turned to his advantage, though, as he sails
off, Columbus-like, from Genoa and other Mediterranean haunts onto
the uncharted new seas of the 'free spirit' period.[19] One might have
expected that he would identify all the more with the 'befreiender
Genius' of Luther during his own period of 'protestant' revolt, but
Luther was part of the baggage he needed to leave behind, and he
consequently comes to theorise the Reformation in a radically
different way from that 'erster dionysischer Lockruf' of *Die Geburt
der Tragödie*. The context which Nietzsche now establishes for
Luther is suddenly very different – the plot is abruptly switched, so to
speak, and Luther becomes a protagonist in a historical narrative
which no longer sweeps through from the Greeks to the present with
majestic vagueness but focuses more directly on Luther's immediate
historical context. Specifically, as Nietzsche's appreciation for the
Enlightenment grows, so, too, does his respect for the noble
humanism of the Italian Renaissance, which he sees as its cradle, and
as a consequence Luther's Protestant Reformation becomes vilified as
the baneful antithesis of those noble flowers, Renaissance values, its

---

18   See my articles '"The Freest Writer": Nietzsche on Sterne', *The Shandean*, 7
      (Nov. 1995), 9–29, and 'Nietzsche's Shakespearean Figures', in Alan D. Schrift
      (ed.), *Why Nietzsche Still? Reflections on Drama, Culture, and Politics*
      (Berkeley, Los Angeles and London: University of California Press, 2000), pp.
      45–65.
19   On Nietzsche's identification with Columbus, see my 'Nietzsche and the Figure
      of Columbus', *Nietzsche-Studien*, 24 (1995), 162–83.

'manliness' a sad mockery of Renaissance *virtù*, its overall success one great cultural calamity.

The first signs of his new attitude appear, as one might expect, in the first volume of *Menschliches, Allzumenschliches* in 1878. In the opening section, 'Von den ersten und letzten Dingen', Nietzsche introduces his first overt criticism of Schopenhauer's metaphysics by way of his first overt criticism of Luther, in the paragraph '*Die Reaction als Fortschritt*':

> So zeugt zum Beispiel Luther's Reformation dafür, dass in seinem Jahrhundert alle Regungen der Freiheit des Geistes noch unsicher, zart, jugendlich waren; die Wissenschaft konnte noch nicht ihr Haupt erheben. Ja, die gesammte Renaissance erscheint wie ein erster Frühling, der fast wieder weggeschneit wird (MA I 26).

This relatively tentative first shot (the Renaissance *seems* like an early spring *almost* snowed away again) gives way in section 237, on '*Renaissance und Reformation*', to a full-blown critique of the Reformation and a lament for the glorious cultural possibilities on which it foreclosed. Here Nietzsche contrasts the Italian Renaissance – 'das goldene Zeitalter dieses Jahrtausends' – with what came to assail it, 'die deutsche Reformation':

> ein energischer Protest zurückgebliebener Geister, welche die Weltanschauung des Mittelalters noch keineswegs satt hatten und die Zeichen seiner Auflösung, die ausserordentliche Verflachung und Veräusserlichung des religiösen Lebens, anstatt mit Frohlocken, wie sich gebührt, mit tiefem Unmuthe empfanden. Sie warfen mit ihrer nordischen Kraft und Halsstarrigkeit die Menschen wieder zurück, erzwangen die Gegenreformation, das heisst ein katholisches Christen-thum der Nothwehr, mit den Gewaltsamkeiten eines Belagerungszustandes und verzögerten um zwei bis drei Jahrhunderte ebenso das völlige Erwachen und Herrschen der Wissenschaften, als sie das völlige In-Eins-Verwachsen des antiken und des modernen Geistes vielleicht für immer unmöglich machten. Die grosse Aufgabe der Renaissance konnte nicht zu Ende gebracht werden, der Protest des inzwischen zurückgebliebenen deutschen Wesens (welches im Mittelalter Vernunft genug gehabt hatte, um immer und immer wieder zu seinem Heile über die Alpen zu steigen) verhinderte diess (MA I 237).

This is Nietzsche's new critique of the Reformation as a movement already fully worked out: it was a reactionary *political* phenomenon above all, a northern, all-too-northern movement of boorish cultural retards (cf. FW 148–49); as Nietzsche will put it in section 50 of *Jenseits von Gut und Böse*, 'der ganze Protestantismus entbehrt der südlichen delicatezza'. Not only did the Reformation, as Nietzsche had argued back in 1865, not reject enough of the medieval world-view, it was actually a regressive force compelling a *return* to that medieval world-view: in the medieval period itself the German church had had the good sense to climb over the Alps to Rome for frequent spiritual sustenance (mountain-climbing will always represent good sense to Nietzsche!); now, ironically, precisely when times have moved on and the medieval world-view is at last beginning to crumble, the anachronistic German Reformers have the temerity to reverse the direction of cultural influence and inflict their cisalpine stupidities on the eternal city in a re-run of its sacking at the hands of the barbarian hordes. These Reformers took everything too *seriously* (in which they were consummately German) and failed to grasp the point that it was far better the church should luxuriate its way into decadence, secularism and corruption – that way it would abolish itself. As Nietzsche muses in a subjunctive fantasy from *Der Antichrist*, the Reformation deprived the world of 'ein Schauspiel, so sinnreich, so wunderbar paradox zugleich, dass alle Gottheiten des Olymps einen Anlass zu einem unsterblichen Gelächter gehabt hätten – *Cesare Borgia als Papst...*' (AC 61). What actually happened instead was that, through an unfortunate combination of power-political circumstances, Luther was not burned at the stake like Jan Hus, and consequently the church was able to regroup at the Council of Trent, launching a Counter-Reformation which prolonged the benightedness of Europe for a further two or three hundred years.[20]

---

20 Bornkamm (pp. 58–59) recognises the influence of Burckhardt here, but in my view he takes this argument much too far, seeing in Nietzsche's 'Bündel wilder Äußerungen' on Luther 'kaum etwas originell'.

Such a lament for the premature demise of the Renaissance and consequently delayed onset of the Enlightenment is perhaps a typical position for *Menschliches, Allzumenschliches* – a text published in some haste in April 1878 so as to coincide with the centenary of the death of Voltaire, its dedicatee; the text in which Nietzsche first openly turns his back on what he now dismisses as the 'Artisten-Metaphysik' of *Die Geburt der Tragödie* and seeks to practise instead a new kind of 'historische Philosophie' taking its cue from the methodology of the natural sciences (MA I 1). Nietzsche's lament here is, however, a theme which endures throughout his work from now on, right up to the last months of 1888, where in *Der Antichrist* we find him writing: 'es gab bisher keine entscheidendere Frage-stellung als die der Renaissance, – *meine* Frage ist ihre Frage' (AC 61), and in *Ecce homo* we find him still arguing: 'Die Deutschen haben Europa um die Ernte, um den Sinn der letzten *grossen* Zeit, der Renaissance-Zeit, gebracht' (EH 'WA' 2). Something about Nietzsche's attack on the Reformation does change along the way, though, and that is its personalisation, his focusing on the figure of Luther, who becomes metonymic of 'the Germans' in all their failings. Thus, the *Ecce homo* passage quoted above continues:

> Luther, dies Verhängniss von Mönch, hat die Kirche, und, was tausend Mal schlimmer ist, das Christenthum widerhergestellt, im Augenblick, *wo es unterlag* ... [...] Luther, ein unmöglicher Mönch, der, aus Gründen seiner "Unmöglichkeit", die Kirche angriff und sie – folglich! – wiederherstellte ... Die Katholiken hätten Gründe, Lutherfeste zu feiern, Lutherspiele zu dichten... (ibid.).

In fact this focusing of Nietzsche's attack on the figure of Luther sets in very early, and an important contributory factor is his reading of Johannes Janssen's *Geschichte des deutschen Volkes seit dem Ausgang des Mittelalters* (1878–88) – he bought the first volume on New Year's Eve 1878 (KSA 14/381), the second volume the following year. Janssen's voluminous history is vehemently and unremittingly anti-Lutheran: he presents Luther the man in an invariably poor light, as a tortured soul who emerges from a troubled childhood a dangerous fanatic who finds it impossible to live at peace

with himself, a fundamentally violent man with psychopathic tenden-
cies who consequently vents his spleen on the poor unfortunates
willing to be duped by his particular brand of piety, which is nothing
more than personal *Angst* writ large. Janssen enjoys 'setting the
record straight' and correcting some of the many 'misunderstandings'
which have arisen around the figure of Luther: thus, Luther was
wrong about salvation by good works, because the Catholic Church
had always stressed that the most important element of faith was
belief and trust in the risen Christ; Luther was wrong on the sale of
indulgences, too, for Tetzel was in fact an upright man who did not
just give them away like confetti as soon as he heard the jangle of
coins in his collecting box, etc., etc.

All this, of course, was grist to Nietzsche's mill, and the impact
of Janssen's history on him can be gauged from some correspondence
of his with Heinrich Köselitz (aka Peter Gast) in October 1879. In
response to a letter from Köselitz in which Nietzsche's friend seeks
his opinion on Luther while himself praising Luther as a great
benefactor of the Germans, the opinion Nietzsche gives is devastating:

> Lieber Freund, über Luther bin ich nach längerer Zeit außer Stande, in *ehr*licher
> Weise etwas Verehrendes zu sagen: die Nachwirkung einer mächtigen
> Materialsammlung über ihn, auf die mich J. Burckhardt aufmerksam machte.
> Ich meine Jans[s]en Gesch[ichte] des deutschen Volkes Bd. II. in diesem Jahre
> erst erschienen (ich besitze es) Hier redet einmal *nicht* die verfälschte
> *protestant[ische]* Geschichtsconstruktion, an welche wir zu glauben angelernt
> worden sind. Augenblicklich scheint es mir nichts mehr als Sache des
> *nationalen* Geschmacks in Norden und Süden, daß *wir* Luther als Menschen
> dem Ign[atius] Loyola *vorziehen*! Die gräßliche hochmüthige gallig-neidische
> Schimpfteufelei Luthers, dem gar nicht wohl wurde, wenn er nicht vor Wuth auf
> jemanden speien konnte, haben mich zu sehr angeekelt. [...] – Übrigens sind *Sie*
> in der billigeren Stimmung gegen ihn. Geben Sie mir Zeit! (KSB 5/451)[21]

21 The profound impact of Nietzsche's reading of Janssen is first noted by
    Emanuel Hirsch in his 1921 *Luther-Jahrbuch* article 'Nietzsche und Luther'
    (reprinted with a postface by Jörg Salaquarda in *Nietzsche-Studien*, 15 (1986),
    398–439). As Salaquarda points out, though (pp. 436–37), Hirsch's extreme
    view – that the shift in Nietzsche's perspective on Luther can be wholly
    ascribed to his reading of Janssen – was subsequently qualified in studies by

But Nietzsche's attitude to Luther did not change with time: in fact
thereafter he effectively declares open season on Luther's character,
and his many subsequent passages on Luther bristle with personal
invective directed against Luther's inadequacies as a man. Whereas in
1865 he had been prepared to dismiss Luther as but a child of his time
and effectively sideline him, now Luther very much assumes centre
stage and is held personally responsible for the calamity of the
Reformation, seen as a direct result of his character flaws, marked
and marred by his dysfunctional personality. The Reformation
becomes one immense psychodrama, with Luther the sole protagonist.
Nietzsche, it should be noted, says next to nothing about the
other Reformers in his works: there are a few passing remarks about
Calvin (MA I 101; MA II/2 85; M 113; GM II 7; KSA 9/245, 269),
the one reference to Jan Hus which I have quoted is the only one
in his writings (MA I 237); there is likewise only one reference
to Melanchthon (MA II/2 66), and there is nothing at all on, say,
Zwingli or Knox. Instead we are given a litany of abuse aimed at
Luther alone: Luther was irascible (he himself admitted he needed to
be angry in order to write well);[22] he was also obstinate – at the
Regensburg conference in 1541, 'der knöcherne Kopf Luther's, voller
Verdächtigungen und unheimlicher Aengste, sträubte sich', and any
chance of reconciliation was lost (MA II/1 226). He was 'de[r] große
"ungeistige Mensch"' (KSA 11/679), 'ein nordischer Barbar des
Geistes' (JGB 46), indeed a pathological fanatic (AC 54) who brought
about 'eine zeitweilige Brutalisirung der Geistlichkeit' (M 60).
Whereas in 1872 Nietzsche had praised this horny-handed son of
toil, now Luther is condemned as 'coarse' ('grob' – M 207; KSA
12/489; 13/156), 'uncouth' ('ungeschlacht' – M 511), 'peasant-like'

Ernst Benz ('Nietzsches Ideen zur Geschichte des Christentums und der
Kirche', *Zeitschrift für Kirchengeschichte*, 56 (1937), 169–313) and Heinz
Bluhm ('Nietzsche's Idea of Luther in *Menschliches, Allzumenschliches*',
PMLA, 65 (1950), 1053–68).

22 See KSA 8/111, quoting one of Luther's 'Tischreden' from January 1532:
'wenn ich wohl dichten, schreiben, beten und predigen will, so muss ich zornig
sein'.

('bäurisch' – M 88; JGB 50; FW 358; GM III, 22; AC 53; KSA 11/82, 200; 12/271), 'plebeian' ('pöbelhaft', 'plebejisch' – GM I, 16; KSA 11/242), a 'lout' ('Rüpel' – KSB 6/479; GM III, 22). Typically, Nietzsche's only comment on Luther in the anniversary year of 1883 is: 'Luther verräth in der Art, wie er *Feind* ist, seine bäurische Abkunft und Gemeinheit, Mangel an Vornehmheit' (KSA 10/257).[23]

These personal attacks reach their apogee in the section of the fifth book (1887) of *Die fröhliche Wissenschaft* entitled '*Der Bauernaufstand des Geistes*', where Luther is described as a 'Mann aus dem Volke, dem alle Erbschaft einer herrschenden Kaste, aller Instinkt für Macht abgieng' (FW 358). Luther puts his foot wrong at every turn, Nietzsche tells us here – at each stage he actually achieved the opposite of what he had intended, 'so dass sein Werk, sein Wille zur Wiederherstellung jenes Römer-Werks, ohne dass er es wollte und wusste, nur der Anfang eines Zerstörungswerks wurde. [...] er zerschlug ein Ideal, das er nicht zu erreichen wusste, während er die Entartung dieses Ideals zu bekämpfen und zu verabscheuen schien.' One could certainly say that Luther was a man of contradictions, but Nietzsche says more than that, for in a surprisingly generous gesture he concedes that Luther cannot be held responsible for the con-sequences of his exploits: 'Er ist an Allem unschuldig, er wusste nicht was er that'. This Christ-like 'magnanimity' only sets the stage for Nietzsche the psychologist to get to work, however, and understand Luther for him: beneath the surface invective, there is a more serious side to Nietzsche's later appraisal of Luther. In fact Nietzsche completely disempowers Luther – he takes the deterministic emphasis in Luther's theology, twists it and turns it against him, for he was but the slave of his *drives*. As Nietzsche remarks in *Der Antichrist*: 'Der "Glaube" war zu allen Zeiten, beispielsweise bei Luther, nur ein Mantel, ein Vorwand, ein *Vorhang*, hinter dem die Instinkte ihr Spiel

---

23   The same year, he gives away his copy of Luther's *Tischreden* to Walter Janicaud's father. See Sander L. Gilman (ed.), *Conversations with Nietzsche: A Life in the Words of His Contemporaries*, trans. David J. Parent (New York and Oxford: Oxford University Press, 1987), p. 142.

spielten –, eine kluge *Blindheit* über die Herrschaft *gewisser* Instinkte' (AC 39). And Nietzsche will make it the task of his unparalleled psychological flair to sense what was actually going on at the instinctual level behind Luther's screen.

Luther as Psychological Type

In a section on the art of biography in *Zur Genealogie der Moral*, Nietzsche reflects – now by way of contrast with Janssen's portrayal – on what a truly penetrating psychological study of Luther might bring to light:

> Gedenken wir noch des komischen Entsetzens, welches der katholische Priester Janssen mit seinem über alle Begriffe viereckig und harmlos gerathenen Bilde der deutschen Reformations-Bewegung in Deutschland erregt hat; was würde man erst beginnen, wenn uns Jemand diese Bewegung einmal *anders* erzählte, wenn uns einmal ein wirklicher Psycholog einen wirklichen Luther erzählte, nicht mehr mit der moralistischen Einfalt eines Landgeistlichen, nicht mehr mit der süsslichen und rücksichtsvollen Schamhaftigkeit protestantischer Historiker, sondern etwa mit einer *Taine*'schen Unerschrockenheit, aus einer *Stärke der Seele* heraus und nicht aus einer klugen Indulgenz gegen die Stärke? [...] (GM III, 19).[24]

Nietzsche considered himself, of course, the pre-eminent 'wirklicher Psycholog', and although he himself never wrote such a biography, nevertheless his scattered pronouncements on Luther do allow us to

---

24 Although Nietzsche's enthusiasm for Janssen's iconoclastic, warts-and-all portrayal of Luther is evident from his 1879 letter to Köselitz, even before then, when drafting what would become MA I 35, he had intended citing Janssen as an example of the kind of 'lächerlich-enge, altjungfernhafte Bücher' so superficial in their psychological characterisations (KSA 14/125); by 1884 he is expressing his 'Geringschätzung gegen das jetzige Deutschland, welches nicht Takt genug hat, solche Klatschbasen-Bücher, wie das von Jans[s]en, einfach abzulehnen' (KSA 11/216).

reconstruct a portrait of the kind of 'wirklichen Luther' he envisages.[25] I want now to isolate four particular strands in Nietzsche's psychological characterisation of Luther: his irrationalism, his nihilism, his 'Ressentiment' and his dialectical bad manners. I also want to argue, though, that in each case Nietzsche is attributing to Luther a psychological trait which he more usually applies to some other of his *bêtes noires*. I hope by this to demonstrate that Nietzsche pieces together his analysis of Luther through a series of more or less explicit analogies with other figures, psychologically stronger than he and thus better able to serve Nietzsche as case studies in individual character types. The point of Nietzsche's analysis of Luther is that he was a typically Christian, self-divided composite of competing drives over which he was precisely *not* able to gain the kind of self-mastery Nietzsche attributes to certain other figures for whom he consequently has a greater interest and appreciation. In more senses than one, Luther in Nietzsche's eyes is not his own man.

To take my first example, in the preface to *Morgenröthe* Nietzsche argues that by privileging faith over reason – his infamous insistence that the righteous Christian would gain redemption 'by faith alone' (*'sola fide'*) – Luther laid the foundations for the irrationalist streak in all those German philosophers whose grandfathers were the Protestant pastors he inspired. Luther is described here as:

> jene[r] ander[e] grosse Pessimist, der es einmal mit der ganzen Lutherischen Verwegenheit seinen Freunden zu Gemüthe führte: 'wenn man durch Vernunft es fassen könnte, wie der Gott gnädig und gerecht sein könne, der so viel Zorn und Bosheit zeigt, wozu brauchte man dann den *Glauben*?' [...] credo *quia absurdum est*: – mit ihr tritt die deutsche Logik zuerst in der Geschichte des christlichen Dogma's auf (M Preface 3; cf. M 22).

---

25 Again I would disagree with Baeumer, who concludes that 'Nietzsche's estimate of Martin Luther is basically superficial and conceived exclusively under the notion of German nationalism' ('Nietzsche and Luther', p. 160).

If one wonders who the other great pessimist was, the answer is Kant, and this connection is spelt out again later in the book, in section 207 (*'Verhalten der Deutschen zur Moral'*): 'Lange vor Kant und seinem kategorischen Imperativ hatte Luther aus der selben Empfindung gesagt: es müsse ein Wesen geben, dem der Mensch unbedingt vertrauen könne, – es war sein *Gottesbeweis'* (M 207; cf. KSA 9/113, 223). Kant, Nietzsche will write later in *Götzen-Dämmerung*, is nothing but 'ein *hinterlistige[r]* Christ, zu guterletzt' (GD III 6); 'Der Erfolg Kant's ist bloss ein Theologen-Erfolg' (AC 10), and any attempt he might try making to deny that his faith undermines any claim his ethics might have to a rational basis – that his philosophy is not simply a '"Philosophie der Hinterthüren"' (GD ix 16) – is ... pure cant.

As regards pessimism, though, even Kant is outstripped by his successor Schopenhauer – Nietzsche indeed commonly uses 'unsre Pessimisten' as shorthand for Schopenhauerians (GD ii 1; ix 36) – and it is thus Schopenhauer who provides Nietzsche with his model when he addresses Luther's moments of black self-doubt. Schopenhauer and Luther, Nietzsche tells us, share a 'Grobheit' (KSA 7/618, 811) and 'eine Geschwätzigkeit des Zornes' (FW 97), but more importantly, in a note from summer 1880, Nietzsche constructs Schopenhauer as the patron saint of pessimistic nihilists, with Luther as his forerunner and Wagner his acolyte: 'Der Trost Luthers als die Sache nicht vorwärts gieng, "Untergang der Welt". Die Nihilisten hatten Schopenhauer als Philosophen. Alle die extrem Aktiven wollen die Welt in Stücke gehen lassen, wenn sie ihren Willen als unmöglich erkennen (Wotan)' (KSA 9/125).[26]

---

26 On Nietzsche and Schopenhauer both being influenced by Luther in their
    fatalism, see Brian Leiter, 'The Paradox of Fatalism and Self-Creation in
    Nietzsche', in Christopher Janaway (ed.), *Willing and Nothingness: Schopen-
    hauer as Nietzsche's Educator* (Oxford: Oxford University Press, 1998),
    pp. 217–57 (p. 250, n. 170); repr. in John Richardson and Brian Leiter
    (eds), *Nietzsche* (Oxford: Oxford University Press, 2001), pp. 281–321 (p. 313,
    n. 170).

So Luther's faith was but a fig-leaf covering a childish, narcissistic rage against the world for not conforming to his will – his was no 'Pessimismus der *Stärke*' (GTVS 1); instead, when his back was against the wall, in the language of *Zur Genealogie der Moral* he would rather will nothingness than not will at all. Luther was a man riven by hatred and self-hatred (KSA 9/113, 165, 426; 12/12, 408; 13/202), in which respect, for Nietzsche, he most resembles St Paul, '*Der erste Christ*' (M 68), consumed with hatred of the law (in Luther's case, the priesthood and its ordinances) and of his own inadequacy at fulfilling it (KSA 9/113, 143; 12/547).[27] Ironically enough, then (given Luther's anti-Semitism), just as Paul turned Jewish 'Ressentiment' against itself at the very moment of his founding that greatest of Judaic heresies, Christianity, so there is something profoundly Judaic, for Nietzsche, about Luther's subsequent Reformation: as early as 1880, indeed, Nietzsche is referring to 'der grosse jüdisch-heroische Zug, welcher die ganze Reformations-Bewegung schuf' (MA II/1 171).

Luther is at root a man of 'Ressentiment', and the movement he leads, that 'Bauernaufstand des Geistes', mirrors the 'Sklavenaufstand in der Moral' of *Zur Genealogie der Moral* (GM I, 10) which saw the Jews installed as the masters of this particular form of spiritual perversity (cf. KSA 11/27, 70). In *Zur Genealogie der Moral*, Nietzsche's earlier critique of the Reformation as a reactionary movement sharpens and becomes more distinctively Nietzschean: the Reformation is not so much reactionary as reactive; it represents not just the rebellion of north against south, Germany against Italy, but is one further sorry chapter in the eternal dispute between the Judaic and the classical ideals.

> Allerdings gab es in der Renaissance ein glanzvoll-unheimliches Wiederaufwachen des klassischen Ideals, der vornehmen Werthungsweise aller Dinge: Rom selber bewegte sich wie ein aufgeweckter Scheintodter unter dem Druck

---

27 On the metaphor of Luther as the 'second Paul', see Tim Murphy, 'Nietzsche's Narrative of the "Retroactive Confiscations" of Judaism', in Weaver Santaniello (ed.), *Nietzsche and the Gods* (Albany: SUNY Press, 2001), pp. 3–20 (p. 14), and *Nietzsche, Metaphor, Religion* (Albany: SUNY Press, 2001), pp. 137–39.

des neuen, darüber gebauten judaisirten Rom, das den Aspekt einer
ökumenischen Synagoge darbot und 'Kirche' hiess: aber sofort triumphirte
wieder Judäa, Dank jener gründlich pöbelhaften (deutschen und englischen)
Ressentiments-Bewegung, welche man die Reformation nennt, hinzugerechnet,
was aus ihr folgen musste, die Wiederherstellung der Kirche (GM I, 16).

Because Luther always achieved the opposite of what he set out to do,
for Nietzsche he becomes a kind of dialectician *malgré lui*, and here I
would turn to a fourth and final figure with whom Nietzsche (this time
implicitly) links Luther's fate: Socrates. For 'Das Problem des
Sokrates', as Nietzsche explains in the second chapter of *Götzen-
Dämmerung* by that title, is that he was rabble ('Sokrates war Pöbel'),
and yet his dialectical bad manners (he insisted on the *exposure* of
reasoning just as Luther insisted on speaking 'informally' with his
God – GM III, 22) were seized upon by a decadent Athenian culture
everywhere but a few steps away from excess: Socrates was the
buffoon who got himself taken seriously. He thus succeeded in
carrying out his own 'peasant rebellion of the spirit' with the willing
complicity of the very same noble culture he was overthrowing.
Socrates himself, weary of the sickness called life, was merely
another form of decadent, a fanatic whose patent remedy – rationality
at all costs – just proved more attractive to ailing Greek culture, afraid
that something else might play the tyrant: he was simply the least bad
option available. Like Socrates, then, Nietzsche sees Luther as
inaugurating a new dark age for the European spirit. *Unlike* Socrates,
though, Luther was not in control of the situation, as we have seen –
he had not become master of his drives, which is why he remains for
Nietzsche the conglomerate of ill-accorded instincts I have just
attempted to describe.

Conclusion: Luther's Greatness

This brings me to my conclusion, and to the question of style – a puzzling question in Luther's case, I think, for in the light of what I have just sketched out it would appear that Luther should not have style in the Nietzschean sense, style being precisely that imposition of a personal stamp on the chaos of competing drives which he so admires, for example, in Goethe (GD ix 49). One would expect Nietzsche's view of Luther's style to match his description of Plato's: 'Plato wirft, wie mir scheint, alle Formen des Stils durcheinander, er ist damit ein *erster* décadent des Stils' (GD x 2). At the very least one might expect Nietzsche to react to the (famously 'plebeian') desire Luther expresses in his *Sendbrief von Dolmetschen* to translate the Bible into the language of 'the mother in the house, the children in the street, the common man at the market':

> den man mus nicht die buchstaben inn der lateinischē sprachen fragē / wie man sol Deutsch redē / wie diese esel thun / sondern / man mus die mutter ihm hause / die kinder auff der gassen / den gemeinen mā auff dem marckt drumb fragen / vn den selbigē auff das maul sehen / wie sie reden / vnd darnach dolmetzschen so verstehen sie es den / vn mercken / das man Deutsch mit jn redet.[28]

Yet it is quite clear that Luther's literary style is the one aspect about him which retains Nietzsche's admiration, notwithstanding all his cultural-political misgivings about Luther's psychology which I have been analysing here: as Kathleen Marie Higgins argues, 'For all of Nietzsche's disagreement with Luther's doctrines, he admires Luther as an *artist*'.[29] Indirectly, the mock-biblical style of *Also sprach Zarathustra* is perhaps the greatest compliment Nietzsche could pay

---

28   Martin Luther, *Ein Sendbrief von Dolmetschen und Fürbitte der Heiligen*, ed. H. S. M. Amburger-Stuart (London: Duckworth, 1940), p. 20.

29   Kathleen Marie Higgins, *Comic Relief: Nietzsche's 'Gay Science'* (New York and Oxford: Oxford University Press, 2000), p. 119. See also Robert C. Solomon and Kathleen M. Higgins, *What Nietzsche Really Said* (New York: Schocken Books, 2000), p. 148f.

Luther, but his admiration is also made perfectly explicit, notably
when in *Jenseits von Gut und Böse* he describes Luther's Bible –
without irony – as 'Das Meisterstück der deutschen Prosa' and
'bisher das beste deutsche Buch' (JGB 247). 'Gegen Luther's Bibel
gehalten', Nietzsche writes, 'ist fast alles Übrige nur "Litteratur"' –
almost, but not quite everything else, and there's the rub, for by
conforming to the received wisdom about the superlative qualities of
Luther's Bible translation, by allowing this evaluation to stand in
contradiction to his otherwise unceasing denigration of this bumptious
boor, Nietzsche is setting himself a challenge: write *better* than
Luther! This is a challenge, however, which he knows he has already
met, in *Also sprach Zarathustra*, for as he confesses to Rohde in
February 1884:

> ich bilde mir ein, mit diesem Z[arathustra] die deutsche Sprache zu ihrer
> Vollendung gebracht zu haben. Es war, nach *Luther* und *Goethe*, noch
> ein dritter Schritt zu thun –; sieh zu, alter Herzens-Kamerad, ob Kraft,
> Geschmeidigkeit und Wohllaut je schon in unsrer Sprache *so* beieinander
> gewesen sind. [...] Ich habe die strengere, männlichere Linie vor [Goethe]
> voraus, ohne doch, mit Luther, unter die Rüpel zu geraten (KSB 6/479).

In the last resort, even in his style Luther's 'loutishness' will out, but
on the stylistic level Nietzsche clearly identifies with him and takes
Luther as his educator.[30]

On other levels, too, Nietzsche can be seen to be covertly
identifying with Luther even after the mid-1870s, for as Jörg
Salaquarda points out, the very fact that Nietzsche continues to attack

---

30 See also KSA 11/60 (Spring 1884): 'Die Sprache Luthers und die poetische
    Form der Bibel als Grundlage einer neuen deutschen *Poesie*: – das ist *meine*
    Erfindung!' (cf. KSA 11/548). This theme is sounded as early as the spring of
    1876: 'Es ist die *rechte Zeit*, mit der deutschen Sprache sich endlich artistisch zu
    befassen. [...] Jetzt stehen bis zu Luther's deutschem Stile alle Farbentöpfe zum
    Gebrauche da – es muß nur der rechte Maler und Kolorist hinzukommen' (KSA
    8/279). For an analysis of both JGB 246 and '247a' in the light of this stylistic
    agon, see Laurence Lampert, *Nietzsche's Task: An Interpretation of 'Beyond
    Good and Evil'* (New Haven and London: Yale University Press, 2001), pp.
    250–53.

Luther is a mark of his respect.[31] He may reflect wistfully on what might have become of the Roman Church had Luther not arrived on the scene ('Cesare Borgia als Papst'), but he reflects equally wistfully on what might have become of Luther had he not been so catastrophically misguided: 'Ich empfinde häufig "Mitleid", wo gar kein Leiden da ist, sondern wo ich eine Verschwendung und ein Zurückbleiben sehe hinter dem, *was hätte werden können*. So z. B. in Bezug auf Luther. Welche Kraft und verschwendet auf was für Probleme!' (KSA 11/17; cf. 11:552). Luther may have been a peasant in Nietzsche's eyes, yet in paragraph 88 of *Morgenröthe*, again without irony, he can describe '*Luther der grosse Wohlthäter*', whose 'bäuerische Art, Recht zu behalten' was actually the only way Germans could be freed from the grip of the Christian saints and *vita contemplativa*, just as in the spring of 1884 Nietzsche can admit that 'Bauernblut ist noch das *beste Blut* in Deutschland: z. B. Luther Niebuhr Bismarck' (KSA 11/81). Luther will always *matter* to Nietzsche, for as well as acknowledging the importance of Luther's Bible, Nietzsche also concedes that Luther's Reformation, although the greatest wrong turn in German history, was nonetheless a great event – indeed Germany's most recent world-historic event ('Unser letztes Ereigniß' – KSA 11/56), to be superseded only by the seismic upheavals of his own 'Umwerthung'.

'Ich bin kein Mensch, ich bin Dynamit', Nietzsche writes, famously, in *Ecce homo*, at the opening of the final chapter, but the passage continues: '– Und mit Alledem ist Nichts in mir von einem Religionsstifter' (EH iv 1), which serves as a final emphatic denial of any affinity with Luther. Luther does not figure in any of the lists of names Nietzsche draws up in his last letters from January 1889 which betoken the onset of his insanity – the names of all those he has already been in his previous incarnations on earth – yet that did not prevent others from referring to Nietzsche as a 'second Luther' even during his lifetime.[32] In the introduction to his translation of

31 Salaquarda, 'Emanuel Hirsch', p. 435.
32 See Salaquarda, 'Emanuel Hirsch', p. 437, n. 22.

Zarathustra, Hollingdale takes this identification with Luther to an extreme, arguing that the whole of Nietzsche's mature philosophy is a kind of negative theology, one great abreaction against his Lutheran upbringing, with his 'Umwerthung aller Werthe' being not so much a transvaluation as merely a translation of Lutheran values into secularised form.[33] Hollingdale certainly has a point, even if he pushes it too far;[34] more subtly, David B. Allison has shown how, even in levelling his criticisms at Luther, Nietzsche employs a peculiarly Lutheran 'aposiopetic rhetoric'.[35] Just as Luther's Bible translation continues to provide Nietzsche with a seemingly inexhaustible linguistic resource, then, even after the mid-1870s he remains fascinated by the baneful influence of this fateful figure, 'the

33   R. J. Hollingdale, 'Introduction', in Friedrich Nietzsche, *Thus Spoke Zarathustra: A Book for Everyone and No One*, trans. R. J. Hollingdale, 2nd edn (Harmondsworth: Penguin, 1969), pp. 11–35 (pp. 27–29). In his biography of Nietzsche, Hollingdale more mutedly aligns himself with 'the tendency today [...] to emphasize the conventional aspects in his philosophy and its connection with that "Protestant" tradition of inquiry of which the whole of German philosophy may be said to be a part' (*Nietzsche: The Man and His Philosophy*, 2nd edn (Cambridge and New York: Cambridge University Press, 1999), p. 3).

34   For Giles Fraser, too, 'Hollingdale spoils what is, I think, a genuine and important insight (that Nietzsche is deeply indebted to Lutheran Pietism) by seeking to draw out parallels that are far too specific' (*Redeeming Nietzsche: On the Piety of Unbelief* (London and New York: Routledge, 2002), p. 40). His own more nuanced argument is that 'the paradigm from which Nietzsche thinks the question of God is largely that which is bequeathed by Luther' (p. 34). For further comparisons of Nietzsche's philosophy with aspects of Lutheran theology, see Hirsch, 'Nietzsche und Luther', and more recently Robert Gooding-Williams, 'Zarathustra's Three Metamorphoses', in Clayton Koelb (ed.), *Nietzsche as Postmodernist: Essays Pro and Contra* (Albany: SUNY Press, 1990), pp. 231–45 (pp. 236–37), and *Zarathustra's Dionysian Modernism* (Stanford: Stanford University Press, 2001), pp. 37, 42, 98; Higgins, *Comic Relief*, pp. 110–22 ('Was Zarathustra a Lutheran?').

35   See David B. Allison, 'A Diet of Worms: Aposiopetic Rhetoric in "Beyond Good and Evil"', *Nietzsche-Studien*, 19 (1990), 43–58, and '"Have I Been Understood?"', in Richard Schacht (ed.), *Nietzsche, Genealogy, Morality: Essays on Nietzsche's 'Genealogy of Morals'* (Berkeley, Los Angeles and London: University of California Press, 1994), pp. 460–68.

embodiment of everything German',[36] and the mere frequency with which Nietzsche parodically appropriates Luther's most famous line is sufficient indication that for all his faults this epic forebear continues to serve Nietzsche as a model, perhaps even as a pioneer of *amor fati*: 'Hier stehe ich, ich kann nicht anders. Gott helfe mir! Amen!'[37]

---

36 Baeumer, 'Nietzsche and Luther', p. 158; cf. Salaquarda, 'Emanuel Hirsch', p. 437.

37 Cf. FW 146; Za IV xvi 2; GM III 22; EH iii 2. For 'ich kann nicht anders', see also KSA 8/509; 9/116, 354. Nietzsche rings the changes on this basic phrase and uses it in a variety of other grammatical guises, too, as in: MA I 121 ('er kann nicht anders'); FW 3 ('wir können gar nicht anders'); JGB 9 ('sie kann nicht anders'); JGB 202 ('Was hilft es! Wir können nicht anders'); WA 8 ('man kann nicht anders'); KSA 10/521 ('Zarathustra kann nicht anders!'); KSA 10/525 ('wir können gar nicht anders'); KSA 10/590 ('*Nicht anders können*') and KSB 4/180 ('Da steht er der Arme, Gott helfe ihm, er kann wahrscheinlich nicht anders. Amen.').

Ben Morgan

Fear and Self-Control in *The Antichrist*: Nietzsche's Prussian Past[1]

1. A methodological suggestion

One should not mix up philosophy and life, Walter Kaufmann warned in his attempt to rehabilitate Nietzsche after the war, because philosophical problems have an impetus all of their own which biographical interpretations do not fully acknowledge.[2] Derrida made the same point almost thirty years on in a deconstructive idiom, suggesting an unexpected continuity between post-structuralism and the currents from which it sought to differentiate itself. Anyone who tries naïvely to bridge the gap between philosophical works and a philosopher's life, he argues, will find themselves stranded in an inescapable border country in which neither the subjects nor the philosophical meanings they hoped to bring together unproblematically exist. The separation that for Walter Kaufmann was a mark of philosophical tact becomes, in Derrida's 'Otobiographies', an inevitable part of the textual condition. But it is the same division nevertheless. Kaufmann's inner momentum of philosophical problems, and Derrida's ghostly world of deferral and displacement (or what he calls 'the *dynamis* of that borderline between "work" and the

---

1   This article is a revised version of a paper entitled 'Fear and Ecstasy in "The Antichrist" and the "Dialectic of Enlightenment"', which was presented at the Friedrich Nietzsche Society conference in St Andrews in 1997.

2   See Walter Kaufmann, *Nietzsche: Philosopher, Psychologist, Antichrist*, 4th edn (Princeton: Princeton University Press, 1968), p. 21.

"life'"),[3] are both arguments which drive a wedge between the text and the experience of which it is in some way the record.[4]

The explanation for this separation cannot be found in Nietzsche's own philosophy. Admittedly, Nietzsche partly prepared the ground for it when, in *Ecce homo*, he categorically separated himself from his writings ('I am one thing, my texts are another'),[5] or when, in his analysis of Wagner's *Parsifal* in *The Genealogy of Morals*, he counselled his readers to distinguish a work from its creator and view the artist as just the fertilizing dung from which the creation developed (GM III, 4). At the same time, he flatly rejected any such distinction, rooting philosophy in the life of the person who wrote it (he called philosophy an 'unacknowledged confession').[6] If Nietzsche himself is to offer an explanation for the division, it is not to his texts that we should look, but rather to his madness, or at least to the issues raised by his mental collapse. Foucault suggested that the only adequate reading of Nietzsche would be one which could perceive the continuity from *The Birth of Tragedy* to the final, deluded jottings: 'Nietzsche's madness – that is, the dissolution of his

---

3   Jacques Derrida, 'Otobiographies', in his *The Ear of the Other*, trans. Peggy Kamuf (Lincoln: University of Nebraska Press, 1985), pp. 3–38 (p. 5).

4   The same applies to Alexander Nehamas, *Nietzsche: Life as Literature* (Cambridge, MA: Harvard University Press, 1985), which hopes to conceal Nietzsche's empirical existence behind the masks of his literary self-fashioning: 'In engaging with his works, we are not engaging with the miserable little man who wrote them, but with the philosopher who emerges through them, the magnificent character these texts constitute and manifest, the agent who, as the will to power holds, is nothing but his effects, – that is, his writings' (p. 234). This passage contains two sleights of hand – the first the claim that the philosopher in the texts is consistently magnificent (editing out anything unsavoury from the texts themselves), the second the reductive reading of the will to power which replaces 'effects' with 'literary effects' or writings. Both of these elisions are necessary if Nehamas is to maintain his artificial separation of the 'miserable little man' from his magnificent texts.

5   'Das Eine bin ich, das Andre sind meine Schriften' (EH iii 1: KSA 6/298). Translations from KSA are my own.

6   'das Selbstbekenntnis ihres Urhebers' (JGB 6: KSA 5/19).

thought – is that by which his thought opens out onto the modern world'.[7] What Foucault means by this is that the fact of Nietzsche's collapse challenges his readers to reflect on the conditions and role of philosophical writing, to reconnect philosophy with the context from which it springs. It is just this reconnection that Lesley Chamberlain undertook in her recent account of Nietzsche's last active year, *Nietzsche in Turin*, a book that peoples Nietzsche's world once more with the men and women with whom he was entangled (Wagner, Lou Andreas-Salomé, the semi-fictive Peter Gast), and that offers a sketch of the psychological structures which underpin his work. She concludes: 'In the end we are bound to ask if Nietzsche's seminal contribution to modern philosophy is not the coincidental result of his complex, unevenly weighted, maladjusted character exaggerating the world for us, in order to show it in one of its true lights'.[8] Such a conclusion is doubly difficult for academic philosophy. It sullies a canonical author by suggesting that writings otherwise highly prized are the by-product of emotional difficulties. At the same time, it steers philosophical debate into unfamiliar territory, for it indirectly raises questions not just about Nietzsche's motivations, but about the motivations of his readers and critics ('Why are we fascinated by the products of Nietzsche's maladjustment?'). Chamberlain's approach forces us to ask uncomfortable questions about the relations between abstract argument and the stuff of emotional life.

If such an approach is uncomfortable, it is worth contemplating nevertheless, for it promises to clarify Nietzsche's writings in two ways. It helps in the process of interpreting contradictions in the texts (such as the statements for and against biographical criticism), by drawing attention away from abstract arguments and questions of consistency, to the emotional life which underpins them. It is an

7   Michel Foucault, *Madness and Civilisation: A History of Insanity in the Age of Reason*, trans. Richard Howard (London: Tavistock Press, 1967), p. 288.

8   Lesley Chamberlain, *Nietzsche in Turin: The End of the Future* (London: Quartet Books, 1996), pp. 141–42.

archaeological approach which reconstructs the way of life of which the texts, with all their inconsistencies, are a record. This reconstruction, in its turn, facilitates an evaluation of the philosophy. Equipped with a picture of the underlying way of life, it is easier to see what is at stake in Nietzsche's texts, to grasp what emotional habits are being reproduced or rejected where Nietzsche is interpreted and re-worked.

Yet such an approach appears to bring with it a methodological problem. The technique is psychological in inspiration. It returns us to the emotional situation of which it believes the texts to be a product and a reflection. To return to this situation without the assistance of the individual whose experience it was, is a potentially fruitless undertaking, as Freud noted when he was asked to comment on a series of dreams by Descartes: 'working on dreams without being able to obtain from the dreamer himself any indications on the relations which might link them to one another or attach them to the external world – and this is clearly the case when it is a question of the dreams of a historical figure – gives, as a general rule, only a meagre result.'[9] Worse than a meagre result would be a result that is merely arbitrary, as a critic imposed his or her vision onto the available material. (One such example is Lou Andreas-Salomé's *Friedrich Nietzsche in seinen Werken*, which stylizes Nietzsche as the heroic outsider, presupposing and glorifying his isolation rather than seeking to account for it.)[10] Such arbitrariness is deplorable, but the way to combat it is not to establish a false distinction between readings which impose on their objects, and others which manage magically to avoid foisting

9   '"Some Dreams of Descartes": A Letter to Maxime Leroy', *The Standard Edition of the Complete Psychological Works of Sigmund Freud*, trans. and ed. James Strachey and Anna Freud, 24 vols (London: Hogarth Press, 1953–74), xxi (1961), 199–204 (p. 203).

10   Lou Andreas-Salomé, *Friedrich Nietzsche in seinen Werken* (Dresden: Reissner, 1924). R. J. Hollingdale has rightly criticized attempts to force a romanticized ideal of heroic isolation onto Nietzsche's texts ('The Hero as Outsider', in Bernd Magnus and Kathleen M. Higgins (eds), *The Cambridge Companion to Nietzsche* (Cambridge: Cambridge University Press, 1996), pp. 71–89).

psychological presuppositions upon them. All interpretation, even that which hopes to separate philosophical problems from their psychological origins, presupposes a normative psychological theory. When Kaufmann distinguishes philosophical problems from biography, he is making a psychological statement, based on his assumptions about the appropriate places for discussing emotional complications. He is advocating a particular way of regimenting emotional life (separating emotions from argument), and at the same time conferring more value on the zone without emotion. Derrida's approach presupposes a similarly prescriptive psychology. His arguments don't separate philosophy from emotional experience quite so cleanly, but rather ontologize (and to a certain extent glamourize) emotional confusion, as they declare the state of constant deferral and restlessness to be inescapable. Both these approaches make implicit statements about how they believe emotional life to be organized, but neither fully acknowledges its psychological assumptions. They instead impose them on Nietzsche's texts unreflectingly.

To escape this unacknowledged imposition, it seems preferable to make any psychological assumptions explicit and so start the business of refining them, drawing on the – in the case of Nietzsche ample – biographical and historical material so as to overcome the twin dangers of being too meagre or too arbitrary in one's analysis. Using the published writings, notebooks, letters and anecdotes, but also information about the habits and assumptions of the Prussian society by which Nietzsche was shaped, it is possible to put together a working model of the psychological structures that underpin his work, and thus, as Foucault suggested, to 'open out' Nietzsche's texts onto the modern world. One Nietzsche text that is particularly revealing in this respect is *The Antichrist*. On the one hand, it rounds on and angrily debunks the German Protestant tradition of which Nietzsche, the son of a Lutheran pastor, was himself the product. On the other hand, it contains a portrait of Christ which, read against the grain, reveals in miniature the emotional habits behind Nietzsche's texts, and demonstrates the degree to which he remained ensnared in the tradition, even as he fought to criticize and transcend it. It is this ensnaring that this article will briefly present.

2. From the Will to Power to a Helpless Child

One flaw in Lesley Chamberlain's book is that she identifies too much with Nietzsche. She can show us his frailty, and unmask his self-delusions. But there remains a basic faith in the value of his philosophy that stops her fully accounting for its concepts, and causes her simply to bracket out those points at which the texts become too obviously offensive (such as Nietzsche's denunciation in *Twilight of the Idols* of the sick man as the parasite of society).[11] To avoid such glossing over, one needs to find a perspective that allows one both to include and explain the excesses of the will to power. One needs, in other words, a perspective which stands beyond the will to power and has abandoned it as a conceptual centre or foundation (a move post-modern readings, such as that of Gilles Deleuze, are unwilling to make).[12] Adorno was feeling his way towards this re-orientation as he re-read Nietzsche in the 1940s, preparing for his collaboration with Horkheimer on the text of the *Dialectic of Enlightenment*. In a letter he wrote to Horkheimer in July 1941, he reported: 'I've been thinking a good deal about the will to power [...]. What Nietzsche calls the will

11   Chamberlain, p. 106.
12   Deleuze retains the will to power as the central concept of Nietzsche's philosophy only by sanitizing and abstracting it. He defines the will to power as 'not force but the differential element which simultaneously determines the relation of forces (quantity) and the respective qualities of related forces' (Gilles Deleuze, *Nietzsche and Philosophy*, trans. Hugh Tomlinson (London: Athlone Press, 1983), p. 197). This definition excises the more embarrassing aspects of the philosophy, but at the price of rendering equally abstract the affirmation and creativity that Deleuze hopes to derive from the will to power.

to power is actually nothing but the fear of losing power'.[13] Nietzsche insisted in his later notebooks that one cannot get behind the will to power, that it is the force for which all other explanations are metaphorical circumlocutions.[14] Adorno challenges this assertion and suggests that behind the will to power there lurks in fact just the terror that one might lose one's power or mastery. This suspicion is borne out by the brief re-statement of his position with which Nietzsche begins *The Antichrist*: 'What is good? – everything which increases the feeling of power, the will to power or power itself in the subject. [...] What is happiness – the feeling of power *growing* – that an obstacle is being overcome.'[15] The repeated invocations of power, and the need to feel power constantly growing suggest a relation to power which is neither stable nor self-assured. Instead, the relief which Nietzsche feels at the overcoming of an obstacle could be likened to the relief of a neurotic who, faced with a potentially threatening situation, surrenders to his or her neurotic structure, and so re-establishes a sense of personal order.[16] It is the relief of

---

13   'Ich habe sehr viel über den Willen zur Macht nachgedacht [...]. Was [Nietzsche] den Willen zur Macht nennt, ist eigentlich nichts als die Angst, diese zu verlieren [...]' (letter of 30 July 1941, in Max Horkheimer, *Briefwechsel 1941–1948*, in *Gesammelte Schriften*, ed. Alfred Schmidt and Gunzelin Schmid Noerr, 19 vols (Frankfurt a.M.: Fischer, 1985–96), xvii (1996), 113. The edition includes Adorno's letters to Horkheimer).

14   Nietzsche asserts e.g.: 'that every "purpose", "aim", "intention" is only an expression for, or metamorphosis of the One Will that inheres in all action, the Will to Power' ('daß alle "Zwecke", "Ziele", "Sinne" nur Ausdrucksweisen und Metamorphosen des Einen Willens sind, der allem Geschehen inhärirt, der Wille zur Macht') (NF 1887–88, 11[96]: KSA 13/44).

15   'Was ist gut? – Alles, was das Gefühl der Macht, den Willen zur Macht, die Macht selbst im Menschen erhöht. [...] Was ist Glück? – Das Gefühl davon, dass die Macht *wächst* – dass ein Widerstand überwunden wird' (AC 2: KSA 6/170).

16   Jung would have termed such a reaction a power complex, which he defined as: 'the whole complex of ideas and strivings which seek to subordinate all other influences to the ego, no matter whether these influences have their source in people and objective conditions or in the subject's own impulses, thoughts, and

someone who has the problem 'beneath' him, who has returned to his isolated, Alpine viewpoint, where the air once again is clear – if a little thin.[17]

The motivation for this frightened pursuit of mastery can be found in the portrait of Christ sketched in *The Antichrist*. Nietzsche's presentation of what he calls the 'psychological type' of the redeemer shows us what he is afraid of, as well as revealing the mis-understanding from which this terror springs. Christ, as he is portrayed by Nietzsche, displays all the characteristics of a mystic, or as Gary Shapiro puts it: 'Nietzsche proposes an ahistorical and non-narrative psychology of the redeemer, according to which Jesus was, in our everyday language, "blissed out".'[18] This Christ rejects all structures, be they institutional, or conceptual.[19] He lives in a world without rituals, without even ideas of time or space, a world where the individual is not separated from God by hierarchy or by sin, but in which the individual himself has become divine. Nor is this divinity an abstract, or unreal state. In the heuristic sketch with which Bernard

feelings' (C. G. Jung, *Psychological Types* (Princeton: Princeton University Press, 1971), p. 457).

17   Cf. 'The ice is near, the solitude is monstrous – but how peacefully all things lie in the light! how freely one breathes! how much lies *beneath* one!' ('Das Eis ist nahe, die Einsamkeit ist ungeheuer – aber wie ruhig alle Dinge im Lichte liegen! wie frei man athmet! wie Viel man *unter* sich fühlt!') (EH Preface 3: KSA 6/258).

18   Gary Shapiro, 'The Writing on the Wall: *The Antichrist* and the Semiotics of History', in Robert C. Solomon and Kathleen M. Higgins (eds), *Reading Nietzsche* (Oxford: Oxford University Press, 1988), pp. 192–217 (p. 200). Shapiro is not interested in this bliss as an emotional structure, but as a linguistic one. He sees it as a state so far removed from language that it demonstrates the contingency of every act of naming.

19   Nietzsche's speaks of Christ's 'repugnance for all formulae, all concepts of time and space, for all things that are fixed: custom, institution, church' ('Widerwille gegen jede Formel, jeden Zeit- und Raumbegriff, gegen alles, was fest, Sitte, Institution, Kirche ist') (AC 29: KSA 6/200). For a mystical text which similarly pushes beyond all structures, be they ecclesiastical or conceptual, see Meister Eckhart, *Selected Writings*, trans. Oliver Davies (Harmondsworth: Penguin, 1994), pp. 202–9: *Beati pauperes spiritu*.

McGinn starts his history of mysticism, he reminds us that 'mysticism is always a process or a way of life'.[20] Similarly, for Nietzsche's redeemer the proximity to divinity is what he calls a condition of the heart, a particular way of living out longing in the present, a real-life praxis which is in the world but simultaneously in the presence of God (AC 34).

How Nietzsche knows this state, how he comes to describe this mystical life-style in terms so close to those of its advocates is not clear. (Martin Pernet suggests it is a form of life Nietzsche observed in the revivalist Pietist circles in which he grew up, and which left a lasting, and in Pernet's view, positive impression on him. But Pernet's view of nineteenth century, Pietist practice is very idealized, and does not correspond to the cold, pedagogical and implicitly reprimanding tone evident in many of the letters written by adults to the boy Nietzsche.)[21] What is more important is the way Nietzsche misunderstands this life, even as he so astutely records its forms. For Nietzsche's psychological explanation of this way of life seems to bear little relation to the mystical practice he describes. In Nietzsche's view, the psychological explanation for Christ's behaviour is what he calls an 'instinctual hatred of reality'.[22] Christ, for Nietzsche, is someone for whom all contact with reality, even in self-defence, is so painful, that he withdraws into an inner world for which reality does not exist. This interpretation is flawed on two levels. As a portrait of Christ, it seems simply wrong (of the Christ, for instance, who said give to Caesar what is Caesar's, recommending to his disciples that they live both in the world and with God). But it also appears misguided as an interpretation of the psychological structures Nietzsche is describing, if one takes at all seriously the striking parallel between Nietzsche's Christ and mysticism. For many mystics,

---

20 Bernard McGinn, *The Foundations of Mysticism* (London: SCM Press, 1991), p. xvi.

21 Martin Pernet, 'Friedrich Nietzsche and Pietism', *German Life and Letters*, 48 (1995), 474–86.

22 '*Der Instinkt-Hass gegen die Realität*' (AC 30: KSA 6/200).

the contemplation of God's presence is but one part of a journey which eventually takes the individual back into the world.[23]

Nietzsche's interpretation makes more sense as a statement about the interpreter, Nietzsche himself, than about Christ. To understand what is at stake behind this misinterpretation, it helps to look at an earlier draft of the portrait of Christ. What Nietzsche disapproves of in Christ, it transpires, is his lack of virility: he has no fight in him, no pride, no heroism. Indeed, to Nietzsche, it appears that Christ is retarded and has stayed childishly in the age of puberty.[24] What Nietzsche sees in Christ is an helpless boy unable to defend himself, a child who does not have it in his power to change the structures that assail him, and who so finds refuge in cutting off all contact with the world. To someone who has learnt a more heroic way of defending himself, but to whom, equally, Christ's apparent passivity is an uncomfortable reminder of a former helplessness, Christ is bound to appear a weak and distasteful figure. The question that remains is why Nietzsche should mistake Christ for this helpless boy. To answer this, we need to look at the circumstances of Nietzsche's upbringing, which is to say, we need to look back at the structures that wrote the signature of nineteenth-century Prussia indelibly on the psyche of the developing philosopher.

---

23   See, for example, Meister Eckhart's sermon on the biblical figures of Martha and Mary (*Selected Writings*, pp. 193–202, *Intravit Iesus in quoddam castellum*), which praises Martha precisely because she works even as she enjoys God's presence.

24   'zurückgeblieben [...] und kindhaft im Alter der Pubertät geblieben' (NF 1888, 14[38]: KSA 13/237).

3. Nietzsche's Context

Underlying the pedagogic manuals of the nineteenth century is the repeated insistence that the child not be allowed a will of its own. This process of taming the child's desire for satisfaction was supposed to start even at the mother's breast. As the educationalist Schreber wrote in 1858:

> the child must not be given even the slightest impression that it could force something out of its environment through screaming or unruly behaviour. On the contrary, the child learns very quickly that it reaches its aims only through the opposite behaviour, through an (albeit still unconscious) self-control.[25]

Nietzsche's own childhood was similarly marked by the belief that the child's needs should be met only on the terms of adults. To give one of many possible example: Nietzsche learned to talk relatively late, a fact which a doctor explained in the, for Nietzsche's sister, 'jovial' remark: 'Little Fritz is being served too solicitously and attentively; all his wishes are being fulfilled without delay so why should he bother to speak!'[26] The doctor assumes that for a child to develop and join the adult world, its wishes must be systematically denied.

As well as shaping the child in the image of the parent, the household Nietzsche grew up in was one in which conflict or overt resistance was not allowed. (This taboo on open conflict seems to have been a common characteristic of the Lutheran *Pfarrhaus* of the sort Nietzsche was born into, as the pressure of being an exemplary

---

25   'es muß vom Kind selbst der leiseste Schein ferngehalten werden, als könne es durch Schreien oder unbändiges Benehmen seiner Umgebung irgend etwas abzwingen. Im Gegenteil erkennt das Kind sehr bald, daß es nur durch das entgegengesetzte Benehmen, durch (obschon noch unbewußte) Selbst-beherrschung, seine Absicht erreicht' (quoted in Alice Miller, *Am Anfang war Erziehung* (Frankfurt a.M.: Suhrkamp, 1980), p. 43).

26   Sander L. Gilman (ed.), *Conversations with Nietzsche: A Life in the Words of his Contemporaries*, trans. David J. Parent (New York and Oxford: Oxford University Press, 1987), p. 3.

household for the parish prohibited any ruffling of the family ideal.)[27]
When his mother lost her temper or tried to have her own way,
Nietzsche's father would withdraw into his study and refuse to eat
until his wife had relinquished her demand.[28] Similar tactics were
employed with the child Nietzsche, who learnt when he was angry to
withdraw into a corner, or even to the loo, until his anger was spent.[29]
If he was denied satisfaction when he was angry, the denial was
implicit no less on occasions when he was to be congratulated. A
letter written to him by his uncle Gustav Adolf Oßwald on his seventh
birthday leaves no space for a child who isn't merely the pattern of
adult demands. Nietzsche's birthday was that of the Prussian King,
Friedrich Wilhelm IV. But this coincidence is used only as an excuse
to remind him that he can himself never be King, but should aspire
instead to becoming a pastor like his father. The letter then cautions
the seven-year-old to repay the care that his teachers and his mother
have been so good as to lavish upon him, to give to the adult world
its due. What is lacking from the letter is the sense that the boy
could want anything more than gratefully to conform to adult
structures (the one exception is a fleeting admission that the young
Nietzsche may not want to talk Greek or Latin with a new friend, but
simply to play with him and talk German).[30] That the boy may have
had his own needs, his own inner energy, his own inner rhythm of
desires and longings is apparently inconceivable. As Jørgen Kjaer
emphasizes in his reconstruction of what he calls the 'communicative
pathology' which structured the relations between adults and children

---

27 See Andreas Gestrich, 'Erziehung im Pfarrhaus', in Martin Greiffenhagen (ed.),
    Das evangelische Pfarrhaus. Eine Kultur- und Sozialgeschichte (Stuttgart:
    Kreuz, 1984), pp. 63–82 (p. 66).
28 Curt Paul Janz, *Friedrich Nietzsche: Biographie*, 3 vols (Munich: Hanser,
    1978–79), i, 42.
29 Ibid., 43.
30 Gustav Adolf Oßwald to Nietzsche, 15 Oct. 1851 (KGB I.1 305–06).

in nineteenth-century Prussian society: 'What it means to be a child is a role which is precisely defined by adults.'[31]

Nietzsche's Christ is exactly this child whose desires have no space, whose every stirring meets with resistance or denial, and for whom consequently every encounter with reality leaves a scar. Yet Nietzsche didn't remain this helpless boy, what he learnt instead was to check his own desire, to become himself the monitoring power. The most graphic example of the violence which this self-regulation required can be seen in an incident from Nietzsche's first year at Schulpforta, the ascetic and disciplinarian boarding school to which he was sent at the age of thirteen. Nietzsche's response to a discussion of the Roman Mucius Scaevola, who let his hand be burnt, was himself to light a bundle of matches on the palm of his hand, and let them burn there while his fellow school boys looked on, as his sister Elisabeth would have us believe, in 'horror and admiration' (Janz, i, 82–83). But Nietzsche's identification with the regulatory powers isn't only visible in this incident. It can be seen in the nineteen-year-old's conviction that the discipline of his schooling has done him good (ibid., 118). But it can also be seen in the adult Nietzsche, who, as Lukács noted in *The Destruction of Reason*, enthusiastically supported Prussian militarism, volunteering for service in the Franco-Prussian war of 1870–71, and taking the discipline and self-control of the Prussian soldier as his positive model in the notebooks from the period of autumn 1873 when he was working on the essay *The Uses and Disadvantages of History for Life*: 'My starting point is the Prussian soldier. Here a genuine convention is to be found, here too are compulsion, seriousness, discipline, also in questions of form.'[32]

---

31 'Das Kindsein ist eine Rolle, die von den Erwachsenen genau definiert wird.' (Jørgen Kjaer, *Friedrich Nietzsche. Die Zerstörung der Humanität durch Mutterliebe* (Opladen: Westdeutscher Verlag, 1990), p. 278, p. 60). For a clear presentation of what Kjaer calls the 'grammar' of miscommunication between adults and children in Nietzsche's era, see pp. 53–60.

32 'Mein Ausgangspunct ist der preussische Soldat: hier ist eine wirkliche Convention, hier ist Zwang, Ernst, Disciplin, auch in Betreff der Form' (NF 1873, 29[119]: KSA 7/685). Nietzsche's enthusiasm for Prussia is discussed by

This identification with violence continues even after Nietzsche is disillusioned with the Prussian state. It returns in Zarathustra's celebration of a self-imposed yoke (Za I xvii), or *Ecce homo*'s declaration that progress in philosophy is inseparable from a certain hardness against oneself (KSA 6/259). It returns too in the notebooks, in the praises of the hardening and strengthening character of war,[33] or in the declaration that Nietzsche's natural allies are still the Prussian army: 'When I look for my natural allies, then they are primarily officers; with military instincts in one's body one *cannot* be a Christian.'[34] The identification with, and praise of, violent self-control returns as a refrain again and again.

This simple structure underpins Nietzsche's entire philosophy. The child who has learnt to regulate his every impulse has also learnt to recognize every stirring of affect or vulnerability in the people and philosophies he meets. If Nietzsche was more discerning than his contemporaries, it is perhaps because he was himself an extraordinarily perceptive child. He seems on two occasions unconsciously to have registered an impending disaster in his family, prefiguring in dreams the deaths of both his younger brother and his grandfather (Janz, i, 47, 85). At the same time, the affects he uncovered in others or in himself were for him only ever signs of weakness, something disgusting that made him want to put on gloves, and protect himself, as he admits in *Ecce homo* (EH Preface 3), or indeed that he found positively life-threatening. To share another's feelings, to open himself up to pity or empathy, was for Nietzsche to find his very identity threatened: 'Through pity suffering itself becomes infectious.'[35]

Lukács in 'Nietzsche als Begründer des Irrationalismus der imperialistischen Periode', in *Die Zerstörung der Vernunft: Der Weg des Irrationalismus von Schelling zu Hitler* (Berlin: Aufbau, 1954), pp. 244–317 (pp. 256–57).

33   NF 1888, 18[1]: KSA 13/531.

34   'Wenn ich nach meinen natürlichen Verbündeten frage, so sind das vor Allem die Offiziere; mit militär[ischen] Instinkten im Leibe *kann* man nicht Christ sein [...]' (NF 1888–89, 25[11]: KSA 13/642).

35   'Das Leiden selbst wird durch das Mitleiden ansteckend' (AC 7: KSA 6/173).

Nietzsche could never recognize himself in the suffering he came across. He could never let through the knowledge that he shared the misfortune he condemned as degenerate. Or rather, the moment when this knowledge finally became irresistible was the moment when his identity as Friedrich Nietzsche collapsed. The story of the horrified philosopher falling on the neck of a beaten horse may be no more than hear-say or myth-making (Janz, iii, 34). At the same time, it perfectly captures the change which generated Nietzsche's insanity. On the street in Turin, Nietzsche seems suddenly to have identified with the tortured animal. But to let through the pain which this recognition brought with it seems to have been more than his conscious identity was willing to bear. It seems it could bear it only by pushing his inflated identification with violence to its limit, by becoming God and giving up all responsibility for the real and vulnerable Friedrich Nietzsche:

> The world is transfigured, for God is upon the earth. Can you not see how all the heavens rejoice? I have just taken possession of my kingdom, I shall throw the pope into prison, and have Wilhelm, Bismarck and Stöcker shot. – The Crucified.[36]

---

36 'Die Welt ist verklärt, denn Gott ist auf der Erde. Sehen Sie nicht, wie alle Himmel sich freuen? Ich habe eben Besitz ergriffen von meinem Reich, werfe den Papst ins Gefängniß und lasse Wilhelm, Bismarck und Stöcker erschießen. Der Gekreuzigte' (letter to Meta von Salis, Turin, 3 Jan. 1889 (KSB 8/572)).

Christopher Janaway

Schopenhauer as Nietzsche's Educator[1]

1. Schopenhauer as . . .

'Nice letter from Prof. Nietzsche, though informing us that he now rejects Schopenhauer's teachings!' – thus wrote Cosima Wagner in her diary for 24 December 1876,[2] her exclamation elicited by the following communication sent from Sorrento on 19 December:

> Would you be amazed if I confess something that has gradually come about, but which has more or less suddenly entered my consciousness: a disagreement with Schopenhauer's teaching? On virtually all general propositions I am not on his side; when I was writing on Schopenhauer, I already noticed that I had left behind everything concerning dogma; for me what mattered was the *human being* (KSB 5/210).

This announcement would have surprised many of Nietzsche's acquaintances and marks a pivotal point in his career. Of around one hundred references to Schopenhauer in his letters during the previous eleven years none is critical in the slightest: Nietzsche had felt himself

---

1   This paper was first published in Christopher Janaway (ed.), *Willing and Nothingness: Schopenhauer as Nietzsche's Educator* (Oxford: Oxford University Press, 1998), pp. 13–36, and is reproduced here by kind permission of the publisher. It is a later version of the paper ('Nietzsche as Schopenhauer's educator and subtext') read at the Friedrich Nietzsche Society conference in St Andrews in 1997. Works by Schopenhauer are abbreviated as follows: PP – *Parerga and Paralipomena* (*Parerga und Paralipomena* 1851); WWR – *The World as Will and Representation* (*Die Welt als Wille und Vorstellung* (I – 1819; II – 1844)).

2   *Cosima Wagner's Diaries*, ed. Martin Gregor-Dellin and Dietrich Mack, trans. Geoffrey Skelton, 2 vols (London: Collins, 1978–80), i, 938.

at the centre of a small but growing band of 'Schopenhauerians' and had consistently praised Schopenhauer, sometimes in extravagant terms.

The well-known preface to *On the Genealogy of Morals* points back to the same pivotal period. Nietzsche recalls the time he started writing *Human, All Too Human*, 'begun in Sorrento during a winter when it was given to me to pause as a wanderer pauses and look back across the broad and dangerous country my spirit had traversed up to that time',[3] and later he adds:

> What was at stake was the *value* of morality – and over this I had to come to terms almost exclusively with my great teacher Schopenhauer, to whom that book of mine [...] addressed itself as if to a contemporary (for that book, too, was a 'polemic') (GM Preface 5).

Texts from the period begun by *Human, All Too Human* and continuing with *Daybreak* and *The Gay Science* bear out Nietzsche's description. Some of Schopenhauer's main philosophical ideas are here subjected to strong criticisms: his attempt to ground morality in pity or compassion, his claim to provide a metaphysics of the 'thing in itself', his belief that beneath their various dogmas the major religions contain important truths, and his claims about the human will, freedom, the inalterability of character, artistic genius, the fundamental unreality of the individual, and the negativity of pleasure, a doctrine on which Schopenhauer's negative assessment of life is founded.[4]

However, the conventional oversimplification, that Nietzsche straightforwardly accepted Schopenhauer's philosophy from his first acquaintance with it (in 1865) until this critical winter of 1876–77, and rejected it wholesale thereafter, should be resisted. First, we should not ignore Nietzsche's frequent re-interpretations, reliable or unreliable, of his earlier writings. Secondly, some positive Schopenhauerian elements may persist in the later period despite the

3   GM Preface 2.
4   Cf. MA I 39, 57, 99, 110; MA II/1 5; M 63, 132, 133, 142, 474, 547; and FW 99, 127, 151.

prominent rejection of others. Thirdly, Nietzsche's philosophical questions can remain in close contact with Schopenhauer, even if his answers to them are quite opposed. And finally, Schopenhauer never has just a single role for Nietzsche. Here are some (and only some) of the diverse uses Nietzsche makes of Schopenhauer in his letters, notes, and published writings throughout his career:

1. *Schopenhauer as consolation.* Nietzsche describes the effect of reading Schopenhauer as uniquely comforting: 'The best thing we have is to feel oneself at one with a great mind (*Geist*), to be able to enter sympathetically into his trains of thought, to have found an intellectual home, a place of refuge for troubled hours – we will not wish to rob others of this, we will not allow ourselves to robbed of it. Even if it is an error, even if it is a lie – – –' (to Deussen, Oct.–Nov. 1867: KSB 2/229).

2. *Schopenhauer as master.* In 1869, for example, Nietzsche writes to his friend Gersdorff: 'The portrait of our master, with which you have adorned my room, reminds me to inform you of the foundation of a Societas Schopenhaueriana in Leipzig' (to Gersdorff, 19 Dec. 1869: KSB 3/84).

3. *Schopenhauer as exemplar.* The figure of Schopenhauer functions as an instructive symbol and embodiment of the intellectual life for Germany and Europe: 'Here you have the philosopher – now seek the culture that belongs with him!'[5]

4. *Schopenhauer as authority.* Nietzsche will refer to passages in Schopenhauer in order to establish or support a point of his own. Thus in *The Birth of Tragedy*: 'How is music related to image and concept? Schopenhauer, praised by Richard Wagner for expressing that very

---

5   In 'Das Verhältniss der Schopenhauerischen Philosophie zu einer deutschen Cultur' of 1872 (KSA 1/782).

point with unsurpassed clarity, presents the issue most clearly in the following passage, which I shall reproduce in full: [...]' (GT 16).[6]

5. *Schopenhauer as philosophical opponent.* Nietzsche engages in philosophical debate with Schopenhauer, faulting his reasoning, criticizing his assumptions and the like.[7]

6. *Schopenhauer as antipode.* Striking utterances in Nietzsche's later writings, where Schopenhauer is said to propound and symbolize everything opposite to Nietzsche himself.[8]

7. *Schopenhauer as case-study.* Schopenhauer's writings are seen as symptoms of a particular configuration of psychological needs and drives.

> Of few things does Schopenhauer speak with greater assurance than he does of the effect of aesthetic contemplation: he says of it that it counters *sexual* 'interestedness', like lupulin or camphor [...] Indeed, one might be tempted to ask whether his basic conception of 'will and representation', the thought that redemption from the 'will' could be attained only through 'representation', did not originate as a generalization from this sexual experience (GM III 6).

8. *Schopenhauer as Nietzsche's educator.* As in the *Genealogy*'s preface quoted above, Nietzsche retrospectively assigns Schopenhauer a central role in his own intellectual development.'[9]

---

6   In this essay, citations of *The Birth of Tragedy* use the translation by Shaun Whiteside, ed. Michael Tanner (Harmondsworth: Penguin, 1993), with occasional minor modifications.

7   One of many instances: 'That pity [...] is the *same kind of thing* as the suffering at the sight of which it arises, or that it possesses an especially subtle, penetrating understanding of suffering, are propositions contradicted by *experience*, and he who glorifies pity precisely on account of these two qualities lacks adequate experience in this very realm of the moral. This is what I have to conclude when I see all the incredible things Schopenhauer had to say of pity' (M 133).

8   Thus 'Wagner as much as Schopenhauer – they deny life, they slander it, and in that they are my antipodes' (NW vi: KSA 6/425; my translation).

9   Another prominent example from 1886: 'I then went on to give expression to my reverence for my first and only educator, the *great* Arthur Schopenhauer – I

9. *Schopenhauer as subtext.* In very many passages Schopenhauer is evoked by a choice of vocabulary or argumentative framework. In second part of this essay I shall look in detail at section 12 of the Third Essay of the *Genealogy of Morals*, one of the most important Nietzschean passages to be structured in this way by the presence of Schopenhauer as its unnamed but scarcely disguised subtext.

Schopenhauer appears 'as exemplar', 'as master', and 'as authority' predominantly in the period up to *Schopenhauer as Educator* (1874); and he occurs 'as antipode' only in the later period. But I shall argue that the early 'Schopenhauerian' Nietzsche had ceased surprisingly soon to be an uncritical pupil, while the later Nietzsche never ceased to value his own Schopenhauerian education or to recognize Schopenhauer as a cultural icon of tremendous significance.

According to his own account, in 1865 Nietzsche first picked up Schopenhauer's *The World as Will and Representation* in a second-hand bookshop in Leipzig:[10]

> I do not know what daemon whispered to me: 'Take this book home with you'. [...] At home I threw myself into the sofa corner with the treasure I had acquired, and started to allow that energetic, sombre genius to work upon me. Here every line screamed renunciation, denial, resignation, here I saw a mirror in which I caught sight of world, of life, and of my own mind in terrifying grandeur. Here the full, disinterested, sun-like eye of art looked upon me, here I saw sickness and healing, exile and sanctuary, hell and heaven.[11]

would now express it much more strongly, also more personally' (MA II Preface 1).

10 This incident occurred probably in October 1865. In a recent article Johann Figl contends that Nietzsche had acquaintance with Schopenhauer's philosophy some months earlier. A single sheet of notes which appears to date from Nietzsche's summer semester in Bonn contains an excerpt from Schopenhauer's 'Critique of the Kantian Philosophy' (Appendix to WWR I). See Johann Figl, 'Nietzsches Begegnung mit Schopenhauers Hauptwerk. Unter Heranziehung eines frühen unveröffentlichen Exzerptes', in Wolfgang Schirmacher (ed.), *Schopenhauer, Nietzsche und die Kunst* (Vienna: Passagen Verlag, 1991), pp. 89–100.

11 Translated from FS 3/298; see also EH ii 1.

Over the next few years Nietzsche seems infatuated with Schopen-hauer.[12] The reading of Schopenhauer's works continued to have profound effects on his emotions. Consoling Gersdorff over a bereavement, he wrote:

> Now, dear friend [...] you have experienced for yourself why our Schopenhauer values suffering and tribulations as a wonderful stroke of fate, the *deuteros plous* [second sailing] towards the denial of the will. [...] It is a time when you can ascertain for yourself what truth there is in Schopenhauer's teaching. If at this time the Fourth Book of his main work leaves upon you an ugly, troubling, burdensome impression, if it does *not* have the power to uplift you, to draw you away from severe external pain into the mood – melancholy yet happy – that seizes us on hearing noble music, the mood in which we see the earthly veil fall away from us: then I too want nothing more to do with this philosophy. Only someone filled with pain can and should speak definitively on such things: we others who stand in the midst of the stream of things and of life, merely yearning for the denial of the will as a blissful isle, we cannot judge whether the consolation of such a philosophy is adequate even for times of profound grief (to Gersdorff, 16 Jan. 1867: KSB 2/195–96).

Schopenhauer is revered as the writer who evokes a particular mood: a kind of aestheticized elevation which transforms and ennobles suffering, quieting the will and leading to a renunciation of one's earthly self – an accurate, if brief, restatement of some views found in the Fourth Book of *The World as Will and Representation*. 'Yearning for the denial of the will as a blessed isle' is a strikingly Schopenhauerian sentiment. Nietzsche seems not only to have com-prehended, but to have taken to heart, the culmination of Schopen-hauer's theory of value, in which salvation for humans consists in the spontaneous breaking of their will to life under the pressure of

---

12   Nietzsche calls Schopenhauer a philosophical demi-god in the letter to Deussen, Sept. 1868 (KSB 2/316). He is keen to 'make propaganda' for Schopenhauer, to persuade his friends and acquaintances to join him in his enthusiasm. He wishes for a journal in which brilliant young men write to further the cause of Schopenhauer's philosophy, and feels himself 'in the centre of Schopenhauerian threads that stretch throughout the world'. See letters to Franziska Nietzsche, 31 Jan. 1866 (KSB 2/109); to Deussen, 2 June 1868 (KSB 2/285); and to Gersdorff, 16 Feb. 1868 (KSB 2/258) and 28 Sept. 1869 (KSB 3/60).

inordinate suffering. Schopenhauer himself calls this the *deuteros plous* to salvation (WWR I, §68, 392). The 'first route' is the revelation of one's identity with the world, a transformative knowledge which quietens one's individual will, but is attained only rarely by saints. The more common 'second' way is through pain and sorrow, on which Schopenhauer quotes the words of Meister Eckhart: '"Suffering is the fleetest animal that bears you to perfection"' (WWR II, ch. 48, 633).[13]

During this period Nietzsche became acquainted with Richard Wagner, their relationship cemented by the revelation that the great composer too was devoted to Schopenhauer's philosophy.[14] Nietzsche found his Schopenhauerian mood in Wagner's art, and found in the man himself the epitome of the artistic genius Schopenhauer had described in the Third Book of *The World as Will and Representation*.[15] He wrote to Wagner:

> the best and most elevated moments of my life are linked with your name, and I know only one other man, your great spiritual brother Arthur Schopenhauer, whom I regard with such admiration, even in a kind of religious manner (*religione quadam*) (to Wagner, 22 May 1869: KSB 3/8).

All this suggests that Nietzsche's absorption in Schopenhauer was motivated more by a search for emotional security than by rigorous philosophical engagement. He was aware of the distinction:

> To write an apology for Schopenhauer [...] I have only to convey the fact that I look this life freely and bravely in the face now that my feet have found a place to stand. [...] Of course that is no more than a totally individual apology. But that's how things are. If anyone wishes to refute Schopenhauer for me with reasons, I murmur in his ear: 'But, my dear man, world-views are neither created nor destroyed by logic' (to Deussen, Oct./Nov. 1867: KSB 2/228–29).

Such an outlook explains the fact that, even at the height of his devotion to Schopenhauer 'as master', Nietzsche was aware of gaping

---

13   Nietzsche refers to the same saying, and Schopenhauer's use of it, in UB III 4.
14   See letter to Rohde, 9 Nov. 1868 (KSB 2/340–41).
15   See letters to Rohde, 9 Dec. 1868 (KSB 2/352), and to Gersdorff, 4 Aug. 1869 (KSB 3/35–36).

faults in Schopenhauer's philosophical system. Evidence for this lies in the relatively neglected notes 'On Schopenhauer' of 1868.

In these notes Nietzsche carefully distinguishes between Schopenhauer himself, whose person he wishes to respect, and the philosophical system which deserves criticism. His attitude is that 'the errors of great men are worthy of honour because they are more fruitful than the truths of the small'. The errors revealed are, however, fundamental. First, Schopenhauer's conception of the thing in itself. In Kant's philosophy the notion of the thing in itself was scarcely the strong point. But instead of abandoning it Schopenhauer tries to develop it further and make it the centrepiece of his system, by converting the unknown, shadowy thing in itself into the supposedly more determinate 'will'. Nietzsche complains that this 'will' is 'created only with the aid of a poetic intuition', not reached by any sound argument. Schopenhauer might reply that 'the thinker standing before the riddle of the world simply has no other means than guessing, in the hope [...] that a moment of genius will place on his lips the key to that script [...] which we call world'. But Nietzsche, now in analytical mode, cannot be satisfied with that. We see the 'the weave of the Schopenhauerian system' simply come apart in its author's hands: the world 'does not allow itself to be framed by the system'.

Nietzsche's main point here is that the thing in itself, if we want to use that concept at all, ought to be genuinely beyond our cognition. 'Will' therefore is merely an arbitrary label attached to an un- knowable. And yet Schopenhauer not only claims this labelling of the thing in itself is justified, but defends it by introducing a blatant contradiction. He insists that the thing in itself is never an object of experience for us, on the sound principle that any such object 'is once again [...] mere appearance and no longer thing in itself'. Yet in the same breath he requires the thing in itself 'to be thought of objectively', so that it must 'borrow name and concept from an object'. This flaw Nietzsche sees as wholly vitiating Schopenhauer's metaphysics. While predicates can supposedly be attached with confidence to the thing in itself – it is a single, timeless, groundless will – it is also required to remain a mysterious unknown x. Rather than solving 'the riddle of the world' Schopenhauer has invented a riddle that is more perplexing.

Nietzsche also finds puzzling Schopenhauer's conception of the connection between will and intellect. The intellect arises for Schopenhauer as an outgrowth or instrument of the will. Organisms develop the capacity for cognition, which for Schopenhauer is activity of the brain, as a way of satisfying the will's need for existence. This presupposes, then, that will pre-dates the arrival of any intellect in the world. But to understand the development of brain-based cognition in an organism, we have to picture the world prior to cognition as containing individual things in space and time and operating according to the law of causality: how so, if this law, and the very possibility of spatio-temporal individuation, are themselves dependent on cognition, as Schopenhauer's idealism demands? Schopenhauer concedes only 'hypothetical' existence to 'the geological processes that preceded life on earth': strictly they have 'no existence at all'. So he must either suppose that prior to cognition there existed only will, as undifferentiated non-causal thing in itself, or cheat and adopt a realist doctrine that material things exist and function without being present in the consciousness of a subject.

Thus already in 1868 Schopenhauer appears in Nietzsche's notes as a philosophical opponent, and sustains, as it were, an attack on the central nervous system, an attack that should make us doubt whether Nietzsche ever seriously adhered to Schopenhauer's metaphysics of the will, even in the earliest published writings which ostensibly support and are supported by Schopenhauer, namely *The Birth of Tragedy* (1872) and *Untimely Meditations* with its essay *Schopenhauer as Educator* of 1874.

Nietzsche said of this essay in his letter to Cosima that he wrote it with a clear division in his mind between the 'dogma' and the 'human being': so in the essay we hear of Schopenhauer's alleged qualities of character, but almost nothing about his philosophical position. The topic of *Schopenhauer as Educator* is really education rather than Schopenhauer.[16] At length Nietzsche deplores the contemporary subordination of the institutions of learning to the ends of the German state, and castigates professional university 'philosophers' as mercenary and vacuous – here at least following Schopenhauer's lead.[17] But his chief concern is with fostering a *culture*, whose goal must be 'the procreation of genius' (UB III 3) or 'the production of the philosopher, the artist and the saint within us and without us'. (UB III 5) If we seek to know the nature of a true philosopher (as opposed to the drudge-like scholar or man of learning) then Schopenhauer serves as exemplar: his persona is one of honesty, cheerfulness, and steadfastness (later we hear of his 'inflexible and rugged manliness' (UB III 2 and 7)). He is a true philosopher because of his heroic independence and because his philosophy says: 'this is the picture of all life [...] learn from it the meaning of your own life' (UB III 3).

Nietzsche helps himself, with little explanation, to Schopenhauer's formulations for those individuals capable of supreme moral or aesthetic achievement: the saint and the artistic genius. But if Schopenhauer is used as an authority standing behind Nietzsche's pronouncements in the essay, it is only in the vaguest manner. Nietzsche quotes a passage in which Schopenhauer maintains, '[a] happy life is impossible: the highest that man can attain to is a *heroic one* [...] his will, mortified a whole life long by effort and labour, ill success and the world's ingratitude, is extinguished in

---

16   Nietzsche later says as much in *Ecce homo*: 'What I was fundamentally trying to do in these essays was something altogether different from psychology: an unequaled problem of education [...] was seeking its first expression. Broadly speaking, I caught hold of two famous and as yet altogether undiagnosed types [Schopenhauer and Wagner] [...] in order to say something, in order to have at hand a few more formulas, signs, means of language' (EH 'UB' 3).

17   Michael Tanner's comment on this: 'Schopenhauer had done it far better himself in Parerga and Paralipomena' (*Nietzsche* (Oxford: Oxford University Press, 1994), p. 20); see Schopenhauer's 'On Philosophy at the Universities' (PP I, 139–97).

Nirvana',[18] and in sections 3–4 of the essay there is a sprinkling of Schopenhauerian phrases: 'Profound depression [...] at the value-lessness of his existence', 'sacrifice of the ego', 'a striving [...] which leads towards resignation', 'a kind of denying and destroying that is the discharge of [a] mighty longing for sanctification and salvation'. Constructing any philosophical position out of these materials would demand scrutiny of the system of ideas in which they originate. But it is never really made clear how these ideas cohere, nor how they would help to propagate the kind of culture Nietzsche urges upon Germany. In *Schopenhauer as Educator*, then, the eponymous hero appears primarily as an exemplar, and only obliquely as a philosophical authority and an organizing subtext.

In *The Birth of Tragedy* the presence of Schopenhauer is more essential, if more complex and troubling. Nietzsche summons him as authority to corroborate the assertion that for 'men of philosophy' the world of our experience is a mere appearance (*Schein*), even a collection of phantoms or dream-images. Soon the motif of illusion and dream is taken up by the figure of Apollo, of whom

> we might say [...] in an eccentric sense [*in einem excentrischen Sinne*] what Schopenhauer says of the man caught up in the veil of *mâyâ*: 'Just as the boatman sits in his little boat [...] so in the midst of a world full of suffering the individual man calmly sits, supported by and trusting the *principium individuationis*' [...] we might even describe Apollo as the glorious divine image of the *principium individuationis* (GT 1).[19]

Nietzsche then explains the opposing figure of Dionysus in terms of the fragmentation of this principle of individuation, and the mixture of dread and ecstasy which, again according to Schopenhauer, that fragmentation can induce.

Much of Nietzsche's diction here is Schopenhaueresque: 'the principle of sufficient reason seems suspended', 'subjectivity disappears completely into self-forgetfulness', 'ecstasy [...] rises up from

18   UB III 4 (Nietzsche is quoting from PP II, §§172, 322).
19   Nietzsche quotes from WWR I, §63, 352–53.

man's innermost core, indeed from nature', 'as if the veil of *mâyâ* had been rent and now hung in rags before the mysterious primal Oneness' – demanding the reader's awareness of the metaphysical system in which 'man's innermost core', identical with the whole world, is the one undifferentiated will that lies beyond individuation, and in which aesthetic experience is marked by the suspension of the principle of sufficient reason, the cessation of willing, forgetfulness of one's subjectivity and individuality, and incipient dispersal of the illusion that reality as a whole separates into individuals, a seeing behind what Schopenhauer, borrowing from Indian philosophy, had called the veil of *mâyâ*. Without this key it is hard to interpret Nietzsche's words. And yet Nietzsche's new distinction is only an off-centre analogue of Schopenhauer's. It is only 'in an eccentric sense' (a phrase translators seem to overlook)[20] that Nietzsche can describe Apollo (and by extension Dionysus) using Schopenhauer's terms. He does not propound the doctrine that the thing in itself, lying beneath individuation, is will.[21] His construction of the symbols of Apollo and Dionysus exploits Schopenhauer's opposition between individuation and the world-whole, while the Schopenhauerian system hovers eerily in the background, unasserted but indispensable.

Nietzsche's train of thought moves on to Dionysus' companion, Silenus, whose vision ('the best of all things is something entirely outside your grasp: not to be born, not to *be*, to be *nothing*' (GT 3)) readily suggests Schopenhauer's pessimism as a subtext. Yet in other references to Schopenhauer the term 'pessimism' is applied to something different. Later, as Nietzsche attempts a closer application of his ideas to German culture, Schopenhauer is praised along with Kant for a 'victory over optimism' and for an insight that 'ushered in a culture which I should like to call tragic' (GT 18). This seemingly

---

20   Francis Golffing is an exception; see his translation in *'The Birth of Tragedy' and 'The Genealogy of Morals'* (Garden City, NY: Doubleday, 1956).

21   The discussion by Henry Staten, *Nietzsche's Voice* (Ithaca, NY: Cornell University Press, 1990), p. 192ff., is invaluable here.

concerns not the evaluative view of life adopted by Silenus, but the insight that experience is illusory and only masquerades as knowledge of the world's essence. To the extent that he holds experience to be illusory and to obscure the world's 'essence', Nietzsche is relying on a further use of Schopenhauer as an authority, and through him Kant's transcendental idealism, or Kant's transcendental idealism as read by Schopenhauer.[22] I suppose we might call the resulting view a kind of epistemological pessimism.

Elsewhere in *The Birth of Tragedy* Schopenhauer's theory of music is to the fore. In section 5 Nietzsche openly disagrees with his predecessor for the first time in print, but his rhetoric is still deferential. He proposes to resolve a difficulty in Schopenhauer's view of song 'in his spirit and to his honour', by exploiting 'his profound metaphysics of music'. Schopenhauer had said that song is poised between two opposing states, the will-lessness of aesthetic contemplation and the urgent presence of the subject's own willings as an individual. Nietzsche offers to straighten out the theory using an extension of Schopenhauer's own idea that subjectivity and the will are impediments in the aesthetic realm. But is this what Nietzsche should be saying? He states in full Schopenhauerian mode that art is inconceivable 'without objectivity, without pure contemplation devoid of interest (*reines interesseloses Anschauen*)'. In *Genealogy* III, 12 (as we shall see in Section 2 below) Nietzsche's attitude to Schopenhauer's version of objectivity, and to its *Anschauung ohne Interesse*, is one of vehement opposition. Should he be supporting it even in *The Birth of Tragedy*? According to Michael Tanner, this statement by Nietzsche is 'incongruous and unthinking' since 'the main thrust of [*The Birth of Tragedy*] is that in Dionysiac art we come

---

22 Kant and Schopenhauer are also said to have 'introduced an infinitely more profound and serious consideration of ethical questions and art, which we might almost describe as Dionysiac wisdom in conceptualized form' (GT 19), though it is obscure what their 'wisdom' here consisted in, especially since their views of art, and even more of ethics, are divergent in many respects. Nietzsche rests his case on a breakthrough his predecessor has allegedly made, while leaving its nature dismayingly vague. Note the telling 'almost' in the passage quoted.

as close as possible to identifying with the will'.[23] But Nietzsche
cannot have it both ways: if he fails to assert the connection between
will-lessness and the aesthetic, he fails to save Schopenhauer's view
of poetry from inconsistency, while if he asserts it, he falls into an
inconsistency of his own.

A vital question for *The Birth of Tragedy* is: What lies beyond
individuation? Nietzsche is cagey here, and talks simply of the
'primal Oneness' – an uninformative phrase, since if you think away
the separation of reality into a plurality of things, then what (if
anything) remains cannot but be Oneness. Given Nietzsche's praise
for Schopenhauer's metaphysics of music, we might be forgiven for
inferring that the primal Oneness ('prior to and beyond all
phenomena') is Schopenhauer's metaphysical will, the will as thing in
itself. When Nietzsche asks himself, 'As what does music appear in
the mirror of images and concepts [in lyric poetry]?', he answers: 'It
appears as will, taking the term in Schopenhauer's sense' (GT 6),
making it terribly easy for the reader to think he endorses the view of
music as the direct expression or copy of the metaphysical will in
itself, and *a fortiori* that he endorses the metaphysics which in private
he had already found riddled with holes. However, in this passage he
need not be committing himself to Schopenhauer's metaphysics. The
point is that lyric poetry must represent something in its images and
concepts, and what it represents are *phenomena* of willing. This does
not necessitate a metaphysics of the will as thing in itself, only the
view that *empirical* reality as seized upon by the lyric poet is 'nature,
and himself within it, as eternally willing, desiring, yearning'.[24]

In section 16, though, Nietzsche seems to want his own view of
music to coincide even more closely with Schopenhauer's theory,
indeed *to be* Schopenhauer's theory, which he calls 'the most
important in all aesthetics'. Over seven hundred consecutive words
are quoted straight from *The World as Will and Representation*
(WWR I, §52, 252–53), presenting in all its essentials Schopenhauer's

23   See *The Birth of Tragedy*, ed. Tanner, p. 120, n. 16.
24   See Staten, p. 198, on this issue.

view that music is the immediate copy of the metaphysical will, the thing in itself. Nietzsche does not dispute this doctrine or qualify it, but affirms *propria persona* that 'music is the immediate language of the will'. So he appears to rest passively on Schopenhauer's authority, not raising his earlier fatal criticisms of the metaphysical doctrine of the will. Later in the same section Dionysiac art 'expresses the will in its omnipotence, behind the *principium individuationis*, the eternal life that lies beyond the phenomenal world'. If this is not a restatement of Schopenhauer's view it is hard to know how to construe it at all. One must concur with Henry Staten's verdict that 'Nietzsche apparently tried to write the metaphysical will out of *The Birth of Tragedy* but found, on arriving at section 16, that he could not do it'.[25]

Schopenhauer reappears briefly in section 20 as a steely Düreresque knight who 'lacked all hope, but sought the truth; he is peerless'. In the first impression of the book Nietzsche had also referred in section 1 to 'unser grosser Schopenhauer' ('our great Schopenhauer'),[26] and though 'our' and 'great' were subsequently removed, there is still adulation in the book – something not acknowledged in Nietzsche's well-known retrospective remark about Schopenhauer's peculiar fragrance adhering 'only to a few formulas' (EH 'GT' 1). The remark falsifies the tone of *The Birth of Tragedy* and parts of its substance. Given that Schopenhauer presides over the inauguration of the Apollo-Dionysus distinction, is congratulated for his view that ordinary experience is an illusion, and praised for the pessimism that inaugurates a new tragic age, while the all-important 'spirit of music' can be explained only with the help of prolonged incorporation of his text, his presence amounts to more than a superficial dusting of scent over Nietzsche's position.[27] In sum,

25   Staten, p. 192. Staten points to several passages earlier in GT where 'will' had stood in Nietzsche's corresponding draft in the earlier piece 'Die dionysische Weltanschauung' but had been written out in preparing the book.

26   See KSA 14/46.

27   For completeness let us note a final reference to Schopenhauer in GT 22. Schopenhauer's parable of the porcupines (PP II, §396, 651–52) is used against

Schopenhauer in *The Birth of Tragedy* is something rich and strange: a composite of authority, subtext, exemplar, and master. Whether he enhances the book is an unanswerable question. It is impossible to imagine its existing without him.[28]

For all this, the later Nietzsche is right to regard *The Birth of Tragedy* as already tending in an anti-Schopenhauerian direction. At the foundation of anything of value in Schopenhauer's eyes lie 'the instincts of pity, self-abnegation, self-sacrifice [...] on the basis of which he *said No* to life and to himself' (GM Preface 5), and for him tragedy in particular yields 'knowledge that the world and life can give no true satisfaction, and are therefore not worth our attachment to them' so that its value lies in its leading to resignation.[29] The Nietzsche of 1886–87[30] bristles at this: from the start he had opposed any idea of retreat into nothingness in the face of the world's horrors. Helped by Schopenhauer's conviction that morality, art, and the world religions – at least Christianity, Buddhism, and Brahmanism[31] – all cohere in their ultimate value because they rest on some lapse or abolition of the individual's egoistic will to life, Nietzsche now pinpoints this 'sublimest enticement' as the greatest danger underlying European culture: a perversely self-gratifying seduction to 'nothingness', a self-devaluation in the name of value, a self-destruction in the name of salvation. His horrified scepticism clarifies his own defining trait:

art critics: they must huddle together for warmth, but spring apart again because of their prickliness.

28   'This is the book that could not have been written without Schopenhauer, whether it is obedient to him or whether it flagrantly violates his teachings' (Erich Heller, 'Nietzsche's Last Words about Art versus Truth', in *The Importance of Nietzsche: Ten Essays* (Chicago: University of Chicago Press, 1988), pp. 158–72 (p. 171)).

29   Quoted by Nietzsche from WWR II. 433–34 (GTVS 6).

30   See GTVS 6, and GM Preface 5.

31   See WWR II, ch. 48, 628, 633.

[Around 1876] I grasped that my instinct went into the opposite direction from Schopenhauer's: toward a justification of life, even at its most terrible, ambiguous, and mendacious; for this I had the formula 'Dionysian' (NF Autumn 1887, 9[42]: KSA 12/354-55).[32]

We might say that from his crucial winter in Sorrento onwards Nietzsche comes into his own as the anti-Schopenhauer, and that much of his later thought is tightly integrated around this opposition. Schopenhauer: 'The value of art is its removing us from the realm of willing, desiring, attaining, and suffering'; anti-Schopenhauer: 'No, the value of art is as a great self-affirmation of the will to life, as a stimulus to life, an arouser of the will.' Schopenhauer: 'Beyond the veil of empirical particularities lies a realm of timeless realities'; anti-Schopenhauer: 'There is no beyond, there is merely this world and it is the instinct towards self-slander that prompts us to project a beyond.' Schopenhauer: 'That the world has no moral significance is a pernicious perversity of the mind, personified in religion as the antichrist';[33] anti-Schopenhauer: 'The world has no moral significance, there are merely moral interpretations of the world; so let us affirm this "antichrist".' Schopenhauer: 'Value lies in pity, because in feeling with another I glimpse the illusoriness of individuality'; anti-Schopenhauer: 'Pity is a temptation to be resisted, a self-gratification which diminishes the pitying individual's strength and demeans the pitied.' Schopenhauer: 'Only through the denial of the will to life can this pain-ridden existence be redeemed'; anti-Schopenhauer: 'Only through the affirmation of life with all its pain can strength and greatness be achieved.' Schopenhauer: 'It would be better if I had not existed, if there were no world'; anti-Schopenhauer: 'I love and will everything that has happened, and wish its recurrence endlessly.'

But there is more here than the simple negation of doctrines. Once Nietzsche is secure in this opposition, he is able to acknowledge the intimate and essential role that Schopenhauer, and his own adherence to Schopenhauer, have played in his own thought. Three

32   A version of this fragment appears as note 1005 in *The Will to Power*.
33   This paraphrases PP II, §109, 201.

passages from 1886 contain the most subtle and explicit self-assessments Nietzsche makes with regard to Schopenhauer:

> When, in the third *Untimely Meditation*, I then went on to give expression to my reverence for my first and only educator, the *great* Arthur Schopenhauer – I would now express it much more strongly, also more personally – I was, so far as my own development was concerned, already deep in the midst of moral scepticism and destructive analysis, *that is to say in the critique and likewise the intensifying of pessimism as understood hitherto*, and already 'believed in nothing any more', as the people puts it, not even in Schopenhauer (MA II Preface 1).

> Perhaps [...] I might be reproached with having employed a certain amount of 'art', a certain amount of false-coinage: for example, that I knowingly-wilfully closed my eyes before Schopenhauer's blind will to morality at a time when I was already sufficiently clearsighted about morality [...] Supposing, however, that all this were true [...] what do *you* know, what *could* you know, of how much cunning in self-preservation, how much reason and higher safeguarding, is contained in such self-deception – or of how much falsity I shall *require* if I am to continue to permit myself the luxury of *my* truthfulness? (MA I Preface 1).

> Whoever has endeavored with some enigmatic longing, as I have, to think pessimism through to its depths and to liberate it from the half-Christian, half-German narrowness and simplicity in which it has finally presented itself to our century, namely, in the form of Schopenhauer's philosophy; whoever has really, with an Asiatic and supra-Asiatic eye, looked into, down into the most world-denying of all possible ways of thinking – beyond good and evil and no longer, like the Buddha and Schopenhauer, under the spell and delusion of morality – may just thereby, without really meaning to do so, have opened his eyes to the opposite ideal: the ideal of the most high-spirited, alive, and world-affirming human being who has not only come to terms and learned to get along with whatever was and is, but who wants to have *what was and is* repeated into all eternity, shouting insatiably *da capo* [...] (JGB 56).

Nietzsche reckons he has achieved a stance beyond morality, in the sense that he is able to treat the moral vocabulary always as an object of evaluation, never as itself the medium of evaluation. But (in a nice pun) he presents himself as self-deceived *en route* about Schopenhauer's 'blind will to morality'. The self-deception lay in not seeing how Schopenhauer used an essentially Christian, self-denying morality as a block against the ultimate valuelessness of life, how his interposing of the possibility of selfless compassion between himself and a wholly despairing view of the world was still a way of regarding the world from within the moral mode of evaluation. The 'intensification' or 'deepening' of pessimism consists in not sparing moral evaluations from the same pessimistic gaze, finding them too as symptoms expressing some underlying 'will'. Schopenhauer expresses in extreme and concentrated form the 'will to nothingness' Nietzsche had diagnosed as the driving force behind Christian morality. But now he can say Yes to his own past, his own succumbing to the sickness he needed to suffer and recuperate from in order to discover an opposite ideal. Hence Schopenhauer and his own self-deception about Schopenhauer are embraced, more strongly and more personally than ever, as essential to his becoming himself.

2.   Schopenhauer as Subtext in *Genealogy* III, 12

To show how the Nietzsche of the 1880s thinks both antithetically to Schopenhauer and in Schopenhauerian patterns, I shall concentrate on section 12 of the Third Essay of *On the Genealogy of Morals*. One of Nietzsche's better known passages and the classic locus for his 'perspectivism', this is also a prime example of Schopenhauer's persistent presence as a subtext for the later Nietzsche.

Schopenhauer is not named in this section but (as not every reader seems to notice)[34] he is quoted directly: the words 'pure, will-less, painless, timeless subject of knowledge' comprise Schopen-hauer's exact formula for the subject in aesthetic experience, the subject whose will is blissfully suspended and who remains as a

---

34   For an earlier analysis of GM III, 12, that makes its Schopenhauerian background clear, see John E. Atwell, 'Nietzsche's Perspectivism', *Southern Journal of Philosophy*, 19 (1981), 157–70.

passive 'mirror' of objective reality. The first point to stress is that Nietzsche's prominent use of the term 'objectivity' later in this section gains its energy by tapping into his predecessor's account, in which aesthetic experience is a release from subjectivity and a route to the discovery of Platonic Ideas. In this account the subject of aesthetic experience allegedly leaves behind empirical particulars and survives as the receptor for the eternal Ideas which are the 'adequate objectification' of the thing in itself, or the nearest approach we can make within possible experience to reality 'itself'. At the same time the subject of aesthetic experience loses the sense of himself or herself as an individual and becomes, in Schopenhauer's words, 'the *single* world-eye that looks out from every cognizing being' ('das *eine* Weltauge, was [*sic*] aus allen erkennenden Wesen blickt').[35] Thus, allegedly, the object is raised to the level of the universal, and the subject, by way of a loosening of the sense of his or her individuality, progresses towards an identification with the world as a whole. Aesthetic experience achieves greater objectivity than everyday understanding or scientific knowledge, in that the explanatory connections pertaining among the subject's representations – connections instrumental in attaining the goals of willing – are all dissolved. Because these connections of space, time, and causality are subjective, being forms inherent in the subject, their temporary abeyance yields a cognition closer to 'what truly is', as Plato would put it.[36]

Nietzsche contends that Schopenhauerian objectivity is a sham for two reasons. It makes theoretical mistake about the nature of

35   WWR I, §38, 198.
36   Schopenhauer's motto for the Third Book of WWR is Plato's 'Ti to on men aei, genesin de ouk echon [...]?' ('What is that which always is, and has no coming into being?') The same title page announces 'the Platonic Idea' as 'the object of art'. For Schopenhauer's problematic conflation of Plato's Ideas and Kant's thing in itself, see WWR I, §§31–2, 170–78, and my discussion in 'Knowledge and Tranquility: Schopenhauer on the Value of Art', in Dale Jacquette (ed.), *Schopenhauer, Philosophy, and the Arts* (Cambridge: Cambridge University Press, 1996), pp. 39–61.

knowledge, and it misrepresents its own motivation, concealing through dishonesty or self-deception its own end-directedness, its own specific expression of a 'will'. In both cases, as we shall see, Nietzsche's objection adopts a quasi-Schopenhauerian position in order to counter Schopenhauer. First, as the final paragraph of section 12 makes clear, in demanding the lapse of all active, interpreting powers, and hoping to leave in operation something resembling an eye that looks in no particular direction and from nowhere in particular, Schopenhauerian objectivity demands an impossibility. Such interpreting powers attach necessarily to any striving, embodied being, for whom to lack such powers would be to have no cognition at all. Secondly, the aspiration towards utter will-lessness is self-deluding, since the very act of conceiving such a would-be escape from the desires and attachments of embodiment is itself the fulfilment of an end, the stilling of pressing desire. The theory of pure painless objectivity owes its existence to a need within the theorizer.

But before examining Nietzsche's dispute with the Schopen-hauerian brand of objectivity, let us look beyond aesthetic experience. For related notions carry over into Schopenhauer's ethics and philosophy of religion, and into all his propositions concerning value. In describing those in whom the will to life has turned and who have undergone the ultimate redemption which he calls the denial of the will (the 'blessed isle' for which the younger Nietzsche expressed a yearning), Schopenhauer asks us to recall his characterization of aesthetic experience and imagine the 'pure, will-less, timeless' state prolonged indefinitely.[37] Aesthetic objectivity thus prefigures the disintegration of one's ability to place value in the striving, egoistic, material individual one is – that disintegration which is for Schopen-hauer the sole hope of cheating life of its emptiness of any genuine, positive worth. The connection of this disintegration also with ethical value is made clear when he says that 'the identity of all beings, justice, righteousness, philanthropy, denial of the will to life, spring from *one* root [...] the virtuous action is a momentary passing through

37   See WWR I, §68, 390.

the point, the permanent return to which is the denial of the will to life'(WWR II, ch. 48, 610).

We should read section 12 in the context of the Third Essay's claim to decipher the meaning of ascetic ideals, to provide 'the answer to the question whence the ascetic ideal [...] derives its tremendous *power*' (EH 'GM'). Schopenhauer can help us elucidate both Nietzsche's question and his answer, the claim that humanity would rather will nothingness than not will.[38] For Nietzsche all apparent goals and sources of meaning for humanity have posited objects or states whose value transcends that of our ordinary human existence, and have relied on an attitude of self-denial or self-belittlement, in which one estimates one's own worth as low by comparison with that whose value is supposedly absolute and unconditioned. This belittling of the self simultaneously allows the aspiration to rise above ourselves: we can improve upon the meagre value of our existence and be brought closer to whatever has transcendent value, if only we exercise a severe self-suppression and extinguish many instincts and drives. The object of transcendent value might be God, or the moral law, or truth, or, most relevant here, one's own idealized existence as will-less, objectively mirroring self. Schopenhauer's notion of redemptive objectivity is a paradigmatic instance of the ascetic ideal's combined self-belittlement and self-transcendence. It presupposes that one can cease to acquiesce in one's pre-ordained place as an individuated outlet for the world-will's self-expression, and rise above the disvalue of ordinary human existence towards a state of salvation or redemption (*Erlösung*).

Although Nietzsche's critical conception of the ascetic ideal potentially subsumes almost every aspect of extant culture, Schopenhauer provides the most immediate and decisive model of the ideal – and also the most vulnerable. In Platonism or Christianity, my fallen or embodied existence stands to be redeemed by my continuation as a pure, timeless, immaterial essence, conceived as a return to something that I truly am. For Schopenhauer, by contrast, there is

---

38   See ibid., and GM III, 1 and 28.

no immortal soul, no divine purpose, no rational essence in me or in the world. The only 'order of things' is the brute fact of existence and the blind striving for existence. The 'real self' is the will to life (WWR II, ch. 48, 606). My essence is an unchosen tendency towards perpetuating life, that presses me on from striving to illusory satisfaction and back to more striving. So the only hope is that this *essence* within each human being will manage to gain enough knowledge, or sustain enough suffering, that it is brought to *negating itself.* Schopenhauer's conception of redemptive objectivity (as I have called it) approaches the limit of self-destructiveness, and fulfils its paradigmatic function for Nietzsche because of its very extremity.

I have spoken of objectivity and release from subjectivity, self-belittlement and self-transcendence, and now of self-negation. This may appear to take us far from the aesthetic theory in which the phrase Nietzsche quotes – 'pure, will-less, timeless subject of knowledge' – is at home. How can that aesthetic theory lead us to the 'limit of self-destructiveness'? Why should 'objective knowledge', which requires a knowing subject for whom this state is conceived as blissful, be linked at all with an aspiration towards the extinction of the subject? Unless we can see how these ideas are connected in Schopenhauer, we stand little chance of understanding them as Nietzsche's subtext in the *Genealogy.*

Schopenhauer's philosophy carries out an unfolding of a long continuum of states which redeem what he sees as the absence of positive value in life. Aesthetic experience is at one end of the continuum, extinction at the other. The key to the unity of his thought is the thesis that value can be retrieved *to the extent that the individual embodiment of will abates.* One wills less and less, and locates significance less and less in the individual living manifestation of will that one happens to be. In aesthetic experience willing ceases totally but temporarily, and one ceases to be aware of oneself as individual. In achieving the morally virtuous stance, one makes little or no distinction between self and the remainder of the world, and loses something of the egoistic impulse to satisfy the desires attaching to the individual.

Up to this point the subject of knowledge remains: it apprehends the aesthetic universals, it regards other living things as equal in value to itself. But further along this same continuum of detachment from individuality are states which can be described as extinction. At the furthest point is the individual's death, which Schopenhauer describes as 'the great opportunity no longer to be I' (WWR II, ch. 41, 507). But the state of 'denial of the will' occupies a point poised between objective knowing and extinction. In this state one has not died; one continues to exist, but experiences the saintly or fully resigned vision which eschews assertion of will and identification of self with any individual component of the world-whole. Philosophical analysis must stop here, for Schopenhauer, and yield to mystical utterance or silence. In the final section of his book (WWR I, §71, 408–12) he must describe denial of the will in contradictory ways: 'Only knowledge remains; the will has vanished', and 'such a state cannot really be called knowledge, since it no longer has the form of subject and object'. 'We have before our eyes in perfect saintliness the denial and surrender of all willing', but this 'now appears to us as a transition into empty *nothingness*'. Thus the attainment of objective knowledge, purged of will and independent of individuality, is described as assuming the status of 'pure, painless, timeless subject', but is also the beginning of a movement towards salvation which must eventually come to rest in nothingness.

The sublimely eloquent and unnerving final pages of *The World as Will and Representation* present nothingness as the opposite of willing, and as the radical remedy against it. Nothingness is 'the final goal which hovers behind all virtue and holiness'; we are naturally disposed to fear it, but must learn to embrace it, or face the lack of any consolation:

> Before us there is certainly left only nothing; but that which struggles against this flowing away into nothing, namely our nature, is indeed just the will to life which we ourselves are [...] That we abhor nothingness so much is simply another way of saying that we will life so much, and that we are nothing but this

will [...] Yet this consideration is the only one that can permanently console us, when, on the one hand, we have recognized incurable suffering and endless misery as essential to the phenomenon of the will, to the world, and on the other see the world melt away with the abolished will, and retain before us only empty nothingness (WWR I, §71, 411).

In the Third Essay of the *Genealogy* Nietzsche's pointed expression 'willing nothingness' (*das Nichts wollen*) is all the more deadly for its deliberate misuse of Schopenhauerian terms. In Schopenhauer's language you cannot really talk of 'willing nothingness'. 'Nothingness' and 'willing' are supposed to be mutually exclusive conditions. But Nietzsche is not fooled. Why is nothingness portrayed as the ultimate 'goal'; why is it conceived as offering 'consolation'; why is it posited as the occasion of redeeming value, to be positively welcomed as such? Nietzsche's well-founded allegation is that for Schopenhauer and for the generic Schopenhauerian individual, who stands well this side of nothingness, *the thought of nothingness* is the target of an ardent *will*. The state of nothingness, if it were attainable, might be state of will-lessness. But meanwhile the theorist of nothingness is willing it mightily as the fulfilment of needs of his own.

More precisely, Schopenhauer's system wants or needs some validation to be granted to existence, otherwise it will fold under total despair. We see this need fulfilled when Schopenhauer announces that 'nothing else can be stated as the aim of our existence except the knowledge that it would be better for us not to exist' (WWR II, ch. 48, 605). Life has the point of coming to realize its own pointlessness. Nietzsche's formula 'willing nothingness rather than not willing' expresses this feature of Schopenhauer's axiological system acutely. What propels the Schopenhauerian individual towards wanting and welcoming the prospect of an attenuated existence as pure, painless, timeless subject of knowledge? Surely the need to enact, at least in theory, a peculiarly gratifying form of self-extinction, the extinction of the organic, affective, desiring self.

With the wider picture in place the attentive reader will find Schopenhauerian markers throughout section 12. Nietzsche begins:

> Suppose such an incarnate will to contradiction and antinaturalness is induced to
> *philosophize*: upon what will it vent its innermost contrariness? Upon what is
> felt most certainly to be real and actual: it will look for error precisely where the
> instinct of life most unconditionally posits truth.

The phrase 'will to contradiction and antinaturalness' is a play on
words which takes a stab at Schopenhauer's central idea of 'will to
life'. What Nietzsche calls the 'instinct of life' posits truth in the
tangible particularities of empirical knowledge. But here is a life
form, the ascetic priest (and the philosopher in his commonest guise –
see GM III 10), whose fundamental drive is *against* life. The ascetic
character paradoxically tends towards a kind of survival or continuation of existence, and is in that respect a proper manifestation of
'will to life'. But that whose existence is fostered is the attitude of
negation towards life, an anti-corporeal, anti-sensual, anti-sexual
orientation. And the paradigm of the philosopher who exhibits this
apparently contradictory 'will to life' is Schopenhauer himself – as
witness the case-study in section 5, where he was called the 'genuine
philosopher [who] pays homage to the ascetic ideal'.

Nietzsche continues: 'It will, for example, like the ascetics of the
Vedanta philosophy, downgrade physicality to an illusion; likewise
pain, multiplicity, the entire antithesis "subject" and "object" – errors,
nothing but errors!' Vedanta philosophy is a clear signpost towards
Schopenhauer, since he revered this school of thought and especially
its doctrine of 'exaltation beyond our own individuality'.[39] Schopenhauer remarks that the *Upanishads* describe a state of contemplation
in which 'subject and object and all knowledge vanish' (WWR II,
ch. 48, 611), but he is using Schopenhauerian rather than Vedanta
terms, and the same must be said of Nietzsche. And of course
Schopenhauer's metaphysics itself expressly proclaims that subject
and object, multiplicity, physicality (dependent on the subjective
forms of space, time, and causality), and pain (dependent on one's
embodiment in, and attitudinal identification with, an individual
willing being) are illusions from the point of view of reality *in itself.*

---

39   See WWR I, §39, 205–06; §63, 355; II, ch. 49, 639.

Nietzsche continues:

> To renounce belief in one's ego, to deny one's own 'reality' – what a triumph! not merely over the senses, over appearance, but a much higher kind of triumph, a violation and cruelty against *reason* – a voluptuous pleasure that reaches its height when the ascetic self-contempt and self-mockery of reason declares: '*there is* a realm of truth and being, but reason is *excluded* from it!'[40]

'Renouncing belief in one's own ego' reflects two aspects of Schopenhauer's position, one descriptive, the other evaluative. As we have seen, Schopenhauer finds value in the loss of one's self-identification as 'I'. But this is not only a redemptive release. It realigns us with the true state of things. In his analysis of the self he says that the knowing and conscious I 'has only a conditioned, in fact, properly speaking, a merely apparent reality. Far from being the absolutely first thing (as Fichte taught, for example), it is at bottom tertiary, since it presupposes the organism, and the organism presupposes the will' (WWR I, ch. 22, 278). The will is ontologically basic and un-individuated. To move away from regarding the 'I' as a secure primary entity is to be relieved of an error and to come nearer to the 'realm of truth and being'.

Next Nietzsche turns and affirms this apparently self-denying movement:

> But precisely because we seek knowledge, let us not be ungrateful to such resolute reversals of accustomed perspectives and valuations with which the spirit has, with apparent mischievousness and futility, raged against itself for so long: to see differently in this way for once, to *want* to see differently (*anders-sehn-wollen*), is no small discipline and preparation of the intellect for its future 'objectivity' – the latter not understood as 'intuition (*Anschauung*) without interest' (which is a nonsensical absurdity), but as the ability *to control* one's

---

40 Here Nietzsche directs an aside at Kant's conception of 'intelligible character', of which, he says, we can comprehend only its incomprehensibility to us. Even this has a connection with Schopenhauer, for whom 'intelligible character' rates as one of Kant's 'masterly' notions; see esp. WWR I, §55, 286–90. Schopenhauer treats the intelligible character as an atemporal metaphysical essence underlying the empirical character of each of us, and as the true locus of freedom.

For and Against and to dispose of them, so that one knows how to employ a *variety* of perspectives and affective interpretations in the service of knowledge.

Three brief points here: (1) '*Anschauung* without interest' is a semi-Kantian formula for Schopenhauer's notion of will-less contemplation in aesthetic experience – Schopenhauer's rather than Kant's, because it is in Schopenhauer that the artistic genius has the specifically cognitive value of attaining heightened 'objectivity'.[41] The Schopenhauerian genius possesses an intellect that can sever its moorings in the bodily will and cast off to a greater extent than usual its subjective, will-serving mode of experience. (2) Nietzsche's word 'objectivity' is placed in quotation marks because it is borrowed ironically from Schopenhauer's account in which objectivity increases proportionately with progression towards will-lessness and escape from individuality. Nietzsche's notion of objectivity situates itself as the antithesis of Schopenhauer's. (3) 'For' and 'Against' are movements of the will which, though they must interfere with the quest for Schopenhauerian objectivity, are for Nietzsche both ineliminable and valuable components of knowledge.

We come now to the famous culmination of section 12, in which the subtext at last breaks through to the surface and becomes quoted text:

> Henceforth, my dear philosophers, let us be on guard against the dangerous old conceptual fiction that posited a 'pure, will-less, painless, timeless subject of knowledge'; let us guard against the snares of such contradictory concepts as 'pure reason', 'absolute spirituality', 'knowledge in itself': these always demand that we should think of an eye that is completely unthinkable, an eye turned in no particular direction, in which the active and interpreting forces, through which alone seeing becomes seeing *something*, are supposed to be lacking; these always demand a nonsense and an absurdity of an eye. There is *only* a perspective seeing, *only* a perspective 'knowing'; and the *more* affects we allow to speak about one thing, the *more* eyes, different eyes, we can use to observe one thing, the more complete will our 'concept' of this thing, our 'objectivity',

---

41   For the contrast between these frequently assimilated aesthetic theories, see my 'Kant's Aesthetics and the "Empty Cognitive Stock"', *Philosophical Quarterly*, 47 (1997), 461–63.

be. But to eliminate the will altogether, to suspend each and every affect, supposing we were capable of this – would that not mean *castrating* the intellect?...

Readers should scarcely need reminding of Schopenhauer's use of the eye metaphor: the subject of pure passive will-less contemplation is not the individual, but the 'clear eye of the world', viewing it as if from nowhere. This is an attempt to free the intellect entirely from the will. The driving force behind all ordinary cognitive transactions with the world is the will, which constrains the intellect to follow the needs and interests of the organism, some of them unconscious. That is why escaping the will demands a kind of 'pure' cognition which is quite extraordinary. Schopenhauer polarizes will and intellect, and likes to tell us that while the brain is the focus of the intellect, the genitals are the focus of the will. Hence Nietzsche's 'castrating the intellect' is a direct assault on Schopenhauer's polar distinction, replacing it with the idea of the intellect as *essentially* will-driven, rather than obstructed by, or at the mercy of, a will that is alien to it. While Schopenhauer's ideal is to eliminate or suspend the will, remaining as a pure, painless intellect, Nietzsche not only doubts that one could remain at all in such a state, but suggests it would destroy the capacity for knowledge.

There is an argument fairly near the surface in this final passage: (1) all knowledge is active interpretation rather than passive reception of data; (2) all active interpretation is in the service of the will; so (3) all knowledge is in the service of the will. Hence Schopenhauer's beloved will-lessness could not be a state of knowledge. But note how impeccably Schopenhauerian the assumptions of this argument are. It was Schopenhauer, following Kant, who initially insisted on premiss (1): the human intellect actively shapes the objects of knowledge. Then Schopenhauer added the powerful idea of his own that the intellect is an instrument of the embodied will to life: the intellect must be rooted in a living, striving entity, and the forms it imposes on experience understood as subserving the functions of organic life, ultimately grounded in the requirements of survival and reproduction. So Schopenhauer himself should have reached (3) as his conclusion, and indeed he did in a way: all *empirical* knowledge, all knowledge that I can reach as an ordinary individual member of the human species, is in the service of the will. But he could not rest there, impelled, as Nietzsche would say, by a drive to reject and despise the willing self, and posit a timeless, painless realm of which this self has hitherto fallen short.

So we learn that Schopenhauer's redemptive, will-less objectivity is an impossibility. Anything we could call knowledge is inescapably conditioned by the will we manifest as empirically situated individuals. Add to this Nietzsche's notion that personhood is not ontologically basic, and that each human being is constituted by a plurality of drives and affective states, and we arrive at the notion of 'perspectivism', whose central claim, in this section at least, is that all knowledge is in the service of one or more of the many drives that make up the knower, so that the greater the plenitude and integration of the drives served by an interpretation, the more knowledge is increased.[42]

As I said earlier, Nietzsche uses Schopenhauerian means to counter Schopenhauer. The thesis of the dependence of intellectual knowledge on the will is Schopenhauer's own achievement. For him there should have been no will-less objectivity. Why did he seek it?

---

42   Brian Leiter's detailed reading of GM III, 12 yields – without mentioning Schopenhauer – the following partially similar formulations: 'Knowledge of objects in any particular case is always conditioned by particular interpretive interests that direct the knower to corresponding features of the object of knowledge' (what he calls 'the perspectivist thesis (proper)'), and 'The more perspectives we enjoy – for example, the more interests we employ in knowing the object – the better our conception of what the object is like will be' ('the plurality claim') (Brian Leiter, 'Perspectivism in Nietzsche's *Genealogy of Morals*', in Richard Schacht (ed.), *Nietzsche, Genealogy, Morality: Morality: Essays on Nietzsche's 'Genealogy of Morals'* (Berkeley, Los Angeles and London: University of California Press, 1994), pp. 334–57 (pp. 351 and 345)). I agree with Leiter's central claim that GM III, 12 does not support the 'Received View' of Nietzsche's perspectivism – that all concepts and theories are 'mere' perspectives, all equally lacking in epistemic privilege and all equally failing to correspond to any determinate reality.

Because he could treat it as redemptive in a way nothing else could be. His own intellectual activity was driven by a hidden 'will': his need to embrace the promise that pure knowledge could, at the limit, prepare the way for the extinction of the human individual, whose cognitive enterprise and very existence were otherwise spoiled by his or her essence, the will to life.

Yet once again it would be wrong to speak of an outright rejection of Schopenhauer. Nietzsche should want us to judge his teacher while fully in command of our impulses *for* and *against*. When he suggests that the urge to affirm the notion of selfless objectivity can be put to positive use because it reverses 'accustomed perspectives and valuations', he appears to implement his own perspectivism, hinting that the exploitation of a rejected, antipodean philosophical system can be a source of cognitive strength and an occasion for gratitude.

Hans-Gerd von Seggern

Nietzsches (anti-)naturalistische Ästhetik in der *Geburt der Tragödie*[1]

I.

Friedrich Nietzsches Rezeption der ästhetischen Konzeptionen der Weimarer Klassik scheint im deutschsprachigen Raum mit einem Tabu belegt. Abgesehen von der verdienstvollen Studie Carsten Zelles *Die doppelte Ästhetik der Moderne*,[2] die sich freilich auf Nietzsches Schiller-Lektüre beschränkt, scheint es in der neueren Forschung ein stillschweigendes Abkommen zu geben, eine Diskussion dieses heiklen Stoffes zu umgehen.[3] Einschlägige Arbeiten von Nicht-Muttersprachlern sind in Deutschland bislang kaum rezipiert worden. Zu nennen wäre etwa Giuliano Baionis

---

1   Der vorliegende Aufsatz ist die erheblich überarbeitete Fassung eines Vortrags, der bei der 7th Annual Conference der Friedrich Nietzsche Society im September 1997 in St Andrews gehalten wurde. Eine ältere Version des Vortrags ist erschienen in meinem Buch *Nietzsches Philosophie des Scheins*, (Weimar: Verlag und Datenbank für Geisteswissenschaften, 1999), S. 27–38, und wird hier mit freundlicher Genehmigung des Verlages abgedruckt.

2   Carsten Zelle, *Die doppelte Ästhetik der Moderne. Revisionen des Schönen von Boileau bis Nietzsche* (Stuttgart: Metzler, 1995).

3   Eine bemerkenswerte Ausnahme bilden Wilfried Barners Hinweise auf den typologischen Gegensatz von 'klassischem Stil' und 'Barockstil' bei Nietzsche, den er in Bezug setzt zu einschlägigen Gedanken Goethes in dessen frühem Baukunst-Aufsatz von 1795 unter Verweis auf beider Abhängigkeit von Kategorien der Rhetorik. Vgl. Wilfried Barner, *Barockrhetorik. Untersuchungen zu ihren geschichtlichen Grundlagen* (Tübingen: Niemeyer, 1971), S. 3–21.

brillanter Essay *La filologia e il sublime dionisiaco*,[4] der es mit
beträchtlichem philologischem Aufwand – wenngleich streitbaren
methodologischen Prämissen – unternimmt, Nietzsches Schriften in
den Kontext des ästhetischen Diskurses um 1800 einzubetten. Zu
nennen wäre die Studie *Nietzsche and Schiller*[5] des britischen
Literaturwissenschaftlers Nicholas Martin, die mit umfassender
Textkenntnis eine 'Umwertung' des für gewöhnlich antagonistisch
gedachten Verhältnisses Nietzsches zu Schiller vornimmt; 'two
writers, who are usually regarded as chalk and cheese'[6], wie Martin
nicht ohne Ironie vermerkt. In jüngster Zeit haben Paul Bishop und
R. H. Stephenson noch einmal Nietzsches Ästhetik als eine 'new
and revitalising formulation' der klassischen Kunstdoktrin der
Weimarer Dioskuren gewürdigt.[7] Der vorliegende Beitrag versteht
sich in Ergänzung der genannten Beiträge europäischer Forscher als
ein Baustein zu einem notwendig stets unvollständig abbildbaren
Diskurs, in dem sich die Ästhetik Nietzsches bewegt.[8] Im Mittelpunkt

---

4   Giuliano Baioni, 'La filologia e il sublime dionisiaco. Nietzsche e le
     "Considerazioni inattuali"', in: Friedrich Nietzsche, *Considerazioni inattuali*,
     hg. von Sossio Giametta und Mazzino Montinari (Turin: Einaudi, 1981), S. vii–
     lxiii. Vgl. auch den Beitrag Mazzino Montinaris zu einigen verblüffenden
     Parallelen im Geschichtsdenken des späten Goethe und Nietzsches ('Aufklärung
     und Revolution: Nietzsche und der späte Goethe', in: *Nietzsche lesen* (Berlin
     und New York: de Gruyter, 1982), S. 56–63. Vgl. weiter Sandro Barbera,
     'Apollineo e dionisiaco. Alcune fonti non antiche di Nietzsche', in: *Linguistica
     e letteratura*, 13–14 (1988–89), S. 125–45, und Aldo Venturelli, 'Das
     Klassische als Vollendung des Sentimentalischen. Der junge Nietzsche als Leser
     des Briefwechsels zwischen Schiller und Goethe', in: *Nietzsche-Studien*, 18
     (1989), S. 182–202.
5   Nicholas Martin, *Nietzsche and Schiller: Untimely Aesthetics* (Oxford:
     Clarendon Press, 1996). Ders.: 'Nietzsche's "Schillerbild": A Re-Evaluation',
     in: *German Life and Letters*, 48 (1995), S. 516–39.
6   Martin, *Nietzsche and Schiller*, S. 5.
7   Paul Bishop und R. H. Stephenson, 'Nietzsche and Weimar Aesthetics', in:
     German Life and Letters, 52 (1999), S. 412–29.
8   Vgl. Roger Chartier, 'Geistesgeschichte oder *histoire de mentalités*?', in:
     Dominick LaCapra und Steven L. Kaplan (Hg.), *Geschichte denken.*

wird dabei Nietzsches Rekurs auf Schillers Spätschrift *Der Gebrauch des Chors in der Tragödie* (1803)[9] stehen, dem theoretischen Prolog zur *Braut von Messina*, in dem Schiller auf knappstem Raum noch einmal seine Tragödienpoetik reformuliert.

II.

Eine Notiz zur Konzeption der *Geburt der Tragödie* deutet auf den starken Eindruck, den die ästhetischen Versuche Schillers beim jungen Nietzsche hinterlassen haben müssen:

> Der Kultus der Natur – Wesen der neueren Kunst – die Aufhebung der Naturwirklichkeit kommt aus derselben Wurzel. Die *Flucht* zur *Natur ist unsre Kunstmuse*: [...] Es ist eben die *Göttin Natur*, zu der wir flüchten, nicht die gemeine empirische (NF 1871 9[76]: KSA 7/302).

Mit der scharfen Ablehnung der Nachahmung der empirischen Natur – der 'Naturwirklichkeit' – verweist Nietzsche auf einen Grundkonsens Johann Wolfgang Goethes und Friedrich Schillers *in aestheticis*, denn: 'Die Weimarer Klassik ist die erste Klassik, die ihre Kunsttheorie an den Stil-Begriff bindet.'[10] Der Begriff des Stils wird von beiden abgegrenzt gegen den der 'Manier' und den der 'einfachen Nachahmung'. So hat Goethe in seinem Aufsatz *Einfache Nachahmung, Manier, Stil* (1789) die einfache Nachahmung der Natur als Arbeit im 'Vorhofe des Stils' zwar gewürdigt, sie aber

---

Neubestimmung und Perspektiven moderner europäischer Geistesgeschichte (Frankfurt a.M.: Fischer, 1988), S. 41.

9   Friedrich Schiller, *Sämtliche Werke*, hg. von G. Fricke und H. G. Göpfert, (München: Hanser, 1981) (im folgenden zitiert als: SSW), Bd. 2, S. 815–23.

10   Zu diesem Fazit kommt jedenfalls Claudia Kestenholz in ihrem instruktiven Aufsatz 'Emphase des Stils. Begriffsgeschichtliche Erläuterungen zu Goethes Aufsatz über "Einfache Nachahmung der Natur, Manier, Stil"', in: *Comparatio. Revue Internationale de Littérature Comparée*, 2–3 (1991), S. 36–56.

letztlich den 'zwar fähige[n], aber beschränkte[n] Natur[en]'[11] vorbehalten. Der Manierist hingegen entferne sich von der Natur, denn

> es verdrießt ihn, der Natur ihre Buchstaben im Zeichnen nur gleichsam nachzubuchstabieren; er erfindet sich selbst eine Weise, macht sich selbst eine Sprache, um das, was er mit der Seele ergriffen, wieder nach seiner Art auszudrücken. (HA 12/31)

Mit dem Begriff der Manier bezeichnet Goethe hier wie später in *Der Sammler und die Seinigen* (1799) das Vorherrschen von subjektiver Eigenheit, Originalität, gelegentlich auch Einseitigkeit einer individuellen Formensprache in der Kunst. Bei aller prätendierten Zurückhaltung gegenüber einer Bewertung der drei unterschiedlichen Kunstformen scheint Goethe doch die selbstvergessene Objektivität des Nachahmers der weltlosen Subjektivität des Künstlers der Manier vorzuziehen. Ganz ähnlich begründet auch Schiller in den 'Kallias-Briefen' (1793) seine Reserve gegenüber dem Manieristen: 'Leidet die Eigentümlichkeit des darzustellenden Objekts durch die GeistesEigentümlichkeit des Künstlers, so sagen wir, die Darstellung sei manieriert'.[12] Den Begriff des Stils verwendet Goethe in *Einfache Nachahmung Manier, Stil* denn auch, 'um den höchsten Grad zu bezeichnen, welchen die Kunst je erreicht hat und je erreichen kann' (HA 12/34). Es lassen sich also mit Goethe drei Typen künstlerischer Produktion ausmachen: 'unreflektierte

---

11   *Goethes Werke* [Hamburger Ausgabe], hg. von Erich Trunz (München: Beck, 1981) (im folgenden: HA), Bd. 12, S. 30. Zur Geschichte der (Fehl-)Rezeption des Mimesis-Begriffs der *Poetik* des Aristoteles allgemein vgl. Jürgen H. Petersen, '"Mimesis" vs. "Nachahmung". Die Poetik des Aristoteles – nochmals neu gelesen', in: *Arcadia*, 27 (1992), S. 3–46; ders.: '"Nachahmung der Natur": Irrtümer und Korrekturen', in: *Arcadia*, 29 (1994), S. 182–98.
12   Friedrich Schiller, *Werke und Briefe*, ed. Otto Dann, 12 Bde (Frankfurt a.M.: Deutscher Klassiker Verlag, 1988–2002) [im folgenden: SFA], Bd 8: *Theoretische Schriften* (1992), hg. von Rolf-Peter Janz, S. 325.

Objektivität ("einfache Nachahmung"), reflektierte Subjektivität ("Manier") und reflektierte Objektivität ("Styl")'.[13]

Einen vergleichbaren Rang, wenn auch mit divergierender theoretischer Fundierung, behauptet der Stil-Begriff in den ästhetischen Schriften Schillers: 'Das Gegenteil der Manier ist der Stil, der nichts anders ist, als die höchste Unabhängigkeit der Darstellung von allen subjektiven und allen objektivzufälligen Bestimmungen' (SFA 8/325). Eine eindeutig wertende Stufung des künstlerischen Vermögens wird im folgenden an Stil, Manier und Nachahmung festgemacht:

> Der große Künstler [...] zeigt uns den Gegenstand (seine Darstellung hat reine Objektivität), der mittelmäßige zeigt sich selbst (seine Darstellung hat Subjektivität) der schlechte seinen Stoff (die Darstellung wird durch die Natur des Mediums u. durch die Schranken des Künstlers bestimmt (SFA 8/326).

In seiner Vorrede zur *Braut von Messina* rechtfertigt Schiller die Wiedereinführung des Chors in die moderne Tragödie als Element der Stilisierung. Der Chor diene als 'Hauptwaffe' gegen den 'gemeinen Begriff des Natürlichen', bzw. gegen den 'Naturalism in der Kunst' (SSW 2/818–19). Nur scheinbar paradox geht es Schiller, der in *Über naive und sentimentalische Dichtung* (1795) von 'allen Dichtern' sagt, sie 'werden [...] entweder Natur *sein*, oder sie werden die verlorene *suchen*' (SFA 8/728), um die Aufhebung der Naturwirklichkeit. Schiller schreibt, 'daß der Künstler kein einziges Element aus der Wirklichkeit brauchen kann, wie er es findet, daß sein Werk in *allen* seinen Teilen ideell sein muß, wenn es als Ganzes Realität haben und mit der Natur übereinstimmen soll' (SSW 2/818). Im Rahmen seiner am Idealismus Platons orientierten Ästhetik unterscheidet Schiller von einer 'gemeinen', empirischen Natur, die aus dem Bereich der Kunst zu verbannen sei. Der 'Geist der Natur' dagegen genießt als eigentliches Objekt der Kunst höchste Dignität. Begriffe wie 'Wahrheit', 'Natur' und 'Leben' bezeichnen somit

---

13 Vgl. Norbert Christian Wolf, *Streitbare Ästhetik. Goethes kunst- und literaturtheoretische Schriften 1771–1789* (Tübingen: Niemeyer, 2001), S. 376.

einmal das Maß der wahren Poesie, ein andermal deren Gegenwelt. [...] Wahrheit, Natur, Leben sind erst aufgrund ihrer Brechung im Medium des Scheins gültige ästhetische Werte. Nur wenn ihre Strahlen ungebrochen in die Kunst dringen, der Brechungswinkel beim Übergang von der Realität in die Fiktion zu klein oder gar nicht vorhanden ist, erscheint das Leben als roh, die Natur als gemein.[14]

So erklärt sich auch Schillers in der Tradition der *Hamburgischen Dramaturgie* Lessings stehende Kritik an der *tragédie classique*, bzw. an Corneille, der in unzulässiger Weise Dichtungsnormen in die aristotelische *Poetik* projiziert habe.[15] In der Kunstwelt des Dramas ist 'alles [...] nur ein Symbol des Wirklichen', dagegen

> haben die Franzosen, die den Geist der Alten zuerst ganz mißverstanden, eine Einheit des Orts und der Zeit nach dem gemeinsten empirischen Sinn auf der Schaubühne eingeführt, als ob hier ein anderer Ort wäre als der bloß ideale Raum, und eine andere Zeit als bloß die stetige Folge der Handlung (SSW 2/818).

Dem Natürlichen im 'gemeinen Sinne' Vorschub geleistet zu haben, diesem Vorwurf entgeht also – aller 'frostigen Dezenz' zum Trotz – selbst die *tragédie classique* nicht. Als Fortschritt auf dem Weg zur 'poetischen Tragödie' der Moderne bewertet Schiller die 'Einführung einer metrischen Sprache'. Nicht zuletzt der Rhythmisierung der Sprache hatte Schiller bereits im Briefwechsel mit Goethe die Qualität zugeschrieben, selbst dem 'prosaischen Stoff' des *Wallenstein* eine 'poetische Natur zu geben',[16] ihm zu

---

14 Dieter Borchmeyer, "'... dem Naturalism in der Kunst offen und ehrlich den Krieg zu erklären...'': Zu Goethes und Schillers Bühnenreform', in: Wilfried Barner u. a. (Hg.): *Unser Commercium. Goethes und Schillers Literaturpolitik* (Stuttgart: Cotta, 1984), S. 365.

15 Vgl. hierzu Dieter Borchmeyers Studie über 'Corneille, Lessing und das Problem der "Auslegung" der aristotelischen Poetik', in: *Deutsche Vierteljahrsschrift für Literaturwissenschaft und Geistesgeschichte*, 51 (1977), S. 422-35.

16 An Goethe, 01. Dez. 1797, in: *Der Briefwechsel zwischen Schiller und Goethe*, hg. von Emil Staiger (Frankfurt a.M.: Insel, 1977), S. 504 (im folgenden: *Briefwechsel*).

'poetische[r] Dignität'[17] zu verhelfen, da der Rhythmus 'alle Charaktere und alle Situationen nach Einem Gesetz behandelt' (ebd.): 'Er bildet auf diese Weise die Atmosphäre für die poetische Schöpfung, das Gröbere bleibt zurück, nur das Geistige kann von diesem dünnen Elemente getragen werden.'[18] Die moderne Restitution des Tragödienchors ist Schiller

> der letzte, entscheidende Schritt – und wenn derselbe auch nur dazu diente, dem Naturalism in der Kunst offen und ehrlich den Krieg zu erklären, so sollte er uns eine lebendige Mauer sein, die die Tragödie um sich herumzieht, um sich von der wirklichen Welt rein abzuschließen und sich ihren idealen Boden, ihre poetische Freiheit zu bewahren. (SSW 2/819)

Der Chor als Hilfsmittel im Kampf gegen den 'gemeinen Begriff des *Natürlichen*' in der Tragödienpoetik (SSW 2/818) – hiermit wird von Schiller in erster Linie seine Restitution in der modernen Tragödie legitimiert.

War die Realität in der Antike 'poetisch', der Chor ein 'natürliches Organ', wird er in der Moderne 'zu einem Kunstorgan', das die Poesie hervorzubringen helfen soll, indem er die Fabel des Dramas 'in jene kindliche Zeit und in jene einfache Form des Lebens' zurückversetzt (SSW 2/819). Die Abstraktheit der spruchhaften Lehren des Chors, der als 'einzige ideale Person' (SSW 2/823) im Kontrast steht zur Individualität der agierenden Charaktere, wird komplementiert von einer 'sinnlich machtvollen' Art des Vortrags. Abstraktion und Sinnlichkeit müssen im Gleichgewicht sein, wenn der Chor seine Aufgabe erfüllen soll, die 'naivsten Motive'

---

17 An Goethe, 24. Nov. 1797 (*Briefwechsel*, S. 497).
18 An Goethe, 24. Nov. 1797 (*Briefwechsel*, S. 498). Vgl. dazu Nietzsches 'falsche' Textparaphrase in *Die Geburt der Tragödie*: 'Auch [!] für diese Anfänge der tragischen Kunst hat Schiller Recht: der Chor ist eine lebendige Mauer gegen die anstürmende Wirklichkeit, weil er – der Satyrchor – das Dasein wahrhaftiger, wirklicher, vollständiger abbildet als der gemeinhin sich als einzige Realität achtende Culturmensch.' (KSA 1/58). Aus dem 'Auch' des Zitats geht zweifelsfrei hervor, daß Nietzsche *bewußt* Schillers Chor-Modell auf die Antike überträgt und dies auch seinem Leser kenntlich macht, was Borchmeyer leugnet.

hervorzutreiben. Wird das Gleichgewicht zugunsten einer der beiden Seiten aufgehoben, geht das Poetische zugrunde, dessen Bereich im 'Indifferenzpunkt des Ideellen und Sinnlichen' angesiedelt ist (SSW 2/821). Die 'lyrische Sprache des Chors' ist es schließlich, die den Dichter zu einer 'Erhebung des Tons' berechtigt, die 'das Ohr ausfüllt, die den Geist anspannt, die das ganze Gemüt erweitert. Diese eine Riesengestalt in seinem Bilde nötigt ihn, alle seine Figuren auf den Kothurn zu stellen, und seinem Gemälde dadurch die tragische Größe zu geben' (SSW 2/822).[19]

III.

Die 'moderne gemeine Welt' in die 'alte poetische' verwandeln, *qua* Reflexion zur Naivität: zweifellos steht auch hier (unausgesprochen) der Begriff des 'Sentimentalischen' im Hintergrund.[20] Ganz ähnlich hatte Schiller in dem berühmten Geburtstagsbrief von 1794, der zentrale Gedanken der späteren Abhandlung antizipiert, den 'Gang des Geistes' des 'naiven' Dichters Goethe zu beschreiben versucht. Nur vermittels der 'Nachhülfe der Denkkraft' nämlich war es dem deutschen Poeten möglich, sich über die Mängel der modernen Wirklichkeit und der 'schlechteren' nordischen Natur hinwegzusetzen und so 'auf einem rationalen Wege ein Griechenland zu gebären'.[21] Um zur Naivität zu gelangen hatte der neuzeitliche Dichter Goethe

---

19   Vgl. hierzu Nietzsches Paraphrase: 'Der *Chor* ist es, der die ideale Sprache der Tragödie festsetzt: wie dies Schiller empfunden hat' (NF 1871, 9 [104]: KSA 7/312).
20   Zum 'sentimentalischen' Charakter des Chors: 'Richtiges Gefühl *Schillers* über den Chor und *Tiecks* Äußerung: das gänzlich *Unnatürliche* (gegenüber unsrer Natur) ist das Ergreifendste' (Nachgelassene Fragmente 1871, 9 [126], KSA 7/321).
21   An Goethe, 23. Aug.1794 (*Briefwechsel*, S. 34).

eine Arbeit mehr, denn so wie Sie [scil. Goethe] von der Anschauung zur Abstraktion übergingen, so mußten Sie nun rückwärts Begriffe wieder in Intuitionen umsetzen und Gedanken in Gefühle verwandeln, weil nur durch diese das Genie hervorbringt.[22]

Eine ähnliche Gedankenbewegung beschreibt Goethes Protagonist in *Der Sammler und die Seinigen*, um den Weg zum 'hohen Stil'[23] zu kennzeichnen, wie er sich auch in *Shakespeare und kein Ende* (1813) des Schillerschen Vokabulars bedient.[24] Die Figur des Sentimentalischen wird später auch Nietzsche umschreiben, wenn er sagt: 'Einfach und natürlich' zu sein ist das höchste und letzte Ziel der Cultur: inzwischen wollen wir uns bestreben, uns zu binden und zu formen, damit wir zuletzt vielleicht ins Einfache und Schöne zurück-kommen' (NF 1873, 29 [118]: KSA 7/685). Das Postulat Schillers geht dahin, den Bereich empirischer Befangenheiten unter sich zu lassen, um durch die Kunst in eine Sphäre zu gelangen, in der Geist und Natur auf einer höheren Stufe koinzidieren. Dies ist der Sinn künstlerischer Idealisierung. Im Medium des Scheins wird so ein Zustand antizipiert, nach dem der Mensch in der Wirklichkeit 'aufgefodert [ist] zu ringen', wenngleich er ihm sich nur in einem 'unendlichen Fortschritte zu nähern hoffen' darf (SFA 8/708): Die 'Übereinstimmung zwischen seinem Empfinden und Denken', die einst '*wirklich* statt fand, existiert jetzt bloß *idealisch* [...] als ein Gedanke, der erst realisiert werden soll' (SFA 8/734). Der Dichter soll

alles Unmittelbare, das durch die künstliche Einrichtung des wirklichen Lebens aufgehoben ist, wieder herstellen und alles künstliche Machwerk an dem Menschen und um denselben, das die Erscheinung seiner innern Natur und seines ursprünglichen Charakters hindert, wie der Bildhauer die modernen Gewänder, abwerfen, und von allen äußern Umgebungen desselben nichts aufnehmen, als was die Höchste der Formen, die menschliche, sichtbar macht (SSW 2/820).

22 Ebd. (*Briefwechsel*, S. 35).
23 'Ein schönes Kunstwerk hat den ganzen Kreis durchlaufen, es ist nun wieder eine Art Individuum, das wir mit Neigung umfassen, das wir uns zueignen können' (HA 12/84).
24 Vgl. HA 12/291.

Dem Gebot der Idealisierung entspricht in der Plastik, wie hier von
Schiller angedeutet, die Darstellung des nackten Menschen. In seiner
Studie zur Laokoon-Gruppe begründet Goethe die Wertschätzung der
Bildhauerkunst eben damit, daß sie

> den Menschen von allem, was ihm nicht wesentlich ist, entblößt. So ist auch bei
> dieser Gruppe Laokoon ein bloßer Name; von seiner Priesterschaft, von seinem
> trojanisch-nationellen, von allem poetischen und mythologischen Beiwesen
> haben ihn die Künstler entkleidet (HA 12/59).

'Idealische Masken' nennt Schiller daher die Charaktere der antiken
Tragödie und bewundert diese, da sie von der 'schlechten' Subjektivität leibhaftig-empirischer Individuen ebensoweit entfernt sind, wie
davon, 'bloßen logischen Wesen' zu entsprechen.[25] Vom Stoff der
geschichtlichen Wirklichkeit und der Natur im empirischen Sinne soll
also abstrahiert werden zugunsten einer überhistorisch-idealen
Sphäre, in der die Form des 'rein Menschlichen' sichtbar werde.
Die Braut von Messina ist daher als Schillers 'geschichtsfernstes'
Stück interpretiert worden, da es sich im Rahmen massiver
'klassizistische[r] Ambitionen'[26] am entschiedensten von der
empirischen Geschichte abwendet. Auch Peter Szondi spricht in
Bezug auf das Drama vom Klassizismus in 'seiner konsequentesten
Form' als einer Art idealtypischen Experiments.[27]

---

25   An Goethe, 04. Apr.1797 (*Briefwechsel*, S. 364).
26   Rolf-Peter Janz, 'Antike und Moderne in Schillers *Braut von Messina*', in:
      Barner u. a. (Hg.), S. 338.
27   Peter Szondi, *Poetik und Geschichtsphilosophie II* (Frankfurt a.M.: Suhrkamp,
      1974), S. 53.

IV.

Allein die 'Kunst des Ideals' – so hieß es bei Schiller – kann 'wahrer sein als alle Wirklichkeit und realer als alle Erfahrung' (SSW 2/818). Die Aufhebung der Naturwirklichkeit wird von Schiller als Voraussetzung einer Darstellung der Naturwahrheit bestimmt. Die 'Naturwahrheit' ist es nun wiederum, die bei Nietzsche der dionysisch verstandene Chor der gesellschaftlichen 'Culturlüge' entgegenhält. Auch von Nietzsche wird hier auf den Topos des nackten Menschen angespielt:

> Die Sphäre der Poesie liegt nicht ausserhalb der Welt, als eine phantastische Unmöglichkeit eines Dichterhirns: sie will das gerade Gegentheil sein, der ungeschminkte Ausdruck der Wahrheit und muss eben deshalb den lügenhaften Aufputz jener vermeinten Wirklichkeit des Culturmenschen von sich werfen (GT 8: KSA 1/58).

Der 'falsche Begriff der Mimesis', mit dem sich Schiller so intensiv auseinandersetzt, wird im Nachlaß auch von Nietzsche – wiederum mit deutlichen Schiller-Anleihen – reflektiert. Die Stilisierung erscheint hier als Korrektiv einer falsch verstandenen Nachahmung:

> Das Charakteristische – das neue Zauberwort für Sophokles, d.h. die Nachahmung der wirklichen Charaktere. [...] Die Kunstgestalten sind realer als die Wirklichkeit, die Wirklichkeit ist die Nachahmung der Kunstgestalten: ist die wachende Welt eine Nachahmung der Traumwelt? (NF 1871, 9[133]: KSA 7/323).

Nietzsche stellt Platon vom 'Kopf' der metaphysischen Ideen auf die 'Füße' irdischen Scheins. Seine frühe Ästhetik steht im Zeichen einer Inversion des Platonismus. Wenn in obigem Zitat der Schein der Realität defizitär erscheint, dann bedeutet das keine Abwertung gegenüber den Ideen, sondern vielmehr eine Aufwertung des potenzierten Scheins der Kunst.[28]

---

28 Vgl. Verf.: *Nietzsches Philosophie des Scheins.*

Gegenüber Schillers Begriff des Ideals, das einer Harmonie von Reflexion und Sinnlichkeit entsprang, gibt es aber einige wichtige Unterschiede. Nietzsche projiziert Schillers Beschreibung des restituierten Chors zurück in die Antike, worauf etwa Dieter Borchmeyer hingewiesen hat, gibt aber dabei das Moment der Reflexion preis.[29] Die dionysische 'Musik des Chors' bezeichnet er als 'jene nur empfundenen, noch nicht zum Bilde verdichteten Kräfte' (GT 8: KSA 1/64). Die 'sinnlich machtvolle' Seite des Chors wird also anders als bei Schiller isoliert. Der wohlfeile Hinweis Borchmeyers auf Nietzsches Wagner-Verehrung kann an dieser Stelle kaum zur Klärung der Sachlage beitragen. Joachim Latacz hat dagegen gezeigt, daß die Betonung der grundlegenden Bedeutung der Musik für die Entwicklung der griechischen Lyrik wie der späteren Dramatik vielmehr einen weithin gültigen Grundkonsens der zeitgenössischen Gräzistik darstellt:

> Daß am Anfang der Tragödie die Musik stand, war damals eine allgemein geteilte Überzeugung, nicht nur unter Fachgräzisten, sondern auch im gebildeten Publikum [...]; gerade ein Gräzist bedurfte nicht erst Richard Wagners, um zu dieser Einsicht zu gelangen.[30]

Das Erklärungsmodell des Chors, nach dem dieser das Volk (bzw. die 'constitutionelle Volksvertretung') vertreten habe, wird von Nietzsche 'für die uns bekannte classische Form des Chors bei Aeschylus und Sophokles für Blasphemie' erachtet, 'jegliche politisch-sociale Sphäre' wurde hier 'ausgeschlossen' (GT 7: KSA 1/52). Hier glaubt sich Nietzsche einig mit Schiller, radikalisiert aber tatsächlich den idealistischen Ansatz der programmatischen Vorrede. Zwar ist es – wie oben dargelegt – die Aufgabe des Chors, als 'lebendige Mauer' die schmucklose Wirklichkeit der Moderne aus der Kunstsphäre der

---

29 Vgl. Dieter Borchmeyer, *Das Theater Richard Wagners. Idee – Dichtung – Wirkung* (Stuttgart: Reclam, 1982), S. 168.

30 Joachim Latacz, 'Fruchtbares Ärgernis: Nietzsches "Geburt der Tragödie" und die gräzistische Tragödienforschung', in: ders., *Erschließung der Antike. Kleine Schriften zur Literatur der Griechen und Römer* (Stuttgart und Leipzig: Teubner, 1994), S. 485.

Tragödie fernzuhalten, allerdings versteht Schiller den Chor sehr wohl (im Sinne der von Nietzsche zurückgewiesenen 'geläufigen Kunstredensarten' (ebd.)) als Repräsentanten der Öffentlichkeit. Er verkörpert nach Schiller das Volk, die 'sinnlich lebendige Masse', die in der modernen Realität, 'wo sie nicht als rohe Gewalt wirkt, zum Staat, folglich zu einem abgezogenen Begriff geworden' sei und damit ihren in der Antike vorhandenen poetischen Charakter eingebüßt habe (SSW 2/820).

Nietzsche verschweigt angeblich (vgl. Anm. 18), daß die Funktionsbestimmung des Chors bei Schiller 'gerade nicht für den griechischen, sondern ausschließlich für den modernen (restaurierten) Chor gilt'.[31] Erst die 'Übermacht der Prosa' der modernen Verhältnisse zwingt – nach Schiller – den Dichter dazu, die Kunst gegen die Prosa der Wirklichkeit abzuschirmen.[32] Es mag daher zutreffen, daß Nietzsche Schillers Konstruktion vereinfacht. Doch zu einfach macht es sich, wer deshalb behauptet, Nietzsche habe

> Schillers differenzierte Beschreibung des Chors [...] zu einer einzigen Feststellung zusammenschrumpfen lassen, in der die Differenz zwischen der originalen und der zeitgenössischen Wieder-Verwendung des Chors nicht mehr erkennbar ist (ebd.).

Denn – mit Ausnahme Martins – hat die Forschung bislang Nietzsches strategische Aneignung der Schillerschen 'Umwertung' des Nachahmungsbegriffs im Sinne einer fortgesetzten 'Kriegserklärung' an den Naturalismus schlicht ignoriert. Nur unter Einbeziehung dieser Gesichtspunkte kann die Bedeutung der Schrift *Über den Gebrauch des Chors in der Tragödie* für Nietzsches *Geburt der Tragödie* angemessen gewürdigt werden.

Nietzsche fordert, über Schiller hinauszugehen: Der 'Begriff des *Naiven* und *Sentimentalischen* ist zu steigern. Völlige Verschleierung durch Trugmechanismen ist "naiv", die Zerreissung derselben, die den Willen zu einem Nothgespinst nöthigt, ist "sentimentalisch"' (NF

---

31 Borchmeyer, *Das Theater Richard Wagners*, S. 168.
32 Schiller an Herder, 04. Nov. 1795; zitiert nach Borchmeyer, *Das Theater Richard Wagners*, S. 168.

1870–71, 7 [173]: KSA 7/206). Im Nachlaß wird also die Begrifflich-
keit Schillers mit Schopenhauerscher Willensmetaphysik kontaminiert
und dementsprechend umdefiniert: Nietzsche scheint hier nämlich
jene 'herrliche Schillersche Terminologie' (scil. die Begriffe 'naiv'
und 'sentimentalisch') nicht hinzureichen, um 'das ganze weiteste
Bereich aller Kunst' zu erklären (NF 1870–71, 7 [126]: KSA 7/184).
Als 'naiv' definiert Nietzsche 'rein apollinisch', den 'Schein des
Scheins' (ebd.). Das 'Naive' gilt ihm hier als 'das ewige Merkmal
einer allerhöchsten Kunstgattung' (ebd.). Für unzulänglich erklärt er
hingegen den Begriff des 'Sentimentalischen' zur Erklärung aller
'nicht-naiven Kunst': 'Welche Verlegenheit bereitet uns, falls wir das
wollten, z.B. die griechische Tragödie und Shakespeare! Und gar die
Musik!' (ebd.). Die eigene Terminologie wird der Schillerschen
regelrecht aufgepfropft, und zwar mit pastoralem Pathos:

> Dem 'Sentimentalisch' muß ich sogar vom höchsten Richterstuhle aus die
> Geltung eines reinen Kunstwerks versagen, weil es nicht wie jene höchste und
> dauernde Versöhnung des Naiven und des Dionysischen entstanden ist, sondern
> unruhig zwischen beiden hin- und herschwankt, und ihre Vereinigung nur
> sprungweise, ohne bleibenden Besitz erreicht, vielmehr zwischen den ver-
> schiedenen Künsten, zwischen Poesie und Prosa, Philosophie und Kunst,
> Begriff und Anschauung, Wollen und Können eine unsichere Stellung hat. Es ist
> das Kunstwerk jenes noch unentschiedenen Kampfes, den es zu entscheiden
> sich anschickt, ohne dies Ziel zu erreichen; wohl aber weist es uns, wie z.B. die
> Schillersche Dichtung, zu unsrer Rührung und Erhebung, auf neue Bahnen hin
> und ist somit 'Johannes' der Vorläufer all' Volk der Welt zu taufen (ebd.).

Als 'vollen Gegensatz des "Naiven" und des Apollinischen', die
geradezu als identisch definiert werden, versteht Nietzsche dagegen
das 'Dionysische', 'd.h. alle Kunst, die nicht "Schein des Scheins",
sondern "Schein des Seins" ist, Wiederspiegelung des ewigen Ur-
Einen' (ebd.). Das 'Sentimentalische' gilt ihm damit als 'Vorläufer'
seines eigenen Begriffs des 'Dionysischen'. Im publizierten Text der
Geburt der Tragödie – und hierin liegt eine der Pointen dieser Schrift
– erscheint dann das 'Naive', die vielbeschworene 'Heiterkeit' der
griechischen Kultur, als Resultat der Wirkung des Apollinischen, als
'der vollkommene Sieg der apollinischen Illusion' (GT 3: KSA 1/37).

V.

Nietzsche bewertet Schillers idealistische Ästhetik deutlich höher als die zeitgenössischen naturalistischen und realistischen Programmatiken, die von ihm mit Häme bedacht werden. Seine Schiller-Lektüre zusammenfassend schreibt Nietzsche:

> Eine solche Betrachtungsart ist es, scheint mir, für die unser sich überlegen wähnendes Zeitalter das wegwerfende Schlagwort 'Pseudoidealismus' gebraucht. Ich fürchte, wir sind dagegen mit unserer jetzigen Verehrung des Natürlichen und Wirklichen am Gegenpol des Idealismus angelangt, nämlich in der Region der Wachsfigurencabinette. Auch in ihnen giebt es eine Kunst, wie bei gewissen beliebten Romanen der Gegenwart: nur quäle man uns nicht mit dem Anspruch, dass mit dieser Kunst der Schiller-Goethesche 'Pseudoidealismus' überwunden sei (GT 7: KSA 1/54-55).

Die 'Verehrung des Wirklichen', wie sie sich für Nietzsche etwa in den Schriften Julian Schmidts, den Werken Gustav Freytags oder Berthold Auerbachs manifestiert, gilt ihm als 'Gegensatz zu der Zucht des Klassischen' und als 'Protest der Photographie gegen das Gemälde' (NF 1870–71, 8[113]: KSA 7/266). Im Spätwerk geht es dann gegen die Frères de Goncourt, die bekanntlich auch durch ein Kapitel in den *Essais de psychologie contemporaine* Paul Bourgets, die Nietzsche wiederholt zitiert, gewürdigt werden. In diesem Zusammenhang sei erinnert an Nietzsches Kritik am Konzept des *roman expérimental* bei Zola. Dieses fordert vom Schriftsteller 'connaissance scientifique', um 'la littérature de notre âge scientifique' zu schaffen.[33] Die Skepsis gegen die 'servile Naturnachahmung'[34] bzw. das 'peinliche Abkonterfeien der Wirklichkeit' (GT 7: KSA 1/55), die sich bei Schiller zunächst gegen die bürgerliche Trivialdramatik und die Ausläufer des Sturm-und-Drang-

---

33   Emile Zola, *Le roman expérimental*, zitiert nach Theo Meyer, *Nietzsche. Kunstauffassung und Lebensbegriff* (Tübingen: Francke, 1991), S. 448.
34   An Goethe, 29. Dez. 1797 (*Briefwechsel*, S. 529).

Theaters richtete,[35] wird dagegen bei Nietzsche offensichtlich lebendig gehalten und bis ins Spätwerk fortgeführt. Seine Kritik an Realismus und Naturalismus – in der *Geburt der Tragödie* wie später – ist letztlich als ein Produkt seiner frühen Schiller-Lektüre zu begreifen. Kritik am Naturalismus: in der deutlichen Sprache des späten Nietzsche heißt das: 'Zola: oder "die Freude zu stinken"' (GD ix 1: KSA 6/111).

Den 'matten Religionsvelleitäten' seiner Zeit setzt Nietzsche den 'höchsten energischen Idealismus' entgegen. Die 'Kunstperiode' erscheint in diesem Zusammenhang gar als 'Fortsetzung der *mythen*- und *religion*bildenden Periode' (NF 1871, 9[94]: KSA 7/309). Rhythmisierung der Sprache und Einführung des Chors im Wortdrama Schillers erscheinen Nietzsche als Vorstufen zum Musikdrama Wagners: 'Was Schiller vom Chore erwartet, leistet im höheren Maße die Musik' (NF 1871, 9[75]: KSA 7/302). Durch die Einführung des Begriffs des Dionysischen wird die 'Schillersche Vorstellung unendlich vertieft!' (NF 1871, 9[11]: KSA 7/277). Es sollte daher nun weniger überraschend erscheinen, daß selbst die kulturrevolutionäre Pointe der Tragödienschrift, nämlich die Erwartung einer '*Wiedergeburt der Tragödie*' aus dem Geist der (Wagner-)Oper (GT 19: KSA 1/129), in einem Brief Schillers an Goethe antizipiert wird. Schiller begründet im Briefwechsel aus der Ablehnung der 'servilen Naturnachahmung' sein 'gewisses Vertrauen zur Oper, daß aus ihr wie aus den Chören des alten Bacchusfestes das Trauerspiel in einer edlern Gestalt [sich] loswickeln sollte'.[36] In der Oper werde die 'gemeine Nachahmung' erlassen, und 'obgleich nur unter dem Namen von Indulgenz könnte sich' 'auf diesem Wege das Ideale auf das Theater stehlen' (ebd.). Im *Mahnruf an die Deutschen* wendet sich Nietzsche noch einmal in offensichtlicher Bezugnahme auf den Brief vom 29.12.1797 in Bezug auf das Projekt 'Bayreuth' an alle,

---

35   Vgl. hierzu Borchmeyer, in Barner u. a. (Hg.), S. 352.
36   An Goethe, 29. Dez. 1797 (*Briefwechsel*, S. 529).

denen die Veredlung und Reinigung der dramatischen Kunst am Herzen liegt und die Schillers wunderbare Ahnung verstanden haben, dass vielleicht einmal aus der Oper sich das Trauerspiel in einer edleren Gestalt entwickeln werde (KSA 1/896).

Goethe erklärt den Stil als Resultat des Bemühens des Künstlers um eine Fundierung des Kunstwerks auf den – freilich je unterschiedlich deutbaren – 'tiefsten Grundfesten der Erkenntnis, auf dem Wesen der Dinge', einem eingehenden Studium der Natur, das von den ephemeren Eigenheiten der Erscheinung abzusehen gelernt hat (HA 12/32). Im Hinblick auf Nietzsche nun ließe sich mit Richard Shusterman von einem radikalen ästhetischen 'Naturalismus' sprechen,[37] der freilich nichts mit 'einfacher Naturnachahmung' noch mit dem üblichen literarästhetischen Epochenbegriff gemein hat. Der frühe Nietzsche versteht Kunst nicht als 'Nachahmung der Naturwirklichkeit, sondern gerade [als] ein metaphysisches Supplement der Naturwirklichkeit [...], zu deren Ueberwindung neben sie gestellt' (GT 24: KSA 1/151). Nietzsches Rekurs auf ästhetische Konzepte der Weimarer Klassik dient nicht nur der Bezugnahme auf 'unbezweifelbare Autoritäten'. (Ein Verfahren, das Nietzsche wie ganz nebenbei bekannt sein dürfte ohnehin äußerst selten verwendet. Am entschiedensten wendet sich Nietzsche überdies von den zuvor noch mit peinigenden Elogen bedachten 'Mentoren' Schopenhauer und Wagner ab, deren Einfluß auf sein Werk nicht zu leugnen ist. Es liegt auf der Hand, das Ähnliches für Schiller gilt.) Vielmehr stellen diese eine Matrix dar, vor der die eigenen ästhetischen Auffassungen Kontur gewinnen. Die Adaption zentraler ästhetischer Begriffe der Weimarer Klassik dient der Abgrenzung der eigenen Positionen gegen die zeitgenössische Literarästhetik und der Ausformulierung der eigenen Literaturpolitik.

---

37   Richard Shusterman, 'Tatort: Kunst als Dramatisieren' in: Josef Früchtl und Jörg Zimmermann (Hg.), *Ästhetik der Inszenierung* (Frankfurt a.M.: Suhrkamp, 2001), S. 129ff.

Paul J. M. van Tongeren

Nietzsche's Naturalism

Whoever looks more carefully than has often been done at what
Nietzsche says about 'race' and 'breeding', finds that he almost never
uses those words in their 'modern' meaning which is related to a
reprehensible racism.[1] Race for Nietzsche means 'people' or 'human
being' in general, rather than 'race' in the racist sense; the characteristics of 'races' are social and cultural, rather than biological;
'breeding' is more related to education than to the breeding of
animals, etc. Nevertheless, Nietzsche does use a vocabulary with
biological connotations of which he is certainly aware, and physiological factors are according to his opinion important in this
educational breeding and in the development of 'races' or people: in
their rise as well as in their decline. So even if there is no justification
for suspecting Nietzsche of racist positions, let alone of an alliance
with, or predecessorship of, Nazi ideology in this respect, the question
remains why he is so fond of using a 'biological', 'physiological',
or – to put it in more general terms – a 'natural' or 'naturalistic'
terminology.

There seems to remain something irritating and alarming,
especially for philosophers, in this bias towards the language of these
natural sciences (the 'life-sciences'), even if we know that Nietzsche
– who, after all, wanted to be a physician of culture[2] – in this respect
is also a product of his time, a time in which the term physiology was

---

1   See Gerd Schank's essay in this volume. His paper and mine were presented
       together at the 7th Annual Conference of the Friedrich Nietzsche Society at the
       University of St Andrews in 1997.
2   See KSA 7/545, 23[15], and FW, Preface, 2. Nietzsche's published writings are
       cited from Walter Kaufmann's translations (see Bibliography).

sometimes used as equal in meaning to 'the science of man'.[3] Far from claiming to give an exhaustive interpretation of Nietzsche's physiological language,[4] in this paper I want to address – only very briefly – three questions with respect to his 'naturalism', i.e. his apparent reduction of the cultural to the natural, where this 'natural' is conceived of in terms of the modern natural sciences, especially physiology: first I will ask whether this naturalism is not a complete abandonment of philosophy, and its surrender to science; second I will go into Nietzsche's concept of nature and question whether it deserves the term 'reductionism'; and third I will enquire into the normative implications of this concept of nature when applied to the development of the human being, as implied in many of Nietzsche's texts, such as the following note: 'To breed a race with strong instincts – that is what morality wants.'[5]

1. The scientist, the physician and the philosopher

Just like early nineteenth-century medicine,[6] Nietzsche advocated physiology in opposition to a religiously and theologically dominated philosophy of man and morals. His criticism of what, in *Beyond Good and Evil*, he called 'the prejudices of the philosophers' is well known; these prejudices are according to Nietzsche almost all determined by

---

3   L. S. Jacyna, 'Medical Science and Moral Science: The Cultural Relations of Physiology in Restauration France', *History of Science*, 25 (1987), 111–43 (p. 119). See also: 'the concept of physiology as a science of man capable of making a crucial contribution to ethics and social policy was prominent in medical literature between 1800 and 1830' (p. 116).

4   For a discussion of this physiological language, see Michel Onfray, *Le ventre des philosophes: critique de la raison diététique* (Paris: Grasset, 1989), ch. 6.

5   'Eine Rasse mit starken Instinkten züchten – das will die Moral.' (KSA 9/115, 4[67])

6   Cf. Jacyna, 115.

religious or moral motivations. His criticism consists for a large part in showing a more fundamental force behind or under these moral motives: the actual causes behind the secret motives. And these actual causes are often said to be of a physiological nature: 'Behind all logic and its seeming sovereignty of movement, too, there stand valuations or, more clearly, physiological demands for the preservation of a certain type of life' (JGB 3). In a similar way we find in *Beyond Good and Evil* such diverse matters as philosophy in general (JGB 20) and scepticism in particular (JGB 208), the tempo of the style of languages (JGB 28) and the language-unit of a period (JGB 247), the democratic movement of the Europeans (JGB 242) and the German profundity (JGB 244) explained in terms of physiological causes. Nietzsche sees it as his task to 'translate man back into nature' (JGB 230), and this apparently makes him often use the language and conceptuality of physiology.

To understand this correctly, however, we should note at least two things. First, physiology is not the only science Nietzsche resorts to and, second, the physis to which Nietzsche's physiology relates is not nature in the current scientific sense of the word.

Next to physiology, we find medicine, linguistics, philology and, probably most important of all, psychology, sometimes physio-psychology (JGB 23). And all of these sciences have in Nietzsche's understanding a strong historical bias; they describe the physiological, medical, linguistic, psychological and other conditions of the development of a phenomenon. Sometimes Nietzsche gathers all these different methodologies under the term 'natural history' ('Natur-geschichte') as, for example, in Part V of *Beyond Good and Evil*, until, in 1886, he gives his method the name 'genealogy'.

One of the reasons that Nietzsche uses the names of different sciences, and that he searches for a new and proper name for his own use of them, is that he wants to distance himself from these sciences as they are currently conceived. We should not forget, after all, that the same sciences to which Nietzsche resorts are all criticized by him. Physiology should not be taken in the sense in which the physiologists take it, who interpret the organism in terms of an instinct of self-preservation, but in Nietzsche's sense, i.e. in terms of a theory of the will to power (JGB 13).[7] Psychology should be taken in a sense in which nobody has yet taken it, i.e. as 'morphology and *the doctrine of the development of the will to power*' (JGB 23).

In order to translate the human being and human culture 'back into nature' (JGB 230), Nietzsche uses a physiology, a *logos* (science) of *physis* (nature), which conceives of nature as will to power. That means that in order to understand Nietzsche's recourse to 'natural sciences', we have to understand his theory of the will to power, which certainly is not a science in the modern sense of the word, but a philosophical or even 'metaphysical' theory, albeit with quotation marks and certainly not in the sense in which Heidegger calls Nietzsche the last metaphysician. Nietzsche does not replace philosophy with some scientific theory, but rather makes use of several sciences to present a new type of philosophical interpretation.

In order to clarify further the distinction between Nietzsche's theory of the will to power and a scientific understanding of nature, and to elucidate the normative or educational pathos in Nietzsche's 'naturalism', I will elaborate a little more on Nietzsche's concept of nature.

2. Nature and plurality

Nature plays an important role in part V of *Beyond Good and Evil*.[8] Nietzsche takes morality as a part of nature, and therefore he presents his analysis of morality as a 'Natural History of Morals'.[9] 'Natural

---

7   See Longinus J. Dohmen, *Nietzsche over de menselijke natuur: Een uiteen-zetting van zijn verborgen antropologie* (Kampen: Kok, 1994), pp. 93–94.

8   Cf. also Leo Strauss, 'Note on the plan of Nietzsche's "Beyond Good and Evil"', *Interpretation*, 3 (1973), 97–113.

9   The German title is 'Zur Naturgeschichte der Moral'. The preposition 'zur' reduces the pretensions. It indicates that the following is meant as part of, or preparatory to, the actual and complete 'Naturgeschichte'. The same preposition is used in the title of *Zur Genealogie der Moral.*

History' is a name for Nietzsche's genealogical analysis, as we saw. There may be many reasons for Nietzsche's use of this expression 'Natural History'. He probably thought of Goethe's 'Natur-philosophie': the outline of a basic structure of nature, and from there on of its many different forms in a 'morphology' and a 'history of their evolution',[10] terms that remind us of Nietzsche's description of his 'psychology' 'as morphology and *the doctrine of the development of the will to power*' (JGB 23).

A more important reason is that through this expression Nietzsche polemicizes against the naturalism of the Darwinists and the social Darwinists who were both very popular and controversial in nineteenth-century Germany.[11] Their genealogy, which explains morality (like everything else) from a natural 'struggle for survival' and 'development by means of adaptation', is according to Nietzsche no scientific explanation of morality from nature, but precisely the opposite: a moral distortion of nature by means of alleged science. Darwin's theory is an expression of prevailing morality, the morality of the weak. They survive by means of adaptation and then justify their strategies by means of this morality: 'the Darwinian beast and

10   Cf. J. W. Goethe, *Gedenkausgabe der Werke, Briefe und Gespräche*, ed. Ernst Beutler, 2nd edn (Zurich: Artemis, 1964). Goethe's *Naturwissenschaftliche Schriften* (scientific writings) are in Vols 16 and 17. See esp. Vol. 17, p. 711.

11   Cf. Alfred Kelly, *The Descent of Darwin: The Popularization of Darwinism in Germany 1860–1914* (Chapel Hill, NC: University of North Carolina Press, 1981), and W. M. Montgomery, 'Germany', in Thomas F. Glick (ed.), *The Comparative Reception of Darwinism* (Austin and London: University of Texas Press, 1974), pp. 81–116. A clear example of Darwin's influence on contemporary moralists is Paul Rée's book on *The Origin of the Moral Sensations*. In the preface the author states that for those readers who do not agree with Darwin it is useless to read his book, because it draws only the conclusions from Darwin's theses! Cf. also GM, Preface 4. For a discussion of the difference between Nietzsche's naturalism and the idea of a naturalistic morality in the sense of sociobiology (and especially of Emerson), see Hans Seigfried, 'Nietzsche's natural morality', *The Journal of Value Inquiry*, 26 (1992), 423–31.

the ultramodern unassuming moral milksop who "no longer bites" politely link hands' (GM, Preface 7).

Nietzsche wants to do the opposite: instead of grounding prevailing morality in nature, he attempts to strip away all self-evidence from this dominant morality. And precisely for this purpose he uses the term 'nature'. He wants to 'translate man back into nature' (JGB 230), convinced as he is that nature is much richer than its moral interpretation suggests. 'Natural history' is an older name for the science of biology, from the time when it consisted of the gathering, description and arranging of the many forms which nature had produced.[12] That is exactly what Nietzsche proposes to do with regard to morality: 'to collect material, to conceptualize and arrange a vast realm of subtle feelings of value and differences of value which are alive, grow, beget, and perish –' (JGB 186).

Nietzsche's 'naturalism' is no reductionism which levels reality to one pattern, but the opposite: it is an attempt to bring the prevailing uniformity of cultural products back to nature, nature being conceived of as a plural wealth of possibilities, as a polymorphic and variable ground for various and changing forms, i.e. as 'will to power'.

But although nature indicates for Nietzsche a plurality of possible forms, it nevertheless does not really exist except in some particular form. The tension between plurality and particular identity in nature is elaborated in section 188 of *Beyond Good and Evil*, where we find it as the tension between nature and morality! Let us look more carefully for a moment at this important section.

Every morality, Nietzsche says, forces the human being into one specific form. Therefore we can say morality oppose the plurality of nature and tyrannizes it. 'Every morality is [...] a bit of tyranny

---

12 An influential source might also have been W. E. H. Lecky's *History of European Morals from Augustus to Charlemagne*, 2 vols (London, 1869), which was studied by Nietzsche carefully and which opens with a long chapter (160 pages) entitled 'The Natural History of Morals'. In this chapter, Lecky presents a typology of morals: 'a brief enquiry in the nature and foundations of morals', in which they are divided in 'two opposing groups' that can be observed throughout history. (cf. Lecky, i, 1).

against "nature"'. But as such morality is very useful and even necessary. For the many possibilities of nature remain only possibilities as long as they are not reduced – through morality – into one that is realized. Nietzsche sums up the many things that originated as a result of this tyranny: the great linguistic creations by poets and orators, science, philosophy, politics and everything else that 'has been on earth of freedom, subtlety, boldness, dance, and masterly sureness, whether in thought itself or in government, or in rhetoric and persuasion, in the arts just as in ethics' (JGB 188).

Nature urges of itself to such determinations. Therefore Nietzsche says that this tyrannical (and in a certain sense anti-natural) morality is itself natural. In this section the reader is lead along different concepts of this so-called 'nature': 'nature' as being tyrannized by morality, 'nature' as being tyrannical itself, the indifferent magnificence of 'nature', 'nature' in morality. All of these concepts of 'nature' apparently need quotation marks! Only at the very end of section 188, where Nietzsche introduces his last concept of nature, in which nature and morality are fully integrated, are there no more quotation marks to the term nature: '"You shall obey – someone and for a long time: else you will perish and lose the last respect for yourself" – this appears to me to be the moral imperative of nature'. Nietzsche leads the reader from opposed concepts of morality and nature to a naturalized concept of morality, and a concept of nature which results from his doctrine of the will to power. The opposition between nature and morality is transformed into the tension or struggle between different wills to power.

This 'moral imperative of nature' addresses 'peoples, races, ages, classes – but above all [...] the whole human animal'. In discussing Nietzsche's conception of the human being as a special kind of animal, we might find a further clarification of his naturalism, and how it fits with the normative, educational pathos of his philosophy.

3. Human and animal

For Nietzsche the human being 'is the *as yet undetermined animal*'.[13]
On the one hand the human being is an animal: nature, corporeal,
driven by instincts, etc. But, on the other hand, the naturalness of this
being is not complete and encompassing. Human beings are not
completely determined by their instincts, they are not classified once
and for all into one particular pattern. They do not have a fixed and
definite identity, but maintain many possibilities: 'the type we are
representing is one of our possibilities – we could form many persons
– we do have the material for that in us. –' (KSA 11/107, 25[362]).[14]

Nietzsche uses the traditional form of the anthropological
definition (the human being is a special kind of animal) in an ironical
way. For him the *differentia specifica* which distinguishes this animal
(this species) from the other ones (the other species of the same
genus) is not its rationality (nor its language, its laughing, its upright
stature, and whatever else has been proposed), but precisely its
*in*determinacy.

To understand more fully what this means, we should realize that
the traditional definitions of the human being were usually meant to
be not merely descriptive but at the same time normative. They were
always part of some sort of naturalistic teleological ethics according

13   JGB 62. See also GM III, 13: 'For man is more sick, uncertain, changeable,
      indeterminate than any other animal, there is no doubt of that – he is *the* sick
      animal: how has that come about? Certainly he has also dared more, done more
      new things, braved more and challenged fate more than all the other animals put
      together: he, the great experimenter with himself, discontented and insatiable,
      wrestling with animals, nature, and gods for ultimate dominion – he, still
      unvanquished, eternally directed toward the future, whose own restless energies
      never leave him in peace, so that his future digs like a spur into the flesh of
      every present – how should such a courageous and richly endowed animal not
      also be the most imperiled, the most chronically and profoundly sick of all sick
      animals?'
14   See also: KSA 11/17, 25[21], where Nietzsche speaks about 'the plurality of
      characters [...] which is in any of us'.

to which human beings must become what they are. The task for human beings is to realize their humanity, which is characterized by the indicated *differentia specifica*.[15]

Nietzsche's variant of this traditional definition, when used for an ethics of self-realization, turns out to be paradoxical, because it says that every form to which the human being would determine himself or herself, would at the same time do harm to what he or she is, i.e. 'the *as yet undetermined animal*'. On the one hand the human being cannot live with this indeterminacy. Therefore humans are called 'as yet' undetermined. Self-determination is required and unavoidable for this 'most endangered animal' (FW 354). On the other hand every determination is an identification that wrongly conceals its own one-sidedness, and thus stands in contrast with the proper nature of this animal. As soon as the human being has become what it has to become, it is no longer what it most properly is, i.e. 'as yet undetermined'. We recognize again the tension between indeterminacy and determination which, as we already saw, holds in nature in general.

Nevertheless, Nietzsche's definition can still be used in a normative way. We could say that his definition of the human being allows him to distinguish between higher and lower types of self-realization. Among the ways in which the human being identifies itself, those that most comply with its being undetermined will be higher, i.e. those that are most open to many possibilities.[16] To the

15 Nietzsche was familiar with this idea of self-realization, as we may conclude from the subtitle of his 'autobiography' *Ecce homo*: 'How One Becomes What One Is'. In an unpublished note we read: 'The principle according to which man mastered animals, will probably also be the principle which determines "the highest man"' (KSA 11/135, 25[459]).

16 Lee F. Kerckhove ('Re-thinking ethical naturalism: Nietzsche's "open question" argument', *Man and World*, 27 (1994), 149–59) elaborates this point in a discussion with A. MacIntyre's thesis that we have to make a choice between 'Nietzsche or Aristotle', seen as mutually exclusive alternatives. Kerckhove writes: 'What MacIntyre has neglected to notice is that Nietzsche's naturalism is ultimately the same *in spirit* as Aristotle's naturalism. For it is clear that Nietzsche, like Aristotle, believes that our tables of what is good should

moral and religious fanaticism which is dominated by 'a single point of view and feeling', Nietzsche opposes a freedom which is 'practiced in maintaining (itself) on insubstantial ropes and possibilities' (FW 347).

Although the human being is nature, nature yet has double roles. On the one hand, nature is always determined and urging for determination. On the other hand, it is always as yet undetermined and transcending every determination. Without a reduction into specific forms the human animal is nothing but possibility; however, every concretization represses and destroys many of its possibilities: 'for here, as everywhere, "nature" manifests herself as she is, in all her prodigal, and indifferent magnificence which is outrageous but noble' (JGB 188).

Nature is will to power: a plurality of possible forms, possibilities which fight and repress each other. Nature lives as long as this struggle continues, as long as nature does not become rigid in one of her possibilities. To save nature from thus becoming rigid, be it in scientific theories or in moral doctrines, is the normative task of the philosopher.

This inner tension of nature is nowhere more forcefully represented than in the human being. For that reason Nietzsche concentrates on the development of the human being. That the human being is in essence '*as yet undetermined*' (JGB 62) and always has to be determined, that is 'the real problem of humankind' (GM II 1).

conform to what we essentially are, i.e. to our "nature". [...] Where Nietzsche and Aristotle differ is that Nietzsche believes that we don't yet know what our nature is.' (p. 157) It is my contention that Nietzsche's point is not that we do not yet know what our nature is, but that (our) nature is essentially not yet determined.

Jim Urpeth

Nietzsche and the Rapture of Aesthetic Disinterestedness: A Response to Heidegger

Heidegger, in a section of his first lecture course on Nietzsche entitled 'Kant's Doctrine of the Beautiful: Its Misinterpretation by Schopenhauer and Nietzsche', argues that Nietzsche's criticism of Kant's notion of aesthetic disinterestedness rests on a mis-understanding of it.[1] Nietzsche's failure in this regard is due, Heidegger suggests, to the influence of Schopenhauer's, in Heidegger's view flawed, interpretation of Kant's aesthetics. Nietzsche's dependence on Schopenhauer's appropriation of Kant's notion of aesthetic disinterestedness is, Heidegger claims, particularly un-fortunate in that there is, in fact, an affinity between Nietzsche's and Kant's conception of the beautiful which Nietzsche was unable to recognize.

In what follows, Heidegger's text will be taken as a foil to develop an alternative to his account of Nietzsche's response to Kant's notion of aesthetic disinterestedness. Although Heidegger's claim – that Nietzsche's conception of art can itself be said to contain a notion of aesthetic disinterestedness – will be endorsed, a different conception of which aspects of Nietzsche's thought can be thus conceived will be proposed. The strategy implicit in what follows will consist in finding Nietzsche's conception of art to be the consummation of a nascent radicality in Kant's aesthetics nurtured much more effectively, for all its faults, in Schopenhauer's response

---

1   See Martin Heidegger. *Nietzsche: Volume One*, trans. D. F. Krell (New York: Harper and Row, 1984), pp. 107–14.

to it than in the avenue of post-Kantian thought, originating with Hegel, which Heidegger valorizes in the text in question.[2]

After a brief critical review of the claims made in Heidegger's text, the two key occasions on which Nietzsche addresses Kant's notion of aesthetic disinterestedness will be discussed. As the texts in question are, intriguingly, drawn respectively from what is often categorized in terms of the 'early' and 'late' (or 'mature') periods of Nietzsche's thought, the interpretation offered here, in which Nietzsche's thought seemingly *declines* in radicality, will appear somewhat unorthodox. This will set the scene for the closing elaboration of an alternative account to that suggested by Heidegger of the sense in which Nietzsche's conception of art inherently develops, rather than rejects, the notion of aesthetic disinterestedness.[3]

I.

Although the overall contours of Heidegger's argument in the text under consideration are impressive, his implicit view that Nietzsche's critique of Kant's aesthetics is rendered impotent by its dependence upon Schopenhauer's reading of it is questionable. Similarly, Heidegger's account of wherein lies the proximity between Nietzsche's

2   See ibid., p. 107. As regards interpreters of Kant's aesthetics, Heidegger reserves the highest praise for Schiller (ibid., p. 108). For related comments on the relative value of Hegel (and 'German Idealism' in general) and Schopenhauer respectively see ibid., pp. 62–63. It is, of course, Hegel's problematic of the 'end of great art' which particularly concerns Heidegger both in the text in question (see ibid., pp. 84–85), and in the contemporaneous lecture series 'The Origin of the Work of Art'; see Martin Heidegger, *Poetry, Language, Thought*, trans. A. Hofstadter (New York: Harper and Row, 1971), pp. 17–87.

3   A familiarity with Kant's account of the notion of aesthetic disinterestedness and Schopenhauer's appropriation of it is, due to limitations of space, presupposed in what follows.

and Kant's discussions of art can be challenged. A more convincing implication of Heidegger's argument is that Nietzsche's critique of the notion of aesthetic disinterestedness is far more applicable to Schopenhauer's, much more unproblematically ascetic, conception of it than Kant's. Yet however questionable Schopenhauer's appropriation of Kant's notion of disinterestedness might be, it at least foregrounds the theme of asceticism. Although Heidegger correctly upbraids both Schopenhauer and Nietzsche for interpreting Kant's conception of disinterestedness as an ascetic notion (which, of course, each thinker evaluates very differently), it is precisely Nietzsche's diagnosis of the source of Kant's (and Schopenhauer's) uncritical endorsement of the *value* of the 'ascetic ideal' that characterizes the 'genealogical' nature of Nietzsche's critique of their work. Heidegger, obsessed with 'ontological' concerns, failed to appreciate the 'genealogical' nature of Nietzsche's critique of metaphysics.

Heidegger, given his preference for *The Will to Power*, does not, in the text considered here, discuss either of Nietzsche's most important and extended statements on aesthetic disinterestedness, found in *The Birth of Tragedy* and *On the Genealogy of Morality* respectively. Instead, Heidegger bases his claims on *Nachlass* material contemporaneous with *On the Genealogy of Morality*. In the absence of Heidegger's consideration of the relevant texts it can be noted that the enthusiastic stance Nietzsche adopts towards the notion of disinterestedness in *The Birth of Tragedy*, combined with a criticism, albeit tentative and deferential, of Schopenhauer, contests Heidegger's claims.[4] However, Nietzsche's fiercely critical comments on Kant's notion of aesthetic disinterestedness in *On the Genealogy of Morality* would seem to reinforce Heidegger's view, even if Nietzsche's explicit critical independence from Schopenhauer in this text disturbs it somewhat.

---

4   See GT 5 (Friedrich Nietzsche, *The Birth of Tragedy*, trans. Walter Kaufmann (New York: Vintage, 1967), pp. 51–52).

Heidegger, quite correctly, condemns the interpretation, which he accuses Schopenhauer of propagating, that conceives Kant's notion of disinterestedness as a merely negative state of 'indifference'.[5] Heidegger stresses the inherently active nature of the comportment of 'unconstrained favouring' which, for Kant, characterizes the aesthetic relation to the object of beauty. For Heidegger, the suspension of all empirical, utilitarian and moral 'interests', be they primary or derived, that characterizes, for Kant, a disinterested, purely aesthetic, relation to an object requires the, 'supreme effort of our essential nature, the liberation of ourselves for the release of what has proper worth in itself'.[6] Heidegger thus appreciates the process of affective *intensification* Kant identifies with disinterested contemplation and compares this positively with the effect of de-intensification which Schopenhauer associates with beauty in his valorization of art as a redeeming 'denial of the will to live'.

Heidegger reminds us that Kant's conception of aesthetic feeling and the judgment of taste based upon it is concerned with gaining access, precisely through the suspension of all empirical and moral interests in the 'existence of the object', to the 'pleasure of reflection'.[7] This reading allows Heidegger to demonstrate that Kant, no less than Nietzsche, conceived beauty in profoundly *non-ascetic* terms. Kant's insistence on aesthetic disinterestedness as a necessary element of a 'pure judgment of taste' serves to clarify a specific source of 'higher pleasure' rather than negate pleasure *per se*. Hence Heidegger, having cited a passage from the *Nachlass* (which resonates conveniently with his own problematic!), in which Nietzsche describes the experience of beauty as the 'thrill of being in *our* world now' (*das Entzücken, jetzt in unserer Welt zu sein*) proposes the following identification, 'what Nietzsche describes as the thrill that

---

5   See Heidegger, *Nietzsche*, pp. 108–10.
6   Ibid., p. 109.
7   For confirmation of Heidegger's claim, see Immanuel Kant, *Critique of Judgment*, trans. W. S. Pluhar (Indianapolis: Hackett, 1987), §39, p. 158; §44, p. 173.

comes of being in our world is what Kant means by the "pleasure of reflection".[8]

Of course, the affinity Heidegger detects between Kant's and Nietzsche's conceptions of beauty concerns his 'ontological' critique of metaphysics and excavation of a, hitherto concealed, configuration of being, appearing and the beautiful. For Heidegger the beautiful is conceived as the pre-eminent manifestation of presencing as such, the 'shining-forth' of a singular being in such a way that the self-concealing character of being itself (synonymous, for Heidegger, with the 'difference between being and beings') is disclosed. The radiance of the beautiful object is how, Heidegger contends, being explicitly conceals itself, how its self-concealing character becomes overt in a non-privative manner.[9] From this perspective Kant's and Nietzsche's (and particularly, Plato's) aesthetics are read by Heidegger in terms of traces detectable within 'their' texts, at the 'end of philosophy', of the 'truth of being', 'unconcealment' (*aletheia*), the 'relation between being and human being' etc.

Yet, however illuminating Heidegger's text might be with regard to Kant it displays many of the shortcomings that mar his reading of Nietzsche. One of the most significant deficiencies in this respect is Heidegger's treatment of the explicitly 'physiological' orientation of Nietzsche's thought in general, and overtly 'biological' conception of art in particular. Indeed, Heidegger's failure to comprehend the 'transcendental' nature of Nietzsche's materialism is, arguably, *the* 'Achilles' heel' of his entire reading and a symptom of a failure to consider the possibility that the 'ontological' might be conceivable, non-reductively and without objectification, in 'materialist' terms. Heidegger never interrogates critically the inherited assumptions he makes throughout his thinking concerning the nature, capacity and

8   Heidegger, *Nietzsche*, p. 112.
9   For Heidegger's powerful exposition of the *Sein-Schein-Schön* relation through-out the text under consideration see his *Nietzsche*, pp. 142–220, and also 'The Origin of the Work of Art' (op. cit.). There is, of course, a considerable affinity between Kant's 'disinterestedness' and Heidegger's *'Gelassenheit'*.

limits of materiality or expresses any self-critical suspicion about the sources of his pre-given 'anti-naturalism'.[10] Hence Heidegger can only express, in the text under consideration, an incredulity regarding Nietzsche's 'physiology of art' evident in the claim that, 'what is strange and almost incomprehensible is the fact that he tries to make his conception of the aesthetic state accessible to his contemporaries, and tries to convince them of it, by speaking the language of physiology and biology'.[11]

The interpretative stance adopted here, more attuned to both Nietzsche's 'materialism' and the 'genealogical' nature of his critique of metaphysics, thematizes the relation between Nietzsche's and Kant's aesthetics in a markedly different way to that sketched by Heidegger. The claim pursued below is that Nietzsche's conception of the nature of art is not, contrary to appearances, incompatible with the notion of disinterestedness *per se* and that, in fact, it is a theme which illuminates essential aspects of his views. Through a transvaluative critique of Kant's and Schopenhauer's aesthetics, Nietzsche implicitly

---

10   Heidegger does, of course, accord notions such as the 'earth' a significant status in his later thought and gives many illuminating phenomenological descriptions of a variety of natural phenomena throughout his texts. However, it is always taken as given in such analyses that an 'ontological', non-reductive 'materialism' is an impossibility.

11   Heidegger, *Nietzsche*, p. 113. See also ibid., p. 91. An overall assessment of Heidegger's treatment of the 'physiological' and 'biological' register of Nietzsche's thought cannot, of course, be attempted here. The most important section of Heidegger's text in this respect is 'Rapture as Aesthetic State' (ibid., pp. 92–106). Other relevant comments occur at ibid., pp. 126–27, 219. In general terms the crucial 'materialist' tenor of Nietzsche's thought is, in order to save it from positivism, scienticism, empirical psychology etc., sacrificed by Heidegger and a highly 'phenomenologised' language of 'embodying attunement' (ibid., p. 106) substituted instead. Of course Heidegger's treatment of this aspect of Nietzsche's thought in the first lecture course is not uniformly weak. I discussed the impressive 'Rapture as Form-engendering Force' (ibid., pp. 115–23) and 'The Grand Style' (ibid., pp. 124–37) sections of Heidegger's text in 'The Vitalisation of Aesthetic Form: Kant, Nietzsche, Heidegger, Focillon', in S. Brewster et al. (eds), *Inhuman Reflections: Thinking the Limits of the Human* (Manchester: Manchester University Press, 2000), pp. 72–87.

develops a radicalized, 'extra-moral' and affirmative conception of aesthetic disinterestedness even though he was increasingly unable to endorse the term as such. In short, it will be argued that a form of disinterestedness is inherently contained in Nietzsche's claim that, 'for art to exist, for any sort of aesthetic activity or perception to exist, a certain physiological precondition is indispensable: *rapture* (*der Rausch*)'.[12] The most significant and extended discussions of aesthetic disinterestedness in Nietzsche's texts must now be considered.

II.

In seeking the 'first evidence' of the union between the 'Apollonian' and the 'Dionysian' in ancient Greek culture, Nietzsche addresses the problem of how, on the basis of the terms of reference of 'modern aesthetics', it is possible to account for the status, equal to that of Homer, the Greeks accorded Archilochus the lyrist, the quintessential 'Dionysian artist'. The question Nietzsche addresses is how such an unashamedly 'subjective' artist as Archilochus is conceivable at all. In framing this 'problem', Nietzsche's endorsement of the notion of disinterestedness is explicit and unequivocal,

> [...] we know the subjective artist only as the poor artist, and throughout the entire range of art we demand first of all the conquest of the subjective, redemption from the 'ego', and the silencing of the individual will and desire; indeed we find it impossible to believe in any truly artistic production, however insignificant, if it is without objectivity, without pure contemplation devoid of interest [*reines interesseloses Anschauen*]. Hence our aesthetics must first solve the problem of how the 'lyrist' is possible as an artist – he who, according to the

---

12   GD ix 8 (Friedrich Nietzsche, *Twilight of the Idols*, trans. R. J. Hollingdale (Harmondsworth: Penguin, 1968), p. 71). On the translation of 'der Rausch' as 'rapture' (here modified from Hollingdale's 'intoxication'), see D. F. Krell's translator's note to Heidegger, *Nietzsche*, p. 92.

experience of all ages, is continually saying 'I' and running through the entire chromatic scale of his passions and desires.[13]

What is striking about this passage is that Nietzsche clearly insists upon identifying the seemingly contradictory domains of intense passion and disinterestedness or objectivity. To comprehend this apparently contradictory association of terms it is crucial to recall Nietzsche's overtly impersonal, and radically anti-utilitarian, conception of the 'Dionysian' forces which engulf and determine the lyric poet. Hence, it transpires that the 'outbursts of desire' that characterize Archilochus' verse have a fundamentally *a-subjective* source and that the insistent 'I' that resounds throughout lyric poetry is essentially non-egoic.[14] In this context the first-person pronoun does not designate an 'ego' or self-identity but marks a site wherein fundamentally anonymous processes occur. Nietzsche states his insistence on the priority of such impersonal creative forces over the 'subjectivity' of artist in the following passage:

> The artist has already surrendered his subjectivity in the Dionysian process. The 'I' of the lyrist therefore sounds from the depth of his being: its 'subjectivity', in the sense of the modern aestheticians is a fiction [...] it is not his passion alone that dances before us in orgiastic frenzy... The lyric genius is conscious of a world of images and symbols – growing out of his state of mystical self-abnegation and oneness [...] he, as the moving centre of this world, may say 'I': of course, this self is not the same as that of the waking, empirically real man [...] Archilochus, the passionately inflamed, loving, and hating man, is but a vision of the genius, who by this time is no longer merely Archilochus, but a world-genius expressing his primordial pain symbolically in the symbol of the man Archilochus – while the subjectively willing and desiring man, Archilochus, can never at any time be a poet.[15]

Nietzsche's further identification in this passage of aesthetic objectivity or disinterestedness with intense, yet a-subjective, affect is the basis of his criticism of Schopenhauer's conception of lyric poetry. Nietzsche claims that Schopenhauer, due to his oppositional

13   GT 5 (p. 48).
14   Ibid., p. 48.
15   Ibid., pp. 49–50.

conception of the relation between 'willing' (for Schopenhauer, the 'unaesthetic') and 'pure contemplation' (for Schopenhauer, the 'aesthetic') is forced to conceive lyric poetry as merely, in Nietzsche's phrase, a 'semi-art' in which desire and disinterestedness are only 'wonderfully mingled' rather than fused.[16] This leads Nietzsche into a concluding burst of radical impersonalism:

> We contend [...] that the whole opposition between the subjective and the objective, which Schopenhauer still uses as a measure of value in classifying the arts, is altogether irrelevant in aesthetics, since the subject, the willing individual that furthers his own egoistic ends, can be conceived of only as the antagonist, not the as the origin of art. Insofar as the subject is the artist, he has already been released from his individual will, and has become [...] the medium through which the one truly existent subject celebrates his release in appearance [...] Only insofar as the genius in the act of creation coalesces with this primordial artist of the world, does he know anything of the eternal essence of art [...] he is at once subject and object.[17]

Clearly therefore Nietzsche's discussion of the nature of the ancient Greeks' lyric poetry posits an alignment, rather than an opposition, between disinterestedness and the 'Dionysian'. This suggests the possibility of a trajectory for the overcoming of selfish interest through artistic creation and aesthetic experience other than that proposed by either Kant or Schopenhauer. At least in the case of the comparison between Kant and Nietzsche the issue is not accurately thematized in terms of an opposition between self-denial and egoism but rather concerns a contrast between different economies of intense aesthetic feeling which, in both cases, concern the displacement of the empirical self in a resurgence of pre-egoic creative processes.[18] In *The Birth of Tragedy* Nietzsche identifies the

---

16   See ibid., pp. 51–52.
17   Ibid., p. 52.
18   I attempted to portray this contrast between Kant's and Nietzsche's aesthetic sensibilities in 'A "Sacred Thrill": Presentation and Affectivity in the Analytic of the Sublime', in A. Rehberg and R. Jones (eds), *The Matter of Critique: Readings in Kant's Philosophy* (Manchester: Clinamen Press, 2000), pp. 61–78.

aesthetic state of disinterestedness with the affirmation of the 'Dionysian'. This achieves a radical transvaluative realignment of Kantian-Schopenhauerian aesthetics based upon the uncovering of a primordial level of 'nature', the 'will', the 'body', the 'unconscious' etc., that cannot be described as inherently 'selfish' or said to be determined by lack, want or need. Nietzsche thereby overcomes the interpretation of the fundamental nature of 'desire' that forms the foundation of the value-system that constitutes Platonic-Christian metaphysics and provides the basis for the status it accords to the 'ascetic ideal' in its 'moral' guise.

In his dissatisfaction with Schopenhauer's account of the lyrist, Nietzsche demonstrates that, even in his 'early' texts, he had developed a conception of the 'will' that breaks with the model of 'desire as lack' found in both Kant's utilitarian conception of the 'interests' of the 'empirical' order and Schopenhauer's description of the 'affirmation of the will-to-live' as a cycle of 'pain and boredom'. This is why, unlike Nietzsche, neither Kant nor Schopenhauer can equate the overcoming of egoic interest with an affirmation of the most fundamental instinctual bases of material life. Nietzsche rejects German Idealism's vision of the teleological unification of man and nature and develops an 'extra-moral' alternative in which the capacity for aesthetic disinterestedness plays a similarly crucial role. However, in Nietzsche's case, the aesthetic condition gestures towards the dissolution of subjectivity into self-expending economy of anonymous intensities and affects, an 'extra-moral' and non-reductive materialization of spirit rather than a 'moral' and reductive spiritualization of matter.[19]

---

19 For a reflection on the 'lyrist' in Nietzsche's later thought, see GD ix 11 (*Twilight of the Idols*, pp. 73–74). For another, implicit, positive evaluation and rethinking of the notion of disinterestedness, on this occasion regarding historical consciousness, from an 'early' text, see Friedrich Nietzsche, *On the Advantage and Disadvantage of History for Life*, trans. P. Preuss (Indianapolis: Hackett, 1988), pp. 34–35. Claudia Crawford provides a good contextualization of Nietzsche's early conception of disinterestedness in *The Beginnings of Nietzsche's Theory of Language* (Berlin and New York: de Gruyter, 1988), pp.

III.

The treatment of the theme of aesthetic disinterestedness found in Nietzsche's later texts fails to sustain the radicality of *The Birth of Tragedy*. Nietzsche no longer valorizes a Dionysian form of disinterestedness and retreats from such an ambitious 'transvaluative' synthesis into a simpler oppositional framework in which the notion of disinterestedness is exclusively identified with asceticism. In his later texts Nietzsche finds no radical resources in the notion of disinterestedness relevant or applicable to his conception of art. Typical statements of the later Nietzsche's negative evaluation of disinterestedness include its identification with the 'emasculation of art today'[20] and the claim that it is 'a fat worm of basic error' (GM III 6).[21]

Nietzsche addresses the theme of aesthetic disinterestedness in *On the Genealogy of Morality* in the course of his investigation of the 'meaning of the ascetic ideal' in the case of the philosopher.[22] Here the familiar reasons for Nietzsche's rejection of the Kantian-Schopenhauerian conception of disinterestedness are expressed – the nihilism of its 'denial of life', its source in the psycho-physiological economy of the 'slave', the 'weakness' inherent in such expressions of desire for the transcendent, etc. Nietzsche's claim is that the Kantian-Schopenhauerian conceptions of disinterestedness are instantiations of the 'ascetic ideal' which as such presuppose, either implicitly (Kant) or explicitly (Schopenhauer), pessimism and

---

175–76, 188–92. For an excellent 'impersonalist' interpretation of the 'Dionysian' in Nietzsche's early thought, see D. B. Allison: 'Some Remarks on Nietzsche's Essay of 1871, "On Words and Music"', *New Nietzsche Studies*, 1 (1996), nos. 1–2, 15–41.

20   JGB 33 (Friedrich Nietzsche, *Beyond Good and Evil*, trans. R. J. Hollingdale (Harmondsworth: Penguin, 1973), p. 46).

21   Friedrich Nietzsche, *On the Genealogy of Morality*, trans. Carol Diethe (Cambridge: Cambridge University Press, 1994), p. 78.

22   See ibid., pp. 78–85.

negation in relation to the 'will', the 'body' etc. Nietzsche also condemns the purported claim to objectivity (in the Kantian sense of the universalisable *a priori* dimensions of subjectivity) inherent in the notion of disinterestedness. For Nietzsche any claim to aesthetic disinterestedness merely expresses, in a self-deluding fashion, the interests and self-preservative motivations of a particular, and decidedly enfeebled, type of will and its perspective on life.[23] Yet although Nietzsche applies the full resources of his insights into 'perspectivism' against the notion of 'contemplation without interest', he also anticipates, for those so constituted as to be capable of it, the advent of a 'future 'objectivity'' founded upon the acknowledgment, rather than the exclusion, of 'difference in perspectives and affective interpretations' (GM III 12).[24]

The claim made here is that Nietzsche's later critique of the notion of disinterestedness is applicable only to the Kantian-Schopenhauerian, 'moral' or ascetic *interpretation* of it. Furthermore it is suggested that Nietzsche's later thought also contains, albeit implicitly, an alternative, *affirmative* form of aesthetic disinterestedness conceived as the expression of a 'noble' rather than a 'slave' aesthetic affective economy. It is crucial to establish the credibility of the, *prima facie* implausible, possibility that Nietzsche tacitly develops a notion of aesthetic disinterestedness if clichéd misinterpretations of his thought in 'subjectivist' terms are to be contested. Hence covertly contained in Nietzsche's later critique of proponents of a transcendent conception of aesthetic disinterestedness is the excavation of an *immanent* variety of it aligned with the affirmation, through and as art, of a non-utilitarian dimension of the sensuous in which egoic interests are dissolved. One of Nietzsche's most abiding and important projects is thereby furthered, namely, the overcoming of ingrained 'Platonic-Christian' assumptions concerning

---

23   See JGB 220 (*Beyond Good and Evil*, p. 131). The 'genealogical' provenance of the notion of disinterestedness is hinted at in GM I 2 (pp. 12–13).

24   Nietzsche, *On the Genealogy of Morality*, p. 92.

the allegedly 'selfish' orientation of the primary processes of desire, the 'body' etc., a necessary presupposition of the 'moral world view'.

A key feature of Nietzsche's critique of the notion of disinterestedness in his later thought is the diagnostic exposure of the interests of the psycho-physiological economy that masquerades behind it. Although in general Nietzsche bemoans the emphasis placed in modern aesthetics on the spectator rather than the artist, he also evaluates the relative 'health' of different spectators.[25] Hence one of Kant's formulations of disinterestedness is compared negatively by Nietzsche with Stendhal's formulation, 'beauty promises happiness'. (GM III, 6)[26] He also expresses a preference for Stendhal's conception of beauty, which he interprets as the *'excitement of the will* (*die Erregung des Willens*) ("of interest")' over Schopenhauer's account of it as a 'calming of the will' (ibid.).[27] On the basis of his conception of the relative 'health' and 'sickness' of these individuals' respective relationship to their sexuality, Nietzsche applauds the 'happily adjusted personality' of Stendhal over that of the 'country parson' Kant and the 'tortured' Schopenhauer (ibid.).[28] Thus the universalist pretensions inherent to Kant's notion of disinterestedness are rejected and a diagnostic reflection on the 'sexual experience' of particular individuals is offered instead (ibid.). Clearly the later Nietzsche seems to forsake the radical synthesis suggested in *The Birth of Tragedy* between, on the one hand, a 'Dionysian' dimension of existence such as sexuality and, on the other hand, the possibility of aesthetic disinterestedness. Instead a merely oppositional stance is presented in which disinterestedness and the 'excitement of the will' are negatively

25   See GM III 6 (p. 78), and *The Will To Power*, trans. Walter Kaufmann and R. J. Hollingdale (New York: Vintage, 1968), §811, pp. 428–29.

26   Nietzsche, *On the Genealogy of Morality*, p. 78 and p. 80.

27   For an account of the appearance of Stendhal at this point in Nietzsche's thought, albeit one that adopts the received view of the latter's conception of disinterestedness, see Brian Domino: 'Stendhal's Ecstatic Embrace of History as the Antidote for Decadence', in John Lippitt (ed.), *Nietzsche's Futures* (London: Macmillan, 1999), pp. 48–61.

28   Nietzsche, *On the Genealogy of Morality*, pp. 79–80.

contrasted with Nietzsche favouring the latter over the former. Hence the later Nietzsche seems only capable of an *inversion*, rather than a *transvaluation*, of a metaphysical opposition such as that between disinterestedness and instinctual desire.

An appeal could be made at this point to a, albeit hermeneutically banal, periodization of Nietzsche's thought. It might be claimed that Nietzsche's evaluation of the theme of aesthetic disinterestedness is governed by the degree of his deference to Schopenhauer and, as this wanes, so does the deployment of such traditional terminology. Hence, it may be argued, as Nietzsche's thought matures, his assessment of a theme such as disinterestedness becomes ever more critical, culminating in a rejection of it as part of the unequivocal condemnation of Schopenhauer's aesthetics found in his later texts. However, in addition to the shortcomings inherent to such objectivist hermeneutic schemas, the complexities of the relevant contrasts in Nietzsche's case tend to invalidate such a simplistic account of his changing evaluation of the theme of disinterestedness.[29] Whatever the subsequent fate in Nietzsche's texts of the 'aesthetical metaphysics' adumbrated in *The Birth of Tragedy*,[30] it is argued here that the notion of disinterestedness remains relevant and applicable to the conception of the nature and role of art found in his later texts. Indeed Nietzsche's perfectly justified, insistence in his later texts on the fundamental differences between his and Schopenhauer's aesthetics tends to blind him to the radical resources nascent within Kant's

---

29   For an exceptional account of the Nietzsche-Schopenhauer relation in the early Nietzsche, see John Sallis, *Crossings: Nietzsche and the Space of Tragedy* (Chicago: Chicago University Press, 1991), pp. 60–75, 148–49. See also Jacques Taminiaux's excellent 'Art and Truth in Schopenhauer and Nietzsche', in *Poetics, Speculation, and Judgment: The Shadow of the Work of Art from Kant to Phenomenology*, trans. Michael Gendre (Albany: SUNY Press, 1993) pp. 111–26. Also impressive, on the key section of *The Birth of Tragedy* under discussion here, is Andrzej Warminski, *Readings in Interpretation: Hölderlin, Hegel, Heidegger* (Minneapolis: University of Minnesota Press, 1987), pp. xliii–xlv.

30   See GT 5 (p. 49).

conception of aesthetic disinterestedness.[31] Hence Nietzsche is unable to explicitly acknowledge the extent to which his conception of 'affirmative' art implicitly contains a radicalized version of the notion of disinterestedness.[32]

Yet in his late texts Nietzsche does, albeit only in a gesture of critique rather than affirmative appropriation, overcome a dualistic interpretation of the relation between disinterestedness and desire. This he achieves by offering a naturalistic account of disinterestedness in pursuit of a non-reductive materialist interpretation of 'culture'. On a general level this is an example of Nietzsche's insistence on the self-contradictory character of the 'ascetic ideal' which, far from being a 'denial of life', functions as a key pragmatic strategy serving the self-preservative drives and 'self-interests' of particular types of will (the 'artist', 'philosopher', 'ascetic priest', 'scientist' etc). It signifies an acute affective paradox which finds its most intense expression in the lives of the 'degenerate' who derive an extraordinarily intense yield of pleasure from an unrestrained indulgence in self-denial.[33]

31 A clear example of this is the following condemnation by the later Nietzsche of his earlier thought, 'I obscured and spoiled Dionysian premonitions with Schopenhauerian formulations' in GTVS 6 (*The Birth of Tragedy*, p. 24).

32 Michael Tanner provides a typical statement of the received view concerning Nietzsche's adoption in his first book and subsequent jettisoning in his later texts of the notion of aesthetic disinterestedness when he states, in an editorial note on the topic: '[...] this is an incongruous and unthinking adoption on Nietzsche's part of the Kantian and Schopenhauerian view [...] he was later to castigate "disinterested contemplation" as a castration of art, as he would have done even at this stage, had he been consistent' (Friedrich Nietzsche, *The Birth of Tragedy*, ed. Michael Tanner, trans. Shaun Whiteside (London: Penguin, 1993,) n. 16, p. 120). For a more interesting reflection on this topic, see M. S. Silk and J. P. Stern, *Nietzsche on Tragedy* (Cambridge: Cambridge University Press, 1981) pp. 347–48.

33 See GM III 11 and 13 (pp. 91, 93). I discussed Nietzsche's overcoming of an oppositional relation toward the 'ascetic ideal', in '"Noble" *Ascesis*: Between Nietzsche and Foucault', *New Nietzsche Studies*, 2, nos. 3–4 (Summer 1998), pp. 65–91.

In the course of such a non-oppositional interpretation of the meaning of the 'ascetic ideal' in the life of the philosopher, Nietzsche offers the following account of Schopenhauer's notion of dis-interestedness, '[...] the aesthetic condition might well descend from the ingredient "sensuality" [...] sensuality is not suspended as soon as we enter the aesthetic condition, as Schopenhauer believed, but is only transfigured and no longer enters the consciousness as a sexual stimulus' (GM III 8).[34] Nietzsche states that such insights are part of a *'physiology of aesthetics'* (ibid.).[35] This 'naturalized' interpretation of Kantian-Schopenhauerian conceptions of disinterestedness is clearly entirely critical in nature. Nonetheless, although it offers no explicit account of a transvalued conception of disinterestedness akin to that found in *The Birth of Tragedy*, it gestures toward the resources required for its development. The interpretative question that arises at this point is whether Nietzsche's unmasking of the libidinal nature of the 'ascetic ideal', a perspective which contests the dualistic, 'moral' self-interpretation of its advocates, entails that his thought has a merely negative agenda which aims at nothing beyond the exposure of the naiveté and fraudulence of such, seemingly intrinsically idealist, notions such as disinterestedness. Is it not the case, rather, that such critique has a necessary but merely provisional status in Nietzsche's attempted overcoming of nihilism which undermines merely 'moral' varieties of notions such as aesthetic disinterestedness as a prelude to the development of 'extra-moral' inhabitations of them? In short, can an affirmative, in a sense 'non-sublimated', conception of disinterestedness conceived as a non-redemptive process of artistic 'transfiguration', be said to be implicit in Nietzsche's 'physiology of art'?

34   Nietzsche, *On the Genealogy of Morality*, p. 85.
35   In GD ix 21–23 (pp. 79–81) Nietzsche again criticizes Schopenhauer's self-misinterpretation, in ascetic terms, of the notion of disinterestedness. On this occasion, Nietzsche appeals to Plato's conception of beauty (clearly referring to *Symposium*) in order to insist on a relation between 'sensuous' and 'suprasensuous' manifestations of beauty.

IV.

Arguably the fundamental conception of the nature and role of art found in *The Birth of Tragedy*, in which the notion of disinterestedness is endorsed, is retained by Nietzsche throughout his thought. In the preface to the second edition (1886) of *The Birth of Tragedy*, a text contemporaneous with *On the Genealogy of Morality*, Nietzsche notes how he increasingly forged a language which allowed the inherent radicality of his first book to emerge.[36] Undeniably, the notion of disinterestedness, laden with the ascetic and pessimistic overtones of Schopenhauer's thought, was a casualty of this process of stylistic maturation. As Nietzsche admits, 'I tried laboriously to express by means of Schopenhaurian and Kantian formulas strange and new valuations which were basically at odds with Kant's and Schopenhauer's spirit and taste!' (GTVS 6).

That the theme of the 'Dionysian' retained its central place throughout the course of Nietzsche's discussions of art and aesthetic experience is uncontentious. If anything, the role of the 'Dionysian' expands in Nietzsche's thought and tends to eclipse the 'Apollonian' in that it is also ultimately conceived in terms of 'rapture'.[37] The most significant and obvious development of Nietzsche's discourse on art is an increasingly overt insistence on a 'physiological' register through which to thematize it. Nietzsche employs this both critically, as in *On the Genealogy of Morality*, to undermine the idealism of his predecessors' aesthetics but also, more importantly, in the elaboration of his own conception of art. This 'physiology of art' is given its most extended exposition in the *Nachlass* material collected in *The Will to Power* under the heading 'The Will to Power as Art'. A recurring theme in these notes is the identification of art

36   See GTVS 3 and 6.
37   See GD x 4–5 (pp. 108–111), and *The Will to Power*, §799, p. 420. I discussed this issue in 'The Vitalisation of Aesthetic Form: Kant, Nietzsche, Heidegger, Focillon' (op. cit.).

with the most primordial material and instinctual processes of 'life'. The following passage provides a typical example:

> Art reminds us of states of animal vigor; it is on the one hand an excess and overflow of blooming physicality into the world of images and desires; on the other hand, an excitation of animal functions through the images and desires of intensified life; – an enhancement of the feeling of life, a stimulant to it.[38]

Nietzsche conceives the fundamental processes of 'life' in terms of 'self-overcoming' and argues that nature exhibits a primary prodigality and profligacy that precedes and excedes utilitarian and teleological processes.[39] For Nietzsche the human animal is inextricably embroiled, without remainder, in the gratuitous flow of impersonal materiality. Art is valorized by Nietzsche as the 'cultural' phenomenon most primordially rooted within the prodigious and primary interpretative force of material life. These fundamental elements of Nietzsche's thought form the basis for the claim made here that the notion of disinterestedness resonates profoundly with his later conception of art.

Nietzsche implicitly radicalizes Kant's insight into the specificity of the 'aesthetic attitude' in an attempt to dissociate art entirely from all utilitarian and teleological perspectives and align it with the influx of an irretrievably 'unproductive' material excess. This aspect of disinterestedness must be disentangled from the Kantian-Schopenhauerian 'moral' appropriation of it in which it is conceived in terms of a project of purification from material contamination in support of a theologico-humanist system of value. If a fundamental aspect of Nietzsche's radicalization of the Kantian-Schopenhauerian project of critique is the attempt not merely to recognize but to overcome anthropomorphism, then his thought could be said to display a radical disinterestedness in the promotion of the 'human' as a rational-moral entity essentially distinct in kind from 'nature'. In turn, Nietzsche rejects any philosophical

---

38   Nietzsche, *The Will to Power*, §802, p. 422.
39   See, for example, JGB 15, and *The Will to Power*, §370, p. 200; §650, p. 344; §666, pp. 351–52; §688, pp. 366–67.

project which appropriates art and aesthetic experience in terms of a teleological interpretation of nature as a domain ultimately orientated to theologico-moral ends (even when critically disciplined). Nietzsche refuses to contribute to the pragmatic projects and self-sustaining illusions of the species he only nominally belongs to and instead prioritizes the 'interests' of 'life' over those of the 'human' arguing that the former has primacy over the latter within a fundamentally a-symmetrical relation. In identifying art with the 'stimulation of life', Nietzsche implicitly radicalizes Kant's insights into disinterestedness by uncoupling it from even the critically restrained teleological perspective of the third *Critique*.

Yet surely, it might be objected, Nietzsche's 'biological' account of aesthetic experience entails an ineradicable role for instinctually based perspectival evaluations, a view radically incompatible with *any* notion of disinterestedness? In an important statement of such a view Nietzsche also insists, however, upon a crucial distinction,

> [...] the beautiful and the ugly are recognised as *relative* to our most fundamental values of preservation. It is senseless to want to posit anything as beautiful or ugly apart from this. *The* beautiful exists just as little as does *the* good, or *the* true. In every case it a question of the conditions of preservation of a certain type of man: thus the *herd* man will experience the value feeling of the beautiful in the presence of different things than will the exceptional or overman.[40]

This passage distinguishes between, in effect, 'noble' and 'slave' aesthetic sensibilities. If some of Nietzsche's basic characterizations of the 'overman' are recalled, then it is clear that the self-preservation of the 'noble' type is synonymous with a process of 'self-overcoming', an incessantly reinvoked immanent, rather than transcendent, self-transcendence, a self-dissolution *via* immersion in, rather than redemption from, 'this world'. The 'conditions of self-preservation' of the 'noble' aesthetic sensibility will, unlike the utilitarian instincts of the 'slave', find aesthetic pleasure in the

---

40   Nietzsche, *The Will to Power*, §804, p. 423.

resurgence of dysteleological forces. The aesthetic taste of the 'noble' affective economy warms to the artistic display of the ultimate irreducibility of 'life' to the theoretical and practical order of the 'human', the perpetual dashing of all (even critically delimited) fantasies concerning the teleological alignment of 'nature' and rational-moral humanity. Nietzsche described the qualities of such a 'noble' affective economy in terms of the '*joy in destruction*' (GD x 5) that characterizes an affirmative response to the 'tragic'. The energetic economy from which such aesthetic evaluations arise is, as Nietzsche constantly stresses, not founded upon utility but upon a primary superabundance and excess; the 'self-preservative' aesthetic sensibility of those in whom the instinct of affirmative self-expenditure predominates. This is an economy of anti-utilitarian 'interests' within which 'self-interest' consists of self-abandonment.

Many of the claims that have been pursued here are illustrated in one of Nietzsche's most important statements on art found in *Twilight of the Idols* (GD ix 24).[41] The subtitle of the text in question identifies the theme Nietzsche is critically assessing, namely, '*l'art pour l'art*', a stance which might seem to be akin to Nietzsche's own given his hostility to the '*moralizing* tendency in art' (ibid.). Nietzsche's response to the charge of aestheticism demonstrates the transvaluative character of his thought:

> When one has excluded from art the purpose of moral preaching and human improvement it by no means follows that art is completely purposeless, goalless, meaningless, in short *l'art pour l'art* [...] what does all art do? does it not praise? does it not glorify? does it not select? does it not highlight? By doing all this it *strengthens* or *weakens* certain valuations [...] is it not the prerequisite for the artist's being an artist at all [...] Is his basic instinct directed towards art, or is it not directed towards the meaning of art, which is *life*? towards a *desideratum of life*? – Art is the great stimulus to life: how could it be thought purposeless, aimless, *l'art pour l'art*? (ibid.)

41   *Twilight of the Idols*, pp. 81–82.

The significance of this passage lies in its definitive rejection of both moralism *and* aestheticism. It provides clear evidence that Nietzsche implicitly developed, largely unknowingly, a transvalued conception of some of the principal themes of Kant's aesthetics.[42] Nietzsche concludes the text in which the passage above appears with a restatement of the anti-pessimistic perspective of the tragic artist who displays a *'fearlessness* in the face of the fearsome and questionable' (GD ix 24).[43] Nietzsche refuses therefore, to contain his thought within the inherited oppositional schemas it attacks. Hence, Nietzsche's critique of the nihilistic nature of the teleological appropriation of art does not entail a commitment to its 'purpose-lessness'. Instead, in a radicalization of Kant's theme of the 'purposiveness without a purpose' of aesthetic experience and judgment Nietzsche defines the 'purpose' of art in terms of the affirmation of anti-teleological forces. Art, for Nietzsche, is conceived as the reassertion of a primal, plenitudinous meaningfulness which, whilst irreducible to meaning, is not to be conceived privatively. Nietzsche valorizes art as the natural-cultural hybrid through which the reduction of life to thought is perennially frustrated. Art derives its politico-critical force from an ultimate undermining of all appropriative gestures in terms of human communal sentiment which it contests through its advocacy of a politics of impersonal life forever at odds with the petty human concern for recognition and identity. It is this alignment of art with the resistance to human utilitarian endeavour in all its forms that signals the transvalued notion of disinterestedness implicitly operative in Nietzsche's later conception of art.

It has been argued that Nietzsche's later texts implicitly develop in overtly physiological terms what is explicitly contained in *The Birth of Tragedy*, namely, an affirmative conception of aesthetic disinterestedness. This surpasses, in a gesture of appropriative

---

42 One might say that the 'Kantian' concepts unfold and radicalize themselves in 'Nietzsche's' thought.

43 *Twilight of the Idols*, p. 82.

radicalization, Kant's and Schopenhauer's 'moral' interpretation of the aesthetic condition. Although, therefore, Heidegger's identification of Nietzsche's 'rapture' with Kant's 'pleasures of reflection' is suggestive, in many ways his overall treatment of the role of aesthetic disinterestedness in Nietzsche's thought reveals many of the limitations of his interpretation of Nietzsche's conception of art. Heidegger remains untouched by a 'materialist' current that, beginning with themes in Kant's aesthetics, runs, *via* Schopenhauer, to its fulfilment in Nietzsche's texts wherein a naturalistic conception of 'aesthetic experience' in terms of *enraptured disinterestedness* can be located. Through its role as the site of the affirmation of primary material forces art, for Nietzsche, attains to an absolute form of disinterestedness that contests the physical and spiritual interests of the integrated 'human' organism.

Gerd Schank

Race and Breeding in Nietzsche's Philosophy

Recent years have seen important advances in the clarification of a 'precedence' in Nietzsche for the ideology of the Nazis.[1] This problem also calls for a closer examination of the concepts 'Rasse' (race) and 'Züchtung' (breeding) in Nietzsche's texts and thought. Such an examination has been carried out in the philosophy department of the Katholieke Universiteit Nijmegen.[2] A brief account of the main results of this examination will now be given.

1. The concept of race in Nietzsche

In the first place it is important to note that Nietzsche himself gives his own explanation of the race concept: peoples living for a longer time in a specific environment ('Umgebung') and developing a 'Charakter' of their own in such environments are called 'races' ('Rassen') (NF Spring 1884, 25[462]: KSA 11/136). The 'Charakter' they develop comprises certain physiologically based values appropiate to ensure life ('Dasein') under these conditions. Environ-

---

1   See Rudolf Kreis, *Nietzsche, Wagner und die Juden* (Würzburg: Königshausen & Neumann, 1995), Arno Münster, *Nietzsche et le nazisme* (Paris: Kimé, 1995), and Weaver Santaniello, *Nietzsche, God and the Jews: His Critique of Judeo-Christianity in Relation to the Nazi Myth* (Albany: SUNY Press, 1994).

2   See Gerd Schank, *'Rasse' und 'Züchtung' bei Nietzsche* (Berlin and New York: de Gruyter, 2000).

ment ('Umgebung') is specified by Nietzsche in the language of warmth ('Wärme'), cold ('Kälte'), climate and so on.

Nietzsche could have found such a race concept in the writings of F. A. Lange and Rudolf Virchow.[3] Virchow did special research on the question of races in Europe, in which he refuted the concept of biologically based races for the populations of Europe, stating that there are no such races in Europe, Europe being an 'old mixed country' ('altgemischtes Land') and European people being defined only by their cultural development. This claim can also be found in Nietzsche's texts.

The word 'Rasse' occurs about two hundred times in Nietzsche's texts.[4] Three meanings can be assigned to the word 'Rasse' in these texts: in most instances it means 'people' ('Volk'), corresponding to Nietzsche's own explicit explanation of the word 'Rasse'; often it also means 'social classes' ('Stände'); and it can also refer to human beings in general ('Mensch', 'Menschheit', 'Menschentyp').[5] The word 'Rasse' does not occur in *Zarathustra*. In *Beyond Good and Evil* alone, on the other hand, there are twenty-two passages containing the word 'Rasse'. In this work, Nietzsche treats the problem of modern Europe, and the word 'Rasse' is mostly used synonymously with the word 'Volk' ('people'). The modern biological meaning of the word 'Rasse' was also known to Nietzsche. It occurs mainly in those texts where Nietzsche polemicizes against well-known anti-Semites like Dühring, Fritsch and Treitschke.[6] In the *Genealogy of Morals* he uses it once when treating the question whether there could be a relation between European decadence and the beginnings of democracy in

---

3   F. A. Lange, *Geschichte des Materialismus und Kritik seiner Bedeutung für die Gegenwart*, 3rd edn, 2 vols (Iserlohn: J. Baedeker, 1876–77). For Rudolf Virchow, see: E. H. Ackerknecht, *Rudolf Virchow: Arzt, Politiker, Anthropologe* (Stuttgart: Enke, 1957). For more details, see Schank, pp. 28–46.

4   One third of the 'Rasse' references can be found in Nietzsche's published works, two thirds in the unpublished notes. For a complete list of references, see Schank, pp. 442–51.

5   For instance, in JGB 262 (KSA 5/216).

6   For Nietzsche's criticism of Treitschke, see EH 'WA' 2 (KSA 6/358). For his criticism of Fritsch, see NF Summer 1886 – Autumn 1887, 5[52] (KSA 12/205).

Europe (GM I 5). But further on in the same text he gives an alternative diagnosis of this problem where the word 'Rasse' no longer occurs in a biological sense, but conforms to his own explanation of the race concept (GM III 12–21).

2. 'Race' as 'people' ('Volk') in Nietzsche

We have seen that for Nietzsche 'races' mean 'peoples', developing their 'character' in the environments where they stay and live over extended periods of time. Similar ideas on race *qua* people can be found in eighteenth- and nineteenth-century idealist and materialist philosophers and scientists such as Kant, Herder, Goethe, Ludwig Büchner and Sir Francis Galton.[7] What may be specific to Nietzsche is the introduction of physiology ('Physiologie') as the link between environment ('Umgebung') and the 'character' of a people: the 'external' environmental conditions influence the physiological constitution of people, and the physiological condition of the people finds its expression in cultural phenomena as religion, morals, and so on, understood as 'sign languages' ('Zeichensprachen'), which define the character of the people. Social factors also have an influence on the relation between environment, physiology and the character of the people.

Nietzsche's concept of physiology seems to draw on ancient Greek ideas on digestion ('Stoffwechsel', 'Verdauung') on the one hand and nineteenth-century French physiological concepts on the other. A good digestion, for instance, favours a strong will and faciliates affirmation

7   See Immanuel Kant, 'Bestimmung des Begriffs einer Menschenrace', in *Kants Werke. Akademie-Ausgabe*, 9 vols (Berlin: de Gruyter, 1968), viii, 89–106. For Herder, Goethe, Ludwig Büchner and Galton, see Paul Weindling, *Health, Race and German Politics between National Unification and Nazism, 1870–1945* (Cambridge: Cambridge University Press, 1989).

of the world 'as it is' ('die Welt, wie sie ist').[8] The cultural rank ('Rang', 'Höhe') of a people does not solely depend on these factors; of equal importance is the educational 'work' ('Arbeit') which it carries out on itself. Nietzsche stresses the 'beauty' ('Schönheit') of the Greeks, their 'good taste' ('guter Geschmack'), and their 'nobility' ('Vornehmheit'), all stemming from their will to 'self-control' ('sich nicht gehen lassen').[9] He calls this will the highest guideline ('oberste Richtschnur') for (their) culture. The same can be said regarding the noble French culture of the seventeenth century. The rank of a people does not derive from a biologically understood genealogical descendance, as in Gobineau. Nietzsche rejects such genealogies; between the Germans of today ('Deutsche') and the old 'Germanen' there is for him no kinship ('Verwandtschaft'), either conceptually or consanguineously.[10] Ideas of biological purity are rejected; the 'Germans' of today ('die Deutschen') must 'de-Germanize' themselves ('sich entdeutschen') in order to become real Germans, the mixture of people and cultures being for Nietzsche the 'source of great culture' ('Quell grosser Cultur') (NF 1885–86, 1[153]: KSA 12/45). The hierarchy of peoples depends on their cultural achievement, on their will to self control ('sich nicht gehen lassen'). In Europe, the Greek, the Jews, the Polish and the French peoples stand at the peak of cultural development.

3. The problem of European 'decadence'

Noble Greek culture is based on the health of the body ('Leib') and on their 'Arbeit an sich selbst', their will to self-control.[11] The Jews are the people who still believe in themselves ('an sich selbst glauben'),

---

8   See, for instance, GM III 16 (KSA 5/376–77), and EH i 6 (KSA 6/272).
9   See GD ix 47 (KSA 6/148f).
10   See GM I 11 (KSA 5/276).
11   See GD ix 47 (KSA 6/148–49).

still have 'Lust an sich selbst', and project this 'Lust an sich selbst' into a God to whom they can be thankful ('dem sie dafür danken können') (NF May-June 1888, 17[4]: KSA 13/523). This self-affirmation and freedom from *ressentiment* are the basis of the high rank of the Jews. The first Christians too, the 'little people of the Diaspora' ('die kleinen Leute der Diaspora'), are still free of 'Rancune' against life; ascetism ('Asketismus') does not form the essence of their life (NF Autumn 1887, 10[92]: KSA 12/508-9).

The weakening and falling-ill of the body and of the will-power have their beginnings in Greek culture,[12] not in Jewish culture. In the *Genealogy of Morals* Nietzsche gives a diagnosis of this phenomenon (GM III 12–21). He distinguishes two phases in this process of debilitation. The first stage is a physiological falling ill of the body ('Leib') that finds its expression in the symptoms of apathy ('Unlust') and depression ('Depression'). In making this diagnosis Nietzsche also uses the word 'Rasse', but always in accordance with his own explanation of the race concept; as a people living for a length of time in a specific environment. Thus the falling ill of the body ('Leib') is being brought about by sudden changes of the external conditions of life, by changes in climate and social factors. This decadence is physiological in essence and can only be cured by medical and other appropriate measures.

The second stage of illness is caused by the ascetic priest; ignoring the physiological nature of the illness he concentrates his 'medication' ('Medikation') on the soul, increasing the feelings of guilt ('Schuldgefühle') of the sick, implanting a feeling of ressentiment towards life, thus bringing about a further weakening of will and will power resulting in a paralyzing of the will ('Willenslähmung'). The power of will necessary for self-control is lost. It is important to keep in mind that in this diagnosis Nietzsche does not make use of the biological race concept, but of his own, and that, further on, the Jews do not play a part in it. The ascetic priest does not, as Nietzsche states, belong to the Jewish people: he does not

---

12   GD x 3 (KSA 6/157); and NF Spring-Summer 1875, 5[195] (KSA 8/95).

belong to any particular 'race' ('Rasse'), or time ('Zeit') or social class ('Stand') at all; he is always 'possible' ('er ist immer möglich') (GM III 1). Nietzsche does not regard European decadence as a final stage, as the ruin of European culture. He is not, as Hannah Arendt stresses, 'fascinated by decline'.[13] Nietzsche, rather, shows confidence. The illness can be cured. Europe will emerge out of it 'richer' and in a 'new synthesis' ('in einer neuen Synthese').[14] French nobility, for instance, was limited by its incapacity to appreciate Homer sufficiently (JGB 224). The newly acquired 'historical sense' ('historischer Sinn') will make nobility richer and more extensive ('umfänglicher').

4. Towards a new elevation of humankind

A new elevation of humankind is possible. In order to achieve this goal, will-power must be restored. Apathy and depression must be overcome. Humankind must learn again to stand alone ('allein stehen können'), without taking refuge to the herd ('Herde'). He must win back the power of self-control ('sich nicht gehen lassen'), the capacity to define goals ('sich Ziele setzen können') (NF 1885, 35[24]: KSA 11/518–20). He must learn to affirm the multiplicity of modern existence in a new 'synthesis'.[15]

One way to reach this goal consists in 'self-elevation' ('Selbsterhöhung') of humankind, as Nietzsche points out in *Beyond Good and Evil* (JGB 256: KSA 5/203). The 'Tantaluses of the will' ('Tantalusse des Willens') are an example (Goethe, Beethoven, and so

---

13   See Hannah Arendt, *Elemente totalitärer Herrschaft* (Frankfurt a.M.: Piper, 1986), p. 287.
14   JGB 256 (KSA 5/201).
15   See the concept of 'der synthetische Mensch', in Wolfgang Müller-Lauter, *Nietzsche. Seine Philosophie der Gegensätze und die Gegensätze seiner Philosophie* (Berlin and New York, de Gruyter, 1971), pp. 181–82.

on). They can teach the new concept of the 'higher man' ('den neuen Begriff des höheren Menschen') (ibid.). Methods of biological breeding are rejected, as Nietzsche's critique of the doctrines of the Darwinists shows.[16] Darwinian 'selection' for instance, does not contribute to an elevation of man in Nietzsche's sense. When Nietzsche uses Darwinian terms, such as 'selection', he uses them with a new metaphorical meaning. In speaking of 'selection', he speaks of an 'Auswahl' of appropriate books and friends, or of choosing a favourable climate (NF Spring-Autumn 1881, 11[43]: KSA 9/457–58). There must also be kept in mind that the word 'Züchtung' in Nietzsches usage means 'education', not biological breeding. He calls Schopenhauer his 'Zuchtmeister', paraphrasing this term with 'Lehrer' and 'Bildner' (UB III 1).

There is in Nietzsche a second way to a new elevation of humankind, that is education, the educational task to be fulfilled by his teaching of 'Eternal Recurrence' ('Ewige Wiederkehr') which Nietzsche qualifies as his 'great breeding thought' ('seinen grossen züchtenden Gedanken') (NF Summer-Autumn 1884, 26[376]: KSA 11/250). The word 'züchten' here means 'erziehen' ('educate'). This teaching gives expression to his 'pessimism of strength' ('Pessimismus der Stärke'): that is the will and the power to affirm all aspects of life, even those hitherto condemned (NF Autumn 1887, 10[3]: KSA 12/455). That means a rejection of all selective morals.The 'Dionysian yes' (das 'dionysische Ja') affirms the world 'as it is' ('wie sie ist'), and that includes self-affirmation ('Selbst-bejahung'). For this interpretation of the teaching of 'Eternal Recurrence' Moles gives the formula: 'live as you must want to live again.'[17]

Humankind will only be capable of such an affirmation of the world 'as it is' when the paralysis of the will (die 'Willenslähmung')

16 See Nietzsche's note 'Anti-Darwin' of spring 1885 (NF, 14[133]: KSA 13/315–17).

17 See Alistair Moles. *Nietzsche's Philosophy of Nature and Cosmology* (Frankfurt a.M.: Lang. 1990), p. 324.

has been overcome. Then humankind will again have the power of will necessary for self control ('sich nicht gehen lassen'), the power to self-affirmation and the power to affirm the world 'as it is'. This would be the new noble humankind.

5. 'Great politics': the philosopher as a physician

Since physiology and the body ('Leib') play a major part in Nietzsche's diagnosis of the European illness, Nietzsche as a physician tries to create conditions that would make a new strengthening of will and will-power possible. He sketches his programme of 'Great Politics' ('Grosse Politik'), which is not to be confused with the nationalist and imperialist 'Great Politics' of the Hohenzollern. His own 'Great Politics' attends to the recovery of the physiological processes in humankind (not in 'races') by stressing the importance of food, clothing and so on ('Ernährung, Kleidung, Kost [...]').[18] A closer reading of further texts makes clear that his programme for physiological recovery does not imply that racist or eugenic measures should be taken. As a physician, Nietzsche is concerned with the 'normal' health of humankind and peoples, and with the means of strengthening will-power so as to regain capacity to say a 'Dionysian yes' to the world 'as it is'.[19]

18 See the note 'Die grosse Politik' (NF Dec. 1888 – Jan. 1889, 25[1]: KSA 13/637–38).
19 For further comments on physiology in Nietzsche's thought, see Paul van Tongeren's article in this volume.

Malcolm Humble

Heinrich Mann and Arnold Zweig: Left-Wing Nietzscheans?

Heinrich Mann (1871–1950) and Arnold Zweig (1887–1968) do not yet belong to the the small group of German-speaking writers of the first half of the twentieth century who have achieved international recognition. As the author of *Der Untertan* (1918) and *Professor Unrat* (1905) (filmed in 1930 as *Der blaue Engel* (*The Blue Angel*)) Heinrich Mann has achieved a reputation as a satirist, while Arnold Zweig (not to be confused with his Austrian contemporary and namesake Stefan) is largely remembered for the novel *Der Streit um den Sergeanten Grischa* (1927), which exposes a miscarriage of justice perpetrated on a Russian POW on the Eastern Front during the First World War. Both writers were, however, prolific in novels, dramas and essays, and their response to Nietzsche is evident in all these genres in all phases of their respective careers.[1]

The notion of a left-wing Nietzschean is debatable, because Nietzsche has been for so long associated with the Right by both the Left and sections of the Right. It would be easy to adduce passages from Nietzsche's works to support the view that he was always firmly against humanitarian, egalitarian, communitarian and collective plans and panaceas for the future of mankind. However, three broad surveys published in the most recent phase of Nietzsche research are devoted wholly or in part to the reception of Nietzsche by thinkers, polemicists and politicians associated with the Left, whether one

---

1   This article first appeared in *Journal of Nietzsche Studies*, 13 (Spring 1997), 40–52, and is reproduced here with permission.

defines it as anarchist, bohemian or utopian.[2] From the relevant parts of these studies it is possible to gain an impression of what in Nietzsche appealed to the Left. If the Right is viewed as the traditional conservatism embodied in the Wilhelmine establishment or as the radical populism drifting more and more towards racism (especially antisemitism), aggressive imperialism and a wholesale rejection of modernity, and the Left as a dogmatic Marxism which in its emphasis on the collective and the class war stifles the individual, then the personalities involved share an uneasy position between these forces. Non-terroristic anarchism exercises a strong influence, especially on the intellectuals of the Berlin Friedrichshagen group (Bruno Wille, the brothers Heinrich and Julius Hart), the anti-Marxist Socialist Gustav Landauer and the leader of the activist wing of Expressionism Kurt Hiller. Although some of these figures occasionally bore witness to phases of their intellectual development in the form of lyric poetry and prose fiction, their contributions to the debate for and against Nietzsche consist largely of polemical essays on socio-political questions. Yet the later work of Mann and Zweig in fiction, as well as in polemic, is best understood against the background of this left-wing response to the issues raised by Nietzsche, because in providing a running commentary on the social and political development of Germany in the years up to the Nazi seizure of power and after it extends and broadens the debate initiated in these circles.

Arnold Zweig's novel *Versunkene Tage: Roman aus dem Jahre 1908* (*Submerged Days: A Novel of 1908*), published by the Querido

---

2   See R. Hinton Thomas, *Nietzsche in German Politics and Society 1890–1918* (Manchester: Manchester University Press, 1983); Steven E. Aschheim, *The Nietzsche Legacy in Germany 1890–1990* (Berkeley, Los Angeles and London: University of California Press, 1992) – German edn, *Nietzsche und die Deutschen: Karriere eines Kults* (Stuttgart: Metzler, 1996); and Seth Taylor, *Left-Wing Nietzscheans: The Politics of German Expressionism 1910–1920* (Berlin and New York: de Gruyter, 1990).

Verlag in Amsterdam in 1938,[3] does not conform to the usual categories of exile literature. Neither an examination of the closing years of the Weimar Republic nor a historical novel, it traces the life of Carl Steinitz, a young man with literary ambitions engaged in desultory study and a series of minor love affairs in Munich during the years immediately preceding the First World War. Zweig successfully reproduces the atmosphere of these golden years, in which members of a carefree generation had the leisure to pursue their intellectual interests without too much concern for their professional future or the political rumblings which presaged the storm to come. On a trip into the Bavarian countryside the hero has a chance encounter with a figure described as follows:

> He seemed to be about forty, doubtless an aristocrat from Holstein or Oldenburg, of whom there were supposed to be some among the artists. His narrow skull, with high temples, was extended by an imperial beard and divided by a moustache in the English style. [...] His steady and penetrating gaze [...] involuntarily recalled that of a wise elephant.[4]

In their ensuing conversation the older man asks Carl whether he has been abroad to educate himself, and on learning that the loss of both his parents in a train accident has made him reluctant to travel, declares that solitude liberates and free persons are rare in Germany, before deploring the lack of true freedom for writers and artists in the Reich of Wilhelm II. Carl replies that he ignores newspapers and politics in general in favour of Schiller's aesthetic education of the human race, because, as he puts it, the moral life, the taming of man the beast is so far advanced that in the whole of Europe only domestic animals remain, democratic herds of cattle – useful and boring and arousing anything but concern. When the older man then asks Carl whether he believes that the workers, the masses lack more than just the aesthetic, he insists that they are ugly, coarse, common and hostile

---

3   It appeared as *Verklungene Tage* in 1950 in the Federal Republic and in 1955 in the GDR.

4   *Novellen um Claudia. Verklungene Tage*, in Arnold Zweig, *Ausgewählte Werke in Einzelausgaben* (Berlin: Aufbau, 1962), vii, 258.

towards the intellect. The conversation ends with the older man's rebuke:

> Young man, if you should succeed in seeking Geist and yearning for Geist in life and not in collected works, such as those of poor Nietzsche, you will perhaps notice how much bread and hope someone needs before his education to beauty can be considered. Farewell.

As he leaves, Carl silently but mockingly utters the words: 'Off you go, praeceptor germaniae' (p. 261). When the older man is named as Heinrich Mann in the following paragraph, the narrator from the point of view of a later date refers to Carl's ensuing shame at the memory of the conversation and his readiness to give his former interlocutor the same title without the irony which had accompanied his first reaction to his admonishment.

The episode throws light on the relations between the two writers, for they have much in common in their progression from a Nietzschean aestheticism to a growing concern with politics under the pressure of events and other intellectual influences. However, because of the differences between the two in age and, to some extent, in background, their developments were not synchronised. Furthermore, there is no question in the end of a simple rejection of a Nietzsche who had been a role model in youth and was then perceived to be deficient as both grew to maturity, even if the passage quoted may convey that impression in the case of Zweig. Instead Nietzsche remains for both a source of fascination, at least until the period of their exile, spent by Mann in France and the USA and by Zweig largely in Palestine. Both show evidence in their relation to Nietzsche rather of constant shifts and manoeuvres. In this they are not alone, as is indicated by the more complex case of Thomas Mann, as well as by others (Kafka, Brecht, Rilke and perhaps Musil), whose changing reception of Nietzsche is governed by similar factors, above all by their relation to German society as it was transformed by war, defeat, revolution, impoverishment, and by the political polarisation that marked the closing years of the Weimar Republic and continued within the anti-Nazi front during the exile period.

Heinrich Mann's reception of Nietzsche has already been the subject of thorough investigation, but a confused picture emerges, partly because of the discovery of new evidence, partly because scholarly controversy can easily arise when the step is taken from demonstrating a knowledge of Nietzsche to tracing his effect, first on debate in essays in which explicit reference is made, then on creative writing. In the case of the latter the reader is faced with the problem of distinguishing between characters who express views which recall Nietzsche or who represent in their personality and actions a desire to live out Nietzschean precepts (more or less successfully), and narrative commentary which places these figures, their words and actions in a broader perspective. Consequently four possibilities emerge: that the author accepts Nietzsche's philosophy and thought and writes from a Nietzschean perspective; that he shows himself critical of Nietzsche by demonstrating his effect on characters whom he openly satirizes or implicitly criticizes; that the Nietzschean characteristics of satirized characters show him to be a critic of a Nietzsche reception which differs from his own; that the author's response changes and his initial reception (whether or not it is part of a broader current) is later modified or revoked.[5]

Heinrich Mann knew Nietzsche's works well, especially *Beyond Good and Evil* and *The Genealogy of Morals,* and a note scribbled on the latter[6] indicates a concern with the relation between the moral and the aesthetic, which was to become the guiding thread of his early work: 'meaning: the morally ugly and the *morally* beautiful, but "beauty" in itself is surely not a moral value? moral ugliness can under circumstances be aesthetically beautiful?'[7] The notes from the

5   See Elke Emrich, *Macht und Geist im Werk Heinrich Manns. Eine Über-
      windung Nietzsches aus dem Geist Voltaires* (Berlin: de Gruyter, 1981), and
      Renate Werner, *Skeptizismus, Ästhetizismus, Aktivismus. Der frühe Heinrich
      Mann* (Düsseldorf: Bertelsmann, 1972).

6   Friedrich Nietzsche, *Zur Genealogie der Moral,* 2nd edn (Leipzig: Naumann,
      1892), p. 82.

7   Sigrid Anger (ed.), *Heinrich Mann 1871–1950. Werk und Leben in Dokumenten
      und Bildern* (Berlin: Aufbau, 1977), p. 70.

manuscript of *Minerva*,[8] the second part of the trilogy *Die Göttinnen*, consist of extracts from a section of *Nachlaß der achtziger Jahre* (*Fragments of the 1880s*) in which 'Rausch' (intoxication), 'Lust' (sexual desire), 'Macht' (power), 'Schönheit' (beauty) are linked: 'Artists, if they are any good, are (also) physically strong, with surplus energy, animals with power, sensitive, etc.',[9] but Heinrich Mann adds 'talent = vampire', which recalls the following:

> Every talent is a vampire, which sucks blood and strength from other powers, and an exaggerated production can bring even the most gifted person to madness. [...] People subject themselves out of habit to everything which desires power.[10]

Artists are not persons of great passion, whatever they may claim to us and themselves. And for two reasons: they lack shame towards themselves (they observe themselves, as they live; they lie in wait for one another, they are too curious) and they lack shame towards the great passion (they exploit it as artists). Secondly however, their vampire, their talent, usually begrudges them that spending of power which is passion. With a talent one is the victim of one's talent. One does not come to terms with one's passion by presenting it: rather one has *already* come to terms with it *when* one presents it.[11]

   Die Göttinnen oder die drei Romane der Herzogin Assy (*The Goddesses or The Three Novels of the Duchess Assy*), of 1903, is a three-volume tour de force which gathers together all the topoi and themes of decadence. These, however, are embodied not in the central figure Violante von Assy but in the crowd of artist hangers-on who surround her in her progress through three incarnations: romantic revolutionary, aesthetic idealist and sexual libertine. Although her ageing and death at the end make it clear that even she is subject to

---

8 Bruno Hillebrand (ed.), *Nietzsche und die deutsche Literatur* (Tübingen: Niemeyer, 1978), pp. 133–34.

9 Friedrich Nietzsche, *Werke*, ed. Karl Schlechta, 3 vols (Munich: Hanser, 1954–56), iii, 756. Cited henceforth as *Werke*.

10 *Werke*, i, 605.

11 *Werke*, iii, 622–23.

the limits of human nature, she is throughout contrasted with a series of characters who appear deficient in comparison because they represent the psychology of the artist as presented in the quotations from Nietzsche Mann had summarized. Indeed, it can be claimed that *The Goddesses* realizes more convincingly than any other novel which does not cross the boundary into pure fantasy the ideas of Nietzsche on the Superman (here a Superwoman) and the metaphysics of art. Only d'Annunzio, with whom Heinrich Mann was inevitably compared when the trilogy appeared, achieved a study of the decadent artist of comparable range and depth.

The Goddesses therefore appeared to contemporary readers, whether they praised it or attacked it, as a celebration of amoral aestheticism which ignored the moral questions raised by the interaction of characters subject to the normal constraints of the human condition and judged them instead on the basis of their ability to realize Nietzsche's Dionysian aesthetic of superfluity in their lives as opposed to the decadence of the pseudo-artists whose energies are absorbed by their work.

A contrast of characters similar to that in *Die Göttinnen* appears in the novels *Die Jagd nach Liebe* (*The Pursuit of Love*) and *Zwischen den Rassen* (*Between the Races*), but here neither the embodiments of Nietzschean values nor the decadents appear as positive figures, largely because Heinrich Mann here abandons the fantasy realm of Mediterranean feudalism and international *haute volée* which he had devised for *The Goddesses*. At the same time, while in the long essay *Eine Freundschaft: Gustave Flaubert und George Sand* (*A Friendship: Gustave Flaubert and George Sand*) he bases his approach to Flaubert on Nietzsche's critique of decadence in *Nietzsche contra Wagner*, the positive contrast is represented not by the amoral Superwoman but by the humanitarian realism of George Sand. The move towards realism culminates in *Die kleine Stadt* (*The Small Town*) (1909), its small-town setting implying the greater social awareness advocated in the influential essay 'Geist und Tat' ('Intellect and Deed') (1910), in which Nietzsche is presented as having prostituted 'Geist' (intellect) to 'Macht' (power).

The reception of this essay by the Expressionist generation as a manifesto for political commitment and social concern can hardly be overestimated, but requires careful definition in the context of our theme. As Seth Taylor puts it:

> While there is no doubt that 'Intellect and Deed' represents a partial repudiation of Nietzsche, that repudiation has been misconstrued by some scholars who portray Mann as a born again adherent of reason and democracy who turned away from the irrational and antidemocratic hero of his youth, now recognized as the source of militarism and reaction in Germany. [...] The point here is that while Mann repudiated Nietzsche's antidemocratic teaching and even began to fear the influence of Nietzsche's philosophy on German society, he never came to associate Nietzsche himself with the forces of militarism and reaction.[12]

This conclusion is confirmed on the whole by the references to Nietzsche in another essay, 'Kaiserreich und Republik' ('Empire and Republic') (1919). Here he is defined as one who in the conditions of the Reich could only achieve an impact by being made to conform to aims which were beneath him. Indeed Nietzsche is said to anticipate the Zeitgeist of the Second Reich, viewed as a repulsive amalgam of political aggression, materialistic saturation and ideological conformity which was to prompt a powerful reaction across the entire Left–Right spectrum in its closing years. However, Mann also relates the philosophy to the dynamic force activating the Reich, viewing Borgia as a mask for Bismarck. He then adds that Nietzsche did not fight with the troops who might have carried *Thus spake Zarathustra* in their knapsacks.[13] One detects uncertainty here on Nietzsche's role in a society which had debased aspirations he had unwittingly defined.

The need to clarify the difference between what Nietzsche meant and what had been made of him by the Right became imperative during the Third Reich, in view of the distortions and falsifications perpetrated by his sister and her team at the Nietzsche-Archiv in Weimar and the appropriation of his legacy by at least one strand of

---

12   Taylor, pp. 33–34.
13   Hillebrand (ed.), pp. 194–95.

National Socialist opinion. As part of his rescue operation for German culture during his exile Mann edited the anthology *Es kommt der Tag: Deutsches Lesebuch* (*The Day will Come: A German Reader*) (Zurich: Europa Verlag 1936), in which by his choice of passages (for example 'What Europe owes the Jews' and 'The Germans and the Jews') he clearly aims to provide an alternative view. More significant is the commentary he provided in 1939 for his own selection, *The Living Thoughts of Nietzsche*, part of a series published in London to which several exiled writers contributed. Here the emphasis is placed on Nietzsche's psychological complexity, the provisional nature of his exploratory project, the evidence in it of doubt, contradictions, self-overcoming. Nietzsche in devising a morality acceptable to intellectuals provides an armory which will guarantee immunity against the baseness of contemporary politics. In support of this point Nietzsche's list of four cardinal virtues is quoted: truthfulness to ourselves and to anyone else who is our friend; bravery against the enemy; generosity to the vanquished; politeness. Mann proceeds to reinforce the distinction, between the man and his distorted reception, made tentatively in his earlier essay.

There are points in the introduction where Mann sounds a critical note. He regrets that Nietzsche never once mentioned King Henry IV of France, the subject of a major historical novel in two volumes he composed at this time (*Die Jugend des Königs Henri Quatre* (*Young Henry of Navarre*) (1935) and *Die Vollendung des Henri Quatre* (*Henry, King of France*) (1938)). He alone in his eyes is the Prince of the Renaissance, representing an alternative way of saying yes to life, based on harmony between heart and mind, whereas Nietzsche did violence to his heart, producing an affirmation which sounds shrill. However, Nietzsche's own identification with another French icon, Voltaire, is wholeheartedly endorsed in support of his recommendation to the young. Nietzsche's remarks on the workers as potential exemplars of 'Vornehmheit' are quoted in a clear attempt to make him palatable to left-wing, anti-Fascist readers:

The workers some day must live as the bourgeoisie do now – but *above* them, distinguished by the smallness of their needs, a *higher* caste – poorer and simpler, that is, but in the *possession* of power (*Werke*, iii, 843).

In the end the positive outweighs the negative in the image Mann presents: a humane Nietzsche to challenge the Right and repair the damage it has done to his reputation. He also conveys by what he singles out as Nietzsche's merits and what he rejects aspects of his own philosophy, psychology and aesthetic, such as the good nature and harmony between thought and feeling represented by Henri IV.[14]

In *Ein Zeitalter wird besichtigt* (*View of an Age*) (1945) Heinrich Mann, while taking final stock of the intellectual forces of his lifetime, especially in their relation to politics, repeats that Nietzsche did not (necessarily or consistently) mean what the Germans took him to mean:

Nietzsche and Wagner have allowed the Germans the freedom to choose from their work what suited them: the firm sense, the dubiousness, solely the genuine or above all the seductive. The Germans have chosen.[15]

In the case of Zweig a similar pattern emerges. Autobiographical comments made during exile, in which he reminisces about his student days, confirm the retrospective view of Nietzsche provided in *Submerged Days*. He points to his political naivety, resulting from the success with which his social conscience had been stifled by Nietzsche, and his consequent share in guilt for the war, accepted by him and his fellows, pupils of Nietzsche-pupils, as an inevitable component of a human nature with its roots in the animal species.[16]

However, at the same time Zweig fails to note his involvement in that strand of left-wing Nietzscheanism which came to the fore briefly during the transition from the First World War to the Weimar

---

14   See Heinrich Mann, 'Nietzsche', *Maß und Wert*, 2 (1939), 277–304, repr. in
      Hillebrand, pp. 262–71, and his introductory essay in *The Living Thoughts of
      Nietzsche* (London: Cassell, 1939), pp. 1–34.
15   Heinrich Mann, *Ein Zeitalter wird besichtigt*, in Hillebrand, pp. 277–78.
16   Georg Wenzel (ed.), *Arnold Zweig 1887–1968. Werk und Leben in Dokumenten
      und Bildern* (Berlin and Weimar: Aufbau, 1978), pp. 20 and 61.

Republic. Zweig had quoted Nietzsche at the end of a funeral speech for the victims of the counter-revolutionary purge after the failure of the Spartacus uprising in early 1919. His 'Grabrede auf Spartakus' ('Funeral Speech for Spartakus') ends with the quotation of Nietzsche's poem 'Ecce homo', in which man is compared to a flame consuming itself and others.[17] Two other writers associated with left-wing Expressionism, Ernst Toller and René Schickele, refer to Nietzsche at this time and in a similar context when defining their aspirations. Toller, in a speech to Workers and Soldiers' Councils on the murdered Kurt Eisner (Prime Minister of the first Socialist Republic in Bavaria), quotes from *Thus spake Zarathustra*:

> Behold the good and just! Whom do they hate most? Him who breaketh up their tables of values, the breaker, the law-breaker: – he, however, is the creator.
> Behold the believers of all beliefs! Whom do they hate most? Him who breaketh up their tables of values, the breaker, the law-breaker: – he, however, is the creator.[18]

Schickele, who had edited the major Expressionist periodical *Die Weißen Blätter* from neutral Switzerland in order to avoid censorship, is prompted by the events of November 1918 to write:

> Socialism means for me the opposite of class rule, i.e. the final dissolution of classes in that community of unfathomable depth, which Nietzsche hinted at in his remark about the Greeks as dreaming Homers and Homer as a dreaming Greek.[19]

---

17 See Eva Kaufmann, *Arnold Zweigs Weg zum Roman* (Berlin: Rütten und Loening, 1967), p. 53. The speech appeared in the *Weltbühne* (15/4, p. 75) on 23 January 1919.

18 Wolfgang Frühwald and John M. Spalek (eds), *Der Fall Toller. Kommentar und Materialien* (Munich: Hanser, 1979), p. 54. The lines (in the Levy translation) are from Za, 'Vorrede' 9 (KSA 4/26).

19 René Schickele, *Der neunte November*, Tribüne der Kunst und der Zeit, 8 (Berlin: Erich Reiss Verlag, 1919), pp. 69–70, quoted in Friedrich Albrecht, *Deutsche Schriftsteller in der Entscheidung* (Berlin: Aufbau, 1975), p. 89. Hermann Hesse has a section on Spartakus in 'Zarathustras Wiederkehr' (*Gesammelte Werke*, ed. Volker Michels, 12 vols (Frankfurt a.M.: Suhrkamp, 1970), x, 484–86).

In *Bilanz der deutschen Judenheit* (*Balance Sheet of German Jewry*) Arnold Zweig is in accord with Mann in distinguishing between Nietzsche and the use made of him by the racist and populist Right in the years since his death, but a note of uncertainty, also present in Mann, is struck in the attribution to Nietzsche of responsibility:

> The most solitary spirit has been through his own fault reduced to being the patron of those to whom he devoted dozens of pages of the most savage invective. [...] He was accorded the worst fate Zarathustra could conceive: his teachings 'fell victim to the swine'.[20]

Elsewhere, however, in the privacy of correspondence, Zweig openly expressed an admiration which he felt compelled to tone down in his public writings. In several letters to Sigmund Freud he outlined a plan for a novel based on Nietzsche's life which, if it had come to fruition, would have presented him as an exemplary victim of the Wilhelmine *juste milieu*. Equally significant is the attempt by Zweig to confront his mentor with the view of Nietzsche as his principal precursor, first found in the following from a letter of 2 December 1930:

> He (Nietzsche) tried to explain the birth of tragedy; you have done it in Totem and Taboo. He longed for a world beyond Good and Evil; by means of analysis you have discovered world to which this phrase actually applies. Analysis has reversed all values, it has conquered Christianity, disclosed the true Antichrist, and liberated the spirit of resurgent life from the ascetic ideal.[21]

Zweig repeats the comparison three years later in a letter dated 28 April 1934, before briefly portraying the Nietzsche he envisages, in

---

20 Hillebrand (ed.), p. 256.
21 Ernst L. Freud (ed.), *Sigmund Freud, Arnold Zweig. Briefwechsel* (Frankfurt a.M.: Fischer, 1984), p. 35 (Engl. edn, *The Letters of Sigmund Freud and Arnold Zweig*, trans. Professor and Mrs W. B. Robson-Scott (London: Hogarth Press, 1970), p. 23). Page references are to these editions. See also Arie Wolf, 'Der nicht zustande gekommene Nietzsche-Roman (der "Umnachtungs"-Roman) Arnold Zweigs Anno 1934: Zur Geschichte einer Faszination', in Arthur Thilo Alt et al. (eds), *Arnold Zweig: Berlin – Haifa – Berlin. Perspektiven des Gesamtwerks. Akten des III. Internationalen Arnold-Zweig-Symposions Berlin 1993* (Berne: Lang, 1995).

Turin in the last phase of his sane life, away from the inhibiting presence of family and early influences, inspired by 'the intellectual Eros' as represented by Cosima Wagner and Lou Salomé, followed by the descent into madness, and the flight into the new worlds of the Crucified and Dionysus. He confesses however that the plot causes him concern, for 'neither a case history nor the portrayal of a delusion is a plot', thus anticipating Freud's own doubts about the project (pp. 85–86; Engl. edn, pp. 74–76).

The lyrical tone Zweig here adopts to convey his view of Nietzsche as a tender-hearted victim of stifling conformity is intensified a few weeks later in a letter of June 6, as he adds to the plan his intention to relate the man not only to the heritage he received but also to that which he passed on. In pointing to the conflict between brother and sister, with the shadow of Hitler over her, he shows himself aware of Elisabeth's role in the Nazi appropriation, but he also contrasts personality, 'his soft, gentle timidity', and work, 'his thunderous words which anticipate the Nazi era'. For Zweig Nietzsche is a philologist of genius, for whom words were enough to guarantee happiness. 'But alas, that he should have turned them in such a way that they stirred other people to action – and that is exactly what they did do.' In the following lines he proposes to elaborate by a process of empathy the link suggested here between past and present. 'I would like to establish a link between present-day Germany and his doctrines; I would like to transfer my rage, hate and contempt into his person and share his flight into psychosis.' After calling him a love of his youth, admired as a writer of prose and as a thinker, he draws a distinction between the writings preceding *Thus spake Zarathustra* and the later works, which have provoked in him more and more opposition, but which he resolves to read again (pp. 90–91; Engl. edn, pp. 80–81). On 12 August 1934 he returns yet again to the theme of Nietzsche's appropriation by those he despised. The Germany of Bismarck and Hitler destroyed him and distorted some features of his work to the point of absurdity. Nietzsche's person remains however to be admired, described not as Dionysian, but as pure, halcyon, gentle, polite, yearning for 'the vanished Ariadne, an island world of the heart and mind', which contrasts with the Wagnerian din of *Thus spake Zarathustra* (pp. 98–99; Engl. edn, p. 88).

Zweig's presentation of Nietzsche as a proto-Freud was clearly but perhaps naively meant as a compliment. At the same time by treating him as a psychological case, as a victim of domestication through mother and sister by the Wilhelmine *juste milieu*, he indicated that he required for his investigation the tools of analysis provided by Freud. Freud reacted politely but coolly to the plan, with objections to the legitimacy of portraying in fiction a figure whose psychological abnormality is clear but can no longer be satisfactorily diagnosed. At about the same time Zweig wrote for an exile periodical an essay on Freud which in its title ('Apollon bewältigt Dionysos: Zum 80. Geburtstag Sigmund Freuds, 6. Mai 1936' ('Apollo overcomes Dionysos: On Sigmund Freud's 80th birthday, 6 May 1936')) shows not only a debt to Nietzsche, but also a concern to present Freud as one who himself draws on Nietzsche in a spirit of rational scientific enquiry.[22]

Zweig's failure to carry out his intention of writing the novel on Nietzsche cannot be attributed simply to Freud's lack of enthusiasm for the project. Zweig shared with other novelists (such as Heinrich Mann in his later work, D. H. Lawrence in *Women in Love* and other novels and A. S. Byatt in her recent *Babel Tower*) an awareness that narrative fiction, as a democratic art normally wedded to realism, can test and prove the efficacy or validity of ideas devised in the study (or during solitary wanderings) only in a social context, in which such ideas are then often found wanting. It would have been difficult to reconcile his admiration for Nietzsche's personality with such an outcome.

When during the Second World War he came to write the novel *Das Beil von Wandsbek* (*The Axe of Wandsbek*), the context he devised for the introduction of Nietzsche proved to be very different, perhaps because Zweig had decided to follow his own advice as

22   *Das neue Tagebuch* (1936), 18.

presented in an essay published in the exile periodical *Das Wort* in 1938:

> The writer must be deeply embedded in the life of his time, in the attachments and structure of his society. He must have about him something of the human average, such as Tolstoy and Gorki possessed. No-one would have been less equipped to produce epic works of art than Nietzsche with the delusion of his uniqueness.[23]

The Axe of Wandsbek combines two distinct plots: the agreement of a butcher with a declining business to act as executioner for the Nazis after the death sentence has been passed on several Communist underground workers, followed by a struggle with his conscience which ends in his suicide, and the inner emigration of two middle-class figures, Heinrich Koldewey, the governor of the prison in which the Communists are kept, and his intellectually more open and adventurous friend Dr Käte Neumeier. Koldewey is presented as an admirer of Nietzsche who is well able to distinguish between the nervous splendours of his writings and the vulgarisation which has taken place since his death, but who allows this awareness to justify his withdrawal from any action which might undermine the regime. Käte bases her decision to join what turns out to be a half-hearted and impractically organized resistance group on an insight into Hitler's pathological personality provided by Freud, in particular his intro-duction to Daniel Schreber's *Denkwürdigkeiten eines Nervenkranken* (*Memoirs of a Victim of a Nervous Disorder*), to which she adds the social diagnosis and revolutionary impetus of Marx.

Koldewey's view of Nietzsche is presented in terms which plainly resemble the portrait outlined in the letters to Freud, with the emphasis on his aristocratic attitude, his vulnerability and nervous sensitivity, the moral astringency of his manner of thinking, the music of his prose. He represents a refuge in which Koldewey can take cover from the storm of Nazism, viewed as an extension of the Wilhelmine vulgar grandiosity which Nietzsche had attacked so

---

23 'Roman, Realismus und Form', *Das Wort*, 3/10 (1938), 92–95, quoted in Wenzel (ed.), p. 265.

eloquently. When the storm has passed, he hopes, values will progress in a movement marked by patrician, soldierly qualities beholden to Europe; how this might come about, however, he has no idea. Although he has heard of Freud, he feels no urge to concern himself with him, as Nietzsche the psychologist has provided him with all the insights he needs.[24]

Koldewey is for Zweig a typical educated German of his own generation, a latter-day Carl Steinitz, in whose footsteps Zweig himself might have trodden had not the political trends of the times, his own Jewishness and other intellectual preferences pointed in another direction. In response to fellow-novelist and Jewish exile Lion Feuchtwanger, who had suggested in a letter that Koldewey should overcome Nietzsche through Freud, Zweig reveals a growing ambivalence towards Nietzsche which had not been apparent in his earlier correspondence with Freud but which had emerged under the pressure of events.[25] Because Koldewey is conceived as a representative middle-class German who because of the conservative underpinning of his education lacks the will or incentive to take a clear stand against the regime, he cannot be considered to be a projection of Zweig himself at the time of writing. He therefore fails to make the transition to Freud on his own initiative. Zweig assures Feuchtwanger that there are still aspects of Nietzsche he admires but ends by asserting that these had to be eliminated in the novel as part of a necessary simplification, so that Nietzsche's contribution to a syndrome which removed immunity to Nazism, common amongst middle-class intellectuals, could be demonstrated. Koldewey becomes a scapegoat for Zweig's continued fascination with the man he calls a seducer, and another character has to provide an antidote consisting of both Freud and Marx. Only this double dosage, administered by the woman Koldewey loves, proves strong enough to counteract the power of the enchanter and only to a certain degree.

24 *Das Beil von Wandsbek* (Berlin: Aufbau, 1986), p. 264.
25 Letter to Feuchtwanger, 7 May 1945, in *Lion Feuchtwanger/Arnold Zweig, Briefwechsel 1933–1958,* 2 vols (Frankfurt a.M.: Fischer, 1986), i, 336.

Nietzsche may have been deprived of his subversive force in the 'soft' images developed by Heinrich Mann and Arnold Zweig. However, their readings must be seen in the context of the whole range of Nietzsche's reception, especially in the years following the First World War, when the image constructed by the Right became 'harder'. Both endeavor to place Nietzsche in a German tradition which, while clearly alternative to that postulated by Nazi cultural policy, would not, as in Georg Lukács's *Die Zerstörung der Vernunft* (*The Destruction of Reason*) (1954), exclude all that which, from a Marxist point of view, might be branded as irrational and reactionary. Their task was made peculiarly difficult by the circumstances of their time, and the consequences are some special pleading, a highly selective emphasis and a diversion into biography which divides the man from his work. However, in bringing to bear on their subject the psychological acumen of experienced novelists they were able to offer insights lacking in the commentaries of the philosophers and political commentators, including those on the Left (e.g. Landauer, Hiller, Schickele). The bracketing of Nietzsche with Freud has since become commonplace, but in the 1930s it represented a bold move guaranteed to raise the hackles not only of Nietzsche's German supporters (with the important exception of Thomas Mann) but of Freud himself. Heinrich Mann and Arnold Zweig helped their contemporaries to see him from new angles and contributed to the rehabilitation on which the post-1945 development of Nietzsche studies has partly built. For this achievement at least they deserve acknowledgement and respect.

Nicholas Martin

Nietzsche in the GDR: History of a Taboo

[he] was not only dead, he was abolished, an *unperson*.[1]

In 1987 West German intellectuals, who were still recovering from the previous year's acrimonious 'Historikerstreit' concerning the uniqueness of Nazi genocide, found themselves agonizing once more over the recent German past, in the so-called 'Heidegger case'. This fresh controversy was sparked by the publication of new evidence that the philosopher Martin Heidegger had been more sympathetic to National Socialism than previously thought.[2]

At the same time, in 1986–88, a fierce debate was being conducted in the GDR over whether or not to rehabilitate the work and reputation of Heidegger's intellectual godfather, Friedrich Nietzsche. As well as appearing curiously anachronistic to observers in the West, where Nietzsche had long since been 'rehabilitated', the debate in the GDR was a mirror image of the Heidegger controversy, for while the latter centred on an icon under attack, the apparent issue in East Berlin was the rescue of a fallen icon. The debate was conducted in the journal *Sinn und Form* and appeared to mark a

---

1   George Orwell, *Nineteen Eighty-Four* (Harmondsworth: Penguin, 1983), p. 139.
2   The original allegations are contained in Victor Farias, *Heidegger et le nazisme. Morale et politique* (Paris: Editions Verdier, 1987), and the subsequent controversy is analysed in Thomas Sheehan, 'Heidegger and the Nazis', *New York Review of Books*, 15 June 1988, pp. 38–47. The 'Historikerstreit' is documented in Rudolf Augstein et al., *'Historikerstreit'. Die Dokumentation der Kontroverse über die Einzigartigkeit der nationalsozialistischen Juden-vernichtung* (Munich: Piper, 1987) and surveyed by Wolfgang Wippermann, *Wessen Schuld? Vom Historikerstreit zur Goldhagen-Kontroverse* (Berlin: Elefanten Press, 1997).

softening of attitudes towards Nietzsche, a figure who had hitherto been regarded by the official culture of the GDR as 'Feind Nummer eins'.[3] It seemed as though the uncanny guest had come knocking. In truth, however, throughout the GDR's forty-year existence, Nietzsche was not so much an uncanny guest as an unperson. In the words of the late Wolfgang Müller-Lauter:

> In der DDR mit Nietzsche umgehen, hieß aber grundsätzlich: ihn nach Möglich-keit um*gehen* [...] jedenfalls aber immer kritisch Abstand zu ihm halten. Der Philosoph zählte zum 'schlechten Umgang', vor dem man die Bürger des Landes zu bewahren hatte.[4]

As late as 1988, in his contribution to the debate in *Sinn und Form*, Stephan Hermlin was even more forthright: 'Nietzsche existiert nicht in der DDR.'[5]

The belated engagement with Nietzsche in the GDR began with a seemingly innocuous essay, entitled 'Revision des marxistischen Nietzsche-Bildes?', in the 1986 volume of *Sinn und Form* by Heinz Pepperle, a professor of historical materialism at Berlin's Humboldt University.[6] Pepperle's aim was to show that, behind the apparently 'zusammenhanglose und aphoristische Form' of Nietzsche's phil-osophy, there was a unity and coherence of content that marked him out as a 'Philosoph von Rang' (940). Much of what Pepperle wrote would have been familiar to students of Nietzsche in the West, but this readiness to deal with Nietzsche on his own terms provoked

---

3   See Ludwig Marcuse's review of Erich F. Podach's *Nietzsches Werke des Zusammenbruchs, Die Zeit*, 18 Oct. 1961. *Sinn und Form*, the journal of the GDR's 'Akademie der Künste', had been founded by Johannes R. Becher and Paul Wiegler in 1949 and was an official forum for literary and cultural debate in the GDR. In name at least, *Sinn und Form* survived the 'Wende'.

4   Wolfgang Müller-Lauter, 'Über den Umgang mit Nietzsche', *Sinn und Form*, 43 (1991), 833–51 (p. 834).

5   Stephan Hermlin, 'Von älteren Tönen', *Sinn und Form*, 40 (1988), 179–83 (p. 180).

6   Heinz Pepperle, 'Revision des marxistischen Nietzsche-Bildes? Vom inneren Zusammenhang einer fragmentarischen Philosophie', *Sinn und Form*, 38 (1986), 934–69.

strong reactions, both positive and negative, among readers accustomed to a Marxist-Leninist interpretation which tended to dismiss Nietzsche as the intellectual pathfinder of both Hitlerite fascism and the late capitalist system of the postwar West. Nevertheless, says Pepperle, quoting Ernst Bloch, Nietzsche's ideas were undoubtedly '"faschistisch brauchbar"', because he praises strength, hierarchy, brute force, violence and torture. Nietzsche therefore functioned as 'ein geistiger Wegbereiter des Faschismus' (965). These are scarcely the words of a revisionist rehabilitator. Pepperle's is a knowledgeable and even-handed account of the high and lows of Nietzsche's philosophy; while acknowledging the latter's potentially incendiary nature, Pepperle refuses to dismiss Nietzsche out of hand as either a proto-Nazi or an ideological precursor of Western bourgeois capitalism.

Pepperle's reluctance to regurgitate the received Marxist 'Nietzsche-Bild' was met by a fierce counterblast in the 1987 volume of *Sinn und Form* from the literary historian and ideological hardliner, Wolfgang Harich, who placed heavy inverted commas around the title of Pepperle's essay.[7] Harich, alarmed that Pepperle's rejection of Nietzsche was not firm enough, rehearses what appears to be almost a parody of the party line. He argues that Nietzsche was not abused by the Nazis: 'Er war tatsächlich ihr wichtigster, ihr entscheidender geistiger Wegbereiter' (1020). On this point, and others, Harich repeatedly invokes the authority of Georg Lukács, whom he presents as the final arbiter in all disputes concerning Nietzsche. He also attempts to go beyond Lukács, by arguing that the Hungarian thinker did not place sufficient emphasis on either Nietzsche's anti-Semitism or his misogyny (1021–27).[8]

---

7   Wolfgang Harich, '"Revision des marxistischen Nietzschebildes?"', *Sinn und Form*, 39 (1987), 1018–53.

8   Lukács' interpretation helped to shape approaches to Nietzsche in the GDR. The seminal Lukács texts in this respect are: 'Nietzsche als Vorläufer der faschistischen Ästhetik', *Internationale Literatur – Deutsche Blätter* [Moscow], 5 (1935), no. 8, 76–92; 'Der deutsche Faschismus und Nietzsche', *Internationale Literatur – Deutsche Blätter* [Moscow], 12 (1943), 55–64; and

Harich's argument is undifferentiated and vituperative to a degree reminiscent of National Socialist condemnations of ideologically unsound or 'degenerate' literature. He employs a combination of smear and invective, tactics profoundly at odds with the methods of historical materialism which he claims to espouse. Nietzsche's work, for example, is labelled 'diese Riesenkloake' (1035), it reeks of Zyklon B (1025), and Nietzsche the man is dismissed as 'Abschaum' (1053). Harich's vitriolic hyperbole seems boundless: 'Die Ideengeschichte aller Zeiten,' he writes, 'kennt keinen beredteren Künder der Gewalt, keinen passionierteren Kriegstreiber als Nietzsche' (1028). The most notorious assertion in Harich's 'polemic' is: 'Den Mann nicht für zitierfähig zu halten, sollte zu den Grundregeln geistiger Hygiene gehören' (1036). Despite his admiration for Thomas Mann, 'der größte Deutsche des Jahrhunderts' (1049–50), Harich has clearly not heeded Mann's advice when it comes to reading Nietzsche: 'Not only is it art that he offers – it is an art also to read him, and nothing clumsy or straightforward is admissible, every kind of artfulness, irony, reserve is required in reading him.'[9]

Harich's mud-slinging provides no new understanding of Nietzsche. As already indicated, it relies heavily on a selective and debased reading of Lukács' by now dated interpretation of Nietzsche, though this reliance does not extend to employing Lukács' philosophical acumen. Where Lukács was able to distinguish between Nietzsche, the incorruptibly honest social critic, and Nietzsche, the

'Nietzsche als Begründer des Irrationalismus der imperialistischen Periode', in *Die Zerstörung der Vernunft. Der Weg des Irrationalismus von Schelling zu Hitler* (Berlin: Aufbau, 1954), pp. 244–317.

9   Thomas Mann, *Nietzsche's Philosophy in the Light of Contemporary Events* (Washington, DC: Library of Congress, 1947), p. 33. The German version, published a little later, reads: 'Was er bietet, ist nicht nur Kunst, – eine Kunst ist es auch, ihn zu lesen, und keinerlei Plumpheit und Geradheit ist zulässig, jederlei Verschlagenheit, Ironie, Reserve erforderlich bei seiner Lektüre' (Thomas Mann, 'Nietzsche's Philosophie im Lichte unserer Erfahrung', in *Gesammelte Werke*, 12 vols (Frankfurt a.M.: Fischer, 1960), x, 675–712 (p. 708)). Stephan Hermlin quotes these lines in his attack on Harich's reactionary stance ('Von älteren Tönen', *Sinn und Form*, 40 (1988), 179–83 (pp. 180–81)).

prophet of aggressive irrationalism, Harich sees in Nietzsche's work only a heap of (pre)fascist dung. One reason for Harich's excessive zeal is his belief that rejection of Nietzsche is a cornerstone of the GDR's anti-fascist legitimacy. A related fear is that engagement with Nietzsche in the GDR may help to articulate or even increase present discontents: 'In diesem Kontext will der Beitrag Heinz Pepperles gelesen werden. Er leistet dem Übergreifen der Nietzsche-Renaissance auch auf die DDR, und damit auf die sozialistischen Länder überhaupt, Schützenhilfe' (1053). Harich's solution is as drastic as it is unrealistic: 'Lieber sollte dann schon für Friedrich Nietzsche bei uns der Ruf gelten, mit dem Brecht den Feldherrn Lukullus enden läßt: "Ins Nichts mit ihm!"' (ibid.).

It may seem absurd to suggest that Harich's caricature was representative of official attitudes to Nietzsche in the GDR of the 1980s, but the very public intervention in November 1987 by the President of the Writers' Union, Hermann Kant, would appear to support this view:

> Nach [Pech und Schwefel] schmeckt mir ein Beitrag in 'Sinn und Form', dessen Verfasser [Pepperle] uns zwar vor Nietzsche bewahren möchte, die Gelegenheit aber nutzt, *mühsam erreichte Kulturpositionen in Frage zu stellen*. Es geht um unseren Umgang mit Geschichte und kulturellem Erbe und schwieriger Kunst, und da man diesen Aufsatz mehrfach als eine Wegweisung für unseren Kongreß mißdeutet hat, sei klipp und klar erklärt, daß wir mit derlei Polpotterien nichts zu schaffen haben. Niemand braucht zu besorgen, es gehe hier künftig nun, weil untern Linden wieder eine alte Bronze steht, rückwärts nach Preußen hin (my emphasis).[10]

---

10 Hermann Kant, 'Rede auf dem X. Schriftstellerkongreß der Deutschen Demokratischen Republik', *Neue Deutsche Literatur*, 36 (1988), no. 2, 5–34 (p. 27). Kant was President of the Writers' Union of the GDR from 1978 to 1989 and a member of the 'Volkskammer' from 1981 to 1990. The 'alte Bronze' is a reference to the statue of Frederick the Great on Unter den Linden, re-erected in 1986 by the GDR authorities to mark the two-hundredth anniversary of the Prussian king's death.

Under the heading 'Meinungen zu einem Streit', nine articles responding to Harich and/or Pepperle were published in the 1988 volume.[11] Of these, only one endorsed Harich's position unequivocally: 'Nietzsche gehört *nicht* zu unserem Erbe, zum Erbe der Arbeiterklasse, zum Erbe der antifaschistischen DDR.'[12] Another expressed support, in principle, for Harich's view, but added: 'Wie schade aber, daß er sich zu der polemischen Übertreibung hinreißen läßt'.[13] Overwhelmingly, however, the responses expressed bewilderment and barely concealed anger at what one referred to as Harich's 'beste inquisitorische Praxis'.[14] While one contributor, with cautious irony, characterised Harich's intemperate polemic as one of the 'Besonderheiten in der Essaylandschaft der DDR',[15] Klaus Kändler described it as an attempt at 'Erbeaneignung in der DDR',[16] and Gerd Irrlitz diagnosed it straightforwardly as 'Nietzsche-Hysterie'.[17] In his 'Duplik' the originator of the Nietzsche debate, Pepperle, attempted to discredit Harich by appealing to higher authority:

> Lenin, ein in prinzipieller Polemik nicht unerfahrener Autor, wenn er es mit Vereinfachungen, Übertreibungen, mit Eiferern zu tun hatte, erinnert gerne an

---

11 'Meinungen zu einem Streit', *Sinn und Form*, 40 (1988), 179–220 (Stephan Hermlin, 'Von älteren Tönen', 179–83; Rudolf Schottlaender, 'Richtiges und Wichtiges', 183–86; Thomas Böhme, 'Das Erbe verfügbar besitzen', 186–89; Klaus Kändler, '"Nun ist dieses Erbe zu Ende..."!?', 189–92; Gerd Irrlitz, '"Ich brauche nicht viel Phantasie"', 192–94; Hans-Georg Eckhardt, 'Im Schnellgang überwinden', 195–98; Stefan Richter, 'Spektakulär und belastet', 198–200; Manfred Buhr, 'Es geht um das Phänomen Nietzsche! Unsystematische Bemerkungen anläßlich unproduktiver Polemik und halbierter Empörung', 200–10; Heinz Pepperle, '"Wer zuviel beweist, beweist nichts"', 210–20).
12 Buhr, p. 203.
13 Schottlaender, p. 184.
14 Böhme, p. 187.
15 Richter, p. 198.
16 Kändler, p. 189.
17 Irrlitz, p. 194.

ein französisches Sprichwort: Qui prouve trop, il ne prouve rien (Wer zuviel beweist, beweist nichts).[18]

The most pointed and persuasive response to Harich was Stephan Hermlin's brief piece 'Von älteren Tönen', his eloquent barbs sharpened by personal antipathy to Harich (it was mutual), which Hermlin does not attempt to conceal. According to Hermlin, Harich believes that cultural policy should be conducted through proscription and eradication ('Verbote und Vernichtung'). Hermlin continues:

> Sein [Harichs] von Hysterie und einem in doppeltem Sinne zu verstehenden Verfolgungswahn geprägter Aufsatz behandelt Nietzsche und die Tatsache, daß der Philosoph Heinz Pepperle den Versuch gewagt hatte, Nietzsche anders darzustellen, als es nach Harichs Meinung erlaubt sein sollte. Mir fiel auf, daß Harich bei der Beschreibung seines Verhältnisses zu Nietzsche ungefähr ein Dutzend Mal Termini wie 'Haß' und 'verhaßt' verwendet.[19]

As Hermlin readily acknowledges, he himself is no Nietzsche expert, but he argues forcefully that the GDR can ill afford *not* to engage with such an important figure: 'Nietzsche existiert nicht in der DDR; ich halte das für einen Mangel, weil Sozialisten an keiner wesentlichen Gestalt vorbeigehen können' (180).

Harich's talk of 'spätbürgerliche Kulturzersetzung' and the 'Pseudoavantgarde' of the West is, to Hermlin, the language of the early 1950s. 'Ich frage mich', writes Hermlin, 'was ein solcher anachronistischer Müll im Jahre 1987 in der Zeitschrift unserer Akademie zu suchen hat' (181). Hermlin understands, or at least states, more clearly than any of the other participants in the *Sinn und Form* debate, except possibly Harich, what is really at issue. It is not primarily the relatively narrow question of understanding Nietzsche better that is at stake here but, rather, the broad principle of greater openness which would facilitate more enlightened discussion in the GDR, not only of Nietzsche but also of other questions previously considered taboo. Hermlin's conclusion highlights the essence of the

---

18   Pepperle, '"Wer zuviel beweist, beweist nichts"', p. 220.
19   Hermlin, p. 180.

Nietzsche debate as he perceives it, though he does not appear sanguine about its likely outcome:

> [Harich] tadelt streng die DDR, weil sie zu bedeutenden, problematischen Gestalten der Vergangenheit wie Luther, Friedrich der Große und Bismarck ein neues Verhältnis gewinnt. [...] Ihm ist auch unbegreiflich, daß eine Gesellschaft, die der Zukunft zustrebt, sich ihrer Vergangenheit versichern muß. Mancher mag denken, ich hielte mich zu lange mit diesem Nonsens auf und mit jemand, der, was das Politische angeht, sich unter Sozialismus immer nur eine Art Kriegskommunismus, ein System der Repression vorzustellen vermochte. Aber herostratische Naturen sind keine Unikate und nicht zu verachten. Wo eine solche Stimme sich erhebt, warten andere auf ihren Einsatz. Es ist die Stunde der gebrannten Kinder. Auch ich bin ein gebranntes Kind (183).

On a trivial level, the *Sinn und Form* debate simply confirmed the sclerotic condition of state-sanctioned cultural attitudes in the GDR. More significantly, it revealed that the GDR was at a cultural crossroads. However fiercely Harich may have defended Marxist-Leninist cultural positions against the 'imperialist' Nietzsche, the debate was not, ultimately, concerned with choosing between Marx and Nietzsche. It was about the extent to which a confident socialist society could and should tackle its cultural heritage, however problematic, without prejudice or taboo. The Nietzsche debate in *Sinn und Form* was a curiously muted and oblique version of a process which, by 1987, was already well underway in Mikhail Gorbachev's Soviet Union: glasnost.

This sudden flurry of interest in Nietzsche served to highlight the deliberate, officially sanctioned neglect of this thinker over the previous forty years. Nietzsche's voice had been effectively silenced in the GDR and his manuscripts carefully guarded. While it was not impossible to gain access to these, scholars had to tackle a bureaucratic assault course in order to reach them. (It was even harder to gain access to the papers of Nietzsche's sister.) In a practice redolent of 'doublethink', GDR scholars were allowed to work on the Nietzsche material held at the Goethe-Schiller Archive in Weimar but were rarely, if ever, permitted to publish the results of their research.[20] Employees at the tourist information office in Weimar were instructed to play dumb when asked by foreigners about Nietzsche. Only if the questioner was persistent, and only if this interest in Nietzsche appeared to be 'academic', were employees to tell the visitor that Nietzsche's manuscripts were held at the Goethe-Schiller Archive. Published guides to the town, and indeed to the Goethe-Schiller Archive, contained no reference to Nietzsche.[21] With one, belated, exception his published works were not on sale in the GDR, and pre-war editions in public libraries were locked in the 'Giftschrank' ('poison cupboard'), available only to those who could produce an official certificate stating that they needed temporary access to them for an approved research purpose.

The single exception, which tends to prove the rule that cultural officialdom in the GDR was hostile to Nietzsche, was an edition of *Ecce homo*, published simultaneously in East and West Germany in 1985, which was edited with a separate commentary volume by Karl-Heinz Hahn, the long-serving director of the Goethe-Schiller Archive, and Mazzino Montinari, arguably the most distinguished Nietzsche scholar of the day. Priced at 200 DM, however, and with a print-run of only 2,000, this edition was clearly not designed significantly to increase interest in Nietzsche

---

20 See Olaf Wolter, 'Nietzsche-Rezeption in der DDR? Die Geschichte des Weimarer Nietzsche-Archivs 1945–1990', *Weimarer Beiträge*, 40 (1994), 442–49 (p. 446).

21 See Müller-Lauter, 'Über den Umgang mit Nietzsche', pp. 833–34. For further discussion of restricted access to Nietzsche's works in the GDR, see Thomas Rietzschel, 'Warum Angst vor Friedrich Nietzsche? Annotationen zu einem aktuellen Streit um die Grenzen kritischer Rezeption im Sozialismus', *Amsterdamer Beiträge zur neueren Germanistik*, 27 (1988), 259–80 (p. 266), and Wolf Scheller, '"Vordenker der Nazis" auf dem Index', *Nürnberger Nachrichten*, 19 Aug. 2000 <http://www.virtusens.de/walther/nn_19_8.jpg> [accessed 25 Aug. 2002].

in the GDR.[22] The mere fact of its publication was criticised by, among others, Harich, who wrote with characteristic venom:

> Weder in ihr [der Colli-Montinari Ausgabe] noch in irgendeiner anderen ist [Nietzsche] zur Lektüre zu empfehlen. Eine Gesellschaft kann kaum tiefer sinken, als wenn sie die Kenntnis seiner Elaborate zu den Kriterien ihrer Allgemeinbildung rechnet.[23]

The depth and intensity of official hostility to Nietzsche in the GDR can be traced, in part, to the founding ideas and self-understanding of that state. Its claims to legitimacy were based on two closely related ideas. The first was a Marxist-Leninist inter-pretation of historical development, according to which the GDR was the culmination of progressive ('zukunftsweisend') developments in German history. The second was the anti-fascist struggle of 1933–45, which provided the GDR with its immediate *raison d'être*. The presence of the victorious Red Army on German soil, the sacrifices of the Soviet people in repelling the fascist invader, and the martyrdom of German anti-fascists in the Third Reich appeared to provide compelling evidence for both these claims to legitimacy. There was no room for Nietzsche in the 'first anti-fascist state on German soil', as his writings were perceived (and not only by communists) to have been an important underpinning of National Socialism.

In 1945 Germany lay in ruins, physically and morally. Much of her cultural tradition, too, appeared to be in tatters, not least because it had been exploited by the National Socialist regime for its aggressive and murderous ends. By the end of the war many believed that Germany's political and cultural history before 1933 contained within

22   Friedrich Nietzsche, *Ecce homo. Faksimileausgabe der Handschrift*, ed. Karl-Heinz Hahn and Mazzino Montinari, transcribed by Anneliese Claus (Leipzig: Edition Leipzig; Wiesbaden: Dr. Ludwig Reichert Verlag, 1985). See also Steffen Dietzsch, 'Vom Wiederentdecken eines Unvergessenen. Überlegungen zur ersten Nietzsche-Edition in der DDR', *Weimarer Beiträge*, 36 (1990), 1018–26. This account of the only work of Nietzsche's to be published in the GDR appeared in November 1990, after the GDR had ceased to exist.

23   Harich, p. 1036. For an angry response to this characterisation of the *Ecce homo* edition as an 'Elaborat', see Böhme, p. 188.

it the seeds of the Third Reich and its horrors. As a leading English historian observed in 1945:

> [Germany's invasion of the Soviet Union on 22 June 1941] was the climax, the logical conclusion, of German history [...] Germany was at last united. Anti-Bolshevism, anti-capitalism, the conquest of the west, the conquest of the east, German conservatism and German demagogy, were merged in a single cause. This cause was the supremacy everywhere of German arms, of German industry, of German culture, of the German people. [...] But June 22nd, 1941, was not only the climax of German history; it was also its turning point [...] it was in reality the day of Germany's doom.[24]

The Nazis had contributed to this notion of National Socialism's 'historical inevitability' by drawing an improbable line linking themselves to real and mythical precursors as diverse, and incompatible, as Odin, Zarathustra, Heinrich der Löwe, Friedrich II. Hohenstaufen, Meister Eckhart, Copernicus, Rembrandt, Luther, Friedrich der Große, Schopenhauer, Bismarck, Nietzsche and Wagner.[25] While Nietzsche was never regarded, not even by Nazis, as the single most important influence on National Socialist ideology, he was often placed in a select group of immediate precursors ('Vorkämpfer'). The two men chiefly responsible for attempting to sew Nietzsche's writings into the fabric of the Nazi belief-system were Alfred Rosenberg, ideology chief of the NSDAP, and Alfred Baeumler, a professor of philosophy.[26] In a rare example of one of

24   A. J. P. Taylor, *The Course of German History: A Survey of the Development of Germany since 1815* (London: Hamish Hamilton, 1945), p. 223.

25   Alfred Rosenberg attempted such a genealogy of National Socialism in his *Der Mythus des 20. Jahrhunderts. Eine Wertung der seelisch-geistigen Gestaltenkämpfe unserer Zeit* (Munich: Hoheneichen-Verlag, 1930); see Robert Cecil, *The Myth of the Master Race: Alfred Rosenberg and Nazi Ideology* (London: Batsford, 1972), p. 67.

26   From 1934 to 1945 Rosenberg held the position of 'Beauftragter des Führers für die Überwachung der gesamten geistigen und weltanschaulichen Schulung und Erziehung der NSDAP'. He was hanged at Nuremberg in 1946. Baeumler was professor of philosophy at Dresden, and a convinced Nazi, long before 1933. He was rewarded with a chair in Berlin shortly after the Nazis came to power; see Kurt Rudolf Fischer, 'A Godfather Too: Nazism as a Nietzschean

these Nietzschean Nazis commenting on the work of the other, Baeumler wrote as late as 1943:

> Weder Fichte noch Chamberlain, weder Lagarde noch Nietzsche können mit dem Nationalsozialismus in eins gesetzt werden, da es keinen National-sozialismus vor Adolf Hitler gibt. Aber jene Männer haben zusammen mit manchen anderen schon an der Front gestanden, an welcher durch die große Geistesbewegung unserer Zeit der entscheidende Sieg erkämpft worden ist.[27]

Largely as a result of these efforts to turn him into a 'Staats-philosoph', efforts ably assisted by his sister before her death in 1935 and continued thereafter by the board of directors of the Stiftung Nietzsche-Archiv (Nietzsche Archive Foundation) in Weimar, Nietzsche appeared to be heavily incriminated ('schwer belastet'), to use the terminology of the occupying powers' denazification process.[28] Nietzsche, who had died in 1900, could not, of course, be formally arraigned nor were his works ever formally 'denazified' in any of the zones of occupation between 1945 and 1949.

Nietzsche's fall from grace in 1945, at least in the Soviet zone of occupation, was as rapid and complete as that of the National Socialist regime with which, rightly or wrongly, his writings had come to be associated. It was not the Soviets, however, who first raised objections to the continued existence of the Nietzsche Archive, but

"Experiment"', in Jacob Golomb and Robert S. Wistrich (eds), *Nietzsche, Godfather of Fascism? On the Uses and Abuses of a Philosophy* (Princeton: Princeton University Press, 2002), pp. 291–300 (pp. 293–95).

27   Alfred Baeumler, *Alfred Rosenberg und der Mythus des 20. Jahrhunderts* (Munich: Hoheneichen-Verlag, 1943), p. 84; see also Alfred Baeumler, *Nietzsche, der Philosoph und Politiker* (Leipzig: Reclam, 1931). Another important text in this regard is Heinrich Härtle, *Nietzsche und der Nationalsozialismus* (Munich: Eher, Zentralverlag der NSDAP, 1937).

28   Even before the Nazis came to power, Harry Graf Kessler noted that everyone at the Nietzsche Archive, from the doorman to the director, was a Nazi: 'Im Archiv ist alles vom Diener bis zum Major [Max Oehler] hinauf Nazi' (Harry Graf Kessler, *Tagebücher 1918–1937*, ed. Wolfgang Pfeiffer-Belli (Frankfurt a.M: Insel, 1961), p. 681 [7 Aug.1932]).

the Americans, who had occupied Weimar on 12 April 1945, some four weeks before Germany's unconditional surrender.[29] One of the Americans' first acts on occupying the town was to march its inhabitants to the nearby Ettersberg and confront them with the horror of Buchenwald concentration camp. Partly to counter this mood, and partly as a pre-emptive strike, Nietzsche's cousin Max Oehler, who had run the Nietzsche Archive since 1935, drafted an exculpatory letter to the American authorities. In view of the many years he had spent facilitating and propagating conservative-nationalist and, later, National Socialist readings of Nietzsche's work, Oehler's brief sketch of the history and activities of the Archive appears mendacious and self-serving. He writes, for example, of:

> der vom Nietzsche-Archiv stets vertretene Grundsatz, daß die Nietzsche-Forschung frei bleiben und *jede* wie immer geartete Richtung dieser Forschung unterstützt werden müsse und daß es nicht Sache des Archivs sei, eine bestimmte, von irgend welchen weltanschaulichen oder politischen Voreingenommenheiten beeinflußte Nietzsche Auffassung zu vertreten oder gar ein Nietzsche-'Dogma' aufzustellen.[30]

It is not clear what the Americans made of this document or indeed whether it would have influenced their policy towards the Nietzsche Archive. In the event, they were to have no further say in the administration of Weimar; under the terms of the Yalta Agreement, American forces had to withdraw from Thuringia, which formed part of the Soviet zone of occupation. The Russians occupied Weimar on 9 July 1945. By the end of the year the Nietzsche Archive as an institution, and its director, had ceased to exist:

---

29   See Wolter, p. 442.
30   Max Oehler. *Verteidigung des Nietzsche-Archivs gegen den Vorwurf der Reaktion.* GSA 72/2628. quoted by David Marc Hoffmann, 'Zur Geistes- und Kulturgeschichte des Nietzsche-Archivs', in Angelika Emmrich et al., *Das Nietzsche-Archiv in Weimar* (Munich and Vienna: Hanser, 2000), pp. 9–38 (p. 36).

The Nietzsche Archive was high on their [the Russians'] list as a center of Fascist propaganda, and Major Oehler, its custodian, was listed as a member of the Nazi Party. [...] On December 6 [1945], a Russian woman interpreter requested that Major Oehler accompany her to headquarters for interrogation. She did not know how long he would be gone, but there was no need for a change of clothes. Three days later the Nietzsche Archive was locked and sealed by order of the Russian commanding officer. Major Oehler's wife waited anxiously for her husband's return as the days stretched into weeks and the weeks into months. Finally, she left Weimar and went to West Germany. It was more than a decade later before she heard that, after having been condemned to forced labor in Siberia on the day he was arrested, her husband had fallen sick and had been thrown into the basement of a house close to the Nietzsche Archive and left there to starve to death.[31]

In April 1946 the holdings of the Nietzsche Archive were packed into 111 containers and taken away to an undisclosed destination. Only after the intervention of the Land President of Thuringia were they returned. Its contents may been saved, but the Archive itself was to have no immediate future as a research institution. The Soviet Military Administration's hostile attitude towards it was reflected in a number of articles published in Soviet-controlled newspapers and magazines, and the establishment of the GDR in 1949 rendered the future of the Archive, if anything, still more uncertain.[32]

In this cold climate the board of the Stiftung Nietzsche-Archiv met for the first and last time after the Second World War on 26 October 1949, some three weeks after the founding of the GDR. The most important decision reached at this meeting, chaired by Gerhard Scholz, the newly appointed head of the Goethe-Schiller Archive, was

---

31   H. F. Peters, *Zarathustra's Sister: The Case of Elisabeth and Friedrich Nietzsche* (New York: Crown, 1977), pp. 226–27. A detailed account of these and subsequent developments can be found in David Marc Hoffmann, *Zur Geschichte des Nietzsche-Archivs. Elisabeth Förster-Nietzsche, Fritz Koegel, Rudolf Steiner, Gustav Naumann, Josef Hofmiller. Chronik, Studien, Dokumente* (Berlin and New York: de Gruyter, 1991), pp. 120–31.

32   See Wolter, pp. 443–44. The articles hostile to Nietzsche published in the Soviet zone are discussed in Manfred Riedel, *Nietzsche in Weimar. Ein deutsches Drama* (Leipzig: Reclam, 1997), pp. 171–92.

to transfer Nietzsche's manuscripts to that Archive for safekeeping; Nietzsche's library was to be moved to Weimar's Stadtschloss, and Villa Silberblick, the building which had housed the Nietzsche Archive, would be turned into a guest house for the Goethe-Schiller Archive.[33] Though the Stiftung Nietzsche-Archiv was not formally dissolved until 1956, this meeting signalled the end of the Nietzsche Archive as an independent body. In 1953 the Nietzsche holdings, along with all other literary archive material in the town, were placed under the aegis of a new, state-run organisation, the Nationale Forschungs- und Gedenkstätten der klassischen deutschen Literatur in Weimar.[34]

Meanwhile, in the West, Nietzsche's rehabilitation proceeded apace and was complete long before the *Sinn und Form* debate took place in the GDR. It began with Thomas Mann's brilliant, qualified reappraisal in 1947 and continued, with significant differences of emphasis, through Walter Kaufmann's monograph in 1950 and Karl Schlechta's three-volume edition of Nietzsche's works in the mid-1950s.[35] This Nietzsche 'renaissance' in the West was given fresh impetus in France in the 1960s and 1970s by, among others, Gilles Deleuze, Michel Foucault and Pierre Klossowski.[36]

Official attitudes to Nietzsche in the GDR notwithstanding, Western scholars were permitted unconditional access to Nietzsche material in Weimar. Despite his involvement between 1933 and 1942 with a historical-critical edition of Nietzsche's works, Karl Schlechta was granted access to Nietzsche's manuscripts in the early 1950s.

---

33 See *Protokoll der Sitzung des Vorstands der Stiftung Nietzsche-Archiv*, Stiftung Weimarer Klassik: Nietzsche-Archiv, no. 2627.

34 See Hoffmann, *Zur Geschichte des Nietzsche-Archivs*, p. 121.

35 See Thomas Mann, 'Nietzsche's Philosophie im Lichte unserer Erfahrung'; Walter Kaufmann, *Nietzsche: Philosopher, Psychologist, Antichrist*, 4th edn (Princeton: Princeton University Press, 1974); and Friedrich Nietzsche, *Werke* ed. Karl Schlechta, 3 vols (Munich: Hanser, 1954–56).

36 See, for example, Gilles Deleuze (ed.), *Nietzsche. Cahiers de Royaumont* (Paris: Editions de Minuit, 1967).

This enabled him to begin the process of untangling the confusion, some of it deliberate, which had surrounded Nietzsche's 'Nachlass'.[37] Erich F. Podach, another Western scholar, was also permitted to work on Nietzsche's manuscripts. His groundbreaking *Nietzsches Werke des Zusammenbruchs* (1961) was a direct result of this permission. In the words of Karl-Heinz Hahn, director of the Goethe-Schiller Archive from 1958 to 1986:

> Ungeachtet vieler ausgestreuter Fehlmeldungen über die vermeintliche Unzugänglichkeit der Bestände des ehemaligen Nietzsche-Archivs sind diese [seit 1956] immer und immer wieder in oft wochenlangen Aufenthalten eingesehen und ausgewertet worden.[38]

The most significant achievements on the part of Western scholars working in Weimar were undoubtedly Colli and Montinari's critical editions of Nietzsche's works, from 1967, and letters, from 1975.[39]

Reception of Nietzsche in the GDR itself tended to be limited and negative, '[i]ndeed, it is difficult to speak of a Nietzsche reception there at all, if by reception is meant an interest in, and an attempt to come to terms with, a primary text'.[40] There was nothing resembling an open discussion of Nietzsche and his legacy before 1986, and the first Nietzsche monograph to be published in the GDR, by Heinz Malorny, did not appear until 1989.[41] Discussions of

37   For an explanation of the philological principles behind Schlechta's reordering of the 'Nachlass', see his 'Philologischer Nachbericht' and 'Nachwort', in Friedrich Nietzsche, *Werke*, iii, 1383–1452.

38   Karl-Heinz Hahn, 'Das Nietzsche-Archiv', *Nietzsche-Studien*, 18 (1989), 1–19 (p. 18).

39   See 'Works of Nietzsche Cited' for bibliographical details of these editions; for an account of their genesis, see Hoffmann, *Zur Geschichte des Nietzsche-Archivs*, pp. 125–27.

40   Denis M. Sweet, 'Friedrich Nietzsche in the GDR: A Problematic Reception', in Margy Gerber et al. (eds), *Studies in GDR Culture and Society 4: Selected Papers from the Ninth New Hampshire Symposium on the German Democratic Republic* (Lanham, MD, New York and London: University Press of America, 1984), pp. 227–42 (p. 227).

41   Heinz Malorny, *Zur Philosophie Friedrich Nietzsches* (Berlin: Akademie-Verlag, 1989).

Nietzsche were rare, and these tended to focus on his alleged role in paving the way for National Socialism and/or bourgeois imperialism. In 1958, while acknowledging the philological achievement of Schlechta's new edition of Nietzsche's works, Wolfgang Heise warned:

> Die neue, handliche Nietzsche-Ausgabe ist symptomatisch für die zahlreichen Bemühungen um eine Nietzsche-Renaissance innerhalb der bürgerlichen Philosophie. Diese Bemühungen erklären sich aus dem sozialen Inhalt der Philosophie Nietzsches. Er war derjenige deutsche Denker, der in antizipatorischer Weise innerhalb der Philosophie den Übergang vollzog von der Position der liberalen zur Position der imperialistischen Bourgeosie.[42]

The Nietzsche renaissance in the West was viewed as symptomatic of a restoration of attitudes which had led to fascism. From this perspective, fascism and late capitalism were almost indistinguishable, indeed Harich later characterised them as 'eineiige Zwillinge'.[43]

Attempts to challenge Lukács' interpretation of Nietzsche's thought were invariably qualified. The Germanist Hans Kaufmann, for example, stressed the power of Nietzsche's cultural criticism, but added that this criticism had its roots in Nietzsche's extreme subjectivity which entailed anti-democratic, anti-socialist and, ultimately, fascistic consequences.[44] The view of Nietzsche advanced in a one-volume history of German literature, published in 1966, was less nuanced:

---

42 Wolfgang Heise, 'Friedrich Nietzsche: *Werke in drei Bänden*. Herausgegeben von Karl Schlechta', *Deutsche Zeitschrift für Philosophie*, 6 (1958), 653–58 (p. 653).

43 Harich, p. 1020.

44 Hans Kaufmann, *Krisen und Wandlungen der deutschen Literatur von Wedekind bis Feuchtwanger. Fünfzehn Vorlesungen* (Berlin and Weimar: Aufbau, 1969), pp. 39–46.

Verführerisch, weil man hier [in Nietzsches Philosophie] eine scheinbare Kritik an der Gesellschaft brillant formuliert erhielt, die im Grunde eine Kritik von rechts, von reaktionären Grundpositionen aus, war. [...] Hinter der geistreichen Geste des sich unabhängig dünkenden Individualisten und Verfechters einer exklusiven 'Auserwähltheit' lugte die bösartige Fratze der schwärzesten Reaktion hervor. [...] Nietzsches bewußt ahumanistisch gebärdende Haltung, seine barbarische Predigt in dem Werk *Der Wille zur Macht* (1901), die im 'Uebermenschen' gipfelte, haben später dem Faschismus den Weg bereitet.[45]

The aforementioned Heinz Malorny was the GDR's most prolific Nietzsche commentator. In 1980 he contributed an essay to a volume entitled *Faschismus-Forschung*, in which he repeated the claim that Nietzsche was one of the most influential forerunners of Nazism, argued that renewed interest in Nietzsche in the West amounted to a concerted revisionist campaign, and asserted, moreover, that this revisionism was directed at Marxist-Leninist philosophy:

Die Spannweite der Berufung auf Nietzsche reicht heute von den alten und neuen Nazis und den Neokonservativen bis zu den Versuchen einer Synthese von Marx und Nietzsche bei den modernen Revisionisten. Die marxistisch-leninistische Philosophiegeschichtsschreibung wird sich auch in Zukunft allen derartigen Versuchen einer Wiedererweckung der Ideen Nietzsches gegenüber unversöhnlich verhalten, wie sie bisher Nietzsche stets als philosophischen Gegner behandelt hat.[46]

There were, of course, dissenters from this monolithic understanding of Nietzsche's thought but, in view of the virtual ban in the GDR on Nietzsche publications and on open discussion of his texts, it is difficult to detect traces of them. It is known, though, that

---

45 Hans Jürgen Geerdts (ed.), *Deutsche Literaturgeschichte in einem Band* (Berlin: Volk und Wissen, 1966), pp. 464–65.

46 Heinz Malorny, 'Friedrich Nietzsche und der deutsche Faschismus', in Dietrich Eichholtz and Kurt Gossweiler (eds), *Faschismus-Forschung. Positionen, Probleme, Polemik* (Berlin: Akademie-Verlag, 1980), pp. 279–301 (p. 301); for thoughts in similar vein, see Heinz Malorny, 'Tendenzen der Nietzsche-Rezeption in der BRD', *Deutsche Zeitschrift für Philosophie*, 27 (1979), 1493–1500, and his entry on Nietzsche in Erhard Lange and Dietrich Alexander (eds), *Philosophen-Lexikon* (Berlin: Dietz, 1982), pp. 693–98.

Ernst Bloch and Hans Mayer, for example, for whom no philosopher was taboo, did permit free discussion of Nietzsche, albeit behind the closed doors of their seminars at the University of Leipzig.[47] Undogmatic appraisals of Nietzsche can also be found on occasion between the lines of publications devoted to more general topics. A lengthy history of nineteenth-century German literature, for example, published in 1975, discusses Nietzsche twice in some detail. The first discussion admittedly underlines Nietzsche's well-documented hostility to socialism and rehearses standard Marxist-Leninist objections to his philosophy.[48] However, in a later section of this literary history, entitled 'Vitalismus und Dekadenz in der Lyrik Friedrich Nietzsches', there is a remarkably detailed and sensitive discussion of Nietzsche's lyric poetry and the lieder in *Also sprach Zarathustra* and *Dionysos-Dithyramben*, which draws attention to their formal inventiveness and linguistic vigour. Even this observation is not allowed to go unqualified, however. Immediately, the ideological dangers thought to be lurking in Nietzsche's style are underlined. For the politically unaware or gullible, Nietzsche's is a siren voice:

> Die Funktion der 'Lieder', besondere 'Rausch- und Reizwerte' im epischen Kontext zu schaffen, war raffiniert demagogisch, exemplarisch und folgenreich. Dieses im *Zarathustra* angewandte Verfahren verweist auf den Zusammenhang von Ästhetizismus, sensibilisierter Innerlichkeit des Décadents und pro-imperialistischer Ideologie mit ihren antidemokratischen und antisozialistischen Affekten.[49]

---

47 See Rietzschel, p. 274.
48 Kurt Böttcher et al. (eds), *Geschichte der deutschen Literatur. Von 1830 bis zum Ausgang des 19. Jahrhunderts* (Berlin: Volk und Wissen, 1975), pp. 731–32.
49 Ibid., p. 924.

One of the more remarkable Nietzsche 'publications' in the GDR was a dissertation submitted to the Humboldt University by Renate Reschke in 1983.[50] Though Reschke's handling of Nietzsche is certainly careful, and though it is probably correct to say that she remains, in the end, critical of Nietzsche's 'regressive' stance, both the title and the tenor of her text indicate that this is no run-of-the-mill GDR treatment. Implicitly recognising the parlous state of Nietzsche 'studies' in the GDR, and as if to anticipate Harich's reactionary outburst in the *Sinn und Form* debate some four years later, Reschke writes:

> Es genügt auch nicht, sich auf die klassischen Aussagen der frühen marxistischen Kritik zu berufen, diese müssen vielmehr selbst zum Gegenstand kritischer Aufarbeitung gemacht werden.[51]

The Akademie-Verlag initially expressed interest in publishing Reschke's dissertation but then, for whatever reason, lost interest in the project. In a revised and updated form, it was eventually published, but not until the year 2000 – by Akademie-Verlag.[52] Whatever reservations it may have had before 1990, since the 'Wende' this publishing house has become the leading Nietzsche publisher in eastern Germany. It publishes monographs on Nietzsche, as well as *Nietzscheforschung*, the journal of the Nietzsche-Gesellschaft founded in 1991 in Halle.[53]

Other plans to publish Nietzsche-related projects in the 1980s also came to grief. Reclam in Leipzig accepted Friedrich Tomberg's proposal to publish an anthology of Nietzsche texts but the publisher abandoned the plan in 1983. The same publisher planned to issue

---

50   Renate Reschke, *Die anspornende Verachtung der Zeit. Studien zur Kulturkritik und Ästhetik Friedrich Nietzsches. Ein Beitrag zu ihrer Rezeption* (Habilitation, Humboldt University Berlin, 1983).
51   Ibid., p. 14.
52   Renate Reschke, *Anspornende Verachtung der Zeit. Denkumbrüche mit Nietzsche* (Berlin: Akademie-Verlag, 2000).
53   This society's original name was Förder- und Forschungsgemeinschaft Friedrich Nietzsche.

paperback editions of *Die fröhliche Wissenschaft* (edited by Reschke) and the *Unzeitgemässe Betrachtungen* (edited by Tomberg), but in 1986 these plans were postponed indefinitely; the publisher was reportedly unhappy with Tomberg's introduction. Eike Middell's monograph *Nietzsche und die deutschsprachige Literatur*, due to be published by Akademie, also never saw the light of day.[54] As Sweet remarked shortly afterwards, it seems clear that these publication 'difficulties' were largely, though not solely, attributable to 'the letter and telephone-call campaign of an outraged Wolfgang Harich to Reclam, the Ministry of Culture, and the Goethe and Schiller Archive in Weimar, among other places'.[55] Harich was fundamentally opposed to the publication of any work by Nietzsche in the GDR. He was equally energetic in opposing any form of commemorative site for Nietzsche in Weimar, Röcken, or anywhere else. In 1986 Manfred Buhr and others put forward a tentative plan to refurbish and reopen – for Western visitors only – the former Nietzsche Archive building in Weimar. Harich protested to the Prime Minister of the GDR, Willi Stoph, and the plan was promptly shelved. In his letter to Stoph, Harich not only opposed the plan but also suggested that it had been a mistake not to sell Nietzsche's 'Nachlass' to the West for hard currency. He also proposed bulldozing Nietzsche's grave in Röcken, in order to deter unwanted Western visitors.[56]

The first, and last, Nietzsche monograph to appear in the GDR was Heinz Malorny's *Zur Philosophie Friedrich Nietzsches*, published in 1989. This book is anything but an attempt to praise

---

54   For further discussion of these developments, see Denis M. Sweet, 'Nietzsche Criticized: The GDR Takes a Second Look', in Margy Gerber et al. (eds), *Studies in GDR Culture and Society 7: Selected Papers from the Twelfth New Hampshire Symposium on the German Democratic Republic* (Lanham, MD, New York and London: University Press of America, 1987), pp. 141–53, and Riedel, pp. 286–92.

55   Sweet, 'Nietzsche Criticized: The GDR Takes a Second Look', p. 152.

56   See Eckhard Heftrich, 'Auf deinen Namen werden die Buben schwören. Das Leiden an Friedrich Nietzsche war eine Form des Leidens an Deutschland', *Frankfurter Allgemeine Zeitung*, 17 Sept. 1996, p. 40.

Nietzsche and welcome him into a broader socialist discussion. Malorny, a 'wissenschaftlicher Arbeitsleiter' at the Zentralinstitut für Philosophie of the GDR Academy of Sciences, comes instead to bury him. His opening sentence indicates that the official line on Nietzsche in the GDR remained unreconstructed to the end: 'Vorliegende Arbeit stellt sich der Aufgabe, die Tradition der marxistischen Kritik der Philosophie Friedrich Nietzsches zu verteidigen und weiter-zuführen.'[57] To Malorny, the issue is not the correct interpretation of corrupt Nietzsche texts, nor is it about Nietzsche's life and character, his intellectual development or explaining the contradictoriness of his philosophy, even if much bourgeois literature on Nietzsche gives this impression: 'Worum es vor allem geht, das sind die ideologischen Schwergewichte seines Denkens in ihrer Bedeutung für unsere Zeit!'[58] After restating the fundamental position that Nietzsche is to be viewed as a precursor and inspirer of both National Socialism and bourgeois capitalism, and after attacking Nietzsche 'revisionism' in the West, Malorny asks where 'we' should stand with regard to Nietzsche's 'philosophische Grundaussagen':

> Für Marxisten-Leninisten ist diese Entscheidung nicht schwer. Der Gegensatz in den Auffassungen über die weltanschaulichen Fragen, erst recht in den sozialtheoretischen Auffassungen, vor allem hinsichtlich der Überwindung von Klassenherrschaft, Unterdrückung, Ausbeutung und Krieg, von Not, Elend, Unwissenheit und Rechtlosigkeit der Volksmassen ist unüberbrückbar. Die marxistisch-leninistische Wissenschaft wird darum Nietzsche stets als Gegner behandeln.[59]

A more hopeful note was sounded by Karl-Heinz Hahn, the recently retired director of the Goethe-Schiller Archive, in an article in the 1989 volume of *Nietzsche-Studien*. Not without reason, Hahn devotes only two pages of his essay to the history of the Nietzsche Archive since 1945, but he is guardedly optimistic about the future of Nietzsche studies under socialism. He hopes that, one day, there will

57   Malorny, *Zur Philosophie Friedrich Nietzsches*, p. 7.
58   Ibid., p. 248.
59   Ibid., p. 249.

be Nietzsche research in the GDR, and in other socialist countries, which may correct the Western image of Nietzsche as a liberal 'good European'. Like other commentators cited in the course of this discussion, Hahn could not have seen the writing on the Wall, chiefly because it was invisible, except to later observers blessed with hindsight:

> Und so wird es denn auch in den Ländern des Sozialismus, selbst in der DDR, irgendwann Nietzsche-Forschung geben, wobei allerdings vorauszusehen ist, daß hier im Unterschied zur heute gängigen Nietzsche-Rezeption, die sich nur zu gern auf den Europäer und Friedensfreund beruft, alle Ausfälle auf Geist, Kultur und Gesittung, das wahnsinnige Beschwören von Barbarei und inhumaner Selbstbehauptung, die ja unübersehbar auch im Werk Nietzsches begegnen, bereitwillig ausklammert – der *ganze* Nietzsche diskutiert werden wird, die kritischen Akzente nachgetragen werden, die in der Forschung des letzten halben Jahrhunderts weitgehend vergessen wurden. Erst im Prozeß solch 'kritischer Aneignung' [...] wird es möglich sein, Nietzsche umfassend zu rezipieren [...] Ich verspreche mir diese Entwicklung durch eine künftige Nietzsche-Forschung in der DDR, die in Dissenz und Kooperation mit Forschern aus aller Welt zur Bewältigung der mit dem Namen Friedrich Nietzsche zu bezeichnenden geistigen Herausforderung beitragen wird.[60]

Interest in Nietzsche in eastern Germany since the 'Wende' has been strong and diverse, and it is growing. As early as 1990–91 the Nietzsche Archive on the Humboldtstrasse in Weimar was renovated and reopened, with its impressive Jugendstil decor restored. Unfortunately, the first floor, including the room where Nietzsche died in 1900, had been converted to guest accommodation in the 1950s. There is also a thriving Nietzsche-Gesellschaft, and one is encouraged to trace Nietzsche's footsteps on a trail, or 'pilgrimage', from Leipzig to Röcken, Naumburg, Schulpforta and Weimar. The only important Nietzsche 'sites' outside the territory of the former GDR are Basel and Sils-Maria in Switzerland. The Stiftung Weimarer Klassik, the legal successor to the Nationale Forschungs- und Gedenkstätten der klassischen deutschen Literatur in Weimar, was established in October 1991. Since 1993 this foundation has housed

60 Hahn, p. 19.

the Kolleg Friedrich Nietzsche, a centre which energetically promotes scholarly research in this area through a programme of seminars, conferences, scholarships and publications. Interest in Nietzsche in eastern Germany today is so vigorous that the *Sinn und Form* debate less than two decades ago seems to belong to another world. In a sense, of course, it does.

In that other world, antediluvian anti-fascism was the last refuge of Harich and, perhaps, of others. By recreating ancient battle lines and stigmatising Nietzsche as the (pre)fascist philosopher par excellence, Harich attempted, with some success it must be said, to stifle discussion of approaches to Nietzsche which did not adopt doctrinaire anti-fascism as their first principle. Some may be tempted to view the Nietzsche debate in the GDR in the late 1980s as merely a curiosity, as a bizarre, even amusing symptom of that state's ideological senescence. Such a view would be guilty not only of arrogant hindsight but also of failing to recognise the importance of this episode to a proper understanding both of Marxist(-Leninist) approaches to Nietzsche in the twentieth century and of efforts to secure a greater degree of openness in the GDR of the 1980s.

Works of Nietzsche Cited

Frühe Schriften, ed. Hans Joachim Mette et al., 5 vols (Munich: Beck, 1994).

Sämtliche Werke. Kritische Studienausgabe, ed. Giorgio Colli and Mazzino Montinari, 2nd edn, 15 vols (Munich: dtv; Berlin and New York: de Gruyter, 1988).

Werke. Kritische Gesamtausgabe, ed. Giorgio Colli, Mazzino Montinari et al. (Berlin and New York: de Gruyter, 1967–).

Werke, ed. Karl Schlechta, 3 vols (Munich: Hanser, 1954–56).

Briefwechsel. Kritische Gesamtausgabe, ed. Giorgio Colli, Mazzino Montinari et al. (Berlin and New York: de Gruyter, 1975–).

Sämtliche Briefe. Kritische Studienausgabe, ed. Giorgio Colli and Mazzino Montinari, 8 vols (Munich: dtv; Berlin and New York: de Gruyter, 1986).

The Antichrist, in *The Portable Nietzsche*, ed. and trans. Walter Kaufmann (New York: Viking Penguin, 1982).

Beyond Good and Evil, trans. R. J. Hollingdale (Harmondsworth: Penguin, 1973).

Beyond Good and Evil: Prelude to a Philosophy of the Future, trans. Walter Kaufmann (New York: Vintage, 1989).

'The Birth of Tragedy' and 'The Genealogy of Morals', ed. and trans. Francis Golffing (Garden City, NY: Doubleday, 1956).

The Birth of Tragedy, trans. Walter Kaufmann (New York: Vintage, 1967).

The Birth of Tragedy Out of The Spirit of Music, ed. Michael Tanner, trans. Shaun Whiteside (Harmondsworth: Penguin, 1993).

Ecce homo. Faksimileausgabe der Handschrift, ed. Karl-Heinz Hahn and Mazzino Montinari, transcribed by Anneliese Claus (Leipzig: Edition Leipzig; Wiesbaden: Dr. Ludwig Reichert Verlag, 1985).

The Gay Science, trans. Walter Kaufmann (New York: Vintage, 1974).

On the Advantage and Disadvantage of History for Life, trans. P. Preuss (Indianapolis: Hackett, 1988).

On the Genealogy of Morals, trans. Walter Kaufmann and R. J. Hollingdale, and *Ecce Homo*, trans. Walter Kaufmann (New York: Vintage, 1989).

On the Genealogy of Morality, trans. Carol Diethe (Cambridge: Cambridge University Press, 1994).

Thus Spoke Zarathustra: A Book for Everyone and No One, trans. R. J. Hollingdale, 2nd edn (Harmondsworth: Penguin, 1969).

Twilight of the Idols, trans. R. J. Hollingdale (Harmondsworth: Penguin, 1968).

Twilight of the Idols, in *The Portable Nietzsche*, ed. and trans. Walter Kaufmann (New York: Viking Penguin, 1982).

The Will To Power, trans. Walter Kaufmann and R. J. Hollingdale (New York: Vintage, 1968).

Bibliography

Acampora, Christa Davis, 'Re/Introducing "Homer's Contest": A new translation with notes and commentary', *Nietzscheana*, 5 (Fall 1996), i–iv and 1–8.

— 'Nietzsche's Problem of Homer', *Nietzscheforschung*, 5–6 (2000), 553–74.

— 'Nietzsche's *Thus Spoke Zarathustra* as Postmodern *Bildungsroman*', in Endre Kiss and Uschi Nussbaumer-Benz (eds), *Nietzsche, Postmodernismus und was nach ihnen kommt* (Cuxhaven and Dartford: Junghans, 2000).

Ackerknecht, E. H., *Rudolf Virchow. Arzt, Politiker, Anthropologe* (Stuttgart: Enke, 1957).

Albrecht, Friedrich, *Deutsche Schriftsteller in der Entscheidung* (Berlin: Aufbau, 1975).

Allison, David B., 'Some Remarks on Nietzsche's Essay of 1871, "On Words and Music"', *New Nietzsche Studies*, 1 (1996), nos. 1–2, 15–41.

— 'A Diet of Worms: Aposiopetic Rhetoric in "Beyond Good and Evil"', *Nietzsche-Studien*, 19 (1990), 43–58.

— '"Have I Been Understood?"', in Schacht (ed.), pp. 460–68.

Ambros, Paul, and Udo Rössling, *Reisen zu Luther. Wirkungs- und Gedenkstätten* (Berlin and Leipzig: VEB Tourist Verlag, 1983).

Andreas-Salomé, Lou, *Friedrich Nietzsche in seinen Werken* (Dresden: Reissner, 1924).

Anger, Sigrid (ed.), *Heinrich Mann 1871–1950. Werk und Leben in Dokumenten und Bildern* (Berlin: Aufbau, 1977).

Ansell Pearson, Keith, *Viroid Life: Perspectives on Nietzsche and the Transhuman Condition* (London: Routledge, 1997).

Arendt, Hannah, *Elemente totalitärer Herrschaft* (Frankfurt a.M.: Piper, 1986).

Aschheim, Steven E., *The Nietzsche Legacy in Germany 1890–1990* (Berkeley, Los Angeles and London: University of California Press, 1992); German edn: *Nietzsche und die Deutschen. Karriere eines Kults* (Stuttgart: Metzler, 1996).

Atwell, John E., 'Nietzsche's Perspectivism', *Southern Journal of Philosophy*, 19 (1981), 157–70.

Augstein, Rudolf, et al., *'Historikerstreit'. Die Dokumentation der Kontroverse über die Einzigartigkeit der nationalsozialistischen Judenvernichtung* (Munich: Piper, 1987).

Austin, Norman, *Archery at the Dark of the Moon: Poetic Problems in Homer's Odyssey* (Stanford: Stanford University Press, 1975).

Baeumer, Max L., 'Nietzsche and Luther: A Testimony to Germanophilia', in James C. O'Flaherty et al. (eds), *Studies in Nietzsche and the Judaeo-Christian Tradition* (Chapel Hill and London: University of North Carolina Press, 1985), pp. 143–60.

— 'Lutherfeiern und ihre politische Manipulation', in Reinhold Grimm and Jost Hermand (eds), *Deutsche Feiern* (Wiesbaden: Athenaion, 1977), pp. 46–61.

Baeumler, Alfred, *Nietzsche, der Philosoph und Politiker* (Leipzig: Reclam, 1931).

— *Alfred Rosenberg und der Mythus des 20. Jahrhunderts* (Munich: Hoheneichen-Verlag, 1943).

Baioni, Giuliano, 'La filologia e il sublime dionisiaco. Nietzsche e le "Considerazioni inattuali"', in Friedrich Nietzsche, *Considerazioni inattuali*, ed. Sossio Giametta and Mazzino Montinari (Turin: Einaudi, 1981), pp. vii–lxiii.

Barbera, Sandro, 'Apollineo e dionisiaco. Alcune fonti non antiche di Nietzsche', *Linguistica e letteratura*, 13–14 (1988–89), 125–45.

Barner, Wilfried, *Barockrhetorik. Untersuchungen zu ihren geschichtlichen Grundlagen* (Tübingen: Niemeyer, 1971).

Barner, Wilfried, et al. (eds), *Unser Commercium. Goethes und Schillers Literaturpolitik* (Stuttgart: Cotta, 1984).

Benz, Ernst, 'Nietzsches Ideen zur Geschichte des Christentums und der Kirche', *Zeitschrift für Kirchengeschichte*, 56 (1937), 169–313.

Bishop, Paul, and R. H. Stephenson, 'Nietzsche and Weimar Aesthetics', *German Life and Letters*, 52 (1999), 412–29.

Bluhm, Heinz, 'Nietzsche's Idea of Luther in *Menschliches, Allzumenschliches*', *PMLA*, 65 (1950), 1053–68.

Böhme, Thomas, 'Das Erbe verfügbar besitzen', *Sinn und Form*, 40 (1988), 186–89.

Böttcher, Kurt, et al. (eds), *Geschichte der deutschen Literatur. Von 1830 bis zum Ausgang des 19. Jahrhunderts* (Berlin: Volk und Wissen, 1975).

Borchmeyer, Dieter, 'Corneille, Lessing und das Problem der "Auslegung" der aristotelischen Poetik', *Deutsche Vierteljahrsschrift für Literaturwissenschaft und Geistesgeschichte*, 51 (1977), 422–35.

— *Das Theater Richard Wagners. Idee – Dichtung – Wirkung* (Stuttgart: Reclam, 1982).

— '"... dem Naturalism in der Kunst offen und ehrlich den Krieg zu erklären ...": Zu Goethes und Schillers Bühnenreform', in Barner et al. (eds), pp. 351–70.

Bornkamm, Heinrich, *Luther im Spiegel der deutschen Geistesgeschichte: mit ausgewählten Texten von Lessing bis zur Gegenwart* (Heidelberg: Quelle & Meyer, 1955).

Brecht, Martin, *Luther als Schriftsteller. Zeugnisse seines dichterischen Gestaltens* (Stuttgart: Calwer, 1990).

Brobjer, Thomas H., 'Beiträge zur Quellenforschung', *Nietzsche-Studien*, 30 (2001), 418–21.

— 'Nietzsche's Changing Relation to Christianity: Nietzsche as Christian, Atheist and Antichrist', in Weaver Santaniello (ed.), *Nietzsche and the Gods* (Albany: SUNY Press, 2001), pp. 137–57.

Buhr, Manfred, 'Es geht um das Phänomen Nietzsche! Unsystematische Bemerkungen anläßlich unproduktiver Polemik und halbierter Empörung', *Sinn und Form*, 40 (1988), 200–10.

Cargill Thompson, W. D. J., *The Political Thought of Martin Luther*, ed. Philip Broadhead (Brighton: Harvester Press, 1984).

Cecil, Robert, *The Myth of the Master Race: Alfred Rosenberg and Nazi Ideology* (London: Batsford, 1972).

Chamberlain, Lesley, *Nietzsche in Turin: The End of the Future* (London: Quartet Books, 1996).

Chartier, Roger, 'Geistesgeschichte oder *histoire de mentalités*?', in Dominick LaCapra and Steven L. Kaplan (eds), *Geschichte denken. Neubestimmung und Perspektiven moderner europäischer Geistesgeschichte* (Frankfurt a.M.: Fischer, 1988).

Conway, Daniel W., '"The Great Play and Fight of Forces": Nietzsche on Race', in Julie K. Ward and Tommy L. Lott (eds), *Philosophers on Race: Critical Essays* (Oxford: Blackwell, 2002), pp. 167–94.

— '*Ecce Caesar*: Nietzsche's Imperial Aspirations', in Golomb and Wistrich (eds), pp. 173–95.

Crawford, Claudia, *The Beginnings of Nietzsche's Theory of Language* (Berlin and New York: de Gruyter, 1988).

Deleuze, Gilles (ed.), *Nietzsche. Cahiers de Royaumont* (Paris: Editions de Minuit, 1967).

— *Nietzsche and Philosophy*, trans. Hugh Tomlinson (London: Athlone, 1983).

Derrida, Jacques, *Spurs: Nietzsche's Styles*, trans. Barbara Harlow (Chicago: University of Chicago Press, 1979).

— 'Otobiographies', in *The Ear of the Other*, trans. Peggy Kamuf (Lincoln: University of Nebraska Press, 1985), pp. 3–38.

Dietzsch, Steffen, 'Vom Wiederentdecken eines Unvergessenen. Überlegungen zur ersten Nietzsche-Edition in der DDR', *Weimarer Beiträge*, 36 (1990), 1018–26.

Dohmen, Longinus J., *Nietzsche over de menselijke natuur: Een uiteenzetting van zijn verborgen antropologie* (Kampen: Kok, 1994).

Domino, Brian: 'Stendhal's Ecstatic Embrace of History as the Antidote for Decadence', in John Lippitt (ed.), *Nietzsche's Futures* (London: Macmillan, 1999), pp. 48–61.

Ebeling, Gerhard, 'Luther und der Anbruch der Neuzeit', *Zeitschrift für Theologie und Kirche*, 69 (1972), 185–213.

Eberan, Barbro, *Luther? Friedrich 'der Grosse'? Wagner? Nietzsche? ...? ...? Wer war an Hitler schuld? Die Debatte um die Schuldfrage 1945–1949*, 2nd edn (Munich: Minerva, 1985).

Eckhardt, Hans-Georg, 'Im Schnellgang überwinden', *Sinn und Form*, 40 (1988), 195–98.

Eckhart, Meister, *Selected Writings*, trans. Oliver Davies (Harmondsworth: Penguin, 1994).

Emrich, Elke, *Macht und Geist im Werk Heinrich Manns. Eine Überwindung Nietzsches aus dem Geist Voltaires* (Berlin: de Gruyter, 1981).

Farias, Victor, *Heidegger et le nazisme. Morale et politique* (Paris: Editions Verdier, 1987).

Fichte, J. G., *Werke. Auswahl*, ed. Fritz Medicus, 6 vols (Hamburg: Meiner, 1962).

Figl, Johann, 'Nietzsches Begegnung mit Schopenhauers Hauptwerk. Unter Heranziehung eines frühen unveröffentlichen Exzerptes', in Wolfgang Schirmacher (ed.), *Schopenhauer, Nietzsche und die Kunst* (Vienna: Passagen Verlag, 1991), pp. 89–100.

Fischer, Kurt Rudolf, 'A Godfather Too: Nazism as a Nietzschean "Experiment"', in Golomb and Wistrich (eds), pp. 291–300.

Fortlage, Karl, *Genetische Geschichte der Philosophie seit Kant* (Leipzig, 1852).

Foucault, Michel, *Madness and Civilisation: A History of Insanity in the Age of Reason*, trans. Richard Howard (London: Tavistock Press, 1967).

Fraser, Giles, *Redeeming Nietzsche: On the Piety of Unbelief* (London and New York: Routledge, 2002).

Freud, Ernst L. (ed.), *Sigmund Freud, Arnold Zweig. Briefwechsel* (Frankfurt a.M.: Fischer, 1984).

Freud, Sigmund, '"Some Dreams of Descartes": A Letter to Maxime Leroy', in *The Standard Edition of the Complete Psychological Works of Sigmund Freud*, trans. and ed. James Strachey and Anna Freud, 24 vols (London: Hogarth Press, 1953–74), xxi (1961), 199–204.

Früchtl, Josef, and Jörg Zimmermann (eds), *Ästhetik der Inszenierung* (Frankfurt a.M.: Suhrkamp, 2001).

Frühwald, Wolfgang, and John M. Spalek (eds), *Der Fall Toller. Kommentar und Materialien* (Munich: Hanser, 1979).

Fulbrook, Mary, *The Two Germanies, 1945–1990: Problems of Interpretation* (Basingstoke: Macmillan, 1992).

Geerdts, Hans Jürgen (ed.), *Deutsche Literaturgeschichte in einem Band* (Berlin: Volk und Wissen, 1966).

Gestrich, Andreas, 'Erziehung im Pfarrhaus', in Martin Greiffenhagen (ed.), *Das evangelische Pfarrhaus. Eine Kultur- und Sozialgeschichte* (Stuttgart: Kreuz, 1984), pp. 63–82.

Gilman, Sander L. (ed.), David J. Parent (trans.), *Conversations with Nietzsche: A Life in the Words of His Contemporaries* (New York and Oxford: Oxford University Press, 1987).

Goethe, J. W., *Gedenkausgabe der Werke, Briefe und Gespräche*, ed. Ernst Beutler, 2nd edn (Zurich: Artemis, 1964).

Goethes Werke, ed. Erich Trunz, 12th edn, 14 vols (Munich: Beck, 1981).

Golomb, Jacob, and Robert S. Wistrich (eds), *Nietzsche, Godfather of Fascism?: On the Uses and Abuses of a Philosophy* (Princeton: Princeton University Press, 2002).

Gooding-Williams, Robert, 'Zarathustra's Three Metamorphoses', in Clayton Koelb (ed.), *Nietzsche as Postmodernist: Essays Pro and Contra* (Albany: SUNY Press, 1990).

Gregor-Dellin, Martin, and Dietrich Mack (eds), *Cosima Wagner's Diaries*, ed. and trans. Geoffrey Skelton, 2 vols (London: Collins, 1978–80).

Härtle, Heinrich, *Nietzsche und der Nationalsozialismus* (Munich: Eher, Zentralverlag der NSDAP, 1937).

Hahn, Karl-Heinz, 'Das Nietzsche-Archiv', *Nietzsche-Studien*, 18 (1989), 1–19.

Harich, Wolfgang, '"Revision des marxistischen Nietzschebildes?"', *Sinn und Form*, 39 (1987), 1018–53.

Hayman, Ronald, *Nietzsche: A Critical Life* (London: Weidenfeld and Nicolson, 1980).

Heftrich, Eckhard, 'Auf deinen Namen werden die Buben schwören. Das Leiden an Friedrich Nietzsche war eine Form des Leidens an Deutschland', *Frankfurter Allgemeine Zeitung*, 17 Sept. 1996, p. 40.

Hegel, G. W. F., *Phänomenologie des Geistes*, ed. Johannes Hoffmeister, 6th edn (Hamburg: Meiner, 1952).

Heidegger, Martin, *Nietzsche: Volume One*, trans. D. F. Krell (New York: Harper and Row, 1984).

— 'The Origin of the Work of Art', in *Poetry, Language, Thought*, trans. A. Hofstadter (New York: Harper and Row, 1971), pp. 17–87.

Heise, Wolfgang, 'Friedrich Nietzsche: *Werke in drei Bänden*. Herausgegeben von Karl Schlechta', *Deutsche Zeitschrift für Philosophie*, 6 (1958), 653–58.

Heller, Erich, 'Nietzsche's Last Words about Art versus Truth', in *The Importance of Nietzsche: Ten Essays* (Chicago: University of Chicago Press, 1988), pp. 158–72.

Hermlin, Stephan, 'Von älteren Tönen', *Sinn und Form*, 40 (1988), 179–83.

Hesse, Hermann, *Gesammelte Werke*, ed. Volker Michels, 12 vols (Frankfurt a.M.: Suhrkamp, 1970).

Higgins, Kathleen Marie, *Comic Relief: Nietzsche's 'Gay Science'* (New York and Oxford: Oxford University Press, 2000).

Hillebrand, Bruno (ed.), *Nietzsche und die deutsche Literatur* (Tübingen: Niemeyer, 1978).

Hinton Thomas, R., *Nietzsche in German Politics and Society 1890–1918* (Manchester: Manchester University Press, 1983).

Hoffmann, David Marc, *Zur Geschichte des Nietzsche-Archivs. Elisabeth Förster-Nietzsche, Fritz Koegel, Rudolf Steiner, Gustav Naumann, Josef Hofmiller. Chronik, Studien, Dokumente* (Berlin and New York: de Gruyter, 1991).

— 'Zur Geistes- und Kulturgeschichte des Nietzsche-Archivs', in Angelika Emmrich et al., *Das Nietzsche-Archiv in Weimar* (Munich and Vienna: Hanser, 2000), pp. 9–38.

Hollingdale, R. J., 'The Hero as Outsider', in Bernd Magnus and Kathleen M. Higgins (eds), *The Cambridge Companion to Nietzsche* (Cambridge: Cambridge University Press, 1996), pp. 71–89.

— *Nietzsche: The Man and His Philosophy*, 2nd edn (Cambridge and New York: Cambridge University Press, 1999).

Horkheimer, Max, *Gesammelte Schriften*, ed. Alfred Schmidt and Gunzelin Schmid Noerr, 19 vols (Frankfurt a.M.: Fischer, 1985–96).

Irrlitz, Gerd, '"Ich brauche nicht viel Phantasie"', *Sinn und Form*, 40 (1988), 192–94.

Jacyna, L. S., 'Medical Science and Moral Science: The Cultural Relations of Physiology in Restauration France', *History of Science*, 25 (1987), 111–43.

Janaway, Christopher, 'Knowledge and Tranquility: Schopenhauer on the Value of Art', in Dale Jacquette (ed.), *Schopenhauer, Philosophy, and the Arts* (Cambridge: Cambridge University Press, 1996), pp. 39–61.

— 'Kant's Aesthetics and the "Empty Cognitive Stock"', *Philosophical Quarterly*, 47 (1997), 461–63.

— (ed.), *Willing and Nothingness: Schopenhauer as Nietzsche's Educator* (Oxford: Oxford University Press, 1998).

Janz, Curt Paul, *Friedrich Nietzsche. Biographie*, 3 vols (Munich and Vienna: Hanser, 1978–79).

Janz, Rolf-Peter, 'Antike und Moderne in Schillers *Braut von Messina*', in Barner et al. (eds), pp. 329–49.

Jung, C. G., *Psychological Types* (Princeton: Princeton University Press, 1971).

Kändler, Klaus, '"Nun ist dieses Erbe zu Ende..."!?', *Sinn und Form*, 40 (1988), 189–92.

Kant, Hermann, 'Rede auf dem X. Schriftstellerkongreß der Deutschen Demokratischen Republik', *Neue Deutsche Literatur*, 36 (1988), no. 2, 5–34.

Kant, Immanuel, 'Bestimmung des Begriffs einer Menschenrace', in *Kants Werke. Akademie-Ausgabe*, 9 vols (Berlin: de Gruyter, 1968), viii, 89–106.

—— *Critique of Judgment*, trans. W. S. Pluhar (Indianapolis: Hackett, 1987).

Kaufmann, Eva, *Arnold Zweigs Weg zum Roman* (Berlin: Rütten und Loening, 1967).

Kaufmann, Hans, *Krisen und Wandlungen der deutschen Literatur von Wedekind bis Feuchtwanger. Fünfzehn Vorlesungen* (Berlin and Weimar: Aufbau, 1969).

Kaufmann, Walter, *Nietzsche: Philosopher, Psychologist, Antichrist*, 4th edn (Princeton: Princeton University Press, 1974).

Kelly, Alfred, *The Descent of Darwin: The Popularization of Darwinism in Germany 1860–1914* (Chapel Hill: University of North Carolina Press, 1981).

Kerckhove, Lee F., 'Re-thinking ethical naturalism: Nietzsche's "open question" argument', *Man and World*, 27 (1994), 149–59.

Kessler, Harry Graf, *Tagebücher 1918–1937*, ed. Wolfgang Pfeiffer-Belli (Frankfurt a.M: Insel, 1961).

Kestenholz, Claudia, 'Emphase des Stils. Begriffsgeschichtliche Erläuterungen zu Goethes Aufsatz über "Einfache Nachahmung der Natur, Manier, Stil"', *Comparatio. Revue Internationale de Littérature Comparée*, 2–3 (1991), 36–56.

Kjaer, Jørgen, *Friedrich Nietzsche. Die Zerstörung der Humanität durch Mutterliebe* (Opladen: Westdeutscher Verlag, 1990).

Kofman, Sarah, 'Nietzsche et Wagner: Comment la musique devient bonne pour les cochons', in *L'imposture de la beauté et autres textes* (Paris: Galilée, 1995), pp. 75–103.

Kreis, Rudolf, *Nietzsche, Wagner und die Juden* (Würzburg: Königshausen & Neumann, 1995).

Krell, David F., and Donald L. Bates, *The Good European: Nietzsche's Work Sites in Word and Image* (Chicago: University of Chicago Press, 1997).

Lachterman, David R., '*Die ewige Wiederkehr der Griechen*: Nietzsche and the Homeric Question', *International Studies in Philosophy*, 23 (1991), no. 2, 90–91.

Lampert, Laurence, *Nietzsche's Task: An Interpretation of 'Beyond Good and Evil'* (New Haven and London: Yale University Press, 2001).

Lange, F. A., *Geschichte des Materialismus und Kritik seiner Bedeutung für die Gegenwart* (Iserlohn: Baedeker, 1866).

Large, Duncan, 'Nietzsche and the Figure of Columbus', *Nietzsche-Studien*, 24 (1995), 162–83.

— '"The Freest Writer": Nietzsche on Sterne', *The Shandean*, 7 (Nov. 1995), 9–29.

— 'The Aristocratic Radical and the White Revolutionary: Nietzsche's Bismarck', in Jürgen Barkhoff et al. (eds), *Das schwierige neunzehnte Jahrhundert. Germanistische Tagung zum 65. Geburtstag von Eda Sagarra im August 1998* (Tübingen: Niemeyer, 2000), pp. 101–13.

— 'Nietzsche's Shakespearean Figures', in Alan D. Schrift (ed.), *Why Nietzsche Still? Reflections on Drama, Culture, and Politics* (Berkeley, Los Angeles and London: University of California Press, 2000), pp. 45–65.

— 'Nietzsche's Use of Biblical Language', *Journal of Nietzsche Studies*, 22 (Autumn 2001), 88–115.

Latacz, Joachim, *Erschließung der Antike. Kleine Schriften zur Literatur der Griechen und Römer* (Stuttgart and Leipzig: Teubner, 1994).

Lecky, W. E. H., *History of European Morals from Augustus to Charlemagne*, 2 vols (London, 1869).

Leiter, Brian, 'Perspectivism in Nietzsche's *Genealogy of Morals*', in Schacht (ed.), pp. 334–57.

— 'The Paradox of Fatalism and Self-Creation in Nietzsche', in Christopher Janaway (ed.), *Willing and Nothingness: Schopenhauer as Nietzsche's Educator* (Oxford: Oxford University Press, 1998), pp. 217–57.

Lukács, Georg, 'Nietzsche als Vorläufer der faschistischen Ästhetik', *Internationale Literatur – Deutsche Blätter* [Moscow], 5 (1935), no. 8, 76–92.

— 'Der deutsche Faschismus und Nietzsche', *Internationale Literatur – Deutsche Blätter* [Moscow], 12 (1943), 55–64.

— 'Nietzsche als Begründer des Irrationalismus der imperialistischen Periode', in *Die Zerstörung der Vernunft. Der Weg des Irrationalismus von Schelling zu Hitler* (Berlin: Aufbau, 1954), pp. 244–317.

Luther, Martin, *Ein Sendbrief von Dolmetschen und Fürbitte der Heiligen*, ed. H. S. M. Amburger-Stuart (London: Duckworth, 1940).

McGinn, Bernard, *The Foundations of Mysticism* (London: SCM Press, 1991).

McGovern, W. M., *From Luther to Hitler: The History of Fascist-Nazi Political Philosophy* (London: Harrap, 1941).

Macintyre, Ben, *Forgotten Fatherland: The Search for Elisabeth Nietzsche* (London: Macmillan; New York: Farrar, Strauss, Giroux, 1992).

Malorny, Heinz, 'Tendenzen der Nietzsche-Rezeption in der BRD', *Deutsche Zeitschrift für Philosophie*, 27 (1979), 1493–1500.

— 'Friedrich Nietzsche und der deutsche Faschismus', in Dietrich Eichholtz and Kurt Gossweiler (eds), *Faschismus-Forschung. Positionen, Probleme, Polemik* (Berlin: Akademie-Verlag, 1980), pp. 279–301.

— 'Nietzsche', in Erhard Lange and Dietrich Alexander (eds), *Philosophen-Lexikon* (Berlin: Dietz, 1982), pp. 693–98.

— *Zur Philosophie Friedrich Nietzsches* (Berlin: Akademie-Verlag, 1989).

Mann, Heinrich (ed.), *Es kommt der Tag. Deutsches Lesebuch* (Zurich: Europa Verlag, 1936).

— 'Nietzsche', *Maß und Wert*, 2 (1939), 277–304.

— (ed.), *The Living Thoughts of Nietzsche* (London: Cassell, 1939).

Mann, Thomas, *Nietzsche's Philosophy in the Light of Contemporary Events* (Washington, DC: Library of Congress, 1947).

— 'Nietzsche's Philosophie im Lichte unserer Erfahrung', in *Gesammelte Werke*, 12 vols (Frankfurt a.m.: Fischer, 1960), x, 675–712.

Martin, Nicholas, 'Nietzsche's "Schillerbild"': A Re-Evaluation', *German Life and Letters*, 48 (1995), 516–39.

— *Nietzsche and Schiller: Untimely Aesthetics* (Oxford: Clarendon Press, 1996).

Martin, Richard P., *The Language of Heroes: Speech and Performance in the Iliad* (Ithaca, NY: Cornell University Press, 1989).

Meyer, Theo, *Nietzsche. Kunstauffassung und Lebensbegriff* (Tübingen: Francke, 1991).

Miller, Alice, *Am Anfang war Erziehung* (Frankfurt a.m.: Suhrkamp, 1980).

Mills, Charles W., *The Racial Contract* (Ithaca, NY: Cornell University Press, 1997).

Moles, Alistair, *Nietzsche's Philosophy of Nature and Cosmology* (Frankfurt a.m.: Lang, 1990).

Montgomery, W. M., 'Germany', in Thomas F. Glick (ed.), *The Comparative Reception of Darwinism* (Austin and London: University of Texas Press, 1974), pp. 81–116.

Montinari, Mazzino, *Nietzsche lesen* (Berlin and New York: de Gruyter, 1982).

Müller, Johann Baptist (ed.), *Die Deutschen und Luther. Texte zur Geschichte und Wirkung* (Stuttgart: Reclam, 1983).

Müller-Lauter, Wolfgang, *Nietzsche. Seine Philosophie der Gegensätze und die Gegensätze seiner Philosophie* (Berlin and New York, de Gruyter, 1971).

— 'Über den Umgang mit Nietzsche', *Sinn und Form*, 43 (1991), 833–51.

Münster, Arno, *Nietzsche et le nazisme* (Paris: Editions Kimé, 1995).

Murphy, Tim, *Nietzsche, Metaphor, Religion* (Albany: SUNY Press, 2001).

— 'Nietzsche's Narrative of the "Retroactive Confiscations" of Judaism', in Weaver Santaniello (ed.), *Nietzsche and the Gods* (Albany: SUNY Press, 2001), pp. 3–20.

Nagy, Gregory, *Homeric Questions* (Austin: University of Texas Press, 1996).

Nehamas, Alexander, *Nietzsche: Life as Literature* (Cambridge, MA: Harvard University Press, 1985).

Nipperdey, Thomas, et al., *Martin Luther and the Formation of the Germans*, trans. Patricia Crampton (Bonn: Inter Nationes, 1983).

— 'The Protestant Unrest: Luther and the Culture of the Germans', in Nipperdey et al., pp. 7–24.

Novalis, *Heinrich von Ofterdingen*, ed. Wolfgang Frühwald (Stuttgart: Reclam, 1978).

Nussbaumer-Benz, Uschi, 'Bericht über die 7. und 8. Konferenz der englischen Friedrich Nietzsche Society', *Nietzscheforschung*, 5 (2000), 393–97.

Onfray, Michel, *Le ventre des philosophes: critique de la raison diététique* (Paris: Grasset, 1989).

Orwell, George, *Nineteen Eighty-Four* (Harmondsworth: Penguin, 1983).

Outlaw, Lucius T., *On Race and Philosophy* (New York and London: Routledge, 1996).

Owen, David, *Nietzsche, Politics and Modernity* (London: Sage Publications, 1995).

Pepperle, Heinz, 'Revision des marxistischen Nietzsche-Bildes? Vom inneren Zusammenhang einer fragmentarischen Philosophie', *Sinn und Form*, 38 (1986), 934–69.

— '"Wer zuviel beweist, beweist nichts"', *Sinn und Form*, 40 (1988), 210–20.

Pernet, Martin, 'Friedrich Nietzsche and Pietism', *German Life and Letters*, 48 (1995), 474–86.

Peters, H. F., *Zarathustra's Sister: The Case of Elisabeth and Friedrich Nietzsche* (New York: Crown, 1977).

Petersen, Jürgen H., '"Mimesis" vs. "Nachahmung". Die Poetik des Aristoteles – nochmals neu gelesen', *Arcadia*, 27 (1992), 3–46.

— '"Nachahmung der Natur": Irrtümer und Korrekturen', *Arcadia*, 29 (1994), 182–98.

Pfeiffer, Rudolf, *History of Classical Scholarship from 1300–1850* (Oxford: Clarendon Press, 1976).

Porter, James I., *Nietzsche and the Philology of the Future* (Stanford: Stanford University Press, 2000).

Pucci, Piero, *Odysseus Polytropos: Intertextual Readings in the Odyssey and the Iliad* (Ithaca, NY: Cornell University Press, 1987).

Reschke, Renate, *Die anspornende Verachtung der Zeit. Studien zur Kulturkritik und Ästhetik Friedrich Nietzsches. Ein Beitrag zu ihrer Rezeption* (Habilitation, Humboldt University Berlin, 1983).

— *Anspornende Verachtung der Zeit. Denkumbrüche mit Nietzsche* (Berlin: Akademie-Verlag, 2000).

Richardson, John, and Brian Leiter (eds), *Nietzsche* (Oxford: Oxford University Press, 2001).

Richter, Stefan, 'Spektakulär und belastet', *Sinn und Form*, 40 (1988), 198–200.

Riedel, Manfred, *Nietzsche in Weimar. Ein deutsches Drama* (Leipzig: Reclam, 1997).

Rietzschel, Thomas, 'Warum Angst vor Friedrich Nietzsche? Annotationen zu einem aktuellen Streit um die Grenzen kritischer Rezeption im Sozialismus', *Amsterdamer Beiträge zur neueren Germanistik*, 27 (1988), 259–80.

Robson-Scott, Professor, and Mrs W. B. Robson-Scott (trans.), *The Letters of Sigmund Freud and Arnold Zweig* (London: Hogarth Press, 1970).

Rosenberg, Alfred, *Der Mythus des 20. Jahrhunderts. Eine Wertung der seelisch-geistigen Gestaltenkämpfe unserer Zeit* (Munich: Hoheneichen-Verlag, 1930).

Rupp, Gordon, *Martin Luther: Hitler's Cause – Or Cure? In Reply to Peter F. Wiener* (London: Lutterworth, 1945).

Russo, J., 'Homer Against His Tradition', *Arion*, (Summer 1968), 275–95.

Salaquarda, Jörg (ed.), 'Emanuel Hirsch, "Nietzsche und Luther"', *Nietzsche-Studien*, 15 (1986), 398–439.

— 'Nietzsche and the Judaeo-Christian Tradition', in Bernd Magnus and Kathleen M. Higgins (eds), *The Cambridge Companion to Nietzsche* (Cambridge: Cambridge University Press, 1996), pp. 90–118.

Sallis, John, *Crossings: Nietzsche and the Space of Tragedy* (Chicago: Chicago University Press, 1991).

Santaniello, Weaver, *Nietzsche, God and the Jews: His Critique of Judeo-Christianity in Relation to the Nazi Myth* (Albany: SUNY Press, 1994).

Schacht, Richard (ed.), *Nietzsche, Genealogy, Morality: Morality: Essays on Nietzsche's 'Genealogy of Morals'* (Berkeley, Los Angeles and London: University of California Press, 1994).

Schank, Gerd, *'Rasse' und 'Züchtung' bei Nietzsche* (Berlin and New York: de Gruyter, 2000).

Scheller, Wolf, '"Vordenker der Nazis" auf dem Index', *Nürnberger Nachrichten*, 19 Aug. 2000.

Schiller, Friedrich, *On the Aesthetic Education of Man in a Series of Letters*, trans. Reginald Snell (New York: Ungar, 1965).

— *Sämtliche Werke*, ed. G. Fricke and H. G. Göpfert, 5 vols (Munich: Hanser, 1981).

— *Werke und Briefe*, ed. Otto Dann, 12 vols (Frankfurt a.M.: Deutscher Klassiker Verlag, 1988–2002).

Schlechta, Karl, 'Der junge Nietzsche und Schopenhauer', *Jahrbuch der Schopenhauer-Gesellschaft*, 26 (1939), 289–300.

Schlegel, Friedrich, *Schriften zur Literatur*, ed. Wolfdietrich Rasch (Munich: Hanser, 1972).

Scholl, Margaret, *The Bildungsdrama of the Age of Goethe* (Frankfurt a.M.: Lang, 1976).

Schopenhauer, Arthur, *Sämmtliche Werke*, ed. Julius Frauenstädt, 6 vols (Leipzig, 1873–74).

— *Sämtliche Werke*, ed. W. Frhr. von Löhneysen, 5 vols (Frankfurt a.M.: Suhrkamp, 1986).

Schottlaender, Rudolf, 'Richtiges und Wichtiges', *Sinn und Form*, 40 (1988), 183–86.

Seggern, Hans-Gerd von, *Nietzsches Philosophie des Scheins*, (Weimar: Verlag und Datenbank für Geisteswissenschaften, 1999).

Seigfried, Hans, 'Nietzsche's natural morality', *The Journal of Value Inquiry*, 26 (1992), 423–31.

Shapiro, Gary, 'The Writing on the Wall: *The Antichrist* and the Semiotics of History', in Robert C. Solomon and Kathleen M. Higgins (eds), *Reading Nietzsche* (Oxford: Oxford University Press, 1988), pp. 192–217.

Sheehan, Thomas, 'Heidegger and the Nazis', *The New York Review of Books*, 15 June 1988, pp. 38–47.

Shive, David, *Naming Achilles* (Oxford: Oxford University Press, 1987).

Siemon-Netto, Uwe, *Luther als Wegbereiter Hitlers? Zur Geschichte eines Vorurteils* (Gütersloh: Gütersloher Verlagshaus, 1993).

Siemens, Herman, 'Nietzsche's Hammer: Philosophy, Destruction, or the Art of Limited Warfare', *Tijdschrift voor Filosofie*, 2 (June 1998), 321–47.

Silk, M. S., and J. P. Stern, *Nietzsche on Tragedy* (Cambridge: Cambridge University Press, 1981).

Simon, Josef, 'Nietzsche on Judaism and Europe', in Jacob Golomb (ed.), *Nietzsche and Jewish Culture* (London: Routledge, 1997), pp. 101–16.

Söhngen, Oskar, 'The Word of God in Song: The Significance of Luther in the History of Music', in Nipperdey et al., pp. 35–45.

Solomon, Robert C., and Kathleen M. Higgins, *What Nietzsche Really Said* (New York: Schocken Books, 2000).

Späth, Andreas, *Luther und die Juden* (Bonn: Verlag für Kultur und Wissenschaft, 2001).

Staiger, Emil (ed.), *Der Briefwechsel zwischen Schiller und Goethe* (Frankfurt a.M.: Insel, 1977).

Staten, Henry, *Nietzsche's Voice* (Ithaca, NY: Cornell University Press, 1990).

Strauss, Leo, 'Note on the plan of Nietzsche's "Beyond Good and Evil"', *Interpretation*, 3 (1973), 97–113.

Sweet, Denis M., 'Friedrich Nietzsche in the GDR: A Problematic Reception', in Margy Gerber et al. (eds), *Studies in GDR Culture and Society 4: Selected Papers from the Ninth New Hampshire Symposium on the German Democratic Republic* (Lanham, MD, New York and London: University Press of America, 1984), pp. 227–42.

— 'Nietzsche Criticized: The GDR Takes a Second Look', in Margy Gerber et al. (eds), *Studies in GDR Culture and Society 7: Selected Papers from the Twelfth New Hampshire Symposium on the German Democratic Republic* (Lanham, MD, New York and London: University Press of America, 1987), pp. 141–53.

Szondi, Peter, *Poetik und Geschichtsphilosophie II* (Frankfurt a.M.: Suhrkamp, 1974)

Taminiaux, Jacques, 'Art and Truth in Schopenhauer and Nietzsche', in *Poetics, Speculation, and Judgment: The Shadow of the Work of Art from Kant to Phenomenology*, trans. Michael Gendre (Albany: SUNY Press, 1993), pp. 111–26.

Tanner, Michael, *Nietzsche* (Oxford: Oxford University Press, 1994).

Taylor, A. J. P., *The Course of German History: A Survey of the Development of Germany since 1815* (London: Hamish Hamilton, 1945).

Taylor, Seth, *Left-Wing Nietzscheans: The Politics of German Expressionism 1910–1920* (Berlin and New York: de Gruyter, 1990).

Überweg, Friedrich, *Grundriss der Geschichte der Philosophie von Thales bis auf die Gegenwart*, 3 vols (Berlin, 1863–68)

Urpeth, Jim, '"Noble" *Ascesis*: Between Nietzsche and Foucault', *New Nietzsche Studies*, 2, nos. 3–4 (Summer 1998), pp. 65–91.

— 'The Vitalisation of Aesthetic Form: Kant, Nietzsche, Heidegger, Focillon', in S. Brewster et al. (eds), *Inhuman Reflections: Thinking the Limits of the Human* (Manchester: Manchester University Press, 2000), pp. 72–87.

— 'A "Sacred Thrill": Presentation and Affectivity in the Analytic of the Sublime', in A. Rehberg and R. Jones (eds), *The Matter of Critique: Readings in Kant's Philosophy* (Manchester: Clinamen Press, 2000), pp. 61–78.

Venturelli, Aldo, 'Das Klassische als Vollendung des Sentimentalischen. Der junge Nietzsche als Leser des Briefwechsels zwischen Schiller und Goethe', *Nietzsche-Studien*, 18 (1989), 182–202.

Vondung, Klaus, 'Unity through *Bildung*: A German Dream of Perfection', *Journal of Independent Philosophy*, 5–6 (1988), 47–55.

Warminski, Andrzej, *Readings in Interpretation: Hölderlin, Hegel, Heidegger* (Minneapolis: University of Minnesota Press, 1987).

Weindling, Paul, *Health, Race and German Politics between National Unification and Nazism, 1870–1945* (Cambridge: Cambridge University Press, 1989).

Wells, C. J., *German: A Linguistic History to 1945* (Oxford: Clarendon Press, 1985).

Wenzel, Georg (ed.), *Arnold Zweig 1887–1968. Werk und Leben in Dokumenten und Bildern* (Berlin and Weimar: Aufbau, 1978).

Werner, Renate, *Skeptizismus, Ästhetizismus, Aktivismus. Der frühe Heinrich Mann* (Düsseldorf: Bertelsmann, 1972).

Wiener, Peter F., *Martin Luther: Hitler's Spiritual Ancestor* (London and New York: Hutchinson, 1945).

Wilson, John Elbert, *Schelling und Nietzsche. Zur Auslegung der frühen Werke Friedrich Nietzsches* (Berlin and New York: de Gruyter, 1996).

Wippermann, Wolfgang, *Wessen Schuld? Vom Historikerstreit zur Goldhagen-Kontroverse* (Berlin: Elefanten Press, 1997).

Wolf, Arie, 'Der nicht zustande gekommene Nietzsche-Roman (der "Umnachtungs"-Roman) Arnold Zweigs Anno 1934: Zur Geschichte einer Faszination', in Arthur Thilo Alt et al. (eds), *Arnold Zweig: Berlin – Haifa – Berlin. Perspektiven des Gesamtwerks. Akten des III. Internationalen Arnold-Zweig-Symposions Berlin 1993* (Berne: Lang, 1995).

Wolf, Friedrich August, *Prolegomena to Homer*, trans. and ed. Anthony Grafton et al. (Princeton: Princeton University Press, 1985).

Wolf, Herbert, *Martin Luther. Eine Einführung in germanistische Luther-Studien* (Stuttgart: Metzler, 1980).

— 'Pioneer of Modern German: The Significance of Martin Luther in the History of Language', in Nipperdey et al., pp. 25–34.

— (ed.) *Luthers Deutsch. Sprachliche Leistung und Wirkung* (Frankfurt a.M.: Lang, 1996).

Wolf, Norbert Christian, *Streitbare Ästhetik. Goethes kunst- und literaturtheoretische Schriften 1771–1789* (Tübingen: Niemeyer, 2001).

Wolter, Olaf, 'Nietzsche-Rezeption in der DDR? Die Geschichte des Weimarer Nietzsche-Archivs 1945–1990', *Weimarer Beiträge*, 40 (1994), 442–49.

Yovel, Yirmiyahu, *Dark Riddle: Hegel, Nietzsche, and the Jews* (University Park, PA: Penn State Press, 1998).

Zelle, Carsten, *Die doppelte Ästhetik der Moderne. Revisionen des Schönen von Boileau bis Nietzsche* (Stuttgart: Metzler, 1995).

Zweig, Arnold, *Das Beil von Wandsbek* (Berlin: Aufbau, 1986).

Index